Social Cognition

Social cognition is a key area of social psychology, which focuses on *cognitive* processes that are involved when individuals make sense of, and navigate in their *social* world. For instance, individuals need to understand what they perceive, they learn and recall information from memory, they form judgments and decisions, they communicate with others, and they regulate their behavior. While all of these topics are also key to other fields of psychological research, it's the social world—which is dynamic, complex, and often ambiguous—that creates particular demands.

This accessible book introduces the basic themes within social cognition and asks questions such as: How do individuals think and feel about themselves and others? How do they make sense of their social environment? How do they interact with others in their social world? The book is organized along an idealized sequence of social information processing that starts at perceiving and encoding, and moves on to learning, judging, and communicating. It covers not only processes internal to the individual, but also facets of the environment that constrain cognitive processing.

Throughout the book, student learning is fostered with examples, additional materials, and discussion questions. With its subdivision in ten chapters, the book is suitable both for self-study and as companion material for those teaching a semester-long course. This is the ideal comprehensive introduction to this thriving and captivating field of research for students of psychology.

Rainer Greifeneder is professor of Social Psychology at the University of Basel, Switzerland. His research focuses on various aspects of social cognition, such as the experienced ease or difficulty of thinking, and social exclusion.

Herbert Bless is professor of Microsociology and Social Psychology at the University of Mannheim, Germany. His research addresses the construction of social judgment and the interplay of affect and cognition.

Klaus Fiedler is professor of Social Psychology at the University of Heidelberg, Germany. His research interests include judgment and decision making, social cognition, language and communication, behavior regulation, and methodological issues in behavioral science.

"It is terrific to see a Second Edition of this marvelous book. It is a superb review of the literature and a remarkable synthesis of a complex and important area of research. The authors are gifted researchers in the area; they know the relevant work thoroughly; and their perspective throughout is unique and tremendously insightful."
—**Charles M. Judd**, College Professor of Distinction, Department of Psychology and Neuroscience, University of Colorado

"Social cognition is emerging as the hub of many areas of scholarship in the neurological, behavioral, and social sciences. This timely book presents a remarkably comprehensive and integrative review of the important lessons learned over the last few decades from theory, methods, and research findings in social cognition. The authors, world-renowned social cognition scholars, convey the rich tapestry of social cognitive phenomena as well as shed light on the underlying basic mechanisms. The authors unravel for us the mysteries of the social mind and help us understand why sociality and cognition are inextricably interwoven. I strongly recommend this authoritative book as a valuable resource for advanced undergraduate students, graduate students, as well as researchers and practitioners in the behavioral and social sciences."
—**Yaacov Trope**, Professor of Psychology, New York University

"This volume, written by some of Germany's leading social psychologists, provides a invaluable overview of the field of Social Cognition. It is a great book about an endlessly fascinating topic, and it is indispensible for anyone who wants to understand how we perceive and interact with our social world."
—**Ap Dijksterhuis**, Radboud University Nijmegen, The Netherlands

"Congratulations to the authors! This is an excellent introduction to core principles of social cognition. It illuminates how people make sense of the world in which they live and presents key findings and theories in an involving and easily accessible way. The book will be highly appreciated by students and instructors."
—**Norbert Schwarz**, University of Southern California

Social Cognition

How Individuals Construct Social Reality

Second Edition

Rainer Greifeneder, Herbert Bless, and Klaus Fiedler

Routledge
Taylor & Francis Group

LONDON AND NEW YORK

Second edition published 2018
by Routledge

2 Park Square, Milton Park, Abingdon, Oxon, OX14 4RN
and by Routledge
711 Third Avenue, New York, NY 10017

Routledge is an imprint of the Taylor & Francis Group, an informa business

First edition published by Routledge 2003

British Library Cataloguing-in-Publication Data
A catalogue record for this book is available from the British Library

Library of Congress Cataloging-in-Publication Data
Names: Greifeneder, Rainer, author. | Bless, Herbert, author. |
    Fiedler, Klaus, 1951- author. | Bless, Herbert. Social cognition.
Title: Social cognition : how individuals construct social reality /
    Rainer Greifeneder, Herbert Bless, & Klaus Fiedler.
Description: Second Edition. | New York : Routledge, [2018] |
    Revised edition of Social cognition, 2004.
Identifiers: LCCN 2017013795| ISBN 9781138124424
    (hard back : alk. paper) | ISBN 9781138124455
    (paper back : alk. paper) | ISBN 9781315648156 (ebook)
Subjects: LCSH: Social perception.
Classification: LCC BF323.S63 B55 2018 | DDC 302/.1—dc23
LC record available at https://lccn.loc.gov/2017013795

ISBN: 978-1-138-12442-4 (hbk)
ISBN: 978-1-138-12445-5 (pbk)
ISBN: 978-1-315-64815-6 (ebk)

Typeset in ITC New Baskerville Std
by Swales & Willis Ltd, Exeter, Devon, UK

Chapter overview

Detailed contents

Illustrations

Boxes

Tables

Illustrations

Acknowledgments

Numerous people have helped to put together this second edition of *Social Cognition*. We are extremely grateful for their help. We particularly thank Dr. Axel M. Burger for his contribution to Chapter 5. We thank reviewers, colleagues, and our students for valuable feedback. We thank all those at Psychology Press who were part of the process, from the first day to the book's publication. We thank Thomas Dunlap for outstanding copy-editing. We thank Saskia Bollin for her unmatched assistance in all phases of the project. And we thank our partners and families for their ideas, encouragement, patience, and willingness to put up with long hours.

1 Introduction

What is social cognition research about?

Herbert Bless & Rainer Greifeneder

Making sense: constructing social reality

What determines how we think and feel about our social environment? How do we form impressions about other people? What determines our social behavior? For the most part, the social environment of individuals is very complex and dynamic, with no two situations ever entirely alike. But individuals need to understand each and every situation in order to interact successfully with others. And while making sense of social situations often seems easy and simple on the surface, in actuality it poses an enormous challenge. As a consequence, individuals need a highly differentiated system of tools to accomplish this essential task.

To get a sense of the magnitude of this challenge, think of some very simple examples. Imagine yourself at a lively party, similar to the one shown in Illustration 1.1. Some people are standing around in groups carrying on lively conversations, others are dancing. Some of the guests you have known for a long time, others you have never seen or met before. Chatting with some guests, you hear about a person who helped a friend cheat on an exam. Walking through the room you overhear another person exclaiming, "Any time I start a new project, I know I will succeed." In a different corner of the room two friends of yours are engaged in a loud argument, but you have no idea what it is about. Finally, the next day, on your way to class, you see a new acquaintance from the party standing in a group of people, but she does not greet you.

What would your impressions be about the different persons in all these situations? How would you feel? What would you do if you had to interact with them? Answers to these questions would be quite easy if individuals always reacted to a particular objective situation exactly the same way. But as we know from our own behavior, this is not the case. Because individuals are highly flexible in their responses to social situations, the usual answer to such questions is: *It depends*. Among other things, it depends on how the perceiver interprets the specific behavior he or she witnessed. For example, if you assumed that your new acquaintance simply did not see you, you would feel quite differently than if you assumed that she saw you and intentionally avoided greeting you. Depending on your interpretation, you would presumably respond very differently to this person the next time you met her. The notion that the same objective input can be interpreted in very different ways is similarly reflected in the other examples. You might consider the person who helped a friend on the exam dishonest because he was cheating, or helpful because he was supporting his friend. Similarly, someone who claimed that she was successful on every new project could be perceived as haughty and arrogant—or as self-confident.

Illustration 1.1 To interact successfully with others, individuals need to make sense of their
social world

Source: Rawpixel.com/Shutterstock.com

As these examples illustrate, the same stimulus input may result in different interpretations of a given situation. Individuals construct their own subjective social reality based on their perception of the input. It is this construction of social reality, rather than the objective input, that determines how individuals think, feel, and behave in a complex social world. For example, if you believe that your new acquaintance intentionally avoided greeting you, it is this subjective interpretation that guides your behavior—even if objectively your acquaintance simply did not see you. If you have ever had an argument with a friend over some misunderstanding, you will remember how two persons experiencing the same situation may construct very different subjective realities, depending on their own perspectives. Sometimes the differences in interpretations are so glaring, it is hard to believe that the two individuals were reacting to the same situation.

The assumption that individuals construct their subjective social reality and that this construction provides the basis for social behavior leads us to the very heart of social cognition research: How is an *objective* situation translated into *subjective* reality? How do individuals construct social reality? What processes mediate between a specific input situation and behavior? Why does the same input often result in different interpretations? How is the interpretation influenced by prior social experiences and knowledge? Social cognition research is thus concerned with the study of social knowledge and the psychological processes that are involved when individuals construct their subjective reality. The manifold processes pertain to how we encode information, that is, how we give meaning to a situation, how we store information in memory and later retrieve it, and how we form judgments and make decisions.

Different perspectives on the social thinker

The examples from the party situation illustrate that an objective input, for example, the exact wording of an utterance, requires interpretation in order to give it meaning. On the one hand, this interpretation is determined by the input itself. On the other hand, we know from everyday experiences that individuals display considerable flexibility in how they interpret a particular situation. Given this flexibility, it becomes important which general motives are working in the background of individuals' interpretative processes. For example, sometimes we need to arrive very quickly at interpretations and decisions, that is, we operate under enormous time pressure. In these cases, it is crucial that cognitive processes require little time and little effort. At other times, speed may matter less, but it is critical that our interpretation is absolutely correct and accurate. Finally, there may be situations in which our interpretative processes are driven in particular by our general motive to perceive the world as consistent. These three aspects—speed, accuracy, consistency, and combinations thereof—are reflected in different approaches and perspectives of social cognition research.

Consistency seekers

One perspective maintains that individuals try to perceive the world just as they believe it is. In more general terms, individuals act as *consistency seekers* (S. T. Fiske & Taylor, 2017) who strive for consistency between their prior beliefs about the world and their interpretation of a specific new situation. Imagine someone who believes he is smart and has just learned that he did poorly in an exam. In order to create some consistency between his self-image as smart and the poor performance in the exam, he could, for example, discount the diagnostic value of the exam and argue that it tested unimportant peripheral abilities. This interpretation allows him to maintain his prior belief. Research has shown that the need for consistency is a major influence on the way individuals construct social reality. This need is incorporated into many theoretical approaches, most prominently in Festinger's (1957) dissonance theory (see also Vogel & Wänke, 2016). The basic assumption in Festinger's theory (as in many other consistency theories, see Abelson et al., 1968) is that inconsistencies in social thinking can create a negative, aversive feeling. For instance, the two cognitions "I am a smart person" and "I failed an important exam" are inconsistent and should therefore create an aversive state. This aversive state motivates individuals to reduce the inconsistency, for example, by changing one element of it ("After all, the exam wasn't really that important"), or by adding additional elements ("I would have performed better had I not been partying all night before the exam"). The general notion that individuals' processing of information is guided by their goal to obtain a particular outcome is reflected in various phenomena. For example, given that most individuals like to hold positive evaluations about themselves, their judgments often reflect their motivation to perceive the world as consistent with this positive self-view. Therefore, it is not surprising that individuals have been found to be unrealistically optimistic about their future (Shepperd, Waters, Weinstein, & Klein, 2015), and that they often hold positive illusions about themselves and their situation (Taylor & Brown, 1988). For a simple demonstration, one might ask all students in a classroom to take a look around and then estimate their relative position with respect to intelligence, physical attractiveness, or driving ability. Usually, significantly more than 50% of the students claim to be smarter, better looking, and better drivers than the average student in the classroom—which, at least at first glance, seems to contradict normative expectations that, by definition, 50% of the students should rank themselves below average. Such examples illustrate that our social thinking is in part influenced by our motivation to be consistent (see Dunning, 2015; Kunda, 1990, for conceptualizations along this line).

Fortunately, or unfortunately, the social world is not always consistent with our expectations and our wishes. Individuals who strive *only* for consistency and therefore, for instance, alter inconsistent elements (e.g., "After all, the exam wasn't really that important") are prone to inaccurate constructions of social reality. To act successfully in a complex social world, however, accurate perceptions of the world are needed, and inaccurate constructions may turn out to be quite maladaptive (Festinger, 1954).

Naïve scientists

The need to perceive the world accurately is captured in a second perspective on the social thinker. This perspective holds that individuals gather all relevant information unselectively and construct social reality in an unbiased manner. It maintains that the interpretation of the world is barely influenced by any form of wishful thinking, and conclusions are drawn in an almost logical, scientific manner. This perspective sees the human thinker as a *naïve or lay scientist*, and it is articulated especially in attribution theories. Attribution theories address how people explain behavior and events (e.g., Jones & Davis, 1965; H. H. Kelley, 1987; H. H. Kelley & Michela, 1980). For example, to find an explanation for why you failed the exam, you might consider other students' performance in this exam, your performance in other exams, and

Illustration 1.2 In many situations, individuals are overwhelmed with information. Unable to perceive and use all information, they have to use strategies that can simplify and shortcut information processing

Source: Monotoomono/Shutterstock.com

particular situational circumstances that might have caused the failure. The naive scientist perspective holds that we elaborate on the available information and process it in an unbiased manner in order to find out the cause of an event.

Cognitive misers

Research has shown that individuals can act like lay scientists under certain conditions. In many situations, however, individuals are not able or motivated to engage in systematic, elaborative thinking. Indeed, in daily life individuals often need to respond within a reasonable period of time or have to make their judgments very quickly. Moreover, even simple social interactions contain so much information to be processed that individuals are not always willing or able to act as a naive scientist. Instead, individuals have developed mental shortcuts that allow them to simplify their processing. This notion is captured in a third perspective, that of the social thinker as *cognitive miser* (S. T. Fiske & Taylor, 2017). It maintains that individuals, especially when they are under time pressure or confronted with an unusually complex situation, strive to simplify the cognitive processes (for an example, see Illustration 1.2). Like the naive scientist, the cognitive miser is aiming for high accuracy—but now under the constraint of strategies that are faster and require less effort. For example, when watching the numerous advertising spots on television, we are unlikely to process the provided information extensively. Instead, we may often rely on simplifications (e.g., "If this popular celebrity is in favor of the product, it must be good"). Although cognitive misers may sometimes come up with conclusions different from those posited by a lay scientist perspective that is based on a purely logical assessment of the information at hand, the evolved mental shortcuts often serve very well in everyday life. As we shall see, individuals have quite a number of potential shortcuts in their mental storehouse that can be applied to the numerous tasks they are faced with.

Motivated tacticians

Importantly, individuals seem to be quite flexible in their strategies when constructing subjective social reality. Sometimes they act as consistency seekers, sometimes as naive scientists, and sometimes as cognitive misers. This flexibility is captured in a fourth perspective, that of the social thinker as *motivated tactician* (S. T. Fiske & Taylor, 2017). This perspective holds that individuals may have multiple strategies, which can be applied depending on the situational constraints. Given the variety of processing strategies, individuals can rely on more elaborate or on simpler processing strategies, depending on the situation at hand. The general idea of differentiating between elaborative and simple processing routes has received considerable attention and led to the emergence of so-called dual process models, which have been applied to various domains (for an overview, see Chaiken & Trope, 1999). For example, in the realm of persuasion the general logic may run as follows: when individuals perceive a situation as highly relevant to them personally, they are more likely to engage in elaborative processing than act as cognitive misers; conversely, when faced with strong time pressure, individuals are less likely to consider all relevant information as a lay scientist and more likely to rely on available and applicable shortcuts (e.g., Chaiken, 1987; Petty & Cacioppo, 1986). A similar logic has been applied in person perception: individuals may judge other persons on the basis of all possible information at hand, which is, of course, a rather elaborative and time-consuming strategy; alternatively, they may simply base their judgments on prior stereotypes stored in memory (Brewer, 1988; S. T. Fiske & Neuberg, 1990; for an overview, see Macrae & Quadflieg, 2010).

Activated actors

In addition to rather domain-specific dual models, domain-independent models have been proposed that address the general interplay of the different modes (e.g., Strack & Deutsch, 2004; E. R. Smith & DeCoster, 2000; for overviews, see Sherman, Gawronski, & Trope, 2014). Some of these models capture the idea that much of our social thinking and behavior is highly automatic. As automatic processes require little effort and time, they allow for quick assessments of a situation (for overviews, see Bargh, 2006, 2014; Dijksterhuis, 2010). S. T. Fiske and Taylor (2017) have labeled this variant *activated actor*. This perspective holds that cues in the environment automatically bring to mind relevant knowledge about adequate interpretations and behaviors. For example, when the traffic light turns red, we automatically hit the brake—which requires very little processing time.

The five perspectives have received different emphasis at various times in the course of social cognition research (see S. T. Fiske & Taylor, 2017). But regardless of their underlying assumptions about the nature of the social thinker, over the years social cognition researchers have become increasingly interested in the specific *cognitive processes* of the construction of *social* reality. How is social knowledge stored in memory? How do individuals deal with the enormous amount of incoming information? How do they relate new information to their prior social knowledge? In the last two decades, the primary focus in social cognition has rested on the investigation of how social information is encoded, how the information is stored and retrieved from memory, how social knowledge is structured and represented, and what processes are involved when individuals form judgments and make decisions. As already expressed by the term *social cognition*, social cognition research combines *social* and *cognitive* elements. In the next two sections, we will briefly address the importance of these two components.

The cognitive component of social cognition

Social cognition researchers investigate how individuals mentally construct social reality because they believe that social behavior, rather than being directly determined by the external stimulus of a situation, is mediated by the internal mental representation of that situation. Understanding social behavior essentially requires an understanding of these internal mediating processes. Although the investigation of mediating processes seems rather straightforward from such a perspective, psychologists have not always been interested in the hidden link between external stimuli and overt behavioral responses. In particular, behaviorists proposed that (social) behavior can be explained better in terms of reinforcement contingencies (reward and punishment, e.g., Skinner, 1938), or in terms of contiguity (e.g., Watson, 1930) rather than in terms of mediating cognitive processes. Of course, these researchers did not deny the existence of mental processes. They argued, however, that unlike external stimuli and overt behavior, cognitive processes cannot be observed objectively. Consequently, they suggested treating internal processes as *black box* phenomena beyond the realm of psychological science.

Since the time of Watson and Skinner, the focus of investigation has dramatically shifted toward a systematic investigation of internal mental processes, and important research has accumulated in the field of cognitive psychology. Within cognitive psychology, researchers have addressed a large variety of cognitive processes, such as the role of attention, basic and higher order perception, the organization and function of human memory, the crucial role of working memory, logical reasoning, creativity, problem solving, and so on (for in-depth coverage of the basic principles in cognitive psychology, see e.g., J. R. Anderson, 1990; Matlin, 2013). This understanding of "how the mind works" has had an enormous influence on the field of social cognition.

In addition to the fundamentals of human cognition, the general notion that cognitive processes are highly context-dependent has always played a particularly important role in social cognition (E. R. Smith & Semin, 2004). Research on context dependency is deeply grounded in the work of Gestalt theorists (e.g., Koffka, 1935; Wertheimer, 1945). These theorists always emphasized that it is not the stimulus per se that influences our behavior but our perception of it, in other words, the way in which we mentally construct and represent reality. They suggested that a person's response to a particular stimulus depends on the context in which the stimulus is embedded. As a result, the whole is more than the sum of its parts. In very general terms, the context in which a particular stimulus is interpreted may take two different forms: the context may vary as a function of other stimuli that are present in the same situation, or it may vary as a function of the prior (social) knowledge that is used to interpret the target stimulus. Both cases can be illustrated with fairly simple tasks. For example, most people have no problem reading the words depicted in Illustration 1.3. Although objectively identical, the two middle letters in Illustration 1.3 are interpreted differently, either as "H" in THE or as "A" in CAT (Selfridge, 1955).

In the THE CAT example, the interpretation of the same stimulus is altered depending on which other stimuli are present in the situation. As another possibility, prior social knowledge that is brought to the situation may constitute different contexts and may similarly alter the interpretation of a given stimulus. To illustrate, have a look at Illustration 1.4(a), which depicts a rather ambiguous stimulus. This stimulus can be seen as either a young woman or an old woman. Intriguingly, when individuals are first presented with Illustration 1.4(b), they are more likely to see the young woman in Illustration 1.4(a). In contrast, when first presented with Illustration 1.4(c), individuals are more likely to see the old woman in Illustration 1.4(a). Hence, prior social knowledge (here, prior exposure to another stimulus) defines an interpretational context, based on which an ambiguous stimulus is seen either as a young or an old woman. More generally, this example illustrates that prior social knowledge can also define the context or background against which input information is interpreted.

THE CAT

Illustration 1.3 To illustrate the impact of context information, take a closer look at the second letter in each word. Depending on the context provided by each word, the same identical feature is interpreted differently, either as an "H," or an "A"

Source: After Selfridge (1955)

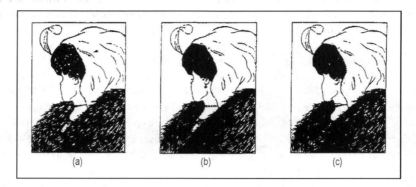

Illustration 1.4 In (b), most individuals perceive a young woman, and in (c), most individuals perceive an old woman; (a) can be perceived either way. What individuals perceive in (a) is therefore more dependent on contextual information

Source: Boring (1930)

The context dependency of social judgment is a highly fascinating phenomenon, and there are numerous examples of how the same stimulus is perceived and evaluated differently, depending on the situational context. For example, in one situation individuals may interpret helping to cheat on an exam as dishonest, and in another situation as helpful. One may argue that this context sensitivity is a flaw of social judgment. As the THE CAT example illustrates, however, context dependency is by no means a flaw of social judgment. On the contrary: context dependency in constructing social reality has a highly important function for adaptive behavior in a complex world. To quote Henri Tajfel (1969, p. 81), one of the most prominent European social psychologists: "the greatest adaptive advantage of man is his capacity to modify his behavior as a function of the way in which he perceives and understands a situation."

Ignoring the cognitive link that causes this context sensitivity would result in a highly impoverished perspective of human behavior. Excluding this link altogether would restrict human behavior to rigid routines. Because human behavior goes far beyond rigid routines, social behavior can hardly be explained without theorizing about the cognitive processes that mediate between an observable input and an observable response.

What is social about social cognition?

Given its emphasis on mediating processes, it comes as no surprise that social cognition research has borrowed heavily from cognitive psychology. Numerous concepts have been taken over and applied to the domain of social perception. Looking at some of the brief illustrations used above, for example, the THE CAT illustration, one might wonder how social cognition is different from cognition about inanimate objects. Is it really necessary to investigate the general principles of information perception, storage, retrieval, and reasoning processes in the domain of social psychology, or could we not simply assume that the general principles can be applied to the social context straightforwardly? While there is substantial overlap, two important differences set social cognition apart from cognitive psychology: the *nature of the stimu-lus* and the *nature of the processing.* Although both aspects are highly intertwined, it makes sense to discuss them separately.

Nature of the stimulus

On the most obvious level, social cognition research is specific because of the *social nature of the stimulus* and its relation to the perceiver. As S. T. Fiske and Taylor (2017) have pointed out, there are quite a number of aspects in which the *target* of social perception is different from the target of non-social perception. For instance, judging the trustworthiness of a person (social perception) is different from estimating the size of a rectangle (non-social perception; see Illustration 1.5).

Presumably, the most pronounced difference between social and non-social perception rests on how *directly* individuals can observe target attributes. In the physical

Illustration 1.5 Different targets—different amounts of constructive processes. First, estimate the size of the squares. Which one is larger? Next, judge the trustworthiness of each speaker. It is obvious that the left square is larger than the right one, since size is a well-defined attribute and can be observed directly. By contrast, not only are we unable to observe trustworthiness directly, but as a concept it is also more vague and controversial than size

Source: Sean Gallup/Getty Images

environment, many stimulus attributes can be directly observed. For instance, individuals can *see* color or size, they can *hear* pitch, they can *smell* scent, and they can *feel* whether something is hot or cold. For social targets, in contrast, many attributes cannot be directly perceived or objectively assessed. For instance, attributes such as intelligence, trustworthiness, love, aggressiveness, or humor cannot be directly seen, heard, smelled, or felt. Indeed, individuals have no sensory receptors for such attributes. Rather, these attributes constitute distal entities that have to be inferred or construed from more proximal cues, and sometimes they have no objective existence at all. For example, we cannot directly observe the *aggressiveness* of a particular person. But we can observe whether the person is hitting someone and then use this observation to *infer* aggressiveness. An important conclusion follows from these considerations: because attributes of social targets cannot be directly observed, their assessment often requires more constructive processing than does the assessment of non-social targets. This constructive processing—this inferring—requires individuals to go beyond the information given (Bruner, 1957a). One might argue that even basic perceptions such as color and size require a considerable degree of inferences. Arguably, however, social judgments require far more inferential processes, and allow for a larger range of outcomes. The large proportion of constructive processes renders social cognition specific and unique.

Two further aspects are directly related to the non-observability of the attributes in social cognition. First, because many attributes of social targets have to be inferred from distal cues, the accuracy of social judgment is often difficult to check. Let's assume that you have seen Person X hitting someone, and you infer from this observation that person X is aggressive. How do you know whether your social judgment is accurate? Because social attributes are often not directly observable, it is often difficult to know how accurate our judgments about social attributes are. Second, the attributes themselves are often ill-defined. For instance, individuals may have very different ideas about what it means to be aggressive. Is every kind of hitting indicative of aggressiveness, or is it a matter of degree? Is aggressiveness only physical, or does it encompass verbal attacks, too? Because social attributes are ill-defined, what is considered the attribute may be different from person to person, and from situation to situation. These two aspects—lack of accurate feedback and the ill-defined nature of many concepts—render social cognition even more unique.

In addition, and partly related, to the non-observability issue, three further aspects constitute important features that are specific to social cognition and make social judgment a very complex task. First, the targets of social perception may change rapidly, and individuals therefore need to adapt their judgments. For example, at the beginning of a conversation a new acquaintance may seem rather shy, but after a while she appears quite extraverted. Second, unlike inanimate objects, people change when they are aware that they are being observed. Finally, persons as judgmental targets often try to influence the perceiver, that is, they want to influence the impression the perceiver is forming. After all, most individuals want to be perceived as smart and trustworthy, for example. To that end, they send signals that are supposed to create a certain impression—but this impression may be wrong.

In combination, various issues related to the nature of social targets, such as indirect observability, lack of direct feedback, ill-defined attributes, or impression management by the target, render *social* cognition a highly inferential and complex task. Social cognition often requires that individuals go far beyond the information given in a particular situation: they need to make many inferences. Given this high level of inferences, even small changes in the context may have a strong influence on final judgments—much more so than for judgments about inanimate objects.

Nature of the processing

The social aspect of social cognition, however, is not restricted to the social nature of the stimulus. Just as a young child could hardly learn her first language from a radio, the processing of social information is a *genuinely social process*. Most obviously, constructing social reality is a highly mutual process. This mutuality emerges in different forms. An individual's construction of social reality is strongly influenced by the constructions of others. Individuals perceive the behavior of others and make inferences about their subjective reality. Conversely, an individual's constructions color the social perception of other people. Although different persons in the same situation may construct quite different social realities, there is a substantial reciprocal relationship between the constructions of these social realities (e.g., Zebrowitz & Montepare, 1992).

Social cognitive processing is also different from the processing of inanimate targets because there is a strong link between the way most individuals think about their social world and the way they think about themselves, that is, their self-conception. Indeed, construction of reality has strong implications for how individuals feel and think about themselves. At least two aspects of self-involvement should be considered here. First, when a person's self is involved and the situation is highly important, individuals are more likely to process incoming information extensively. Because the situation is important to the Self, individuals have a greater need for accuracy, or conversely, a greater fear of invalidity (Kruglanski, 1989, 2004). Personal relevance and importance usually increase the *amount* of processing, a central variable in the processing of information. Second, under certain conditions, self-involvement additionally influences the direction of processing. At times, an accurate construction of social reality can be quite self-threatening. For example, an accurate interpretation of a failed exam could imply that one is not as smart and successful as one thought. As a consequence, the processing individuals engage in can be biased or motivated in one direction or another in order to maintain a particular position. For instance, under certain conditions individuals may prefer to search for and attend to information that is consistent with their prior beliefs and wishes (Dunning, 2015; Festinger, 1957; Kunda, 1990; Alicke & Sedikides, 2011).

Finally, the specific nature of social cognition is reflected in strong time constraints. In most social situations individuals have a fairly limited time to respond. For example, when you are at a party and meet someone for the first time, you need to respond instantaneously. You can hardly stand there and wonder for a long time whether the other person's initial statement had a friendly or an aggressive tone. In any case, your interpretation will influence your response, which in turn influences the other person's subsequent behavior, and so on. Time constraints demand that the amount of processing is reduced to a sufficient level—yet, even under these constraints, individuals' constructions of social reality need to be reasonably adequate for them to act successfully in social situations. As a result, social cognition needs to be highly adaptive and sensitive to the requirements of a situation.

To illustrate how different cognitive processing may be when it is embedded in a social or non-social context, consider a task on logical reasoning abilities: the Wason selection task (Wason, 1966). In order to solve the Wason selection task, individuals must find out which information is needed to test an if–then rule. Extensive research has led to the conclusion that individuals are quite poor at solving this kind of task; reasoning errors persist even when the rule refers to familiar and meaningful content. Basing her argument on an evolutionary approach to logical reasoning, Cosmides (1989; see also Gigerenzer & Hug, 1992) demonstrated that embedding the very same rules within the form of social contracts (e.g., "If someone wants to use public transportation, then he must have a valid ticket") resulted in an enormous increase in correct solutions (see Manktelow, 1999). Findings of this kind suggest that the social context has a very pronounced impact on individuals' processing. They further imply that detaching cognitive tasks from the social context may alter the quality of the underlying process. Detaching the cognitive processes from the social context will thus often result in seemingly poor performance and errors—as in the non-social presentation of the Wason selection task. However, within a social context these errors are not necessarily observable in the form of real mistakes (see Funder, 1987, for the difference between errors and mistakes). For a more detailed description of the Wason selection task within a social versus non-social context, see Box 1.1.

Box 1.1   How introducing a social context may change the mediating processes in logical reasoning

In this task, participants have to check whether a given set of stimuli conforms with a specific rule. In general, the rule has a "if p then q" structure. In the original paradigm introduced by Wason (1966), participants were presented with four cards. They were informed that one side of each card had a letter, the other side a number. The visible symbols were 4, A, L, and 7. The rule participants had to check stated: If there is a vowel on one side of the card, then there is an even number on the other side of the card. Which card would you need to turn, in order to check this rule?

The correct solution is A and 7 (which is p and non-q in the "if p then q" structure). A vowel on the upturned side logically requires an even number on the other side. An odd number on the back side would falsify the rule. The vowel card (A) therefore affords a critical test of the rule. In contrast, the consonant card (L) is irrelevant, for if a vowel implies an even number, this does not logically exclude that consonants may also come with even numbers. Indeed, the rule says nothing about the relationship between consonants and numbers. For the same reason, selecting and turning over the even number (4) is uninformative, because we do not know whether only vowels or both vowels and consonants imply even numbers. The most difficult part is to recognize that the odd number is critical and must be selected to find out whether it has a consonant on the back. If it does, the rule *if vowel then even number* will be violated.

Hundreds of experiments have shown that even intelligent and highly educated student participants have a hard time solving this simple reasoning problem. Even explaining the task extensively does not improve performance. However, Cosmides (1989) suggests that individuals have much less of a problem with this kind of task if it is embedded in a context of social exchange (see also Gigerenzer & Hug, 1992). For example, in one context of social exchange, the rule could be stated as follows: "If a person uses public transportation, he must have a valid ticket." Note that this rule has the same "if p then q" structure as the letter/number example above.

Person has a valid ticket	Person uses public transportation	Person does not use public transportation	Person has no valid ticket

In this scenario, participants check whether the person who uses public transportation has a valid ticket (which is equivalent to turning over A in the task above), and they check whether the person who has no valid ticket uses public transportation (which is equivalent to turning over the seven in the example above). Although the task has the same "if p then q" structure, participants are far better at coming up with the logically correct solutions. In other words, embedding the task in a social exchange context changed the underlying cognitive processes. Our key point here is not the improved performance, but the fact that introducing the social context changes the way the information is processed. While this change improved performance in the present example, it may sometimes also impair performance.

In sum, social cognition is unique in several ways. Most importantly, unlike other judgments, social judgments usually refer to non-observable attributes, rendering social cognition a highly complex endeavor. As a consequence, the constructive aspect plays a particularly important role. In combination with time constraints, motivational aspects, and self-involvement, this "going beyond the information given" (Bruner, 1957a) renders social cognition a unique and fascinating topic.

Overview: the structure of this book

As outlined above, social cognition research investigates how information is encoded, stored, and retrieved from memory, how social knowledge is structured and represented, and what processes are involved when individuals compute judgments and make decisions. Not surprisingly, these different processes are highly intertwined even for simple tasks, and they can hardly be seen in isolation from one another. Before disentangling the various aspects, we will therefore begin with a general overview of the sequence of information processing and an outline of general principles (Chapter 2). Next we look at how social knowledge is perceived and encoded (Chapter 3), as well as stored and retrieved (Chapter 4). Chapters 5 and 6 then focus on how information is used in judgmental processes, with emphasis placed on controlled and automatic processes (Chapter 5) versus heuristic processes, or rules of thumb (Chapter 6). The next two chapters show that feelings play a critical role in all kinds of social cognitive processes, informing and guiding perception, storage, and judgment. Chapter 7 puts the spotlight on mood states, that is, subtle affective feelings of positivity and negativity. Chapter 8 centers on cognitive feelings, that is, the ease or difficulty associated with all kinds of mental processing. Chapter 9 unites a variety of findings on a particularly social part of social cognition: the communication of information. Finally, Chapter 10 illustrates that the social environment fundamentally constrains social processing, and therefore needs to be taken into account to understand human affect, behavior, and cognition. Each chapter focuses on basic theoretical principles, which are illustrated with selective empirical findings.

Chapter summary

1   Social cognition research is concerned with the study of social knowledge and the cognitive processes that are involved when individuals construct their subjective reality. Researchers in social cognition therefore investigate how social information is encoded, stored, and retrieved from memory, how social knowledge is structured and represented, and what processes are involved when individuals form judgments and make decisions.
2   Different perspectives of the social thinker have been proposed: the consistency seeker strives for consistency between various beliefs about the world; the lay scientist gathers information unselectively and constructs social reality in an unbiased manner; the cognitive miser strives to simplify cognitive processes, particularly when under time pressure or in complex situations; the motivated tactician applies multiple strategies depending on the situational constraints; and the activated actor is primarily influenced by environmental cues that bring to mind relevant knowledge about adequate interpretations and behavior.
3   The cognitive component of social cognition emphasizes the role of cognitive processes that mediate between a stimulus and a behavioral response. This mediation is particularly obvious when the objectively identical stimulus results in different responses. The cognitive component allows individuals to modify their behavior as a function of their subjective interpretation of the situation.
4   The social component of social cognition emphasizes the specific aspects of the mediating cognitive processes in thinking about the social world. First, these aspects result from the nature of the social stimulus. Most importantly, the attributes of interests are usually non-observable and require a considerable amount of constructive processes. Second, the processes are highly sensitive to the constraints of the social situation.

Discussion questions/topics

1   What is meant by the phrase "constructing social reality"? In the context of constructing social reality, what is meant by "going beyond the information given"?
2   Describe an example from everyday life in which the same objective input results in different subjective realities as a function of the social context.

3   What different goals might individuals have when they construct social reality? Describe an example in which the different goals will result in different constructions.
4   Present Illustration 1.4(b) to some of your friends, and Illustration 1.4(c) to some other friends. Then show Illustration 1.4(a). Examine how prior exposure may alter the interpretation of Illustration 1.4(a).
5   What advantage lies in the cognitive link between stimulus and response?
6   Describe how judging a person is different from judging an inanimate object.

Recommendations for further reading

Carlston, D. E., ed. (2013). *The Oxford handbook of social cognition*. New York: Oxford University Press. (This book offers an extensive coverage of many topics in social cognition.)

Fiske, S. T., & Taylor, S. E. (2017). *Social cognition: From brains to culture* (3rd ed.). New York: McGraw-Hill. (The book provides an extensive coverage of social cognition research, presumably more adequate for advanced students.)

Kruglanski, A. W. (1989). *Lay epistemics and human knowledge: Cognitive and motivational bases*. New York: Plenum. (The book discusses different motives for how individuals construct their social reality, though somewhat older it still provides an excellent discussion on the various basic perspectives.)

Smith, E. R., & Semin, G. R. (2004). Socially situated cognition: Cognition in its social context. In *Advances in Experimental Social Psychology, 36*, 57–121. (This chapter provides an in-depth discussion on how cognitive processes are affected by social situations.)

2 General framework of social cognitive processing

Herbert Bless & Rainer Greifeneder

This chapter provides a general overview of the social cognition framework. Its main goals are to take a look at social cognition from something of a bird's eye view and to address general principles. It does not focus on complexities and qualifications and puts less emphasis on detailed results from specific studies; rather, it provides a broad overview and lays out the organization of the subsequent chapters. You will therefore notice some degree of redundancy, which we hope will prove beneficial to learning.

We start with a look at the main ingredients that are essential for the way in which individuals construct reality. Next, we outline three general themes that are related to any process involved in the construction of social reality. Lastly, we present an idealized sequence of steps in which information is processed.

Three main ingredients

How does a person go about constructing social reality? On a very general level we can distinguish three different elements or "ingredients" that need to be taken into account (see Illustration 2.1): (i) input from the given situation; (ii) input in the form of prior knowledge that individuals bring to the situation; and (iii) the processes that operate on the input.

(i) Input from the given situation

Obviously, a social situation itself constitutes input for the construction of social reality. Going back to the example of the party situation described in the previous chapter, the input from the situation can be perceived in various forms. We may see someone smiling, we may hear the statement that someone "helped a friend cheat on an exam," we may feel someone touching our hand, or we may feel the cold coming through the open door. These inputs result from sources that are external to the perceiver. (In order to see someone smiling, a number of mental operations must have occurred to transform stimulation of the retina into the perception of a smile. Although these transformations provide the very basis of the input as discussed here, they are beyond the scope of the current discussion.) In addition to these external inputs, there can also be internal ones. For example, we may feel hungry or nervous. It is obvious that when individuals construct their social reality, the situational input plays a key role: whether we detect a smile or a frown on a speaker's face strongly influences our subjective constructions of reality.

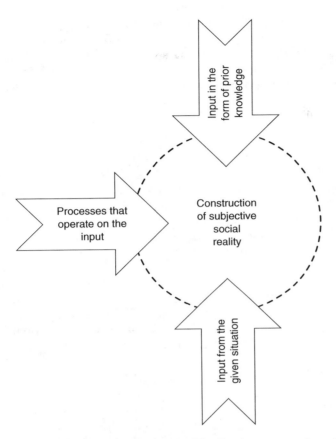

Illustration 2.1 Three main ingredients in the construction of subjective social reality: input in the form of prior knowledge, input from the given situation, and processes that operate on the input

(ii) Input in the form of prior knowledge

Yet, the stimuli from a situation determine its interpretation only in part, since the fate of a particular stimulus input depends also on the prior knowledge the perceiver brings to the situation. This prior knowledge may take very different forms. On the one hand, it may comprise rather general knowledge: individuals have correct or incorrect generalized assumptions about groups of people (e.g., males are assertive), they have knowledge about the usual sequence of social situations (e.g., individuals have a script for the sequence of events when they go to a restaurant), they have general assumptions about what constitutes honesty and trustworthiness (e.g., whether or not a white lie reflects dishonesty), they have knowledge about social norms that apply to social situations (e.g., how one acts when attending church), they have general expectations about how they themselves or how specific individuals react in a given situation, and so on. On the other hand, prior knowledge may also comprise specific episodes. For example, individuals may personally know many unassertive males, they may remember a specific dinner event that did not conform to the script, they may have personal experiences with cheating or being cheated, they may recall their own behaviors or that of others in performance situations, and so on. Prior knowledge thus comes in many forms, and constitutes a source of enormous variance in information that individuals can bring to a situation. For example, the input "helped a friend cheat on an exam" can be related to prior knowledge about honesty, but the same input can also be related to prior knowledge about friendship, thus potentially resulting in very different interpretations of the same input.

(iii) Processes that operate on the input

The third main ingredient in the construction of social reality is the processes that operate on the direct stimuli and prior knowledge. Processes can take very different forms and differ on a variety of dimensions. For example, individuals can process the information very quickly and rather superficially, or they can mull it over for quite a while. Processes can operate automatically or in a more controlled fashion. Moreover, they can be based primarily on the direct input, or they can rely more heavily on prior knowledge.

All three ingredients—the stimuli of the situation, prior knowledge, and the processes operating on them—need to be taken into account when trying to understand how individuals construct their social reality. It needs to be emphasized that the three ingredients are not nearly as distinct and easily distinguished as this preliminary overview might suggest. In fact, further discussion will show that they are highly

Illustration 2.2 When individuals form impressions of their current situation, their subjective interpretation will be influenced by information from the situation (e.g., the woman yells), by prior knowledge (e.g., yelling signals aggression, but not necessarily physical danger), and by cognitive processes that operate on these forms of input (e.g., the extent to which the yelling is scrutinized for being a signal of imminent physical danger)

Source: Ollyy/Shutterstock.com

intertwined and separable only in an idealized presentation. However, simplifying helps understand their respective contribution to the construction. With this in mind, we can now take a more specific look at general themes of social cognition and the sequential order of tasks that constructing social reality entails.

General themes underlying the construction of social reality

Given the complex nature of how social reality is constructed, it is not surprising that theoretical and empirical research has addressed numerous aspects of human information processing. This section will outline three general themes that are involved in all cognitive processes and that, either explicitly or implicitly, play a central role in all sections of the remainder of this book. These three themes pertain to: (a) the limitations of processing capacity and how much processing is allocated to the construction process; (b) the interplay of stimulus information and prior knowledge; and (c) the interplay of automatic and controlled processes.

Theme 1: the limitation of human processing capacity and the allocation of processing resources

When you consider buying a new computer, one of the more important features determining its quality is the size of its working memory, which is where the actual processing is performed. The size of the working memory determines whether programs and processes can be executed at all, and if so, how much time it takes for a specific operation. Similar conceptual assumptions have been made about human information processing. One key assumption of social cognition holds that a person's processing capacity is limited. This limitation implies that individuals cannot process all information that is potentially relevant for the interpretation of a specific situation, especially if time is an issue. And time is almost always an issue, since responding successfully to the needs of a situation often demands quick processing. We thus face two important limitations: that of processing capacity, and that of time. These limitations have a profound influence on almost any aspect of human information processing. Imagine a party situation with different groups of people. Individuals are not able to listen to and interpret all statements that are made. Moreover, when thinking about a particular statement, individuals are usually not able to consider all possible interpretations. And when asked at the end of the party for an impression about a particular guest, individuals are not able to recall all of the guest's statements, how he or she reacted to other people, his or her bodily and facial expressions, and so on. Even if it were possible to do all of these things, considering, weighing, and integrating this information into a judgment would constitute a highly complex and presumably unmanageable task.

The combination of limitations on human processing capacity, on the one hand, and time constraints, on the other hand, constitutes an important challenge for social cognitive processing. Indeed, though there are situations when one of these limitations can be offset by the other (e.g., taking more time to think a specific issue through), most often individuals need to cope with both limitations. One way to respond to this challenge is to simplify processing. Mere simplification, however, is likely not enough. The simplification has to be highly efficient, too, so that the resulting construction of social reality still provides an adequate basis for a person's responses to the social environment. Simplifications that systematically result in wrong interpretations in the real world could have severe consequences.

As we shall see, individuals have developed highly adaptive mechanisms that allow for efficient processing. First, instead of considering all relevant information, individuals may rely on less information: they may not attend to all situational stimuli, and even if a stimulus is attended to, it may not receive enough attention to be processed in greater detail or be stored in memory. In any case, a selection of the information is required. This selection is far from random. In fact, the nature of the situation influences the selection, which results in a highly context-dependent and thus highly adaptive construction of social reality. Research questions resulting from this assumption address the precise mechanism of these selection processes: What determines which stimulus individuals attend to? What determines which concept is used for interpreting a given stimulus?

Reducing the amount of information simplifies processing and is therefore one possible way of dealing with capacity constraints. A second possible way is more directly related to the very processes that operate on the input in a given situation. Cognitive processes differ with respect to the load they impose on processing capacity. Instead of relying on elaborative processes, individuals often rely on less taxing processes, which are referred to as cognitive rules of thumb, mental short-cuts, or heuristics. Here we define a *heuristic* as a cognitive device that enables the social individual to make judgments in ways that require little processing capacity. To illustrate the notion of heuristics, consider the following examples. When forming judgments about other persons, judgments may reflect the integration of all the specific information about the target person. Alternatively, individuals can base their judgment on the stereotype they have about the group or social category the person belongs to. Forming judgments on the basis of stereotypes constitutes heuristic processing and generally requires fewer resources than judgments based on the individuating information about a specific person (cf. Bodenhausen, Macrae, & Sherman, 1999; S. T. Fiske & Neuberg, 1990). Similarly, when deciding which candidate to vote for in an election, individuals may elaborate on the potential implications of the political program. Alternatively, they may simply vote for the candidate who seems friendliest (note that politicians seem to be aware of these alternatives and spend a lot of effort on establishing a friendly image). Again, thinking extensively about the details of a political program requires far more resources than taking a simple cue, here perceived friendliness, as a basis for the decision, which constitutes heuristic processing (cf. Petty & Cacioppo, 1981; Petty & Wegener, 1999).

The different ways of simplifying cognitive processes are a central issue in social cognition research and will re-appear throughout this book (see, in particular, Chapter 6). It is important to emphasize that mere simplification is not enough. To ensure an appropriate construction of social reality, this processing needs to be efficient. Consistent with this premise, reliance on heuristics in social judgment often proves helpful, despite the small amount of processing involved. For example, one rule of thumb in consumer decision making is to gauge the quality of a particular product by comparing its price to that of its competitors. After all, high quality is usually more expensive than low quality. Arguably, this logic holds for the majority of cases and thus constitutes an efficient rule of thumb.

With simplification, however, comes the risk of mistakes. For instance, the quality–price heuristic discussed above may lead consumers astray when quality and price are not aligned. Generally speaking, reliance on heuristics may result in systematic bias under certain conditions. Though these conditions are arguably not representative of all possible situations, a review of social cognition research might create the impression that human judgment is full of flaws and biases. But note that this impression itself is biased because researchers tend to focus on deviations and biases. Researchers argue that investigating deviations, that is, the conditions under which judgments are systematically biased, provides better access to human information processing than merely focusing on conditions in which biases do not occur. While the research focus on biases may thus allow for a particular insight into human processing, it does not allow for the conclusion that human information processing is generally flawed.

Simplifying processes is important and essential, but the way in which individuals shortcut cognitive processes can vary as a function of the situation. Individuals can allocate more or fewer processing resources, depending on the requirements of the situation. Imagine a person at a party doing several things simultaneously: listening to someone else in the group, thinking about what to say next, tasting some food, and noticing a new guest entering the room. All these activities will tax the individual's resources. From a functionalist perspective, it would be highly adaptive if individuals did not simplify all their processes all the time. Presumably, individuals would be better off if they could process the information in either a simplified heuristic manner, or a more elaborative and systematic manner, depending on the demands of the situation. And, indeed, we find that human information processing has an adaptive quality. In fact, the amount of processing can vary enormously. This being the case, the requirement to simplify processing due to the limitation of human processing resources is qualified by a person's ability to allocate more resources to a particular task.

This gives rise to the next question: what determines the amount of processing? Or, to put it differently: what variables influence whether individuals tend to simplify their task or not? First, the amount of processing allocated to a particular task depends on the amount of free resources. How much of the resources is occupied by other tasks? In other words: how much *processing capacity* is available? The smaller the number of other taxing activities, the greater the likelihood that more elaborative processes will occur. In addition to processing capacity, it is *processing motivation* that determines the amount of processing that takes place. Not surprisingly, individuals have a strong processing motivation if the target of their cognitive processes is perceived as interesting or important, particularly when the target has great personal relevance. In these cases, individuals will allocate more processing resources to the task. If the cognitive system is already working at its limits, this may be achieved by withdrawing resources from other tasks. In our example, if the new guest entering the room is of high personal relevance, more resources are allocated to watching that person. This potentially implies, in turn, that resources devoted to other activities are cut back, for example the person will be listening less carefully to what is said in the group.

Many models in social cognition treat processing capacity and processing motivation as key factors influencing cognitive processes. Perhaps most prominently, processing motivation and capacity are conceptualized as central variables in theories on attitude change (for examples, see Eagly & Chaiken, 1993; Petty & Cacioppo, 1986) and person perception (S. T. Fiske & Neuberg, 1990; see also Chaiken & Trope, 1999). Although most of these models treat processing capacity and processing motivation as disjunct aspects on a theoretical level, empirically the two may often be hard to separate. For example, individuals will allocate fewer resources to a particular task (e.g., listening to the lecture) when they simultaneously engage in a second task (e.g., talking to other students). One might argue that the second task is reducing the processing capacity that is available for the first task. However, one might also argue that the student is less motivated to listen to the lecture. The general question concerning the amount of processing will emerge throughout this book in different facets pertaining to different cognitive processes.

Theme 2: top-down and bottom-up processing

We have already noted that the way in which individuals interpret and judge social situations is influenced by the stimuli from a given situation and by prior knowledge. Both aspects are essential ingredients in the process and cannot be seen in isolation. The interplay of situational stimuli and prior knowledge occurs in almost every cognitive process. Imagine, for example, someone at the party saying "Hi, my name is Joanne, I am a librarian." This brief sentence makes sense only if the perceiver can link the word librarian to some prior knowledge. The listener has prior conceptions about what this means, for example that the person works in a library, checks out books, buys new books for public use, and so on. A specific stimulus will not be understood if it cannot be linked to prior knowledge. For example, if Joanna said "I am a heudoi," most people would have no idea what this means. They would be unable to interpret this statement, that is, they could not make sense of it.

The interplay of stimuli from the situation and prior knowledge is similarly present in the subsequent processing that individuals engage in. Let us assume you are supposed to judge how introverted or extraverted the person is who made the statement about being a librarian. You could base your *extraversion judgment* on what you have observed at the party, for example that Joanna has been conversing animatedly with many people, and you could base your judgment at least partly on your stereotype, your prior knowledge that librarians are usually rather introverted (see Illustration 2.3). When the information is stored in memory, new input is related to prior knowledge and thus alters the prior knowledge that individuals bring to the next situation. For example, the observation that this librarian was engaged in lively conversation with many people may change the prior knowledge that librarians are usually rather introverted.

The notion that the interplay of new stimuli and prior knowledge is manifested in virtually every cognitive process does not imply that the relative impact of the two aspects is balanced or constant across situations. On the contrary. Sometimes human information processing is guided primarily by prior knowledge and the expectations individuals bring to a situation. In this case the processing is called *concept-driven* or *top-down processing*. At other times human information processing is influenced primarily by the stimuli from a given situation. In this case the processing is called *data-driven* or *bottom-up processing*. We can illustrate these two ideal types of processing with an example taken from the realm of person perception. In top-down processing, impressions and

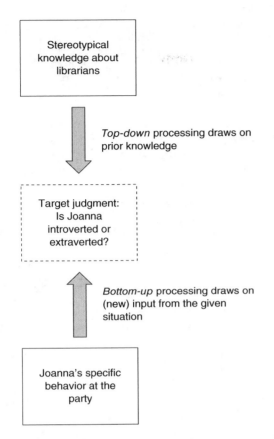

Illustration 2.3 Top-down versus bottom-up processing when evaluating the librarian
Joanna as introverted versus extraverted

judgments about a specific target person are based predominantly on prior beliefs
about the group to which the target person is assigned (e.g., librarians). Prior knowledge
in the form of a stereotype colors the evaluation of a new input (Bodenhausen et al.,
1999; Brewer, 1988; S. T. Fiske & Neuberg, 1990). In bottom-up processing, judgments
about the target person are based predominantly on the implications of the behavior that is observed. In this case, the resulting judgment can be inconsistent with our
prior beliefs. Moreover, the new input may contribute—under certain conditions—to
a change of the stereotype (Hewstone, 1994; Kunda & Oleson, 1995; Weber & Crocker,
1983; Yzerbyt & Carnaghi, 2008). Importantly, top-down versus bottom-up processing
differ with respect to how many processing resources they require. Processes that rely
more heavily on prior knowledge (top-down processes) usually require fewer processing resources than attending more strongly to the information provided by the current
situation (bottom-up processing). Thus, the relative contribution of top-down versus
bottom-up processes is a core element in how individuals can influence the amount of
processing allocated to a particular task.

Theme 3: automatic and controlled processes

Cognitive processes can differ with respect to their automaticity and controllability (Shiffrin & Schneider, 1984). For example, when a new guest arrives at the party, individuals can actively call to mind some particular content from their memory, such as where they saw the person the last time. However, information may also come to mind automatically. For example, by realizing that the new guest belongs to a particular social group (e.g., fraternity member, business major, etc.), the perceiver's general expectations about that group may pop up automatically, unintended, and uncontrolled (Devine, 1989; S. T. Fiske & Neuberg, 1990; Lepore & Brown, 1997).

A number of aspects have been formulated to distinguish cognitive processes on the continuum from automaticity on the one end to controllability on the other. In an ideal type, *automatic processes* are unintentional, require very few cognitive resources, cannot and need not to be controlled, and lie outside an individual's awareness. While automatic processes may differ with respect to how much they match the ideal criteria listed above, it is usually assumed that their initiation and running requires no conscious regulation (Bargh, 1999; Dijksterhuis, 2010; Gawronski & Bodenhausen, 2006). Imagine, for example, someone driving home from the office: all the braking, accelerating, and turning are highly automatized, requiring no intentional control.

Controlled processes, on the other hand, demand considerable resources, their initiation and running requires conscious regulation, and they are potentially within the scope of an individual's awareness. In particular, deviations from a specific automatized sequence of processes, for example taking a detour on the way home to pick up something at the grocery store, require more controlled and intentional processing. Because automatic processes require few resources, and controlled processes require considerable resources, they operate best under different situational conditions. Controlled processes fail particularly when other tasks are taxing a person's resources. For example, despite the driver's need to pick up something at the grocery store, he or she arrives at home having taken the usual route and forgotten to stop. The person obviously did not allocate to the controlled processes the mental resources needed to deviate from the usual routine.

In some cases, controlling one's own processes seems a pretty easy task. For example, for most individuals it is easy to recall where they spent their last vacation. But the attempt to control cognitive processes is not always successful. For example, in an exam students may fail to bring to mind the answer to a question even though they have this information stored in memory. Moreover, avoiding particular thoughts is no simple task, as some intrusive thoughts arise even though a person is intentionally trying to avoid them. Sometimes it seems that the more a person tries to avoid these thoughts, the more they persist and intrude on that person's awareness (Wegner, 1994). For example, people who are worried about a particular problem often cannot stop thinking about it, even though they would like to (Martin & Tesser, 1996). These examples suggest that there are two aspects to the question of control: control pertains to a person's ability to bring a particular content to awareness, as well as to the ability to suppress a particular content. Research and everyday experience suggest that the former kind of control is far more successful than the latter.

As was the case with automaticity, there are different types of controlled processes that match the ideal criteria to varying degrees. It is therefore not surprising that the distinction between automatic and controlled processes is sometimes less sharp than one might expect. This fluid differentiation between automaticity and control is not only one aspect of different processes, but can also be observed within the same process. Mental activities can start out as controlled processes and eventually shift toward highly automatized processes, especially as a result of long practice (C. A. Smith, 1989). For example, driving a car in an unknown city requires a considerable amount of controlled processes—where to turn, what to watch out for, and so on. With more practice and a growing familiarity with the new city, the same processes become more and more automatized, requiring fewer and fewer resources and less awareness.

The general message from this example is that the more familiar individuals are with a particular stimulus situation, the greater the likelihood that automatic processes have a pronounced impact. Controlled processes are more likely to come into play in unfamiliar stimulus situations. This again points to the adaptive and highly efficient nature of human information processing. Because automatic processes require fewer processing resources, the resources they save can be allocated to other tasks. The cognitive system is designed in such a clever way that this saving of resources is most likely in highly familiar situations. When the situation becomes unfamiliar, the system shifts toward the more controlled processing. Note that this aspect, the fact that the required resources are highly context-dependent, directly relates to the limitations of processing capacity and the amount of processing (Theme 1). Automaticity and controllability have become an important aspect in understanding human information processing. Several different facets of this distinction will be touched on implicitly in the remaining chapters, as well as explicitly in Chapter 7.

The sequence of information processing

The task of interpreting a social situation, of making sense of and responding to one's social environment, comprises a variety of highly interconnected sub-tasks. These different sub-tasks can be seen as steps that link the observable input to a person's overt behavior. Following the paradigm of cognitive psychology, we can organize the sequence of cognitive processes into the different stages depicted in Illustration 2.4. To begin with, individuals have to perceive the stimulus events. For example, while talking to someone at the party you recognize that this person is hardly looking at you. Next, perceivers need to extract some meaning from the basic input, that is, they need to *encode* their perceptions. For example, you interpret the fact that the other person is not looking at you as a lack of interest, or, alternatively, as shyness. Because this encoding relies heavily on prior knowledge *stored* in memory, individuals need to *retrieve* prior knowledge. For example, we may retrieve prior knowledge about social interactions where one person was hardly looking at her communication partner. Finally, the encoded perception will be stored in memory and will potentially affect the assessment of future events. Both the newly encoded input and the old knowledge stored in memory will then provide the basis for further processing, leading to *inferences, judgments, and decisions*. For example, you may infer that the other person is not interested in your detailed description of the latest sporting event. Sometimes, but not always, the final outcome of this cognitive process is manifested in an overt *behavioral response*. For example, you might decide to change the topic of your conversation. Following this brief overview, we will now take a closer look at the various steps in the information processing sequence.

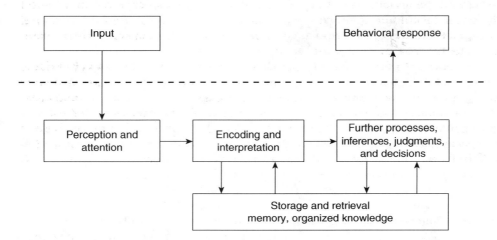

Illustration 2.4 Sequence of information processing

Perception and attention

Let us return to the example of the party situation. Imagine yourself at this party with many people in the same room. Different groups have formed, all carrying on lively conversations. In this situation there is an almost infinite number of stimuli your senses could register. You could attend to what all the different people are saying, the verbal and non-verbal reactions of their partners, the sound of the music, the smell of the different foods, the taste of your wine, and much more. In addition to these external stimuli, you also register internal stimuli. For example, you may feel aroused, happy, sad, or angry, you may feel pain or the contraction of muscles.

In order to act in such a setting, individuals need to construct an internal representation of the situation. Ideally, all the different stimuli could be used for constructing this representation. However, as discussed in Theme 1, the capacity of human information processing is limited. We cannot process all stimuli that reach our sensory system—not even by relying on highly simplified processes. As a consequence, individuals need to select which stimuli enter into further processing. To deal with this essential requirement, individuals have the ability to direct their attention to some aspects of the situation and exclude other aspects from being processed further and thereby taxing resources.

The well-known cocktail-party effect (Cherry, 1953) illustrates this important skill. Suppose at the party you were later asked what the group in the other corner of the room had been discussing. You would probably have no idea. Obviously, the entire conversation of this other group would be lost although it had reached your senses. Indeed, most likely the acoustic sound reached your ear; however, you did not "hear" what was said, because you did not pay attention. Imagine, however, you had overheard someone in that distant group mentioning your name. Even if you continued to converse in your own group, you would probably direct some of your attention toward that other conversation, and later you would be able to recall parts of it.

This example illustrates that individuals have the ability to direct their attention to various aspects of a given situation. This ability is an important mechanism for dealing with the limitations of human information processing captured in Theme 1 (Broadbent, 1958). The attentional processes allow individuals to process only a small and manageable subset of the immense number of stimuli that reach their senses. It is this subset that gets processed further in the next steps.

The important function of attentional processes in the very early stages gives rise to the question of what attracts attention. Our attention is generally attracted by stimuli that stand out, in other words, by stimuli that are distinct or salient in the context of other stimuli. A stimulus can be distinctive in relation to other stimuli in the situational context, it can be salient with respect to an individual's prior knowledge and the expectations the person brings to the situation, or it can be salient because of its special relationship to a person's current goals that guide processing (S. T. Fiske & Taylor, 2017). We will address these three facets of salience in turn.

Clapping of hands

Salience resulting from discrepancy to other stimuli in the situation

A good deal of research suggests that a stimulus attracts more attention if it has a solo status in relation to other stimuli in a given situation. For example, the only female in a group that is otherwise all males will attract more attention than if the context were all females. Conversely, the only male in a group of females will likely draw particular attention (for an additional example, see Illustration 2.5).

This impact of standing out has been demonstrated with respect to a number of variables, such as race or age (for an overview, see S. T. Fiske, 1998). You can test this aspect of salience by wearing some unusual clothes the next time you go to class. For example, wearing a shirt and jeans all in red with yellow dots will attract the attention

Illustration 2.5 Salience of stimuli as a function of the context. Here, both the dog and the sheep with the black head are salient in the context of the other sheep. In the context of dogs, the dog would not be salient, and in the context of black sheep, the sheep with the black head would not be salient

Source: ANADMAN BVBA/Shutterstock.com

of your fellow students. If you put this to the test, however, you might realize that attracting the attention of others does not necessarily imply their approval. Note that the attention toward you will diminish if others start wearing the same type of clothes. Though your clothes are still the same, they cease to stand out and capture less attention—which underscores that it is not the stimulus per se, but its relationship to the situational context that creates salience. There are many other ways in which a stimulus can acquire salience by standing out: for example, the target is moving in the context of a fixed environment, or, conversely, the target is fixed and the other contextual stimuli are moving (McArthur & Post, 1977). Similarly, increasing a target's brightness in an otherwise dark context creates salience (McArthur & Ginsberg, 1981).

Salience resulting from discrepancy to prior knowledge

In order to make sense of a current situation, individuals need to relate the situational stimuli to their prior knowledge, as emphasized in Theme 2. Usually, a particular stimulus that does not match prior knowledge and expectations appears as more distinctive and captures more attention than a stimulus that matches perfectly with a person's prior social knowledge. For example, if you go out for dinner and the waiter is dressed up as Santa Claus on roller skates, he will receive more attention than if he were dressed in the expected outfit. From this perspective it seems clear why it has been argued that infrequent stimuli can attract more attention than frequent and expected stimuli, or that individuals attend especially to extreme and unanticipated behaviors (Hamilton & Gifford, 1976). In general, this mechanism of attention attraction is highly adaptive because it directs a person's focus to those aspects of the situation that are not already incorporated into his or her prior social knowledge. As with most mechanisms that are very adaptive overall, this attention-attraction process may have unwanted side effects. For example, a driver's attention can be attracted by an unusually severe accident on the other side of the freeway. Yet, with less attention devoted to his or her own driving, the risk of causing an accident increases. Similarly, it is no surprise that individuals often gaze at other people who look different from the norm and the expectations the perceiver brings to the situation—for example, because the target is physically disabled, unusually small, tall, large, and so on (e.g., Langer, Fiske, Taylor, & Chanowitz, 1976).

Salience resulting from the relation to goals

Attention to a particular stimulus does not necessarily require a discrepancy with other stimuli or with prior knowledge and expectations. Attention may also arise from the relationship between the stimulus and the perceiver's current goals (see Gollwitzer & Moskowitz, 1996, for a discussion of how goals affect cognition and behavior). For example, if you are very hungry when you come to a party, the food will attract special attention (Bruner, 1957b). Similarly, if your goal pertains to finding a new date, your attention will be directed at party guests who could potentially match your preferences. Because goals can be very diverse, almost any stimulus may receive particular attention from individuals (for examples, see Berscheid, Graziano, Monson, & Dermer, 1976; Erber & Fiske, 1984). For instance, targets that are personally relevant attract more attention than others (Neuberg & Fiske, 1987; Ruscher & Fiske, 1990). Moreover, relevance can be due to external instruction: individuals can be instructed to attend to a particular stimulus in a situation, for example, by teachers or coaches. In the absence of other conflicting goals, instructions can focus an individual's attention on a subset of the potentially observable stimuli (Taylor & Fiske, 1975). To illustrate, consider one experiment in which participants watched a video of two teams of three players each passing a basketball (Simons & Chabris, 1999). One team was dressed in black, the other in white, and participants were instructed to silently count the passes of the white team. Before you go on reading, you may want to try this experiment yourself by watching the video at: https://youtu.be/vJG698U2Mvo.

About 40 seconds into the video, a woman dressed up as a gorilla walked into the picture, faced the camera, and walked out again. Though you won't miss the gorilla once you know that it is there, about 50% of participants missed it when viewing it for the first time (Simons & Chabris, 1999). This experiment illustrates that instructions can focus our attention, and that we miss a lot of things in the perceptual stream our attention is not directed to. As we have seen, attention may arise for different reasons. On the one hand, attention may result almost automatically from the discrepancy between a stimulus and the immediate context or the perceiver's prior knowledge. It is important to realize that in almost every case, the salience of a stimulus is not a property of the stimulus itself; instead, it is the relationship to the context that creates salience. On the other hand, individuals may actively and intentionally direct their attention toward specific stimuli because they are relevant to their current goals. Note that these different causes of salience are related to the issue of automaticity versus controllability (Theme 3). Note also that the highly adaptive functions of attention regulation can hardly be overestimated, because salience channels where our limited processing resources are directed to (Theme 1).

In any case, attention regulation is an essential process with important consequences and ramifications. Indeed, it has been argued that the selection of information itself can sometimes be more consequential than the inferences based on the selection (McArthur & Baron, 1983). Although in some cases the salience of a stimulus is unrelated to its importance, most often a person's construction of social reality based on the "selected" salient stimuli reflects to a high degree his or her current needs and the most important features of a given situation.

Not surprisingly, in everyday life we are exposed not only to a virtually infinite number of social stimuli, but also to countless attempts designed to attract our attention. For example, many advertisers assume that it is an essential step to attract the potential customer's attention before successfully providing further information about a particular product (McGuire, 1985; see Shavitt & Wänke, 2000, on applying the social cognition paradigm to consumer psychology). Similarly, many, though not all, individuals want to attract attention and engage in activities that stand out from the context or the perceivers' expectations.

Encoding and interpretation

After an individual has perceived a stimulus and allocated sufficient attention to it, the next step in the information processing sequence requires the perceiver to *encode* and *interpret* this perception, that is to say, give meaning to the stimulus input. Encoding comprises various processes that are involved when an external stimulus is transformed into an internal representation. Although the boundaries between perception and encoding are fuzzy, encoding usually relies more heavily on prior knowledge than does perception. Individuals accomplish the encoding task by relating the new stimulus to prior knowledge, that is, to information they already know (Theme 2). Much of our prior general knowledge is represented in the form of categories. The term *category* denotes an elementary knowledge structure, corresponding to a singular concept or class of objects (for a more extended discussion of different types of knowledge structures, see Chapter 4). To make sense of a particular input, individuals need to relate the input to some meaningful category. In turn, identifying a perceived target as belonging to a category allows the perceiver to infer more information than is actually provided.

Imagine, for example, that your attention is directed toward an object moving quickly down the road. Based on your prior knowledge, you are able to relate this stimulus input to a meaningful knowledge structure, in this case the category "car." As a consequence, the perception is enriched with stimulus-independent knowledge, and this knowledge information helps to interpret the meaning of the input. You can infer that the car has an engine, most likely runs on gas, has brakes, and that it will stop when the traffic light turns red (at least most of the time). Note that you can see none of these attributes when the object is moving down the road. By adding the information from their prior knowledge, individuals are "going beyond the information given" (Bruner, 1957a). This going beyond the information given is an essential process inherent in any encoding task.

Applying this principle to person perception allows individuals to assign a target to a social category, for example man or woman, the elderly, student, professor, some kind of ethnic group, skinhead, police officer, and so on. Having categorized a target, individuals can use their knowledge of the social category—their stereotype—for subsequent interpretations and inferences. The perceiver could infer personality characteristics or likely behaviors, although—like the engine in the car example—these are not observable in the situation. For example, it could be inferred that the target is slow, aggressive, smart, helpful, and so on—depending on which prior knowledge is associated with the category the target is assigned to. Individuals need to categorize behaviors much as they do objects and persons. How do individuals interpret the behavior of someone who helped a friend cheat on an exam? The behavior is assigned to pre-existing knowledge, for example, to the category "dishonest." The implications of this prior knowledge will influence further storage, retrieval, and inferential and judgmental processes.

In most cases a particular input can be assigned not just to one but to several categories, and these different categories may hold very different implications. For example, the man in Illustration 2.6 may be assigned to the category US-American, or to the category politician, or to the category father, and so on. Similarly, "helped a friend cheat on an exam" can be categorized as dishonest, but also as helpful. Because categorization into one or the other category is highly consequential, social cognition research has placed a lot of emphasis on understanding the encoding and categorization processes. Chapter 3 will address the underlying mechanism, the antecedents, and the consequences in more detail.

Storage and retrieval

When a stimulus has received sufficient attention and has been encoded, it may enter into further cognitive processes. One aspect of these further processes involves the storage of the information in memory. After all, individuals might use the information

Illustration 2.6 When forming an impression about Barack Obama, you can apply different prior knowledge because you might assign him to different social groups (e.g., US citizen, male, politician, African-American, father, husband, Nobel laureate, etc.)

Source: https://upload.wikimedia.org/wikipedia/commons/5/5d/Barack_Obama_family_portrait_2011.jpg

as a basis for their behavior not only in the immediate circumstances, but also in later situations. For example, at the party you make a number of new acquaintances. A few days later you meet one of them in the cafeteria, and most likely your behavior will be guided by what you can recall. Researchers usually investigate the storage process in conjunction with the retrieval process. In most cases, we can infer whether and how some information is stored only by assessing whether and how it is retrieved.

Information should be stored in such a way that it can be recalled easily if needed in a later situation. Moreover, it is obvious that storage of information requires considerable resources. In general, the more processing an individual allocates to a particular stimulus, that is, the more he or she thinks about a piece of information, the more likely it is for the information to be stored in memory. Thus, attention-grabbing information (see above) is more likely to be stored and subsequently retrieved than other information. However, this general statement about the relationship between amount of processing and storage is qualified by the fact that the resources required for efficient storage depend on how the new information is related to prior general knowledge.

If the incoming information is consistent with prior knowledge, it is sufficient to store a link to the prior knowledge structure rather than storing the new information again. For example, when one of the party guests gives an elaborate description of the last time he or she went out for dinner, the listener does not need to store all the details (e.g., that the guest made a reservation, that the waitress escorted them to the table, that she brought the menu, etc.). All this information is already part of the person's general knowledge about "going out for dinner." As a consequence, it is sufficient to store a link to this existing general knowledge structure. When retrieving the information at some later time, individuals simply need to recall "going out for dinner" and they can then reconstruct the details (a reservation was made, the waitress escorted the guests to the table, she brought the menu, etc.). As a result, *consistent information* can be "recalled" easily. Note that we have put "recalled" into quotation marks to signal that when individuals recall consistent information, they may in fact *reconstruct* the original situation on the basis of their general knowledge rather than actually recalling it. The advantage of this "recall" comes at the cost of *intrusion errors*: individuals may also reconstruct information that is part of their general knowledge but was not part of the actual information given. For example, a person might reconstruct that the waitress brought dessert even though this information was never supplied (Graesser, Gordon, & Sawyer, 1979; Snyder & Uranowitz, 1978).

Inconsistent information, by contrast, cannot be reconstructed on the basis of prior knowledge. However, this does not imply that inconsistent information will be lost. Inconsistent information—for instance, that the waitress was wearing inline skates—usually draws more attention (see above), and as a result, individuals allocate more processing resources to deal with the discrepancy between the implications of the stimulus and their prior knowledge. Not surprisingly, the more individuals think about something, the more likely they are to recall the event. Individuals will therefore be able to recall the inconsistent information later, provided they allocated sufficient processing resources during encoding and storing. Thus, both consistent and inconsistent information may have recall advantages, albeit for very different reasons.

Once again the themes outlined in the beginning of this chapter re-emerge. Obviously, storage and retrieval strongly depend on prior knowledge structures (Theme 2) and on the amount of processing (Theme 1). Moreover, the adaptive nature of human cognition becomes clear again. Whenever possible, individuals simplify their processing (in the case of consistent information), and allocate more processing if necessary (in the case of inconsistent information). Chapter 4 will provide a more detailed discussion of how social information is organized in human memory.

Further processes, inferences, judgments, and decisions

Drawing on encoded information and on information retrieved from memory, individuals need to engage in further processing in order to respond to the requirements of the social world. They need to make further inferences, form judgments, and make decisions. Grading an exam, assessing a product presented in a commercial, evaluating the trustworthiness of a politician, judging the likability of a person, weighing a philosophical idea, evaluating the food at the party—any concrete stimulus or abstract concept can be a judgmental target. Judgments usually reflect the fact that the individual is locating the judgmental target along a particular continuum or dimension: a politician is judged to be more or less trustworthy, a product is evaluated more or less favorably, and so on. Decisions often entail that individuals select one of at least two alternatives. These alternatives do not necessarily have anything in common (e.g., if you had the choice, what would you do: go to a movie, eat a bowl of soup, surf the web, or study for the next exam?).

Irrespective of the differences between inferences, judgments, and decisions, they all share one important characteristic: their highly constructive quality. The constructive nature of human cognition, the "going beyond the information given," is particularly pronounced in these stages of processing.

How does this construction work? How do individuals arrive at a particular inference, judgment, or decision? Ideally, individuals would consider all information that is relevant for the respective judgment, think about all the implications, and weigh the information according to its importance. However, given processing constraints (Theme 1) it is rather unlikely that individuals can engage in such exhaustive processing. Imagine, for example, the seemingly simple judgment in response to the question "How satisfied are you with your life in general?" You may retrieve a sheer endless number of aspects and information from memory that are potentially relevant for forming this judgment. Because of processing constraints, however, individuals will not be able to consider or even retrieve all the potentially relevant information. Instead, they can rely on a subset of information (Wyer & Srull, 1989) by truncating the search for relevant information. If so, judgments and decisions will be based on the information that comes to mind before the search process is ended. Chapter 3 addresses what factors determine which information is likely to be considered, and Chapter 5 focuses on how the resulting subset of information is integrated into a judgment or decision.

As a second example, consider one important form of inference that has received considerable attention: how do individuals infer general dispositions or traits on the basis of specific behaviors (observed directly or indirectly)? At the party you may be watching a person who is talking to another guest. You encode his behavior as nervous. Would you conclude that he is an anxious person in general? You could, but you could also take into account potential situational influences. For example, if the person is new in this group and does not know anybody at the party, you would perhaps be less likely to infer that he is generally anxious. Observers often seem to underestimate situational constraints and are more likely to attribute an observed behavior to the actor's disposition ("He is behaving nervously because he is an anxious person in general") rather than to situational influences ("He is behaving nervously because he is in an unfamiliar situation"). The tendency to attribute the behaviors of others to dispositions rather than to situational influence is called the *fundamental attribution error* (Jones & Harris, 1967; L. Ross, 1977). Research suggests that taking into account the situational constraints—which would often result in fewer dispositional attributions—requires additional resources, which individuals are often unable or unwilling to allocate (Gilbert, Pelham, & Krull, 1988). These attributional inferences constitute a very important facet of the way in which individuals process social information.

In many cases, selecting, weighing, and integrating information into a final judgment is a very complex task, even if individuals simplify the process by truncating the search for relevant information. In order to deal with this complexity, individuals have developed additional strategies that allow them to simplify the judgmental task by relying on rules of thumb. As briefly noted above, these cognitive devices are called *heuristics*. Not surprisingly, heuristics capture a wide spectrum of simplifying devices. For example, heuristics include reliance on stereotypes, in that individuals can base their judgments about a social target primarily on their stereotype about the group the target is assigned to (S. T. Fiske & Neuberg, 1990; Bodenhausen et al., 1999). Similarly, when evaluating an advertisement, individuals can rely on a single peripheral cue, such as the attractiveness of a communicator, rather than on an extensive examination of the content of a persuasive message (Eagly & Chaiken, 1993; Petty & Cacioppo, 1996; Vogel & Wänke, 2016).

Interestingly, some of the heuristics pertain to information provided by the processes themselves, that is, individuals rely on procedural knowledge. Most prominently, such a heuristic was introduced by Tversky and Kahneman (1973) in the form of the *availability heuristic*. According to the availability heuristic, individuals can base frequency and probability judgments on the ease with which information comes to mind. The assumption underlying this heuristic holds that if exemplars of a category come to mind easily, there must be many of them. For example, if you can easily retrieve many persons who play hockey, then there must be many people who play hockey; conversely, if it is difficult to retrieve persons who play hockey, then there are probably not that many. While this heuristic generally provides solid results, it can also bias judgments if factors unrelated to the recalled number influence the retrieval processes. For example, if you are a member of a hockey club it is easy to think of many people who play hockey, whereas if you have no connection to the sport you will have greater difficulty recalling exemplars. As a result, you would come up with different judgments about the percentage of people who play hockey. Chapter 6 will provide a deeper coverage of the various forms of heuristics, the conditions of their use, and the consequences for human judgment and behavior.

The selection of a behavioral response

One general notion of social cognition holds that individuals' behaviors are based on their internal representation of the social world, on their inferences, their judgments, and decisions—or as William James (1890, p. 333) noted: "My thinking is first and last and always for the sake of my doing" (see also S. T. Fiske, 1992). The behavioral response can take very different forms.

First, individuals can directly communicate their judgment to other persons. For example, you can tell your friend about your impression of the other guests. Communication about how one perceives and interprets the social world plays a very important role. Obviously, it can facilitate interaction with other individuals. If we know how the other person thinks, we can guide our behavior accordingly. For example, if the other person told us that she did not like a particular guest, we would be hesitant to invite the two persons for dinner at the same time. Moreover, by communicating their interpretation of the situation, individuals are provided with feedback about how others see the situation. Individuals have a strong motivation to compare their world views, not least to receive support for their own view, or to change their view according to other interpretations (Festinger, 1954). From this perspective it is not surprising that on a daily basis we learn about surveys on virtually any issue, and that an entire industry is concerned with assessing individuals' perception of the world.

Second, internal judgments and decisions provide the basis for the whole spectrum of behaviors. Depending on their internal representation of the situation, individuals will engage in different activities: individuals approach or avoid other persons, they help other persons in need, they react aggressively, they ignore others, they purchase certain products, they buy or sell stocks, they vote for a political candidate, and so on—all these behaviors are based on individuals' internal representations.

It is important to note that communicated judgments as well as behaviors do not always correspond with the internally generated representation of the judgmental target. For example, if the guest you don't like is a good friend of the person you are talking to, you will be more hesitant to express your negative impression. Similarly, individuals may sometimes seem to interact in a very friendly manner with a person they do not like.

Clearly, the judgment about the likability of the target person is not the only basis for the way individuals behave. In addition to their interpretation of the target (the other person, a specific product, etc.), individuals will take into account other aspects of the situation. Most obviously, behavior is also guided by social norms, such as not being rude, and these social norms may have different implications for behavior than the interpretation of the target. For example, we may not express a particular attitude or opinion (and perform the corresponding behavior) because the opinion is politically not correct in the current context. The interplay of attitudes and social norms in guiding social behavior is captured in Fishbein and Ajzen's theory of reasoned action (1974; Ajzen & Fishbein, 1980). While attitudes are assumed to influence behavior, it is argued that social norms also enter the equation (see Eagly & Chaiken, 1993; Fazio & Towles-Schwen, 1999 for general discussions of the attitude–behavior link). For example, if the social norm holds that you say nice things to the host of the party, you are likely to talk about how pleasant the party was even though you thought it was in fact quite boring.

In the absence of strong social norms, behavior is assumed to be consistent with individuals' attitudes. Yet, different attitudes held simultaneously may result in different implications for the resulting behavior. For example, you may hold very positive attitudes about cheesecake—which would imply eating a piece of the cake offered at the party (or several pieces). At the same time, you may also hold positive attitudes about eating healthy food—which would imply that you would rather go to the salad bar. This example illustrates that different behaviors are plausible on the basis of individuals' thinking.

Coda

The present chapter's goal was to introduce key ingredients, recurring themes, and a general framework of the information processing sequence. Consistent with this goal, we adopted a very abstract perspective. This abstract perspective allows for a good overview, but may be hard to digest on first reading. The subsequent chapters are different in that they focus more specifically and in rich detail on the various parts of the information processing sequence.

Chapter summary

1   In order to understand how individuals construct their social reality, we have to take into account three different elements: (a) the input from a given situation; (b) the input in the form of the prior knowledge that individuals bring to that situation; and (c) the processes that operate on these two kinds of input.

2   In this chapter three general themes of social cognition were outlined. These themes pertain to (a) the limitations of processing capacity, and how the amount of processing depends on motivation and capacity; (b) the interplay of stimulus information and prior knowledge; and (c) the interplay of automatic and controlled processes.

3   In an idealized model, the sequence of cognitive processes can be separated into different stages. Individuals first *perceive* a stimulus event and then *encode* and interpret this perception. Encoded information will be *stored* in memory so that it can be *retrieved* when required in later situations. Newly encoded input and retrieved prior knowledge provide the basis for further processing, leading to *inferences, judgments, and decisions*. Sometimes, but not always, the final outcome of this cognitive process is manifested in an overt *behavioral response*.

4   Individuals do not have the processing capacity to attend to all stimuli of a given situation. To deal with this shortcoming, individuals have the ability to direct their *attention* to some aspects of the situation and exclude others from being processed.
5   The encoding of a stimulus is heavily influenced by prior knowledge. In order to make sense of an input, individuals need to relate the input to some meaningful concept in memory.
6   Encoded information is stored in relation to prior knowledge. The processes underlying the storage of new information are different depending on whether that information is consistent or inconsistent with prior knowledge.
7   Individuals can rely on different processes when forming judgments and inferences. Depending on the situational constraints, they may select, weigh, and integrate as much relevant information as possible, or they may shortcut the processes by applying heuristic processing strategies.

Discussion questions/topics

1   What are the main ingredients for individuals' construction of social reality? Apply these ingredients to a specific example.
2   What is meant by "top-down" and "bottom-up" processing? Give some examples from everyday life.
3   Discuss some of the introduced concepts (e.g., automatic versus controlled processes, attention processes, heuristics) with respect to how social cognition reflects a high level of adaption toward the requirements of the social world.
4   Select a specific step from the information processing sequence (e.g., encoding, retrieval) and apply it to a specific example. Then relate the three major themes to this example.
5   What could an advertiser do to increase the chances that viewers pay attention to a particular commercial? Derive some specific examples from the considerations about attentional processes. Discuss potential advantages and disadvantages of the strategies.
6   Send the gorilla video (https://youtu.be/vJG698U2Mvo) to a few friends via your social network, with the instruction to count the number of throws. How many of them spontaneously note the gorilla?

Recommendations for further reading

The subsequent chapters of this book will provide greater in-depth coverage of the issues raised in this overview chapter. With the present chapter in mind, it might be worthwhile to see how the social cognition paradigm is applied to different areas. The two contributions listed below provide such an opportunity for the domains of consumer behavior and sport psychology.

Plessner, H., & Haar, T. (2006). Sports performance judgments from a social cognitive perspective. *Psychology of Sport and Exercise, 7*, 555–575.
Shavitt, S., & Wänke, M. (2000). Consumer cognition, marketing, and advertising. In A. Tesser & N. Schwarz (Eds.), *Handbook of social psychology* (pp. 569–590). Oxford: Blackwell.

3   Perceiving and encoding

Herbert Bless & Rainer Greifeneder

In Chapter 2, we outlined the basic principles that underlie the way in which individuals construct social reality. In doing so, we presented an idealized sequence in which information is processed. One central step in this sequence addresses how individuals encode and interpret new information. It was argued that encoding—that is, giving meaning to a stimulus—requires individuals to relate the new information to their prior knowledge. We have seen that, with the help of prior knowledge, new information can be interpreted and, moreover, additional inferences can be drawn. The present chapter addresses this issue in greater detail. We will outline and demonstrate the general principle, then provide selective examples, and finally discuss general background variables that influence encoding processes.

Relating new information to prior knowledge

What is a *heudoi*? Although we used this word in the previous chapter, you probably still have no idea what it could mean. In other words, there is an almost endless number of possible interpretations. You may be able to encode that word letter by letter, but without any prior knowledge you cannot give meaning to it. The endless number of possible interpretations is, of course, an extreme case, but in almost any situation we are faced with the need to specify the meaning within the context of the given situation. Assume you read the word "order." Although you know what it could potentially mean (unlike in the case of heudoi), the word may still have several meanings. Order could mean something like sequence or arrangement, or it could refer to a command. Again, it becomes clear that interpreting an input cannot be solved solely on the basis of the stimulus itself, but that the encoding requires the stimulus to be related to prior knowledge. Very importantly, in most cases a particular input can be related to different kinds of prior knowledge, so that the word "order" receives a different meaning depending on which prior knowledge it is related to. Turning to a somewhat more complex encoding task, assume you learn that someone helped a friend cheat on an exam. Again the semantic meaning is clear, but what does it mean? Would you like or dislike this person? The answer again depends on how you classify "helped a friend cheat on an exam." On the one hand, you could classify the behavior as dishonest, and then, presumably, you would not like this person. On the other hand, you could classify it as helpful, and chances are the person would appear more likable.

   The above examples demonstrate that different prior knowledge can be related to a particular stimulus, and that depending on the prior knowledge, the same stimulus will be interpreted quite differently. A central question of social cognition research directly follows from this perspective. There is broad consensus among researchers that in order for a stimulus to be related to prior knowledge, this knowledge must be applicable and accessible (Higgins, 1996; Higgins & Eitam, 2014; Janiszewski & Wyer, 2014; Wyer & Srull, 1989). *Applicability* refers to whether the knowledge can potentially be used to give meaning to the specific stimulus. For example, whereas prior knowledge about "dishonest" or "helpful" is applicable to the example "helped a friend cheat on the exam," knowledge about "athletic" or "humorous" is hardly applicable in trying to make sense of this particular behavior. In addition to applicability, it has been argued that concept use depends on *judged usability*. Whereas applicability refers to the goodness of fit between a concept and a judgment target, judged usability reflects appropriateness in the given context. This conceptual difference is perhaps best illustrated in the legal domain, where some piece of information may appear applicable but still be ruled inadmissible because it is inappropriate (e.g., testimony based on hearsay). Higgins (1996) emphasized that judged usability goes beyond accessibility and applicability and crucially determines the impact of primed information (see also Greifeneder & Bless, 2010; Higgins & Eitam, 2014).

Accessibility refers to the ease with which prior knowledge can be retrieved from memory. Some information comes to mind quickly, while other information takes longer and requires more processing. Note that accessibility is logically independent of applicability. It is entirely possible that the less applicable category is more accessible and is therefore more likely to be used for encoding than the more applicable category (cf. Förster & Liberman, 2007; Higgins, 1996).

What determines the accessibility of prior knowledge? Two general principles govern accessibility: *recency* and *frequency*. First, information that was recently used is more likely to be retrieved in the next situation than information that was used much longer ago. If an individual recently thought about dishonesty versus honesty, the statement that someone helped a friend cheat on an exam is more likely to be interpreted as dishonest behavior. Information that is accessible at a given time because it was recently activated is also labeled *temporarily* accessible information. Second, information that is used frequently is more accessible than information that is used infrequently. If the "dishonest versus honest" category is used often, the behavior in question is more likely to be interpreted as dishonest. Information that comes to mind easily independent of a particular recent use is also labeled *chronically* accessible information (Förster & Liberman, 2007; Higgins, 1996; Higgins, King, & Mavin, 1982). Perhaps the effect of recency and frequency is best illustrated by way of analogy: think of a box full of different toys, such as dolls, toy cars, robot kits, marbles, and so on. The toys that are on top of the box stand the highest chance of being used. What determines which toys lie on top? The toys that were used recently and those toys that are used frequently (see E. R. Smith, Mackie, & Claypool, 2015).

The recency principle is nicely demonstrated in so-called *priming* experiments, in which recently activated categories have been shown to possess enhanced accessibility. Priming can be referred to as information activation. Perhaps the most prominent study addressing the accessibility and applicability of prior knowledge in the interpretation of data is provided by Higgins, Rholes, and Jones (1977). Participants were asked to judge a target person, Donald, based on a rather ambiguous description of his habits and interests. For example, the following information was given: "By the way he acted, one could readily guess that Donald was well aware of his ability to do many things" (p. 145). Prior to this task, participants were presented with a list of words. The words were subtly embedded in an unrelated verbal learning experiment in which participants were asked to name the color of presented slides and to utter words they were supposed to remember while the slide was being shown. Some of these words were applicable to interpreting the meaning of the behavior descriptions about Donald. These applicable trait categories offered either positive interpretations (independent, persistent, self-confident, adventurous) or negative interpretations (aloof, stubborn, conceited, reckless) of the same behaviors. Participants were not aware of the connection between the two allegedly unrelated experiments, and they did not notice any influence the preceding verbal learning task could exert on later judgments. As can be seen in Illustration 3.1, they neverthe-less provided more favorable judgments of Donald when the primed trait categories had been positive than when the primed traits had been negative. Importantly, when the primed words, positive and negative, were not applicable to the target behaviors (neat, grateful vs. clumsy, listless), judgments by participants showed no differences.

The seminal findings by Higgins and colleagues (1977) inspired much subsequent social psychological research on the role of social priming in understanding human behavior (for overviews, see Förster & Liberman, 2007; Molden, 2014; Strack & Schwarz, 2016). Note that one core interest of social psychology relates to investigating and explaining the context dependency of individuals' behavior. How does the social situation influence individuals? Why do the same individuals sometimes react helpfully and sometimes aggressively in very similar situations? Why do individuals sometimes perceive the glass as half full and sometimes as half empty? The basic answers to these questions are similar to the answer as to why participants evaluated Donald rather differently in the research by Higgins and colleagues. Individuals interpret their current social situation on the basis of information that is accessible at the

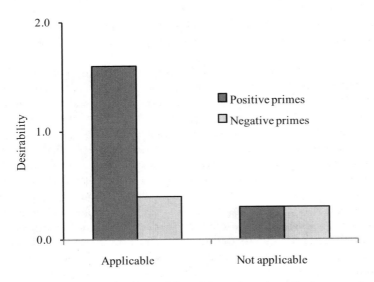

Illustration 3.1 Evaluations of Donald as a function of valence and applicability of activated concepts. Scores range from –5, undesirable, to +5, desirable

Source: Higgins, Rholes, and Jones (1977, Experiment 1)

time the encoding takes place. Context-dependent judgment and behavior is thus a function of which information is made accessible in the situation. In this respect, the concept of information accessibility is at the very heart of understanding why individuals behave differently as a function of the situation they are in.

Conditions that increase and decrease the influence of accessibility on encoding

It has become evident that accessibility plays a central role in how individuals give meaning to their current situation. Though accessibility of information is always involved in the encoding processes, how strongly recently or frequently used information influences individuals' interpretations varies. Among other conditions, the extent of search processes and the ambiguity of the situation itself play a crucial role.

As was discussed earlier, in order for prior knowledge to be used in encoding, it needs to be accessible *and* applicable. The role of accessibility is attributed to the fact that individuals often cannot search for all potential prior knowledge that could be applicable to the current situation. This is because in most situations individuals do not have the necessary resources to engage in a full search of their memory within a given period of time (Higgins, 1996; see Chapter 1, time constraints). To cope with restricted capacity, individuals have been shown to *truncate the search process*, that is, to stop searching once a reasonably applicable piece of information has been found in their memory. Instead of searching for the most applicable prior knowledge, individuals compromise between applicability and accessibility. As a result, accessible information, that is, information that comes to mind more quickly, has a higher chance of getting used in encoding. Note that if processing capacity were not restricted, individuals could potentially search their entire memory for the prior knowledge that is most applicable. Accordingly, subsequent research on the consequences of priming demonstrated that social judgments were in line with recently used information when individuals' processing intensity was limited either by motivational or capacity deficits (e.g., Ford & Kruglanski, 1995; Thompson, Roman, Moskowitz, Chaiken, & Bargh, 1994; for an overview, see Kruglanski, 2004).

Research has further shown that priming is particularly effective when the situation itself is ambiguous rather than clear. By definition, ambiguity implies that different meanings are possible, that is to say, different knowledge is potentially applicable. The more defined and clear a situation is, the smaller the range of different prior knowledge that is applicable. Here the question of which prior knowledge is highly accessible plays a smaller role than in situations in which very different prior knowledge is applicable. Note that the study by Higgins and colleagues (1977) incorporated this idea, as participants were provided with an ambiguous description of Donald's habits and interests. Subsequent research has systematically investigated this aspect and has demonstrated that social judgments are particularly congruent with the valence of primed information when the judgmental target is ambiguous rather than well-defined (Herr, Sherman, & Fazio, 1983; Philippot, Schwarz, Carrera, De Vries, & Van Yperen, 1991). Though research on priming quite frequently relies on fairly ambiguous descriptions of judgmental targets, it needs to be emphasized that almost any social situation can be interpreted in different ways. To illustrate, think of all the misunderstandings in daily life, which often reflect that there are many ways to interpret one and the same (ambiguous) situation.

When taking a closer look at the mechanisms that are involved in information accessibility, it becomes important to differentiate between the stimulus—that is, the prime—and the information activated in memory. In many cases, the prime will elicit information that is congruent with the prime. In the research by Higgins and colleagues (1977) described above, the semantic primes "self-confident" versus "conceited" presumably made information accessible that was congruent with these primes, which in turn resulted in the different evaluations of Donald. Individuals may differ, however, with respect to the knowledge that comes to mind in response to a particular prime. For example, priming individuals with the name of a particular soccer club can bring to mind more positive or more negative concepts, depending on whether or not individuals like that club. Similarly, advertising a product with a celebrity can bring to mind more positive or more negative concepts, depending on whether or not recipients like the celebrity. It is important to note, in line with the general assumptions of the social cognition approach, that individuals' evaluations and judgments are determined by their internal response, and not by the prime itself. A nice demonstration of this aspect within the Donald-paradigm was reported by Konrath, Meier, and Schwarz (2004). Participants were exposed to pictures of US presidents, either George W. Bush or Bill Clinton, and subsequently evaluated an ambiguous description of Donald. The idea was that—at that time—priming President Bush would make accessible information related to aggressiveness. And in fact, Donald was evaluated more negatively after participants were exposed to a picture of President Bush instead of a picture of Bill Clinton. However, this effect was restricted to partisans of the Democratic party, that is, to participants who presumably thought negatively about President Bush to begin with, and was not observed for partisans of the Republican party, who presumably associated positive concepts with President Bush. Thus, the same prime exerted a different influence on encoding processes depending on which information individuals associated with the prime (see also, Cesario, Plaks, & Higgins, 2006; Schwarz, Strack, & Mai, 1991).

What knowledge can be primed?

The answer to this question can be rather simple *and* at the same time rather complex. The simple answer holds that everything stored in memory can be primed, that is, can be made accessible. The more complex answer requires an understanding of how memory is organized and structured, and how memory operates. As Chapter 4 will provide a more detailed look at memory, we will focus on the simple answer in the present chapter, and elaborate further on this basic knowledge in Chapter 4.

Selective examples of priming knowledge

As part of the simple answer, we provide a non-exhaustive selection of examples of the kind of knowledge that can be primed to further illustrate the basic principle, and to illustrate the wide array of possibilities of how making information accessible may influence social judgment and behavior.

As humans, we have stored and organized a sheer endless amount of information in memory. In line with the assumption that this information can be made accessible, numerous studies have demonstrated that priming has important implications for how social situations are perceived and interpreted. In the process, researchers have investigated very different types of priming, that is, different types of knowledge have been made accessible. For example, the research by Higgins and colleagues (1977), described above, relied on priming *semantic concepts* (e.g., adjectives), whereas the research by Konrath et al. (2004) made a particular *target person* accessible, for example, President Bush. Individuals store information about *episodes* in their life—for example, their first day in college—and social cognition research has investigated how making such experiences accessible influences how individuals perceive the current situation. For example, individuals perceived their life in general as more positive when positive episodes rather than negative episodes were activated (e.g., Strack, Schwarz, & Gschneidinger, 1985; for non-experimental evidence, see Suh, Diener, & Fujita, 1996).

When interacting with the social world, individuals rely on information about what they, correctly or incorrectly, expect from groups in the form of *stereotypes*; not surprisingly, this information can be made accessible (Banaji & Hardin, 1996; Devine, 1989) and has consequences for how a situation is perceived (e.g., Correll, Park, Judd, & Wittenbrink, 2002). For example, by assigning a target to a particular group, the corresponding stereotype will be activated and this stereotype will influence individuals' judgments about this target, unless individuals try to counteract this influence (S. T. Fiske, 1998; S. T. Fiske & Neuberg, 1990; see also Chapters 4 and 5).

Researchers have demonstrated that individuals are more likely to comply with social norms when these norms are made accessible (Cialdini & Goldstein, 2004). For example, individuals were less likely to litter when the respective norm was made accessible by the situational context (Cialdini, Reno, & Kallgren, 1990). Moreover, it has been shown that individuals' *goals* can be primed and that making goals accessible renders individuals more likely to act upon them (Bargh, Gollwitzer, Lee-Chai, Barndollar, & Trötschel, 2001; Dijksterhuis & Aarts, 2010). For example, increasing the accessibility of the goal "to socialize" increased participants' effort on tasks that served as means for attaining that goal (Custers & Aarts, 2007).

Going beyond priming specific cognitive content, research has demonstrated that a wide array of feelings can be primed, and that priming such feelings has enormous consequences on how individuals interpret the current situation. For example, individuals have been primed with different *mood* states, for example, by watching a happy or a sad movie. The elicited mood state in turn influences how individuals perceive social situations, and one consistent finding holds that happy individuals report more positive judgments and evaluations than sad individuals (cf. Forgas, 1995b; Schwarz, 2012). Similarly, other feelings and emotional states can be primed. For example, researchers have been interested in how activating *uncertainty* changes individuals' perception of their situation (Van den Bos & Lind, 2002), or how activating the feeling *power* influences individuals' construction of social reality (Magee & Smith, 2013). Furthermore, specific *bodily states* can be activated and this activation in turn alters the interpretation of the current situation (cf. Meier, Schnall, Schwarz, & Bargh, 2012). For example, participants rated the same cartoon as funnier when they were unobtrusively requested to contract muscles involved in smiling (Strack, Martin, & Stepper, 1988), or perceived certain moral actions as less wrong after washing their hands with soap (Schnall, Benton, & Harvey, 2008).

Finally, individuals have stored different *procedures* of how to react cognitively to a social situation, and consistent findings suggest that such procedures can be primed (E. R. Smith, 1994). Making specific procedures accessible may in turn activate different knowledge that is used for interpreting the current situation. For example, individuals can approach a given social situation by searching either for differences or by looking for similarities (Mussweiler, 2003). Though it is "only" the procedure that is primed in this research, the reported findings demonstrate that social situations are interpreted very differently depending on which procedure is used. For example, when searching for similarities to other persons (relative to searching for differences), individuals will perceive others as more similar to themselves, which often results in more liking.

This wide array of examples of what can be primed illustrates that the way in which individuals perceive and encode social information is a function of what information is accessible at the time the perception processes take place. In the remainder of this section, we further illustrate this important general notion of social cognition by applying the priming perspective to phenomena that are prominent in social psychology text books and relate to aggressive behavior, cooperation, and competition.

Media priming of aggressive behavior

In trying to investigate whether and how violent content in media might influence aggression, various accounts have been offered, and these explanations incorporate different mechanisms and causal factors, such as desensitization or the presentation of role models (e.g., Bushman & Anderson, 2001; Krahé et al., 2012). One central element of these explanations entails the idea that violence in media primes individuals with concepts that are linked to aggression. Let us consider the following situation:

Illustration 3.2 Watching violent content on TV can facilitate the activation of aggressive concepts and in turn influence how individuals construct their social reality

Source: Ulrich Baumgarten/Getty Images

after watching a violent movie, a person bumps into another person when leaving the theater. If we apply the priming idea to this situation, several aspects of the above discussion re-emerge.

First, if the violent movie has activated concepts of aggression, these are likely to influence the interpretation of the situation. Thus, the other person's behavior is likely to be interpreted as aggressive. This interpretation in turn increases the tendency to react aggressively, for example, by yelling at the other person (note that if the other person was also watching the violent movie, this yelling is also likely to be interpreted as aggressive, which might further escalate the situation). Research has investigated situational primes that have the potential to increase accessibility of aggression concepts (Engelhardt & Bartholow, 2013). For example, the mere perception of weapons increases aggressive behavior (C. A. Anderson, Benjamin, & Bartholow, 1998).

Second, such short-term effects that are linked to the recent activation due to the movie can turn into long-term effects when aggression concepts are activated frequently, that is, when individuals are frequently exposed to violent movies or video games (Fischer, Kastenmüller, & Greitemeyer, 2010).

Third, it has been shown that the potential of violent media to prime aggression is particularly pronounced in high-trait aggressive individuals—in other words, priming aggression is particularly easy when individuals possess elaborated concepts of aggression, that is, when the prime can be related to extensive knowledge stored in memory (Bushman, 1998). While a violent movie may activate aggression in some, it may activate disgust or fear in others. Again, it becomes obvious that it is not the stimulus per se (here the violent movie) but the internal response that is crucial, as is evident in the above-mentioned study by Konrath et al. (2004), in which Republican versus Democratic partisans reacted differently to the same prime of President Bush.

Priming cooperation versus competition

When individuals interact in group settings, they are often faced with the situation of maximizing either their individual outcomes or the outcome for the entire group. Imagine, for example, a group of students working on a group assignment. In this case, a student may withdraw his or her efforts in the hope that the remaining students will accomplish the task, and allocate the time saved to attending a party. It is clear that when all group members act on this strategy, the group will fail (Van Lange, Joireman, Parks, & Van Dijk, 2013). There are many other examples of these kinds of situations, such as paying taxes or environmentally sustainable behavior. With respect to priming, it has been demonstrated that individuals perceive such social dilemma situations quite differently depending on whether cooperation or competition has been made accessible. V. Liberman, Samuels, and Ross (2004) confronted participants with a social dilemma situation and primed different concepts by describing the situation either as "Wall Street Game" or "Community Game." Presumably because "Wall Street" versus "Community" activated concepts of competition and cooperation respectively, participants applied strategies that reflected their goal of maximizing either their own outcome or that of the group. Similar results were observed when other cues were used to indirectly prime the relevant concepts (e.g., "briefcase," see Kay, Wheeler, Bargh, & Ross, 2004).

These examples illustrate how the perception of a social situation is a function of which concepts are accessible at the time the interpretation takes place, and that the interpretation in turn influences people's subsequent behaviors. Note that these examples recapture the core assumption of social cognition research: namely, that individuals' construction of their reality results from the interplay of the situation and accessible knowledge stored in memory. Starting from these examples, you could now engage in some thought experiments of how social behavior should be affected when situational cues (like the label "Wall Street") make particular knowledge accessible. What happens when we are primed with the concept "money" (Vohs, Mead, & Goode, 2006)? What concepts are activated when people wear uniforms and how would this influence their behavior (Johnson & Downing, 1979)? What cues may activate concepts related to team behavior? What concepts might be activated by different team colors in sports teams (e.g., black vs. blue) and how could this influence referees (Frank & Gilovich, 1988)? The list of such examples is endless, and in fact much of the situational influence on social judgment and behavior eventually results from the context influencing which knowledge is most accessible in any given situation.

General background variables of perceiving and encoding

In the sections above, we outlined the general principles of how individuals make sense of their situation, how they construct meaning on the basis of the input from the situation and their stored knowledge that is accessible. In the remainder of this chapter, we will take a closer look at how general background variables may influence these construction processes. In so doing, we selectively focus on three aspects that have received considerable attention in social cognition research: How does the extent of processing change the individuals' construction of social reality? How does psychological distance to the situation alter perceiving and encoding? Does culture influence how individuals make sense of their social world?

Extent of processing

In the previous chapter we discussed that the amount of processing individuals allocate to the construction of social reality can vary. We argued that the amount of processing depends on individuals' processing motivation and on their processing capacity. In essence, theoretical models that posit the amount of processing as a central element (e.g., Petty & Cacioppo, 1986; S. T. Fiske & Neuberg, 1990; cf. Chaiken & Trope, 1999) suggest that the more elaboration individuals engage in, the more they will search for all kinds of information that is potentially relevant and applicable.

The more individuals think about a social situation, the more information they will consider and in turn evaluate what meaning fits best with the present situation. As we have seen above, the influence of information that has been made accessible results from individuals truncating their search processes. From this perspective it becomes clear that the influence of a particular piece of information that is primed decreases the more individuals search for additional information (Bless & Schwarz, 2010). Perhaps most compellingly, this effect has been demonstrated in research on stereotyping. Activating stereotypes (e.g., due to gender or race) results in judgments that correspond with the stereotype made accessible (cf. S. T. Fiske & Neuberg, 1990; Bodenhausen et al., 1999). However, when the amount of processing is increased (e.g., by increasing processing motivation or processing capacity), judgments correspond less well with the stereotype (e.g., Bodenhausen, 1990; for an overview, see J. L. Hilton & Von Hippel, 1996), presumably because individuals consider additional information as relevant for their judgment.

Similarly, Strack, Erber, and Wicklund (1982) demonstrated that the salience of a target had a pronounced effect on subsequent judgments of causality. This impact of the most accessible information was particularly pronounced when participants were under time pressure. However, when participants were provided with ample time the influence of salience diminished, presumably because individuals not only considered information that came to mind first (due to salience), but also took additional information into account.

Note that the above logic applies to situations in which additional processing increases the chance that any and all information is considered, be it consistent or inconsistent with the activated concept. Sometimes, however, only knowledge that is consistent with the initial prime is activated, and in this case priming effects will likely increase. For instance, this happens if individuals selectively search for some pieces of information. Any additional information is then likely to be consistent with the initial prime, and as a result priming effects may increase when extended search processes are selectively directed (Forgas, 1995a; Igou & Bless, 2007; Mussweiler & Strack, 1999b).

Psychological distance

Everyone has presumably had the experience that situations are perceived differently depending on how close these situations appear to us. For example, consider a scenario in which you have to make a presentation in a seminar you are attending. Imagine that this presentation will take place next year. Now imagine it will take place tomorrow. Most individuals considering these two situations will construct them quite differently as a function of how close (tomorrow) or distant (next year) the situation is to them psychologically. In line with this example, substantial research has demonstrated that psychological distance influences how individuals perceive and encode social situations (N. Liberman & Trope, 2014; N. Liberman, Trope, & Stephan, 2007; Trope & Liberman, 2010). More specifically, this research suggests that when situations are perceived as psychologically close, individuals represent them on a more concrete level, whereas psychologically distant situations are represented more abstractly (see Illustration 3.3). That is to say, what is made accessible changes depending on psychological distance, and this may affect encoding. Against the background of the general assumption that psychological distance determines the level of abstraction on which individuals' construct social reality, the next sections take a closer look at (a) what determines psychological distance, (b) the core elements of concrete versus abstract representations, and (c) some examples of how different levels of abstraction relate to different consequences in social situations.

Construal level theory (Trope & Liberman, 2010) outlines four key dimensions of social situations that influence psychological distance. First, situations may vary with respect to their *temporal distance*. Situations can be remote in time, that is, far in the future or in the distant past. Everything else being equal, these situations elicit more psychological distance than situations that are close in time. Second, the same logic applies to *spatial distance*. Events can occur in places that are either close to or distant from the perceiver's own location. Third, there is *social distance*: persons interact with other individuals that are socially close, for example, a close friend, or socially distant, for example, a casual acquaintance. Finally, construal level theory

Illustration 3.3 The same behavior can be represented at different levels of abstraction, for example as "Looking at another person's answer" or "Cheating on an exam"

Source: Adam Gregor/Shutterstock.com

posits *hypotheticality*: events are psychologically distant when they are unlikely, but psychologically close when they appear more probable.

Though these distances capture different dimensions, they all have a similar effect on individuals' level of construal. Construals become more abstract with increasing psychological distance, and more concrete and enriched with details with decreasing psychological distance. Proverbially speaking, sometimes individuals perceive the input as trees, and sometimes as a forest. On a concrete level, drinking a cup of coffee is more likely to be represented as "lifting a cup to the lips," whereas the same action can be represented on a more abstract level as "getting energized" (Vallacher & Wegner, 1987). To capture the different levels of construal, take a look at Illustration 3.4. What letter do you see first? If you attend to the details (the "trees") you are likely to see the letter "A"; if you attend to the whole and ignore the details, you are likely to see the letter "H" (Navon, 1977).

Going way beyond the basic perception task in Illustration 3.4, Trope and Liberman (2010) have conceptualized how high versus low levels of construals differ from each other. *High-level construals* capture "why" aspects of actions, they emphasize desirability and idealistic concerns, and the primary features of the judgmental target play a key role in its representation. *Low-level construals* are characterized by "how" aspects of actions, feasibility and pragmatic concerns are particularly important, and secondary features of the judgmental target become important in addition to the primary ones.

Different representations result in different interpretations, meanings, and consequently behaviors, and construal level theory has been applied to numerous domains. For example, construal level theory can account for why individuals

```
AAAAAA                AAAAAA
AAAAAA                AAAAAA
AAAAAA                AAAAAA
AAAAAA                AAAAAA
AAAAAA                AAAAAA
AAAAAA                AAAAAA
AAAAAA                AAAAAA
AAAAAAAAAAAAAAAAAAAAAAAAAA
AAAAAAAAAAAAAAAAAAAAAAAAAA
AAAAAA                AAAAAA
AAAAAA                AAAAAA
AAAAAA                AAAAAA
AAAAAA                AAAAAA
AAAAAA                AAAAAA
AAAAAA                AAAAAA
AAAAAA                AAAAAA
```

Illustration 3.4 Example of a Navon figure with a larger shape (H) composed of smaller shapes (A)

underestimate the time they need to accomplish a task, in particular when working on the task is in the distant rather than the near future. Because the distant event is represented more abstractly with fewer details, individuals are likely to ignore activities that are unrelated to the task but still require time and resources (N. Liberman & Trope, 1998). Similarly, construal level can contribute to understanding stereotyping. When other persons are psychologically distant from us, we tend to rely on general, abstract representations—that is, on stereotypes. When other persons are psychologically closer, we also consider more concrete and person-specific information that may eliminate the implications of the stereotype (McCrea, Wieber, & Myers, 2012). Two decades of research inspired by construal level theories have resulted in numerous findings that testify to the importance of distance as a central variable. Trope and Liberman (2010) provide an impressive overview of the wide array of demonstrations of how the level of construal influences social judgment and behavior. For example, distancing oneself from the object of judgment or decision and, hence, engaging in high-level construal enhances self-control (Fujita, Trope, & Liberman, 2010), facilitates causal reasoning beyond the visible effects (Rim, Hansen, & Trope, 2013), leads to highly structured social judgments that vary only on a few dimensions (N. Liberman, Sagristano, & Trope, 2002), induces decision strategies that give more weight to outcome values than to outcome probabilities (Sagristano, Trope, & Liberman, 2002), and reduces the fundamental attribution error, that is, the tendency to explain behavior in terms of a person's internal dispositions rather than situational constraints (Nussbaum, Trope, & Liberman, 2003).

Construal level theory (Trope & Liberman, 2010) is probably the most general and elaborated approach that addresses the role of abstraction in the construction of social reality. Other accounts that have similarly conceptualized mental abstraction have focused on more specific aspects, one example being the linguistic category model, which emphasizes the role of language in social cognition (Semin & Fiedler, 1988, 1991). This model holds that language can capture situations on different levels of abstraction. For example, verbs ("to attack") are considered less abstract than adjectives ("aggressive"). The model has been applied to how individuals describe ingroup versus outgroup members (Maass, Salvi, Arcuri, & Semin, 1989). Outgroup members are described on a more abstract level than ingroup members (assuming that the outgroup is more distant then the ingroup, this observation is consistent with construal level theory). Because abstract statements are vague and more difficult to falsify, these differences contribute to the stability of stereotypes about the outgroup (Maass et al., 1989).

While construal level theory holds that the four core dimensions (temporal, spatial, social, and hypothetical distance) determine the level of abstraction, other variables may also come into play here. For example, research based on action identification theory (Vallacher & Wegner, 1987) suggests that when individuals fail in performing an action, they are more likely to represent this action on a lower level of construal. Similarly, research on how affective feelings influence the construction of social reality has consistently demonstrated that positive affect usually elicits a higher level of construals (Burger & Bless, 2016, note that the findings with respect to failure and affect converge if we equate failure and negative affect; see also Chapter 8).

Culture

There is a broad consensus that the construction of social reality is strongly influenced by culture (Chiu & Hong, 2007; A. P. Fiske, Kitayama, Markus, & Nisbett, 1998; Markus & Kitayama, 1991). Though hard to define, culture can be seen as a general background of traditions and social practices that exert a pronounced influence on human thinking and behavior. While there are many different forms of culture (e.g., nations with different cultures, northern/southern culture, subcultures, organizational culture, etc.), most of the psychological research in social cognition has focused on the differences between East Asian and Western cultures.

The first thing that presumably comes to mind when speculating about the influence of culture is the fact that cultures vary in the "content" they provide. Cultures differ in many beliefs about the social world and about which norms apply to which social situation. For example, Eastern and Western cultures prescribe different norms on whether and how to display emotions in social situations (e.g., Matsumoto, 1990). Other differences pertain to interpersonal distance or eye contact during communication (M. H. Bond & Komai, 1976). Anyone who has experienced a different culture can easily compile an endless list of such differences. From the present perspective, one way to look at cultural influences is to argue that cultures contribute to the accessibility of particular concepts, which in turn guide the perception of social situations. As we have seen above, accessibility of information stored in memory plays a key role in the construction of social reality. Culture thus influences individuals' perception and encoding processes by means of accessibility.

One key difference between East Asian and Western culture that has received considerable attention is the relationship between the individual and the group. In Western societies the focus rests on the individual, who, though part of groups, is perceived as independent and autonomous. East Asian societies, by contrast, put more emphasis on the group and on an individual's relationship to other group members. Thus, the Self is perceived as interdependent and part of a larger whole. Based on these differences, it has been proposed that individualistic cultures foster independent self-construals, whereas collectivistic cultures foster interdependent forms of self-construals (Markus & Kitayama, 1991; Oyserman, Coon, & Kemmelmeier, 2002). Importantly, these self-construals and their different emphases on the relationship to the context have a pronounced influence on how individuals perceive and encode social situations. Specifically, it is assumed that individuals' attention to interdependencies transfers from self-construals to the perception of other situations. Thus, culture may not only influence *what* comes to mind, but may also shape *how* individuals process social information.

Differential attendance to interdependencies, for example, influences the fundamental attribution error. This error reflects the fact that when explaining the behavior of others, individuals tend to underestimate contextual factors and overestimate the role of dispositional factors (L. Ross, 1977). It would appear that individuals with an interdependent self-construal, which is more prominent in East Asian cultures, are more sensitive to relationships in a given context and are more likely to consider context when making sense of the behavior of others. Accordingly, the fundamental attribution error has been found to be less pronounced in East Asian cultures (M. W. Morris & Peng, 1994; for an overview, see Choi, Nisbett, & Norenzayan, 1999), an observation that has led researchers to change the label of the effect from fundamental attribution error to correspondence bias (because it is less fundamental than initially assumed, Gilbert & Malone, 1995). The assumption that individuals with interdependent self-construals pay attention not only to the focal object but also to its relationship to the context has been supported by numerous additional findings (e.g., Chua, Boland, & Nisbett, 2005; Masuda & Nisbett, 2001). These patterns were even observed for very basic attentional aspects, when participants' eye movements were assessed (Chua et al., 2005).

Importantly, from the present perspective on the role of accessibility, these well-documented cultural differences can be attenuated when situational aspects make information accessible that overrides the influence of information made accessible by culture (Oyserman & Lee, 2008). In particular, when an interdependent self-construal was experimentally induced in Westerners and an independent self-construal was experimentally induced in East Asians, the impact of participants' cultural background was reduced, and the information made accessible in the situation determined participants' judgments and behaviors (Oyserman & Lee, 2008; see also Kühnen, Hannover, & Schubert, 2001). Besides demonstrating the role of accessibility, these findings directly point to the possibility of experimentally investigating causal influences of culture (Oyserman & Lee, 2008).

Concluding remarks

This chapter focused on the first step in the idealized sequence of social information processing, namely, on how individuals make sense of a particular situation, that is, how they perceive and encode information. Encoding is critical, because most of the time social situations are not unambiguous and require interpretation. The way we interpret information fundamentally depends on "what comes to mind" (accessibility), and whether this "what" is suitable for interpretation (applicability). The impact of the social situation is thus not to be underestimated, as the many examples from very different domains have illustrated.

Chapter summary

1   In order to perceive and encode information, individuals relate new information to their prior knowledge. The same input can result in different interpretations because it can be linked to different prior knowledge.
2   Which knowledge is applied to encoding depends on accessibility. Accessibility is a function of how recently and how frequently this information was used in prior situations.
3   The role of accessibility in perceiving and encoding is particularly pronounced when the judgmental target is ambiguous and when individuals need to truncate their search for other potentially applicable knowledge.
4   All kinds of prior knowledge can be made accessible by situational cues, for example, semantic concepts, norms, goals, episodes, or stereotypes.
5   Individuals may perceive and encode situations on different levels of abstraction. These different levels of construal may in turn make different aspects of the situation accessible, which may result in different interpretations.
6   Cultures differ on whether the individual is seen as independent from or as interdependent upon other group members. By focusing on the relationship between the stimulus and other aspects of the situation, individuals bring different knowledge to mind, which then influences perceiving and encoding.

Discussion questions/topics

1   Extend the above discussion with an example of your own choice. Select a social situation that is relevant for you and discuss how the encoding of this situation depends on which prior knowledge is applied.
2   Discuss how applicability of prior knowledge and accessibility influence interpretation processes. What situational characteristics contribute to the observation that sometimes prior knowledge is used that is less rather than more applicable?
3   Why are priming effects usually more pronounced for ambiguous targets?
4   Think of an upcoming situation, for example, your next summer vacation. Construct this situation and write down what comes to mind in two steps: first think of this situation as if it were in five months, and then think of it as if it were in five days. How do the two constructions differ?
5   Imagine you are in charge of creating a flyer for a fundraising campaign. What implications do the above considerations have with respect to what you would print on the flyer?

Recommendations for further reading

Subsequent chapters of this book will return to the basic principles discussed in this section. In particular, they will address in greater detail how memory is organized and how it operates (Chapter 4), and how individuals can make differential use of information that is brought to mind (Chapter 5). A more in-depth coverage of various aspects of perceiving and encoding is offered in:

Molden, D. C. (Ed.). (2014). *Understanding priming effects in social psychology*. New York: Guilford Press.

4 Storing and retrieving information

Klaus Fiedler

The first three chapters have revealed that virtually all cognitive processes rely heavily on prior knowledge that is stored in memory. In order to be stored effectively and to be retrievable for later judgments, decisions, and action planning, information has to be structured and organized appropriately. Just as a meaningful word (e.g., FLOWER) is much easier to read and to be held in memory than a random sequence of letters (e.g., REFWLO), social information has a stronger impact on individuals and their behavior if it is organized and embedded in the context of firm world knowledge. Imposing structure on memorized knowledge is as important as an efficient and systematic organization of, for instance, the address book on your smart phone, a computer file directory, or a library. In this chapter we will address in greater detail the role of memory functions in social cognition. In the first section, we will start out with two closely linked questions: How is information stored and organized in memory? What are the structural units and principles used to represent information in memory? A later section will then focus on how previously stored knowledge is retrieved from memory and how retrieval cues result in diverse types of priming effects on social judgments and behaviors. We will discuss conditions that can increase or decrease this impact, and examine how individuals may exert control over seemingly automatic and sometimes unwanted influences of prior knowledge. We will also illuminate how priming and other implicit memory functions are used as diagnostic tools to measure stereotypes, traits, and attitudes. The last section will be devoted to the interplay of old knowledge structures and new information input, which may be consistent or inconsistent with prior knowledge. Special attention will be given to the Self as a multi-faceted knowledge structure, and to the effectiveness of self-determined retrieval processes.

How is information organized in memory?

The key to efficient information processing is a well-organized memory system. Just like a library, a computer directory, or any other store of knowledge, our memory requires a logically sound and efficient organization that allows for economic storage and efficient search and retrieval. The elementary unit of organization in memory is a *category*. Categories constitute abstract representations of entire classes of stimulus objects that share the same defining features. They may refer to object classes in the physical world (e.g., denoting tools such as hammer, pencil, computer) or in the social world (e.g., denoting vocational groups such as salesman, nurse, politician;

or traits such as friendly, dominant, or jealous). They can refer to natural classes (man, woman, child) or to artificial products of human intelligence (automobile, software). And categories may be abstract (dignity, intention) as opposed to relatively concrete in meaning (journal, weapon). However, even when referring to very concrete, visible, physically existing stimulus objects, a category (e.g., weapon) abstracts from many subsidiary features of individual stimuli (e.g., hundreds of different weapons), thus providing a highly economical means of grouping and clustering the environment.

Categories render the world more predictable. By subsuming a newly encountered stimulus object under a meaningful category, the individual can go beyond the information given in the stimulus itself, inferring many other properties and potential uses from prior experience with the category. Understanding a stimulus as belonging to a category affords an elementary model of the interplay of bottom-up processes and top-down processes—one of the basic themes of Chapters 2 and 3. The bottom-up influence of the stimulus is enriched with top-down inferences derived from the meaning and structure of categories. For example, classifying the perception of an object with certain critical attributes as belonging to the category of weapons means that the object is dangerous, that it can serve an aggressive or a defensive function, that it is portable, and that its use may require certain skills. Likewise, the professional category to which a person belongs (e.g., sales person, tennis professional) can be used to predict his or her personality traits, interests, attitudes, and style of living. Ethnic categories help to predict language, religion, appearance, and cultural norms. In many cases, the predictions and inferences derived from categorical knowledge are highly informative and helpful. However, as we shall see below, they may not always be correct, and can be the source of unwarranted and severe fallacies, stereotypes, and superstitious beliefs.

All the above examples refer to stable, commonly shared categories of well-known meaning. Thus, the weapons and tennis professional categories belong to the general world knowledge that we share, and expect to share, with all other people. This holds even more so for many biological categories (mother, race, sex) and mundane categories (car, drink, laughing) that are frequently used in everyday encounters. Apart from such long-established categories, we sometimes face the task of learning new categories that were previously unknown but arise as we deal with new developments, such as bungee jumping, smartphone apps, or driverless cars. Moreover, the human mind has the capacity to flexibly learn new ad-hoc categories that bear little relationship to natural world knowledge, if these ad-hoc categories help to make predictions and discriminations. For example, we can learn the composition of a newly formed group, what sequence of code is valid in an artificial computer language, or what offside is in football. The same categories that adults consider highly familiar are strange and unfamiliar to 18-month-old children who still face the task of learning the meaning of thousands of linguistic concepts. Conversely, however, older people might lack an appropriate understanding of modern categories that play a central role for young people, such as modern social media.

Types of knowledge structures and their representation

Above and beyond the most elementary unit of knowledge categories, social cognition relies on a number of more refined knowledge structures. The technical terms commonly used to denote the most prominent examples of these higher-order knowledge structures are summarized in Table 4.1, along with their defining features and illustrative examples.

Table 4.1 Terminological conventions to denote different types of knowledge structures

Technical term	Defining features	Example
Category	Classes of objects with similar meaning and function	Concrete categories such as hammer and computer, or abstract categories such as dignity and crime
Stereotype	Categories for social groups	Professional (policemen) or ethnic groups (Chinese)
Schema	Knowledge structures linked to adaptive function	Causal schema for making quick causal inferences
Script	Temporally structured behavioral routine	The sequence of behaviors that constitute a visit to the theater
Cognitive map	Spatial organization of concrete objects in visual modality	Visual imagery of and automatic locomotion on one's university campus
Associative network	Highly interconnected structure involving many different concepts	The Self, including all its autobiographic, affective, and semantic aspects

The first entry in Table 4.1, a *category*, as already explained, can be understood as a basic knowledge unit that corresponds to a class of stimulus objects that share certain defining features. As soon as a stimulus is identified as an exemplar of a *category* (e.g., a fluid as *poison*), all defining attributes of the category poison (e.g., dangerous, hard to digest, potentially lethal) are invoked, while abstracting from the other, category-unrelated attributes of the exemplar.

Categories that pertain to social groups or person types are usually referred to as *stereotypes*. A stereotype entails expectations about which attributes characterize a particular group and set it apart from other groups. For example, the stereotype of a skinhead associates this group label with trait categories such as impolite, rude, and dull.

Illustration 4.1 Facial photograph in which baby face features (e.g., large, round eyes; small nose; small chin) have been reduced (left) or enhanced (right) (for details about this method, see Walker & Vetter, 2016)

Source: The original photograph belongs to the Basel Face Database (Walker, Schönborn, Greifeneder, & Vetter, 2017). © Mirella Walker

The meaning of a *schema* comes very close to a category; in fact these terms are often used almost synonymously. However, when additional meaning is given to a schema, it highlights a knowledge structure or behavioral routine that connects one focal category to a number of other categories. For example, a babyface schema (Berry & Zebrowitz-McArthur, 1988) not only describes a class of people with certain facial features, but also links the class of baby-faced people to typical social expectations or reactions, such as protection, care, and leniency, which treat the baby-faced person like an immature child.

Knowledge structures about standard sequences of events and actions in time are referred to as *scripts*, employing a term commonly used to denote the dialogue and stage directions of a theater play. Examples of very common scripts include checking in at the airport, going to church, or buying a hamburger in a fast-food restaurant. Box 4.1 uses the standard airport check-in episode to illustrate the sequential and context-dependent nature of scripted knowledge.

Box 4.1 A script for routinized behavior: checking in at the airport

Checking in at the airport is characterized by the following standard sequence:

> Arriving at the airport (e.g., by train) → looking for a sign leading to the departure hall → searching for the counter or the area belonging to a particular carrier → looking out for machines for ticketing → typing one's name and reservation number into the machine → receiving a boarding pass printed by the machine → moving to the luggage check-in (if one has more than hand luggage) → looking for the direction to the gates → proceeding to the appropriate gate area → holding and presenting passport and flight ticket when entering the security check area → removing all metal objects, belt, and (when required) even shoes → passing these items through the x-ray scanner for hand-luggage → entering the scanners for body security checks → gathering all possessions again after the security check → walking to one's gate.

The standard sequence not only allows us to check in routinely or automatically, without any conscious awareness, while doing or thinking of something completely different, but also to reconstruct a memory protocol of the entire episode using scripted knowledge. For instance, if immediately after checking in we notice that we have lost our credit card or sunglasses, we can mentally traverse the whole way back to the starting point and search for the lost article, even though we did not consciously encode the entire action sequence. Scripted knowledge is not only structured sequentially but also hierarchically. That is, the individual steps, such as presenting passport and flight ticket to the person at the security check area, can be further split into even finer steps, such as → establishing eye contact → saying hello → passing over the ticket and passport → waiting for further instructions, etc. Of course, we may also make characteristic mistakes when relying on scripted knowledge. We might have the passport available when it is not required, or we may erroneously remember having fixed an address label when in fact we did not.

When people form spatial representations of a scenario, the corresponding knowledge structure is often referred to as a *cognitive map*. Most of us have acquired reasonably accurate cognitive maps of our home, the route to work, or the distribution of buttons and icons on a computer screen, so that we can move around and find objects we are looking for rapidly, even when our attention is distracted or when it is dark. The term "cognitive map" is not restricted to geographical orientation and locomotion functions. It can also be expanded to include knowledge that is not literally spatial. We may thus have a cognitive map of the directory of our computer, or a cognitive map of how to navigate through the hypertext representation of Internet providers of encyclopedias.

Complex knowledge structures involving multiple category nodes that are interconnected vertically and horizontally can be referred to as *associative networks*. On the vertical dimension, the nodes of an associative network can be ordered by superordinate and subordinate relationships. As shown by the network depicted in Illustration 4.2, the superordinate sports category can be decomposed into various sports disciplines at a medium level of abstractness, such as swimming, football, ice hockey, or track and field; the latter is further decomposed into finer subordinate disciplines such as decathlon, long jump, or hurdles. Horizontally, the categories at any level are organized by similarity: the more similar two sports disciplines, the smaller the horizontal distance in an associative network. Both the horizontal similarity structure and the vertical inclusion hierarchy render the network organization suitable for memorizing and inference making. Once we remember or know that somebody is interested in track and field, we can infer vertically that he or she is presumably quite informed about, and at least slightly interested in, hurdles, long jump, decathlon, and so on. Moreover, horizontally one can infer that a person who is interested in track and field is presumably interested in other sports disciplines, particularly in disciplines that are similar and therefore close to track and field in the associative network (e.g., football, but less likely car racing).

For various reasons, basic-level categories at a medium level of abstractness are most informative and useful for communication. Very abstract concepts at the superordinate level, such as sports, are applicable to a broader range of stimulus events, but are too unspecific to convey the nature of somebody's interest. In contrast, highly specific concepts at a subordinate level, such as long jump, are overly specific and restricted to a very narrow reference class. Basic-level categories (e.g., track and field, football, gymnastics) seem to provide the best compromise. Indeed, several studies have shown that the basic level is the most preferred and most natural level for representing information in memory (Rosch, Mervis, Gray, Johnson, & Boyes-Braem, 1976). It was also found that in language acquisition, basic-level concepts are learned earlier than superordinate or subordinate concepts. Thus, in first-language acquisition, young children understand and use the words "running," "boxing," or "swimming" well before they use the abstract terms "sports," "politics," and "arts," or the subordinate terms "sprint," "kickboxing," or "butterfly."

An intriguing question is how these structures are represented in memory. The schema or stereotype of disabled people may be represented either in terms of abstracted features (wheelchair, needing help), or in terms of particular exemplars (an acquaintance who is disabled). Whether based on abstract features or exemplars, memory representations can either rely on the category's average values on relevant attribute values, usually called a *prototype* (Cantor & Mischel, 1977), or they can be built on extreme values, usually referred to as ideal types (Barsalou, 1985). For example, the prototype of an athlete can be conceived of as the average of all

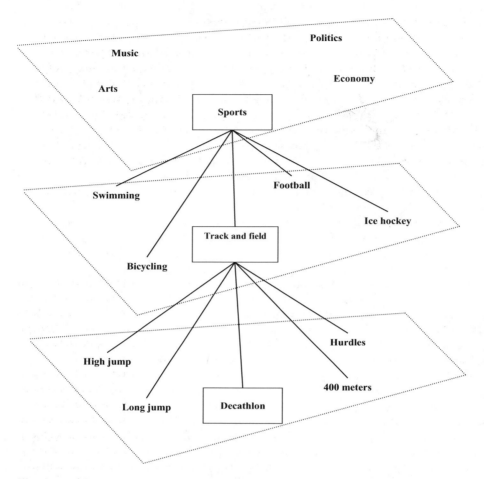

Illustration 4.2 An associative network of knowledge about hobbies and sports. Knowledge
is organized vertically by superordinate–subordinate relationships, and
horizontally by similarity relationships

athletes on such dimensions as body building, dieting, daily hours of training, physical health, and so on. An *ideal type*, however, would be an athlete who represents
extreme, superlative positions on those dimensions (e.g., maximal body building,
extreme dieting, more than six hours of training a day, etc.).

These various formats of mental representations are of theoretical and practical
value because they have distinct implications for the explanation of social-cognitive
phenomena. For example, Judd and Park (1988) assume that knowledge of outgroups
is largely confined to abstract prototypes, whereas cognitive representations of an
ingroup include many concrete exemplars in addition to prototypical knowledge. This
assumption offers a plausible explanation for the phenomenon of outgroup homog-
enization: people usually develop less differentiated and more simplified impressions
of outgroups (which appear to be more homogenous) compared to the richer and
more refined impressions of their own ingroup (Park, Judd, & Ryan, 1991).

Illustration 4.3 Studies suggest that members from outgroups (here: other cultures) appear more homogeneous or similar to each other

Source: Left: Laura Beach/Alamy. Right: Aflo Co., Ltd./Alamy

Cognitive consistency

The Gestalt notion of consistency dominated the early decades of empirical social psychology after World War II. It holds that if similar stimuli fall into the same category and dissimilar stimuli belong to different categories, the consistent pattern that results is easy to memorize and to administrate. Social perception is biased toward consistency because consistent structures are learned more efficiently. Moreover, inconsistent structures are often falsely reproduced as if they were consistent.

Consider the two structures in Illustration 4.4. Let the letters represent persons and let a solid line connecting pairs of persons indicate a liking relationship and a dotted line indicate a disliking relationship between persons and their goals and interests. It is immediately evident that the structure on the left is easier to understand and to learn than the one on the right. On the left, all members of the same subgroup like each other and all relationships between subgroups are of the dislike type. The whole structure can be perfectly understood and reproduced by this single organizing rule. On the right, in contrast, the pattern of liking relationships is much more complex and presumably rather difficult to learn. Given that human processing capacity is limited (see Theme 1, Chapter 2), consistency provides an extremely valuable tool to reconstruct what cannot be perfectly remembered in every detail.

Several studies demonstrate vividly that cognitive structures drift toward consistency. Heider's balance theory (Heider, 1946) predicted that triadic relations should

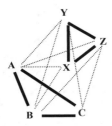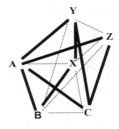

Illustration 4.4 Graphic illustration of the consistency principle

be easier to learn, and more likely to be recalled in memory, if the three bilateral relations in a triad (e.g., involving a person P, another person O, and an attitude object X) are balanced. For example, if P likes O and O likes X, balance implies that P should like X as well. Conversely, if P dislikes O but O likes X, P should dislike X. In general, a triad is balanced if either all three connections are positive, or if only one connection is positive. Imbalance exists when two connections are positive or none are (e.g., P likes O, O likes X, P dislikes X).

De Soto (1960) demonstrated that it is easier to remember a network of balanced relationships between persons than an imbalanced network, implying that selective forgetting should produce a bias in favor of balanced relations. Consistency, as an organizing principle, imposes a highly efficient and economic code on memory. Even when only part of the information is encoded and stored in memory, the remaining parts can be inferred or reconstructed from an internally consistent, balanced structure of positive and negative connections in memory.

Who said what?

To be sure, the drift toward consistency is also the source of errors in recognition and recall, though these errors are revealing about the categorical organization of social memory. In the so-called "Who said what?" paradigm developed by Taylor, Fiske, Etcoff, and Ruderman (1978), participants heard an extended list of statements uttered by six different persons whose photographs were presented along with the statements. The six speakers came from two race categories: three were white and three black. When participants were asked later to remember who said what, not all statements could be correctly assigned to the original speaker. However, incorrectly cued recall responses were not random but tended to reflect confusion within the correct race category. Many statements were erroneously assigned to another speaker of the same race, suggesting that race categories were used to organize the extended list of stimulus statements in memory. An elegant way of analyzing the data arising in a Who-said-what paradigm (using multinomial modeling) was explained and illustrated in a scholarly article by Klauer and Wegener (1998).

Evaluative conditioning

The consistency principle applies not only to semantic and evaluative congruity, but also to spatial and temporal contiguity. For example, learning by conditioning occurs when originally neutral conditioned stimuli (CS) are presented together, in spatial and temporal proximity, with biologically or psychologically important unconditioned stimuli (US). The CS takes on similar affective qualities and elicits similar responses (called conditioned responses) as the US. For instance, in classical conditioning, if the sound of a bell occurs at the same time as and in spatial proximity to an electrical shock, the bell takes on the quality of an aversive signal and elicits similar physiological (e.g., electro-dermal) stress reactions as the shock itself. Similarly, in evaluative conditioning (Hofmann, De Houwer, Perugini, Baeyens, & Crombez, 2010), neutral CS faces or brand names take on the same valence as the positive or negative US stimuli with which they are paired in time and space. Thus, just as two closely related persons (i.e., friends or spouses) are assumed to share similar attitudes and habits, a superficial version of the consistency principle seems to imply that if two stimuli appear together in time and space, they must be of similar affective value.

Note that evaluative conditioning processes that rely on this primitive consistency rule can trigger evaluative learning and the formation of attitudes toward persons, groups, and brand labels, simply as a consequence of contiguity in time and space.

Associative networks

As a natural consequence of the influence of consistency on learning, our most important knowledge structures are organized in a highly consistent fashion. In particular, the consistency principle can explain how associative networks in semantic memory are organized by similarity and contiguity, as we saw earlier (cf. Illustration 4.2). Semantically similar concepts (e.g., referring to hobbies or sports disciplines such as judo/karate; long jump/high jump) that share many common features are expected to co-occur within the same persons, whereas dissimilar concepts (e.g., football/figure skating) are not expected to co-occur within the same people. Such a similarity structure creates a high degree of semantic consistency. In addition to the horizontal organization by similarity relationships, the vertical organization serves to further enhance the consistency of the cognitive organization. Subordinate concepts, which share the same superordinate concepts, inevitably share the defining features of the superordinate concepts, thereby increasing the overall consistency of semantic memory.

How is information retrieved?

When memorized knowledge is used for practical purposes in real life—to comprehend language, to make choices, or to solve technical problems—relevant information must be found in long-term memory and reloaded into working memory for the task at hand. This crucial process is called retrieval. The speed and the effectiveness of the retrieval process, and hence the level of cognitive performance, depend on two major conditions: the clarity and consistency of the memory organization, and the usefulness of the retrieval cues provided in the task context. The organization of memory was the topic of the preceding section; the present section is concerned with the effectiveness of retrieval, which depends on the fit between the available retrieval cues and the knowledge structures required for the current task.

Retrieval cues

The cues that trigger retrieval processes are typically provided in explicit questions or task instructions. Ideally, retrieval cues are easy to understand and restrict the memory search to a single, unequivocal target. Examples of such convergent memory tasks with straightforward retrieval cues include the following: What is the name of the person depicted on this photo? What is the main language spoken in Australia? Where did I park my car this morning? The characteristic feature of these convergent memory search tasks is that clearly defined, concrete objects have to be located and found in memory (e.g., a name, a location) given specific retrieval cues (e.g., a face, a car-parking episode).

Other, divergent memory tasks are characterized by more complex and vague retrieval cues, leaving a much broader search space with many possible outcomes.

Such tasks call for a more creative and malleable retrieval process, which is typically susceptible to contextual influences offering additional retrieval cues. For instance, given the problem of finding an adequate birthday present for a friend, the unspecific retrieval cue "birthday present" is not very helpful because it allows for hundreds of possible answers. Self-generated retrieval cues may offer a creative solution, that is, thinking about the friend's interests and hobbies might result in further retrieval cues that help to narrow down the search space to a few appropriate alternatives.

However, this process of reducing the search space is susceptible to external influence. Having just passed a sporting goods store, we may be primed for a particular category of presents, namely sporting goods. If this category is applicable to our friend, who is perhaps an enthusiastic athlete, we might use an associative network (of the kind presented in Illustration 4.2) to select a present associated with some specific sports discipline. If the sporting goods category is not applicable to this particular friend, we have to search for a different applicable category. We might, for instance, pass a book shop next and be reminded that our friend loves to read literature. It is important to note that this memory search process is not exhaustive; it is typically truncated as soon as a suitable, applicable category or schema is found to solve the problem at hand.

Prospective memory

Many practical memory functions in daily life are prospective in nature. As opposed to only remembering our past experiences or the lessons from prior school classes, prospective memory means remembering to perform intended actions (Einstein & McDaniel, 2005). Typical prospective memory tasks include remembering to take an umbrella if the weather forecast calls for rain, to pick up the kids from kindergarten at the appropriate time, or to take medication at appropriate time intervals. Thus, the typical retrieval structure for prospective memory is a conditional if–then rule. If a glance into the fridge reveals that there is not enough food, an intention must be formed to buy some.

Implementation intentions (Gollwitzer, 1999) constitute one particularly intriguing form of prospective memory functions. People can implement volitional action plans such as "Whenever I am confronted with unhealthy food or drugs, I will engage in a behavior that is incompatible with consumption," or "Whenever I see a member of a stigmatized group, I will not exhibit a hostile response." Such implemented intentions or if–then rules have been shown to afford effective remedies to overcome unwanted impulses, stereotypes, and obsessive tendencies.

A primer of priming research

In any case, whether the task at hand calls for retrospective or prospective memory, the outcomes of divergent, insufficiently pre-determined retrieval processes are subject to all kinds of priming effects. A prime is a stimulus that facilitates the process of memory search by providing additional retrieval cues. The demonstration of such priming effects on judgments, decisions, and cognitive problem solving constitutes a prominent field of experimental research in social cognition (see also Chapter 3). The following "primer of priming research" is meant to introduce the basic methodology of priming experiments, and to explain the differences between different types of priming that impose different constraints on retrieval processes.

In ordinary language, the word "to prime" simply means "to prepare," and a priming effect can in fact be understood very generally as an experimental demonstration that a preceding stimulus serves to prepare the processing of a subsequent stimulus. The preceding stimulus is called the prime and the subsequent stimulus is generally referred to as the target. A typical example of a semantic priming effect consists in the demonstration that the prime facilitates the cognitive processing of a semantically related target. To illustrate: the brief exposure to an angry face as a prime will probably facilitate the subsequent processing of related target words such as "aggression" or "hate." Similarly, a trait adjective ("intolerant") may serve as a prime for an antonymous adjective ("generous"). Completing the word fragment F _ _ R _ _ S _ in a crossword puzzle (to yield FAIRNESS) may increase the rate of cooperative behavior. Or a remote association may effectively prime creative responses on a new task.

The set-up of a typical (sequential) priming task is shown in Illustration 4.5, along with some technical terms used in the pertinent literature. In each trial of an extended series a prime stimulus is presented. Trials are separated by an inter-trial interval. Between prime offset and target onset, a mask is presented in some experiments to prevent prime after-images during target presentation, or to ensure perfectly subliminal priming without any awareness. The time period between prime onset and target onset is called stimulus-onset asynchrony (SOA). Very often, the strength of priming effects decreases as SOA increases. In other words, subliminal priming procedures with a very short SOA (say, less than 70 milliseconds or even less than 50 milliseconds) and mask–prime–mask sequences ("sandwich-masking") often result in stronger priming effects than more enduring, consciously perceived primes.

How can the cognitive processes underlying priming effects be explained? How does the prime facilitate the subsequent target response? A suitable answer is to think of priming as a retrieval cue process. Priming serves to constrain an otherwise open and indeterminate memory search process to those knowledge structures (categories, schemas, scripts, or other structures) that the prime helps to retrieve. The crucial premise here is that world knowledge is rich enough to offer a large number of knowledge structures for interpreting the same behavior in many different ways. Every person belongs to multiple categories, with regard to his or her race, profession,

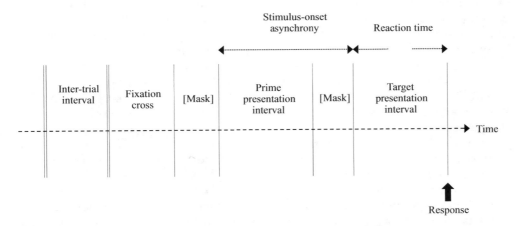

Illustration 4.5 Description of one trial in a priming experiment

religion, age, hobbies, and citizenship, and countless other attributes. Depending on which of these multiple categories is primed, different subsets of knowledge will be retrieved, with the result that the same target person's behavior can be given quite different interpretations. Social knowledge is so rich and multi-faceted that only a small portion of that knowledge is activated at any time. Very often, the currently activated information is appropriate to the problem to be solved in a given context. Sometimes, however, the selectivity of activated world knowledge makes social judgment susceptible to errors and biases.

Let us now consider some pertinent experimental evidence gained from research conducted in different priming paradigms. After an initial outline of basic findings from semantic priming, we will move on to research on action priming, and then to categorical priming. The final section will be devoted to evaluative priming, a special variant of categorical priming that is of particular interest to research in social cognition.

Semantic priming

Consider first the classical paradigm of semantic priming introduced in the seminal experiments by Meyer and Schvaneveldt (1971). In this paradigm, the retrieval cue that constrains the memory retrieval process is a stimulus with a specific semantic meaning to which the subsequent task is sensitive. For example, when the word "nurse" is presented as a prime, the processing of the word "doctor" in the subsequent task would be facilitated. A typical method used to demonstrate facilitation through semantic priming is a lexical decision task. Participants are provided with letter strings that sometimes represent an existing word, but sometimes do not, and they have to respond as fast as possible by pressing one of two response keys denoting "word" and "non-word." The canonical finding says that such lexical decisions about target words are faster when the preceding prime is semantically related rather than unrelated. If this is the case, one can conclude that semantic priming facilitates the lexical access to related concepts in semantic memory.

By analogy, lexical decisions in a semantic priming paradigm have been used by social cognition researchers to study memory processes involved in stereotyping. For example, each trial of a sequential experiment by Wittenbrink, Judd, and Park (1997) started with the presentation of a semantic prime (i.e., WHITE, BLACK, or neutral filler) for a very short period (15 milliseconds), followed by a lexical decision task involving four types of adjectives, representing (a) positive (e.g., playful, humorous) or (b) negative stereotypes (superstitious, lazy) of African Americans; or (c) positive (competitive, educated) or (d) negative stereotypes (boastful, materialistic) of White Americans, as determined in a pilot test. Reflecting negative stereotypes against Black people at that time, the facilitation effect (i.e., the reduction in response latencies on the lexical decision task) was strongest when adjectives representing negative stereotypes of African Americans were preceded by the prime "BLACK," or when adjectives representing positive stereotypes of White Americans were preceded by the prime "WHITE."

While the lexical decision task is used to demonstrate facilitation in lexical access to words in long-term memory, semantic priming can be combined with other tasks to investigate different aspects of memory retrieval. For instance, a word-identification task calls for more complete retrieval than a lexical decision task. Other research on semantic priming has focused on classification decisions, such as gender classifications of male and female names when preceding prime words relate to gender stereotypes (Blair & Banaji, 1996).

Speeded classification tasks afford a major tool for the study of automatic processes in social cognition (see Theme 3, Chapter 2). For instance, in Blair and Banaji's (1996) gender-classification studies, the SOA was manipulated, that is, the time interval between prime onset and target onset was either short (250 milliseconds or 350 milliseconds) or fairly long (2,000 milliseconds). In general, the classification latencies were clearly faster when target names matched the gender meaning of the preceding prime word than when there was a mismatch. In the long SOA condition, the facilitation effect was subject to voluntary control; participants who were instructed to provide responses that counteracted the primed gender cue could still profit from an inverse priming effect. As shown in Illustration 4.6(b), they were now faster in responding to male names after female primes, and to female names after male primes.

Such a reversal in the voluntary use of gender primes was impossible in the short SOA conditions, in which the instruction to counteract the prime led to general impairment and slow response latencies (see Illustration 4.6(a)).

While these findings suggest that short and long SOAs trigger automatic and controlled memory processes respectively, the notion of automaticity has turned out to be more complicated than initially expected (Bargh, 1994). Even very fast and seemingly automatic processes have been shown to be sensitive to controlled higher-order mental influences (e.g., Mussweiler & Neumann, 2000), and even intentional and goal-driven action can be subject to automatic influences (e.g., Aarts et al., 2005), as is evident from the sections below and from the various contrast effects or reversals of priming effects discussed in Chapter 5.

Action priming

Students of social cognition are, of course, particularly interested in whether semantic primes can affect manifest behaviors. Indeed, priming the semantic meaning of the concept "cooperation" has been shown in several studies to trigger cooperative behavior (e.g., in a prisoner's dilemma or in similar competitive games, Smeesters, Warlop, Van Avermaet, Corneille, & Yzerbyt, 2003; Hertel & Fiedler, 1998). Note that the retrieval processes underlying such action priming effects include the full stimulus–response cycle, from the prime stimulus (e.g., words related to cooperation) to routine responses associated with the meaning of the primed semantic concept. Because there are many retrieval cues that can facilitate but also inhibit a concept as abstract as "cooperation," and because there are many different response options to express (or to control for) the exhibition of cooperative behavior, it is not surprising that action priming effects are not as robust and stable as other semantic priming effects.

Indeed, some of the most prominent and widely cited cases of action priming have become the focus of critical debates about the replicability of psychological findings. For instance, Bargh, Chen, and Burrows (1996) found that priming the concept "the elderly" caused participants to walk down the hallway more slowly after the experiment compared to participants in a control condition without such a priming treatment. However, a replication attempt by Doyen, Klein, Pichon, and Cleeremans (2012) failed, or, more precisely, the slowdown was observed only when experimenters were not blind to the hypothesis being tested.

(a)

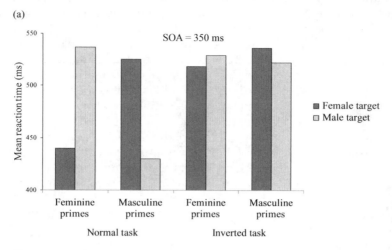

(b)

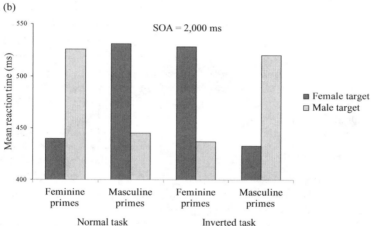

Illustration 4.6 Priming and gender identification, as demonstrated by Blair and Banaji
(1996, Experiment 3)

In a similarly well-known series of experiments, Dijksterhuis and Van Knippenberg
(1998) demonstrated that actual intellectual performance could be enhanced through
priming of intelligent person categories such as "professor." However, when "Albert
Einstein" replaced "professor" as a prime, the facilitation of intellectual performance
was no longer obtained. This suggests that for primes to be effective retrieval cues and
action prompts, they have to be broad and inclusive rather than narrow and exclusive
(see the discussion on applicability in Chapter 3). In any case, direct priming effects
on manifest action and performance appear to be moderated by subtle boundary
conditions, the full complexity of which is only partially understood at the moment.

A final example of a particularly impressive and memorable priming effect
(Gilovich, 1981) is presented in Box 4.2, pointing to the impact of subtle historical cues on political judgments about an international conflict. Rather than priming

elementary semantic concepts, this study invoked knowledge structures consisting of quite elaborate script-like historical analogies (i.e., the opposite lessons taken from World War II and from the Vietnam War, respectively).

Box 4.2   Priming historical knowledge can influence political judgments

That priming influences on judgment and decision can involve rather complex, sophisticated knowledge structures was demonstrated in an experiment by Gilovich (1981) on analogy priming. A number of subtle context cues were used to prime a historical conception of either World War II or the Vietnam War. This manipulation was based, for instance, on the name of the lecture hall where the experiment took place (either "Winston Churchill Hall" or "Dean Rusk Hall"), and on subtle cues in the cover story of the experimental task (e.g., whether the current US president came from New York state, like Roosevelt, or from Texas, like L. B. Johnson). An international conflict was described in which a hostile nation invaded a small country that had an alliance with the US, and the decisive question was whether the US should intervene and help the allied country. Decisions should depend on which historical analogy is activated: World War II, where the historical lesson tells American judges that the US should have intervened earlier; or the Vietnam War, where history says the US should not have intervened. Indeed, a significantly larger proportion of judges decided for military intervention when the priming pointed to World War II.

Note how these priming influences on social judgments differ from the original lexical decision tasks. The dependent measure here is not based on a more or less automatic, reflex-like response to a word recognition task, where the prime is only allowed to affect a single aspect of performance, response latency. Rather than restricting the priming effect to one response dimension, the political problem to be solved in the Gilovich (1981) study leaves considerable freedom for controlled responses. For instance, when historical knowledge of the Vietnam War is primed, the judgment is not yet determined, and the judge can still engage in conscious reflection about various ways of translating the historical analogy into an appropriate decision. The outcome of this higher-order cognitive process is not at all determined by the priming treatment, which could be used quite differently. The judge might trust the Vietnam analogy and conclude that the present conflict has to be treated similarly. However, he or she might also conclude that the present case is different and needs to be treated differently than the Vietnam conflict. In any case, a judgment model is needed in addition to the associative priming effect to explain the ultimate outcome of judgments or decisions.

Categorical priming

Categorical priming is a less restrictive variant of semantic priming. A strong semantic relationship between prime and target may not be necessary for a categorical prime to facilitate the cognitive processing of a target. It may be sufficient that both belong to the same generic category, such as the very broad gender category that encompasses countless individual persons. For example, to demonstrate how a single perceptual cue can facilitate gender categorization, Macrae and Martin (2007) assessed the latencies required for the gender classification of names (John, Julie) preceded by two types of primes, photos of male and female persons, or incomplete photos showing only long or short hair while the remaining parts of the photos had been removed. Primes were presented for 200 milliseconds. The gender classification latency was reduced significantly when the target name matched the primed gender implications, regardless of whether the full face or only a single gender-related cue (hairstyle) was primed.

To further illuminate the time sequence of the categorical priming process, Macrae and Martin (2007) then included all four types of primes resulting from the orthogonal manipulation of hairstyle (long vs. short) and the actual sex of the fully presented face (female vs. male). Clearly, when female (male) faces with long (short) hair were used as primes, this would facilitate the classification of female (male) names. However, what would happen on conflicting trials involving female faces with short hair (suggesting male gender) or male faces with long hair (suggesting female gender)? The authors reasoned, based on relevant previous research, that the salient hairstyle cue should influence the early stages of the process. However, in later stages, after more complete visual information is taken into account, the actual gender of the faces would come to dominate the priming process. Consistent with these expectations, the actual sex of the primed faces facilitated the classification of gender-matching names when the prime presentation time was long (200 milliseconds), but not when primes were presented very briefly (25 milliseconds). In the latter case, priming facilitated the classification of names that matched the gender implications of the hairstyle.

Evaluative priming

An extreme case of categorical priming is evaluative priming (Klauer & Musch, 2003). A very strong assumption here is that the processing of all positive and negative targets is facilitated whenever preceding primes belong to the same valence category. Thus, thousands of positive or negative words, pictures, or feelings are supposed to facilitate the processing of thousands of targets that share only the same positive or negative valence as the prime, independent of any closer semantic relationship.

In a typical evaluative priming experiment (cf. Klauer & Musch, 2003), every trial consists of a positive or negative prime word or picture followed by an evaluative target stimulus that has to be categorized as either positive or negative. Across all trials, the average latency for valence-congruent trials (i.e., positive primes followed by positive targets or negative primes followed by negative targets) is shorter than the average latency for incongruent trials (negative–positive or positive–negative). Such a standard congruity advantage is most apparent with, but not confined to, short SOAs.

Notably, an overall synopsis or meta-analysis of evaluative priming shows that, by and large, across all studies, the evidence seems to support a substantial categorical priming effect, at least when the task is to categorize targets as positive versus negative (Hofmann et al., 2010). In contrast, evidence for evaluative priming on lexical decision tasks (word/non-word) is very weak and questionable, suggesting that evaluative priming influences take place in the post-lexical evaluative judgment stage.

Interesting variants of evaluative priming can be found in many applied areas, such as consumer sciences. Hermans, Baeyens, Lamote, Spruyt, and Eelen (2005) first paired different yoghurt brands with a pleasant or unpleasant odor in an attempt to manipulate the stimulus valence experimentally. Later on, the yoghurt brands were used as primes in an evaluative priming experiment that called for the evaluative classification of clearly positive and negative target words. The results corroborated the expected priming effect. Responses to positive target words were faster, and error rates were lower, when the preceding brand had been associated with a positive odor, and vice versa for brands paired with a negative odor. Not only in consumer sciences, but also in social psychology and decision research, evaluative priming affords an important experimental model of evaluative learning, attitude formation, and the acquisition of preferences.

However, although supportive evidence for evaluative priming has been found in diverse areas, and although very brief exposures to subliminal primes (presented for less than 100 milliseconds and obscured by sandwich-masking) highlight the enormous potential for evaluative priming, it would not be justified to assume that the phenomenon occurs fully automatically. Rather, studies have shown that it is moderated by controlled strategies, voluntary goals, and higher-order cognitive influences. To list but a few relevant moderator effects, the basic congruity advantage in evaluative priming can be reduced, eliminated, or sometimes even reversed (a) when participants are in a sad (vs. happy) mood (Storbeck & Clore, 2008), (b) when stimulus words are common (vs. rare) according to word-frequency counts (Chan, Ybarra, & Schwarz, 2006), (c) when intermediate responses to primes serve to functionally separate targets from the primes (Fiedler, Bluemke, & Unkelbach, 2011), (d) when primes are easy (vs. difficult) to process (Alexopoulos, Fiedler, & Freytag, 2012), and (e) when participants are instructed to counteract the impact of primes (Degner, 2009). A general rule underlying these and many other moderating conditions seems to be that priming effects increase to the extent that the prime encoding task calls for generative and elaborative processing.

In any case, evaluative priming is subject to marked strategic influences. In an impressive demonstration, Spruyt, Hermans, De Houwer, Vandromme, and Eelen (2007) manipulated the proportion (25%, 50%, or 75%) of valence-congruent trials across the stimulus series. Under different SOA conditions (0, 200, and 1,000 milliseconds), they found that the tendency to respond faster on valence-congruent trials decreased markedly with decreasing congruity proportions. Apparently, participants can strategically change their response tendencies (from prime-congruent to prime-incongruent responding) when they recognize that incongruent relationships prevail in a given stimulus environment. In another experiment by Fiedler and colleagues (2011), a higher proportion of incongruent than congruent trials even led to a strong reversal; that is, target evaluation latencies were clearly shorter on incongruent than on congruent trials.

Further evidence for the adaptive plasticity of evaluative priming was found by Henderson and Wakslak (2010) with regard to the moderating influence of psychological distance. Participants in this study were first provided with a word puzzle constructed to include semantic primes that gave either positive connotations to risk-oriented behavior (e.g., bravery, exciting, thrilled) or negative connotations (dangerous, cautious, fear). Afterwards, they were asked to evaluate a skydiving man in a black-and-white picture on four evaluative rating scales (see Illustration 4.7). This photograph and an associated essay were ambiguous in such a way that the behavior could be evaluated both positively (brave) or negatively (reckless). Interestingly, a priming effect—manifested in more positive evaluations after exposure to positive as opposed to negative primes—was obtained only in a low-distance condition, when the skydiver was spatially close to the participant (Experiment 1) or when skydiving was introduced as a common (rather than outlandish) behavior (Experiment 2). In a high-distance condition, by contrast, these priming effects were eliminated, testifying to the strategic malleability of the phenomenon.

Using implicit social cognition for diagnostic purposes

Nevertheless, despite their susceptibility to strategic influences, priming effects promise to open new avenues for diagnostic measurement. Thus, if the speeded classification of positive and negative stimuli is sensitive to valence primes, then this research tool should allow us to diagnose implicit attitudes, defined as associative links between attitude objects and positive or negative valence. Conversely, any stimulus object that, when used as a prime, turns out to facilitate positive target evaluations can be assumed to represent a positive attitude target, whereas any stimulus object that turns out to prime negative evaluations ought to represent a negative attitude target. Accordingly, by using potential attitude objects (e.g., brand names, gender-typed words, group labels)

Illustration 4.7 Is this a likable person? Research by Henderson and Wakslak (2010) suggests that evaluations depend on prior priming episodes and social distance to the target person

Source: Imagemaker/Shutterstock.com

as primes, it should be possible to observe in a subsequent classification task (using clearly positive or negative words or pictures) which prime facilitates positive or negative evaluations, respectively.

The attractiveness of such an implicit procedure for attitude measurement originates in the belief that the resulting measures of response latencies or error rates should be much less susceptible to self-presentation strategies than questionnaire measures or self-reports. It appears easy to conceal one's unwanted attitudes (e.g., prejudice against homosexuals or disabled people) when responding to a questionnaire, but it should be much more difficult to conceal socially undesirable attitudes or traits in an implicit measurement procedure (Wittenbrink & Schwarz, 2007). More specifically, let us briefly discuss three different variants of implicit measures: evaluative priming (Klauer & Musch, 2003), the affect misattribution procedure (B. K. Payne, Cheng, Govorun, & Stewart, 2005), and the Implicit Association Test (Greenwald, McGhee, & Schwartz, 1998).

Evaluative priming

To illustrate how evaluative priming could be used for diagnostic purposes, consider an experiment conducted by Degner and Wentura (2011) in Germany, where many citizens held negative stereotypes about Turks at the time. The authors used pictures of Turks and Germans and of old and young persons as primes, and unequivocally positive and negative adjectives for the target evaluation task. Faster responses to negative (as opposed to positive) adjectives primed by Turks and old people (rather than Germans and young people) provided evidence for implicit stereotypes against Turks and old people in the tested population.

Affect misattribution procedure

The affect misattribution procedure (AMP; B. K. Payne et al., 2005) relies on a slightly different rationale. Again, the potential attitude objects are presented as primes, but rather than measuring classification speed for unequivocally positive and negative targets, the AMP calls for an evaluative response to a maximally ambivalent stimulus. Participants have to indicate their liking or judge the aesthetic value of inkblots, abstract patterns, or Chinese holograms. Positive implicit attitudes toward a stimulus object presented as a prime should be manifested in more positive likability ratings of a subsequently presented neutral and highly ambivalent stimulus. Such a procedure was found to be suitable for measuring racial and political attitudes (B. K. Payne et al., 2005), or attitudes toward relationship partners (Banse, 1999).

Implicit Association Test

The most widely used method for the implicit measurement of attitudes, stereotypes, and self-concepts is the Implicit Association Test (IAT; Greenwald et al., 1998; see also Greenwald et al., 2002). Because it is slightly different from a proper priming procedure and because it has become so highly popular, the IAT procedure is described in some detail in Box 4.3.

Box 4.3   Task setting and sequential design of the IAT

The IAT is freely available on the Internet (https://implicit.harvard.edu/implicit/takeatest.html). It can be easily modified to measure preferences for many different purposes. In its original and simplest application to the assessment of the cognitive underpinnings of a racial stereotype (Greenwald et al., 1998), the IAT starts with a first block of trials in which typically Black or typically White first names are presented on the computer screen, and the participant has to press different response keys for Black and White names under speed instructions. In the second trial block, participants have to sort positive versus negative trait words using the same two response keys (and the reverse is done in the fourth trial block). Then, in the third and fifth block, both race-related category names and valence-related concepts appear in alternating order. This double-sorting task is done under two different instructions. In the third trial block—the stereotype-compatible condition (here: Black, negative)— the task is to sort Black names together with negative terms onto the same response key, and White names together with positive terms. By contrast, in the fifth trial block—the stereotype-incompatible condition—the task is to sort Black and positive together onto one key, and White and negative together on the other key. The measure of interest is the difference in response latencies for these two double-sorting blocks. The test has turned out to be extremely sensitive. For most participants, even those who would emphatically assert being non-racist, it takes longer to sort Black names and positive concepts (and White names and negative concepts) onto the same response key than it does to sort Black and negative (and White and positive) onto the same response keys. Note that the rationale of the IAT is not based on a dyadic association between race categories and valenced concepts, but on the assumption that it is easier to respond with the same response keys to stimuli that share the same valence and meaning.

IAT measures may either converge with or diverge from explicit self-ratings of the same attitude targets. In the latter case, if attitude measures diverge, the important question is whether and under what conditions the IAT affords a better predictor of behavioral intentions and discriminatory behaviors than explicit self-ratings or questionnaire measures. A study by Florack, Scarabis, and Bless (2001) speaks to this point, based on the assessment of German participants' IAT measures as well as their explicit judgments of Turks. The authors posited that the predictive validity of IAT scores is superior when individuals form judgments or behavioral intentions based on intuition or gut feelings, without engaging in deep information processing. Consistent with this expectation, for participants low in need for cognition (Cacioppo & Petty, 1982), who can be assumed not to think extensively about the specific attitude target, the IAT measures did in fact provide a better predictor of evaluations than explicit attitude measures toward Turks in general. In contrast, for individuals high in need for cognition, the explicit judgments about Turks in general allowed for a better prediction than the implicit associations.

Analogous findings have been obtained in diverse areas, such as consumer preferences. For example, Friese, Wänke, and Plessner (2006) assessed implicit (IAT) and explicit measures of food preferences in consumers with somewhat ambivalent attitudes. The IAT provided a better predictor of food choices under time pressure, whereas the explicit measures proved to be better predictors when participants had ample time to make their choices. Apparently, then, the memory functions involved in speeded classification tasks (like the IAT) provide useful tools for predicting behavior under conditions of low processing capacity or processing motivation (such as time pressure or low need for cognition).

More generally, the predictive validity of the IAT has been studied in such diverse areas as racial stereotypes and prejudice, intergroup attitudes, personality traits, sexual orientation, consumer preferences, drug use, and clinical phenomena. In a meta-analysis conducted by Greenwald, Poehlman, Uhlman, and Banaji (2009), IAT measures were substantially correlated with behavioral criteria across all these domains. The average correlation obtained for 14,900 participants in 184 study samples amounts to $r = .274$. By comparison, the average predictive correlation of explicit self-reports (available in 156 studies) was $r = .361$, though reduced for sensitive topics. Although Greenwald and colleagues' generally optimistic appraisal of the IAT's validity may be partially due to a selective review that excluded less auspicious results (see Oswald, Mitchell, Blanton, Jaccard, & Tetlock, 2013), an acceptable conclusion seems to be that the predictive validity of both types of measures is enhanced for those attributes on which IAT and self-report measures converge. This suggests that person attributes vary substantially in predictability, and these differences in predictability seem to affect implicit and explicit measures in similar ways.

Critical note on automaticity

There can be little doubt that retrieval-based implicit measures, such as the IAT or priming procedures, afford a useful alternative to self-report measures in empirical studies that rely on group data. However, for the sake of fairness and responsibility, one should be very cautious in drawing consequential diagnostic inferences from implicit test scores about an individual respondent's prejudice, abnormal status, or guilt (Oswald et al., 2013). There are two major reasons for this note of caution, both related to common misunderstandings of the so-called automaticity of implicit measures.

On the one hand, the constraints imposed by priming cues or IAT task settings on the retrieval and response process are neither absolute nor actually very strong. Several studies have shown that IAT or priming results can be significantly reduced or even reversed when respondents are instructed to fake or to avoid a test result that might reflect undesired person attributes (Degner, 2009; Fiedler & Bluemke, 2005; Teige-Mocigemba & Klauer, 2013). For instance, to avoid being identified as a prejudiced person, one might simply imagine positive thoughts about the target of prejudice to relax and slow down during compatible IAT trials, or simply implement an intention to counteract implicit response tendencies (Gollwitzer, Sheeran, Trötschel, & Webb, 2011). The common denominator of this growing evidence is that implicit measures are not really immune to voluntary self-presentation strategies.

On the other hand, the relationship between person attributes and implicit test scores is asymmetric. Take a look at the base rates. The prevalence of significant test scores on a race IAT with Black and White target categories is over 90%, clearly higher than any reasonable estimate of the true current prevalence of racists with anti-Black attitudes in Western societies. If, however, the base rate of racist IAT scores is higher by an order of magnitude than the base rate of actual racists, this implies that the conditional probability p(racist | racist IAT score), with which racism can be inferred from a racist IAT score, differs by the same ratio as the base rates from the reverse conditional probability p(racist IAT score | racist), with which a racist IAT score can be expected in persons who are actually racist. Thus, assuming that the p(racist IAT score) base rate is ten times higher than the actual racism base rate p(racist), this means that most racists can be expected to score high on an IAT, but that, conversely, only a small proportion of people who score high on an IAT can be expected to be actual racists.

Thus, the typical base rate asymmetry between p(attribute) and p(abnormal test score)—which holds for many diagnostic settings (Fiedler, 2010)—means that diagnostic inferences from test scores to person attributes are very likely inflated, producing many false positives. Such inferences (from a frequent predictor to a rare criterion) can therefore be expected to be much lower than would be indicated by a correlation index. In other words, there must be reasons or causes for a significant IAT score other than a genuinely racist attitude.

This was indeed demonstrated in several clever experimental studies. For instance, Rothermund and Wentura (2004) showed that a sufficient condition for a high IAT score is that one of two group or category labels is more unusual or attention-grabbing than the other (similar to the distinction between figure and ground), and, at the same time, that negative attributes are more unusual or attention-grabbing than positive attributes. In this case, it will be easier to sort unusual (usual) categories and attributes onto the same response key, thus producing a significant IAT effect that mimics a more negative attitude toward the unusual target category. For example, it should be easier to sort together foreign people and negative attributes and familiar people and positive attributes than it would be to sort together what is foreign and positive or what is familiar and negative—even when no attitude is involved. More generally, whenever the two levels of dichotomous variables differ in terms of salience or attention allocation, analogous to the difference between figure and ground (Rothermund & Wentura, 2004), the speeded classification process of the IAT will be faster when sorting together the figure levels and the ground levels of both dichotomies.

As one can see, the underlying cognitive processes are sensitive to factors other than racist attitudes, undesired personality traits, or criminal knowledge. As another example, research by Han, Olson, and Fazio (2006) has shown that IAT measures may reflect extrapersonal knowledge that is independent of prejudice proper. It is also possible that a racist IAT score may arise if a respondent merely knows that from the perspective of a White person, black skin color and negative attributes are more unusual than white skin color and positive attributes (Fiedler, Messner, & Bluemke, 2006). Such extra-attitudinal knowledge may be sufficient to facilitate the speeded sorting of stimuli representing usual and unusual levels of both variables onto the same response keys, thus producing high IAT scores.

Let us close this critical note on automaticity with a broader summary statement that holds for all research on priming and implicit social cognition covered in the two preceding sections. While priming and selective retrieval can exert strong influences on subsequent judgments, decisions, and memory functions, the mere activation of memory content does not impose strong constraints on subsequent behavior.

Although activation increases the chances *that* activated information will be used somehow, there is often considerable freedom in *how* it is used and which behavioral responses lead to which consequences. Chapter 5 will further elaborate on this important distinction between information activation and information use.

Self-generated and knowledge-inherent retrieval cues

So far, the present chapter has been mostly concerned with memory functions triggered by extraneous, experimenter-provided retrieval cues, such as the stimuli used for priming or for an IAT. These extraneous retrieval cues are most often selected, either intuitively or based on pilot testing or semantic catalogues, according to specific semantic association norms, to force the retrieval process into specific associative paths. However, while such experimentally controlled external retrieval cues may be quite useful for measuring the performance on highly restrictive, elementary tasks (such as binary recognition decisions or yes–no decisions), they are unlikely to greatly support higher-order cognitive functions and problem solving. Indeed, memory performance is often hindered, rather than supported, by externally provided retrieval cues that bear no intrinsic relationship to the individual's own knowledge structures. Thus, as emphasized by Mandler (2011), the key to high recall performance and adaptive memory functions is not so much strong and fast standard associations, but the optimal organization of knowledge in memory. Granting this important insight, effective retrieval cues must be naturally tailored to fit the individual's own organization of knowledge. In other words, memory performance will profit most from self-generated retrieval cues that are somehow aligned with the individual's memory organization and the context in which information was acquired and encoded in the first place. To illustrate this abstract statement, let us briefly consider two empirical phenomena: the detrimental influence of externally provided cues and the benevolent influence of self-referent encoding within the individual's own personalized knowledge structures.

Part-list cueing

The first of these two phenomena is commonly known as the part-list cueing effect (A. S. Brown & Hall, 1979; M. R. Kelley, Pentz, & Reysen, 2014). In a typical experiment, several lists of stimulus items are presented first, and participants are then asked to reproduce the lists under two different conditions. No retrieval cues are provided in the control group, whereas a (small) subset of items from each list is provided as retrieval cues in the experimental group. The proportion of correctly recalled items is then assessed in both conditions only with respect to the remaining items that were not cues in either condition. The consistent finding is recall impairment through part-list cueing. Although one might expect the prompted cues to facilitate access to the remaining list context, this is not the case. Instead, it appears that offering somebody else's cues to an individual's retrieval process is disruptive. Relying on one's own retrieval structure leads to superior memory performance.

By analogy, research in legal psychology on the so-called cognitive interview (Fisher, Geiselman, & Amador, 1989) has shown that the quality of eyewitness reports increases if the interviewing police officer or lawyer minimizes the provision of extraneous cues and instead allows the witness to unfold his or her own retrieval structure. Scientifically recommended cognitive-interview rules instruct interviewers not to impose their own structure of pre-determined interview questions on the witness' retrieval process. Thus, the key to higher memory performance in the cognitive interview is to refrain from providing external cues and from the well-intentioned attempt to help the witness unfold his or her memories.

The Self as a powerful knowledge structure

The second phenomenon focuses on the benevolent memory effects of the Self. One of the richest and most elaborate knowledge structures is one's Self (Greenwald & Banaji, 1989), including autobiographic memory, preference structures for appearance, values, goals, attitudes, knowledge of social networks, group membership, family relations, professional expertise, and much other personalized information. It is no wonder, therefore, that self-referent information has a strong memory advantage. An experimental paradigm for demonstrating this self-reference effect was first created by Kuiper and Rogers (1979). A series of trait attributes was presented, and participants were asked to "Rate whether you feel the trait describes you." In a comparison condition, the same trait words were presented and the encoding task was to rate whether the trait described somebody else. A strong *self-reference effect* was obtained across many experiments of this kind, showing a clear-cut recall advantage for adjectives that had been encoded with reference to the Self as an embedding structure. This held in particular for those traits that were accepted as being truly descriptive of the Self.

Generally, self-referent encoding affords an efficient mnemotechnical strategy: to keep in memory what you have learned, for example in a seminar or in foreign language learning, engage in self-referent rehearsal and evaluation. Try to generate your own comments, affective reactions, or autobiographical experiences related to the learned materials, engage in active criticism and translate what you are learning into your own value system and your own private wording, and you will improve your memory performance. A nice experimental demonstration of this basic mnemotechnical rule found that one of the best encoding strategies to optimize memory for faces is to judge faces for attractiveness or sympathy (Bower & Karlin, 1974; Winograd, 1981), that is, to assess faces with respect to one's own evaluative system.

Klein and Loftus (1988) pursued the question of whether the memory advantage of self-referent information actually reflects the organizing function of self-knowledge, or the enhanced elaboration or rehearsal of singular self-referent words. The term *organization* refers to inter-item associations (relating an item to other items in memory), whereas the term *elaboration* refers to the creation of intra-item associations (strengthening memory traces of the individual item to be learned). A memory advantage through organization can only be expected when the items to be learned are imperfectly related. When the relations between stimulus items are already well-organized, an organizing encoding task is of little additional worth. In that case a more efficient encoding strategy could be to elaborate on individual items. Using this rationale (cf. Hunt & McDaniel, 1993), Klein and Loftus (1988) were able to demonstrate that the self-reference effect is due to an increase in both inter-item organization and intra-item elaboration. When the words to be learned were unrelated, subsequent recall improved when the learning task required participants to encode the category structure (i.e., to categorize words as belonging to certain categories). Recall of unrelated items decreased when the learning task promoted the cognitive elaboration of individual items (i.e., providing definitions of stimulus words). However, a third, self-reference task (linking stimulus words to autobiographical events) was equally effective as the organization task.

When an obvious categorical structure was already imposed on the word list (i.e., several items representing countries, occupations, etc.), an elaboration task (word definitions) led to more improvement than an organization task (sorting words into categories that were evident anyway). But once again, the self-reference task was as effective as the elaboration task. Together, these findings suggest that relating stimuli to the Self combines the advantages of both organizational as well as elaborative encoding.

The self-reference effect may also offer at least a partial explanation for the enhanced memory of survival-relevant information (Nairne & Pandeirada, 2008). Klein (2012) reasoned that self-referential processing is a viable component of the encoding of survival-relevant information, and he showed that self-referent processing is similarly effective in producing robust memories of survival-relevant information.

Self-knowledge is like expert knowledge. We are all experts in our Self, and just like an expert (e.g., a stockbroker) can understand and memorize more information in his or her domain (e.g., information on stocks) than a non-expert, we all are particularly prepared to process self-related knowledge in our own personal domain. Contrary to the naive view of human memory as a store house of fixed capacity (like a sector on a computer hard disk), the ability to include further information does not break down when much is already stored in memory. Rather, the more we know in one area, like the Self, the higher our capacity to learn even more.

Interplay of old knowledge and new information

All problem solving and learning progress involves the creative interplay of old and new information. On the one hand, one's knowledge structures ought to be updated continuously in the light of new information and changing environments. On the other hand, old knowledge provides a versatile framework for embedding and assimilating new information. In Chapter 2, we referred to this interplay as top-down versus bottom-up processing (Theme 2). While both are important for memory, this dialectic interplay is usually not symmetric: the top-down influence of older knowledge on the acquisition of new information often dominates the bottom-up influence of new data on old structures. For several reasons, old knowledge is quite resistant to change and quite flexible in assimilating all kinds of new information. One's values and attitudes are organized in a densely interconnected fashion, with the most central attitudes likely to have the most numerous and most consistent relations to other attitudes. A person whose whole life revolves around one central topic, say, religion, will have many interests, hobbies, moral and political preferences, and will seek a job and make many friends that all support this central concern. Given such a powerful, ramified structure of attitudes and related knowledge categories, this person will hardly change her central beliefs and values when confronted with data that cast religion into doubt. Moreover, this person will find it easier than others to learn and memorize new information about religion that can be anchored in the structure of already existing knowledge. Most higher-order learning is of this kind. Efficient learning means being able to encode and embed, and make sense of, new information in the context of older structures.

This discussion of the dialectic interplay between the theories residing in our world knowledge and the stimulus data provided by new experiences raises an intriguing question: How is the conflict resolved when new stimulus input is inconsistent with the expectations derived from prior knowledge? Will unexpected stimulus input be generally neglected, resulting in a global memory advantage for expectancy-consistent information? Or is there also an alternative mechanism that keeps the human mind sensitive to unexpected input and capable of learning about changing environments?

A place for inconsistent information

Once we have acquired interconnected, consistently organized knowledge structures, we are sensitive to both expectancy-consistent and expectancy-inconsistent information, though in different ways. If memory for expectancy-consistent input were maximized unchecked, memory would freeze to include only expected information that fits one's dominant categories and ignore any deviant information. Such a memory system would soon turn out to be maladaptive, unable to deal with new input and changing environments. Fortunately, a refined analysis of evidence on the relative impact of consistent and inconsistent information yields a much more adaptive picture of the self-regulation of human memory.

In spite of the memory advantage for consistent materials that was emphasized throughout this chapter, the role of consistency is actually more flexible and slightly more complicated. Indeed, there is good evidence that stimulus observations that are inconsistent and hard to reconcile with existing knowledge may lead to especially strong memories. For an illustration, imagine your neighbor is a member of Greenpeace. Consistent with this orientation, you observe this person riding a bike, saving energy, eating organic food, liking nature, taking a walk in the forest, and avoiding UV light. Then you observe the same person torturing animals in a manner that is fully incompatible with Greenpeace. Such an inconsistent piece of information is very unlikely to ever be overlooked or forgotten. It will presumably be remembered much better than most expected and "normal" observations. In the same vein, many other observations that are inconsistent with common knowledge will be hardly forgotten, such as a priest involved in a criminal offense, a politician who turns out to be illiterate, or a horse solving mathematical equations.

A seminal and often-cited experiment was conducted by Hastie and Kumar (1979). In each of six person-memory trials, a target person was first characterized by a trait (e.g., intelligent), followed by 20 behaviors that were either consistent with the trait ("won the chess tournament"), inconsistent ("made the same mistake three times"), or irrelevant ("took the elevator to the third floor"). In a subsequent memory test, individuals recalled more inconsistent behavior descriptions (mean recall proportions amounted to 54%) than trait-consistent (43%), or irrelevant behaviors (34%). In another experiment, Hastie and Kumar (1979) varied the proportion of inconsistent behaviors in the list. The proportional recall rate of inconsistent items increased from 59% to 77% as the number of inconsistent items out of 16 decreased from six to one. The more unusual or exceptional an item, the more likely it could be recalled later.

Does this contradict the aforementioned advantage of consistent information? Actually, not really! Sophisticated research on person memory has clarified the distinct conditions under which either consistent or inconsistent information will enjoy a memory advantage. When we try to write down everything that happened during a given day, we can reproduce a number of elementary events that were salient and important enough to be encoded so deeply that they can be recalled individually. However, the entire recall output is by no means restricted to such strong memory traces of isolated salient events. Rather, the largest part of memorized information is reconstructed from superordinate context representations, using systematic world knowledge about what happens normally during a day and what events or behaviors co-occur in common scripts or schemas. Based on such systematic world knowledge, we can reconstruct that we got up in the morning, took a shower, had breakfast, went to the subway, entered the office, drank coffee, and so on. Such a script of a normal work day will at least be used to form hypotheses of what could have happened, which can then be tested against fragments of experience that are still in memory.

Stangor and McMillan (1992) have demonstrated in a meta-analysis that inconsistent observations are likely to grab a lot of attention and be encoded very deeply. To the extent that recall tasks rely on the strength of memory traces of individual items, these outstanding events will have an advantage. However, recall is quite often of the reconstructive, context-sensitive type, such that systematic knowledge is used to reconstruct what must have happened. By definition, this systematic reconstruction gives a clear advantage to information that is consistent with schemas and scripts. Thus, extended bottom-up processing is responsible for the basic recall advantage of inconsistent information, whereas top-down processing explains the reconstruction advantage of consistent information.

Cogent evidence for this interpretation comes from several experiments in which distracter tasks were used to manipulate the amount of available cognitive resources. These experiments were guided by the hypothesis that under memory-load conditions or when cognitive resources are depleted, the extra processing and hence the memory advantage of unexpected information should disappear. Indeed, when participants were required to rehearse an eight digit number during encoding (Macrae, Hewstone, & Griffiths, 1993), or when they were given only 1.8 seconds for encoding (Dijksterhuis & Van Knippenberg, 1995), the extra encoding effort for inconsistent information was precluded and, consequently, expectancy-consistent information was remembered better than inconsistent information. When cognitive resources were not constrained, the advantage of inconsistent encoding could be obtained just as in previous experiments.

In fact, the very advantage of consistent information is that new observations *need not be encoded*. For instance, if tennis player A beats B, and B beats C, we need not lose much time encoding that A beats C, which can be derived through transitivity. The price for this economy are typical reconstructive errors. We may "remember" A beating C although this never occurred. Likewise, if a person is a member of an ethnic group and that group is known to be rather sociable and cheerful, we may "derive memories" of cheerful behavior in that person that was not really observed. In other words, memory for consistent information is not only characterized by many recall hits (correct reconstructions), but also by many false alarms (intrusion errors).

According to this more refined account of the self-regulation of memory, we do not run the danger of being paralyzed in a frozen memory of mutually consistent cognitions. Although, or exactly because, our basic knowledge structures are so tightly organized, being confronted with unexpected, surprising information elicits more attention and more cognitive effort than experiencing and understanding expected observations that are largely redundant with already existing knowledge. Thus, the very economy of a consistently organized memory, which greatly reduces the mental work needed to encode and understand consistent data, enables us to expend more effort on the processing of inconsistent input that does not appear to fit the remaining structure. Although people are often successful in selectively exposing themselves to desired, attitude-congruent information, once they have stumbled across an unexpected event, they can hardly ignore it and have to elaborate on it more than on expected events. How can we make sense of the Greenpeace member, with all his environmentalist and pacifist habits, who is observed torturing animals? We have to go a long way mentally to reconcile this with the remaining knowledge, and this elaboration will create many new connections to older knowledge, leading to strong memory traces of the unexpected event. To be sure, a flexible, mature memory will eventually find a way to reconcile the deviant observation with the remaining knowledge, for instance by inferring that the Greenpeace member is insane or by reinterpreting the alleged torturing episode as black humor, or as a bad joke.

Tightly organized knowledge structures are not only effective at incorporating deviant pieces of information. They even manage to produce false memories (Roediger & McDermott, 1995), which can be induced deliberately by the following experimental procedure. Participants are presented with word lists that revolve around central words, which are however absent from the list. For example, the list would include multiple words related to sleep (such as *bed, rest, awake,* etc.), although the word *sleep* itself is never mentioned. The rate of falsely recalled or recognized central words in this paradigm is almost as high as the hit rate for the best remembered stimulus words. The prevalence of false memories is higher for recognition than for free recall, and it increases with longer retention intervals. Prior active recall increases the subsequent rates of both correct and false memories.

Chapter summary

1   In order to understand how social information is organized in memory, it is useful to distinguish between different types of knowledge structure: categories, schemas, stereotypes, scripts, or associative networks.

2   Because it is impossible to access the entire content of long-term memory at one specific point in time, the actual influence of memory on behavior is contingent on selective retrieval. As memory retrieval depends crucially on appropriate retrieval cues, experimental research is concerned with the question of how to activate memorized information effectively. The so-called priming paradigm affords the major research tool for this endeavor.

3   Different subtypes of priming have been developed within this paradigm, such as semantic priming, action priming, categorical priming, and evaluative priming.

4   Retrieval of knowledge from memory is not only a function of externally provided primes, but is also determined by self-generated retrieval cues. Information that was encoded with reference to the Self has a similar retrieval advantage as other information that has been processed deeply, such as survival-related information.

5   Inconsistent or unexpected information is particularly likely to elicit deep processing in an effort to make sense of the inconsistencies. Accordingly, inconsistent information has a retrieval advantage. Recall of consistent information can also be facilitated if it can be derived from superordinate memory structures.

6 Memory functions not only support the retention of experience and knowledge acquired in the past, but also help us administrate and execute a hierarchy of intentions for present and future action. Research on prospective memory is of theoretical and practical value for self-control and adaptive behavior.

Discussion questions/topics

1 Access an Internet page demonstrating the IAT; for example http://buster. cs.yale.edu/implicit/. Work on one of the example tests. Does the IAT suggest that you are biased? Can you directly experience that "congruent trials" can often be responded to faster than "incongruent trials?" Try to find out whether you can "beat" the IAT.
2 How could subliminal priming be utilized for advertising?
3 Try to find examples for different types of priming within the applied domain of advertising. How can consumer behavior be influenced through priming-like effects?
4 Does information have a better chance of being kept in memory if it is consistent or inconsistent with prior knowledge? Is there a single correct answer to this question?
5 How can self-referent encoding be profitably used for academic learning and textbook reading?
6 Is it psychologically meaningful and practically useful to refer to automatic cognition and behavior? If so, what would be a viable definition of automaticity?

Recommendations for further reading

Greenwald, A. G., & Banaji, M. R. (1989). The self as a memory system: Powerful, but ordinary. *Journal of Personality and Social Psychology, 57*(1), 41–54.

Mandler, G. (2011). From association to organization. *Current Directions in Psychological Science, 20*(4), 232–235.

Nairne, J. S., & Pandeirada, J. S. (2016). Adaptive memory: The evolutionary significance of survival processing. *Perspectives on Psychological Science, 11*(4), 496–511.

Wentura, D., & Degner, J. (2010). A practical guide to sequential priming and related tasks. In B. Gawronski & B. K. Payne (Eds.), *Handbook of implicit social cognition: Measurement, theory, and applications* (pp. 95–116). New York: Guilford Press.

Wittenbrink, B., & Schwarz, N. (Eds.). (2007). *Implicit measures of attitudes*. New York: Guilford Press.

5 Using information

Controlled and automatic processing of information

Herbert Bless & Axel M. Burger

"How trustworthy are the representatives in your national parliament?" "How happy are you with your life in general?" "How satisfied are you with the education at your university?" "How likable is the new acquaintance you met at the party last week?" Individuals form judgments about almost any potential entity and in almost any situation. On the one hand, the formation of these judgments can be triggered by our interaction partners who ask for our judgments. On the other hand, judgments are also formed independent of a particular request from the social situation. Irrespective of what elicits judgmental processes, judgments can take different forms. Sometimes we form *absolute* judgments: How many minutes is it to the train station? What is the current temperature? Most of the time, however, social judgments are not based on objectively defined reference points and dimensions of judgment (such as number of minutes or degrees in Celsius). As a consequence, social judgments are highly context dependent. The same 15 °C (absolute judgment) can be evaluated either as warm or cold—for example, dependent on whether it is observed in January or in July, in Antarctica or in the Sahara. This relative component is clearly evident in judgments that are explicitly relative (e.g., warmer/colder, more/less beautiful), but it is implicitly part of almost any judgment, in particular when it is evaluative: How credible is the salesperson we encounter? Was the movie we just watched entertaining? Is the product we are about to buy environmentally safe? How morally justified is the current policy of our government? Absolute judgments as well as evaluative judgments may capture very different dimensions: we might judge time, temperature, or distance, for example, when forming absolute judgments, while evaluative judgments may refer to any dimension that can be evaluated (e.g., credibility, likability, intelligence, competence, morality, etc.). It is obvious that judgments provide the basis for much of our social behavior—whether we decide which chocolate bar to buy, which friend to meet on the weekend, or which job opportunity to pursue.

In order to form judgments, individuals can apply different mechanisms. One possible way to come up with a judgment is to consciously recall information about the judgmental target and integrate this information into a judgment. In the next section, we outline this possibility and discuss the underlying mechanisms. Subsequently, we discuss the fact that individuals' judgments can be dominated by automatic, less controlled, and less conscious mechanisms. In addition to these divergent options, individuals can rely on heuristics, that is, on mental shortcuts comprised of very simple judgmental rules that are often based on one single cue (this possibility is addressed in Chapter 6). Although in most cases these different possibilities are all involved in an interactive fashion when individuals form judgments, their relative contributions differ from situation to situation. For reasons of presentation we disentangle these facets and address them sequentially in the present and subsequent chapter.

Using what is on your mind

At first glance it may seem reasonable that when evaluating a target, such as a person, a group, a product, a situation, and so on, individuals should consider all potentially relevant information and integrate this information into their judgment. However, we have already learned that due to the complexity of social situations and reduced processing capacity, individuals are hardly able to engage in this seemingly rational procedure. One possible solution to this problem is not to consider all information, but to rely on a subset, specifically the subset of information that comes to mind most easily (cf. Wyer & Srull, 1989). Thus, individuals base their judgments on information that is easily accessible, due to either situational or chronic accessibility (cf. Förster & Liberman, 2007; Higgins, 1996). As Chapter 4 has revealed, automatic processes of activation that spread from one activated concept to other associated concepts play a crucial role here.

To illustrate reliance on accessible information, imagine you are asked to indicate on a seven-point scale how happy you are with your life as a whole. Chances are that you do not have a ready-made answer. Rather, you will need to think about various aspects of your life to form a judgment (Schwarz & Strack, 1999). If individuals do not engage in a *complete* review of all their positive and negative experiences but instead use the information that can be easily brought to mind, their judgments should depend on what they were thinking about previously. Based on this assumption, Strack, Schwarz, and Gschneidinger (1985) asked participants to think about either three positive or three negative events in their present life. When the same individuals had to report their happiness in a different context later on, more positive ratings were obtained if they had been induced to think about positive events, and more negative ratings if they had been induced to think about negative events. In other words, judgments were based on what was on people's mind. One implication of this finding holds, for example, that past life events are most influential on our evaluation of our life when they come to mind easily. As recency is one core determinant of accessibility, recent life events, even though they may not seem all that important, should exert a greater impact than more remote, but perhaps more important events. In line with these considerations, Suh, Diener, and Fujita (1996) found that individuals' judgments of their life satisfaction were predominantly influenced by recent events, whereas more remote events had, overall, a rather limited influence.

The results of the study by Strack and colleagues can be labeled an "assimilation effect"—participants' judgments were made *similar* to the implications of the activated information. *Assimilation* reflects a positive relationship between the implications of accessible information and the resulting judgment (see Bless & Schwarz, 2010): bringing positive information to mind results in more positive judgments, and bringing negative information to mind results in more negative judgments. For example, bringing to mind a positive exemplar of an otherwise negatively stereotyped group results in more positive judgments about this group, that is, it results in stereotype change (e.g., Hewstone, 1994; Kunda & Oleson, 1995; Yzerbyt, Coull, & Rocher, 1999). Similarly, when individuals evaluate the trustworthiness of politicians in general, bringing to mind a scandal-ridden politician reduces participants' evaluations of politicians in general (Schwarz & Bless, 1992b). Also reflecting assimilation effects, heightened accessibility of pro-social thoughts through media exposure increases helpful behavior and decreases aggressive behavior (cf. Greitemeyer, 2011). Examples of these kinds of assimilation effects are manifold and can be found in almost any domain of social psychology.

Relatedly, the fundamental attribution error (L. Ross, 1977; or correspondence bias, Gilbert & Malone, 1995) can be explained by "using what is on your mind." When individuals interpret a target's behavior as aggression, they are likely to assume that the behavior was caused by the target's personality and they neglect situational circumstances. In most cases, the actor is in the perceiver's focus of attention, resulting in an increased accessibility of the actor's personality, while situational circumstances are less accessible, that is, less on the perceiver's mind (Taylor & Fiske, 1978). In line with this interpretation, the fundamental attribution error is reduced when individuals have sufficient time to think about and consider situational circumstances (Gilbert et al., 1988).

In many situations, basing judgments on what comes to mind is a very reasonable processing strategy. First, "using what is on your mind" reduces complexity and thus solves the problem that individuals are hardly able to consider all potentially relevant information. Without truncating your search process, you would probably still wonder about all the aspects that contribute to your life satisfaction in the example mentioned above. Second, accessibility of information is not random but reflects principles of our memory. Indeed, what comes to mind is likely to be relevant, because the activation is the result of the recency principle, suggesting that the activated information has something to do with the present situation; or the result of the frequency principle, suggesting that the activated information is frequently used and is therefore important for the individual in general. Thus, individuals could rely on the activated concepts when interpreting a social situation and would simply need to integrate the accessible information (for a discussion of integration mechanisms, see N. H. Anderson, 1981).

Whether and how to use what is on your mind

While the information that comes to mind provides a solid judgmental basis in many—perhaps even most—cases, this is not necessarily so in every instance. A blind reliance on "using what is on your mind" may thus prove problematic. For example, information may come to mind because it was activated in a prior but totally unrelated situation. Although no longer *relevant*, the activation decays only slowly, thus leaving the concept with a heightened accessibility. In this case, relevance and accessibility drift apart. Furthermore, accessible information may be relevant but may not adequately reflect the judgmental target, and it may thus be atypical. Take penguins, for instance: though technically birds, they are atypical because, unlike birds in general, penguins are unable to fly. Basing judgments about birds on penguins (atypical information) would misrepresent the target. Individuals may therefore avoid relying on information not deemed *representative* for the judgment target. Finally, individuals might refrain from using activated information if they assume that basing their judgment on this information would be inappropriate with respect to *conversational norms*. For instance, assume that in a conversation you had just discussed the positive and negative aspects of your university library. Then, your conversation partner asks you about your satisfaction with university services *in general*. Your satisfaction with the library is highly accessible, but given that you had already provided this information, you would presumably assume that your conversation partner is not

Illustration 5.1 Would you predict assimilation or contrast? How does an outstanding star
on a team influence how other players in the team are evaluated?

Source: Action Plus Sports Images/Alamy

asking for this information again, and you would not base your overall judgment of
university services on your satisfaction with the library services.

The above examples illustrate that accessible information may sometimes impair
judgmental accuracy and thus highlight the need to control the use of accessible
information. Abundant research has addressed this question and demonstrates that
accessible information does not always result in assimilation effects, but sometimes
causes *contrast* effects (for an overview, see Suls & Wheeler, 2007). Contrast effects
reflect a negative relationship between the implications of accessible information
and the resulting judgment (see Bless & Schwarz, 2010): bringing positive information to mind results in more negative judgments, and bringing negative information
to mind results in more positive judgments. Imagine, for example, that people are
watching a TV show with very attractive actors. How would bringing to mind these

exemplars influence the perceived attractiveness of other individuals? Kenrick and Gutierres (1980) demonstrated that after exposure to very attractive exemplars, other targets were evaluated as less attractive. Presumably, this contrast effect results from the highly attractive exemplars serving as a comparison standard. Compared to this accessible high comparison standard, ordinary individuals appear less attractive (for a similar example, see Illustration 5.1).

The inclusion/exclusion model of social judgment

The above considerations emphasize that it is crucial to understand not only what information is brought to mind in a particular situation, but also whether and how accessible information is used. As we have seen, accessible information may result in assimilation or in contrast effects and thus may cause very different outcomes. The inclusion/exclusion model (Bless & Schwarz, 2010; Schwarz & Bless, 1992a) is a general model of social judgment that addresses these issues by integrating a broad set of variables that influence information use (for additional conceptualizations of context effects, see Biernat, 2005; Mussweiler, 2003).

The inclusion/exclusion model holds that evaluative judgments that are based on features of the target require two mental representations, namely a representation of the target and a representation of a standard (Kahneman & Miller, 1986) against which the target is evaluated. Both representations are formed on the spot, drawing on information that is chronically or temporarily accessible. Information that is used in forming a representation of the target results in assimilation effects; that is, the inclusion of positive (negative) information about the target results in a more positive (negative) judgment. For example, when evaluating a group in general, activating information about an exemplar of this group can be included in the representation of the group, and the evaluation of the group will assimilate toward the implications of the exemplar (e.g., Hewstone, 1994).

However, for a variety of reasons, individuals may consider the inclusion of accessible information inappropriate and exclude it from the representation of the target. If so, the excluded information is likely to be used for constructing a comparison standard, resulting in contrast effects. For example, individuals may refrain from including very atypical exemplars into the representation of a group and use them to construct the comparison standard, which results in contrast effects (e.g., Bodenhausen, Schwarz, Bless, & Wänke, 1995). Hence, the very same piece of accessible information can have opposite effects, depending on how it is used (inclusion vs. exclusion). The inclusion/exclusion model holds that three filters channel information use. Information is excluded when individuals assume that (a) accessibility does not result from the judgmental target (relevance filter), (b) the information is not representative of or even applicable to the judgmental target (representativeness filter), and (c) the conversational setting renders using the information inappropriate (for an in-depth discussion, see Bless & Schwarz, 2010; for a concise format, see Bless & Burger, 2016). In the next sections, we will address these aspects in turn.

Filter 1: accessible information and the role of perceived relevance

By default, individuals assume that accessible information is relevant for their task at hand (aboutness principle, see Higgins, 1998), and that accessible information reflects "just their own spontaneous reaction to the stimulus" (Higgins, 1996, p. 150).

This assumption is based on the observation that in most situations accessible information is related to individuals' current situation (Förster & Liberman, 2007). However, in some situations accessibility may not stem from the current judgmental target but from some previous process. For example, imagine being introduced to a new guest at a party. The guest's name, Alex, reminds you of a very unfriendly person you met a couple of years ago. Hence, the name "Alex" brings to mind very negative information. However, this negative information has nothing to do with the new guest you just met and is thus not *relevant* when evaluating him.

Various approaches address the conditions that make it likely that individuals become aware of a potentially unwanted influence on and contamination of their judgments (see Bless & Schwarz, 2010; Strack & Hannover, 1996; Wilson & Brekke, 1994; Wilson, Gilbert, & Wheatley, 1998). These conceptualizations share the assumption that one factor that triggers attempts by individuals to avoid or reduce unwanted influences is related to their becoming aware of the priming episode. In other words, individuals realize that accessibility does not arise from the current situation and judgmental target but from some unrelated source.

These considerations are nicely demonstrated in priming experiments, such as the one reported by Higgins and colleagues (1977). In these experiments, participants typically take part in two ostensibly unrelated studies, with the priming disguised in the "first" study, and the impact of the priming assessed in the second, allegedly unrelated study. Relying on such a two-experiment paradigm, Lombardi, Higgins, and Bargh (1987) demonstrated that when individuals become aware of the priming procedure, they no longer rely on the activated concepts to interpret a subsequent situation.

More direct evidence was reported by Strack, Schwarz, Bless, Kübler, and Wänke (1993), who experimentally directed participants' attention to the priming episode. In particular, participants were required to perform what they thought was a series of perceptual and cognitive tasks. In the ostensible first task, participants were exposed to words with either a positive (e.g., helpful) or a negative valence (e.g., dishonest) while listening to tones, and they were asked to classify these tones as high or low. In the ostensible second task, participants had to form an impression of a target person. The target's behavior was ambiguous (e.g., stole exam questions for a desperate friend) and open to interpretation in terms of the positive ("helped a friend in need") or the negative primed concepts ("stealing is dishonest"). To manipulate participants' attention toward the priming episode, half of the participants were asked to answer some questions about the word-tone task (e.g., how successful they had been in discriminating the tones) before forming their impressions. This interpolated task served to remind participants of the priming episode that had caused the positive or negative words to be highly accessible.

As can be seen in Illustration 5.2, when participants were not reminded of the priming episode, the obtained findings replicate earlier priming studies (e.g., Higgins et al., 1977): the target was evaluated more positively when positive rather than negative information was made accessible, reflecting assimilation to the activated concepts. However, when participants were reminded, the activated concepts were not used as a basis for impression formation. Instead, a contrast effect was obtained: participants gave more positive ratings if the prime words were negative, and vice versa. These findings suggest that if judges are aware that a concept has been activated by an event that is not relevant for the judgment, they may not use the concept for interpreting the target (see also Lombardi et al., 1987), even if the concept is highly accessible.

Given that a heightened memory for the priming episode reduces assimilation effects and makes contrast effects more likely, one can explain why, in many situations,

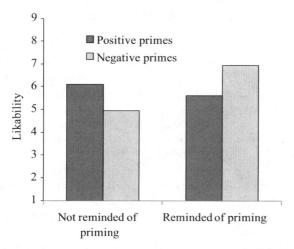

Illustration 5.2 Evaluation of the target person as a function of the valence of activated concepts and participants being reminded about the priming episode; scores range from 1, dislikable, to 9, likable

Source: Strack et al. (1993)

the force of an influence is negatively correlated with its success. Increasing the strength of an influence also increases the chances that recipients become aware of the influence, which in turn elicits mechanisms that counteract the influence if it is perceived as unwanted. In support of this assumption, it has been demonstrated that assimilation turns into contrast if features of the prime or the priming episode increase individuals' attention toward the unrelated source of the increased accessibility. For example, Herr (1986) demonstrated that assimilation effects were more likely for moderate primes, whereas contrast effects emerged for extreme primes (see also Moskowitz & Skurnik, 1999). Similarly, subtle priming procedures (for the extreme case of subliminal priming, see Bargh & Pietromonaco, 1982; cf. Dijksterhuis, Aarts, & Smith, 2005) usually elicit assimilation effects, whereas priming the same information very blatantly causes contrast effects (for a systematic investigation, see Martin, 1986; Martin, Seta, & Crelia, 1990). Moreover, when individuals perceive the priming task as easy or fluent, the activated concepts are likely to trigger assimilation, but contrast effects emerge when the priming task is perceived as difficult or disfluent (Greifeneder & Bless, 2010). Presumably, extremity of the prime and blatancy of priming, as well as perceived disfluency, direct individuals' attention toward the unrelated source of the accessible information. As individuals in these cases do not perceive the relevance of the accessible information, they exclude it from the judgmental target and can use it to construct the standard, which accounts for the observed contrast effects.

Filter 2: accessible information and the role of representativeness and applicability

In order to provide a solid basis for judgment, accessible information must not only be relevant, but should also adequately represent the judgmental target. If information is deemed non-representative, individuals should exclude it from their mental representation of the target. For example, assume you wanted to evaluate how introverted computer experts are in general. A good friend of yours is a computer expert and she is very extraverted. On the one hand, she is an expert (highly accessible information); on the other hand, however, you know her to be very extraverted and realize that this is a rather atypical trait for computer experts. As a result, you may perceive your friend as not representative when evaluating computer experts in general. This example illustrates that even when accessible information is perceived as having been prompted by the judgmental target, individuals may refrain from basing their representation of the judgmental target on this information (exclusion).

Obviously, the perceived typicality of the activated information for the judgmental target plays a crucial role in whether or not individuals rely on accessible information. Evidence for this assumption is provided, for example, by research in the stereotype-change domain. An activated exemplar (e.g., a specific target) is more likely to cause a change in judgments about the group when the exemplar is perceived as typical rather than atypical (Bless, Schwarz, Bodenhausen, & Thiel, 2001; Hewstone, 1994; Kunda & Oleson, 1995, 1997; Weber & Crocker, 1983). In the case of atypical exemplars (e.g., the atypical computer expert), contrast effects emerge: it would appear that in this case the exception to the rule (the extraverted computer expert) proves the rule (computer experts are introverted) even more; for a meta-analytic support of this finding see McIntyre, Paolini, and Hewstone (2016). Relatedly, Bodenhausen, and colleagues (1995) observed that bringing to mind famous and well-liked African Americans (e.g., sport celebrities such as Michael Jordan) who are financially very successful did not reduce but increase perceived discrimination against African Americans. Directly addressing the role of typicality, Bless and Wänke (2000) demonstrated that activated information perceived as typical results in assimilation effects (i.e., activated positive information results in more positive judgments), whereas activated information perceived as atypical results in contrast effects (i.e., activated positive information results in more negative judgments).

Indirectly related to these findings, Herr and colleagues (Herr, 1986; Herr et al., 1983) found in their studies that a target (an animal or a prominent person) was judged as more hostile when presented in the context of another moderately hostile exemplar (assimilation), but was judged as less hostile when presented in the context of an extremely hostile exemplar (contrast). They argued that assimilation and contrast depend on the extremity of the context information. Assuming that extreme exemplars not only draw more attention (as discussed above) but are also perceived as atypical, whereas moderate exemplars are perceived as typical (see also Philippot et al., 1991), these findings converge with the conclusion that perceived typicality plays a crucial role in whether and how individuals rely on activated information (see also Lambert & Wyer, 1990; Maurer, Park, & Rothbart, 1995; for an overview, see Bless & Schwarz, 2010).

Perceived representativeness implies that the prime can, in principle, be included in the representation of the target. However, depending on the structural relationship between the activated information and the judgmental target, potentially relevant information might simply not be applicable to the judgment in question. Imagine, for example, you are asked to rate the trustworthiness of a *specific politician Smith*, and due to some other previously performed task the scandal-ridden politician Miller comes to your mind. Obviously, this information could be relevant. However, the scandal-ridden politician Miller cannot easily be "included" in the politician Smith. In this case, Miller can serve as a standard against which Smith can be compared. As a consequence, Smith seems more trustworthy than without the activation of Miller. Since an exemplar (here: Miller) of one category cannot be included in another exemplar (here: Smith) of the same category (here: politicians), lateral rather than hierarchical structural relationships between prime and target render a (direct) inclusion impossible and result in contrast effects (see also the above example on how exposure to attractive media celebrities results in contrast effects, Kenrick & Gutierres, 1980). Illustration 5.3 (right) illustrates how the activated information about the scandal-ridden politician is used for constructing the comparison standard, resulting in contrast.

To illustrate the importance of the structural relationship between the prime and the judgmental target, imagine a slightly different judgmental task. Instead of evaluating the specific politician Smith, you are asked to rate the trustworthiness of *politicians in general*. In this case, scandal-ridden Miller can be included in the category in question (because he is a politician), and consequently, you would consider politicians in general as less trustworthy when the scandal-ridden politician is activated. Illustration 5.3 (left) illustrates how the activated information about the scandal-ridden politician is now used for constructing the judgmental target, resulting in assimilation.

Evidence reported by Schwarz and Bless (1992b) demonstrates this seeming paradox that the same activated exemplar can cause contrast when individuals evaluate other exemplars but assimilation when they evaluate the superordinate category the exemplar belongs to. Specifically, participants were or were not primed with a scandal-ridden politician and were subsequently asked to evaluate either the trustworthiness of other specific politicians not involved in the scandal (lateral structural relation), or the trustworthiness of the category politicians in general (hierarchical structural relation).

As can be seen in Illustration 5.4, activating the scandalous politician increased the trustworthiness of other politicians but decreased the trustworthiness of politicians in general. In line with these findings, assimilation effects are more likely when the judgmental target reflects a wide rather than a narrow category (e.g., Strack et al., 1985) and when the perceived variability within the target category is high rather than low (Johnston & Hewstone, 1992; Lambert & Wyer, 1990), because in these situations the activated information can be included more easily. The logic that activated information needs to be applicable to the judgmental target is also inherent in the finding that judgments about a target person are likely to reflect assimilation effects when the prime is an abstract trait category, whereas contrast effects are likely to emerge when the prime is a concrete, specific person (Moskowitz & Skurnik, 1999). This makes sense because an abstract trait category is likely applicable to more judgmental targets than a specific exemplar.

Imagine you are a member of a soccer team and a new, exceptionally good player joins your team. The above findings suggest that the new star player would increase the evaluation of the team as a whole (assimilation), while at the same time reducing the evaluation of your own performance (contrast; see also Illustration 5.1). Interestingly, the contrast effects usually elicited by other exemplars ("Compared to this brilliant player, your own achievements seem rather mediocre") can be eliminated under some conditions. When common aspects of the context and the judgmental target are emphasized, contrast effects are reduced or even eliminated (see Wänke, Bless, & Igou, 2001). For example, participants in research by Brown, Novick, Lord, and Richards (1992) rated themselves as less physically attractive after being exposed to physically attractive targets. Importantly, this contrast effect turned into assimilation—that is, participants rated themselves more attractive after exposure to attractive targets—when similarities between themselves and the target were emphasized (e.g., same birthday, interest in the same sport).

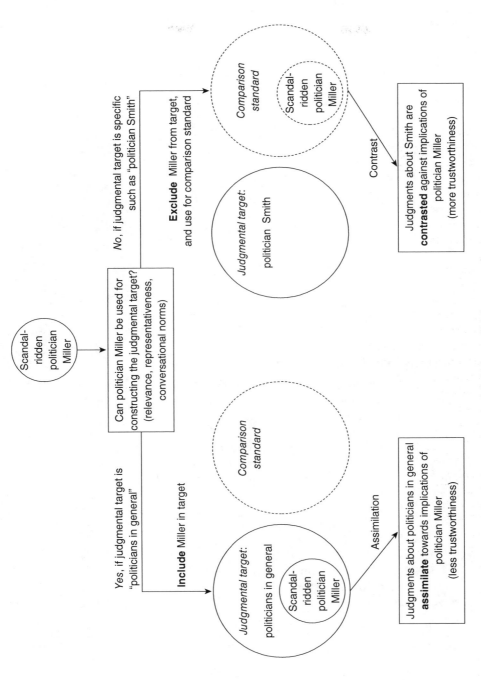

Illustration 5.3 Illustration of inclusion/exclusion in the scandal-ridden politician example

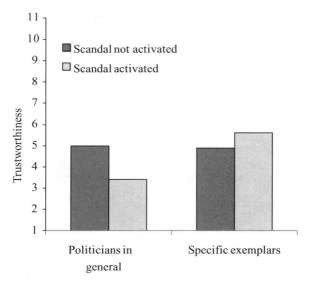

Illustration 5.4 Judgments of trustworthiness as a function of activation of a scandal-ridden politician and type of judgment (politicians in general versus three specific politicians); scores range from 1, not at all trustworthy, to 11, very trustworthy

Source: Schwarz and Bless (1992, Table 1)

Filter 3: accessibility and the role of conversational relevance

Many of our daily judgments are prompted by our social interactions. For example, your friend may ask you about your evaluation of a political party. In order to communicate successfully, you and your friend need to agree on the judgmental target (the political party) and on the applied comparison standard (cf. Schwarz, 1996). Assume, for example, that your friend's question is raised during a discussion of local politics, or, alternatively, during a discussion of foreign policy issues. Obviously, you would adjust your mental representation of the target (the political party) to the conversation's topic. As a consequence, in the context of the local community you would exclude representatives of this party who are not involved in local politics, even though such representatives may be highly accessible. Thus, the social definition of the target (here between you and your friend) can override the influence of mere accessibility (for empirical evidence on this issue, see Schwarz, Strack, & Mai, 1991; Strack, Martin, & Schwarz, 1988).

Moreover, successful communication also requires that communication partners agree on which standard is applied. In the above example it seems plausible that different standards could be applied to local politicians and politicians involved in foreign policy. In line with this assumption, research has demonstrated that standards shift systematically as a function of the underlying category that constitutes the common ground of the communication (Biernat, 2012). For example, Biernat and Manis (1994) provided participants with a target's performance in a verbal skill test. Verbal skill tests are stereotypically associated with poorer performance of males compared to females. The very same performance was evaluated more positively for supposedly male rather than female targets. Presumably, the male target was evaluated relative to other males (for an overview see Bettencourt et al., 2016). The importance of the communicative context of social cognition (cf. Schwarz, 1996) that is evident in these examples will be addressed in more detail in Chapter 9.

Motivational determinants of information use

So far, our discussion has focused on the role of information accessibility. How much and which information comes to mind and how it is used further depends on motivational influences. Sometimes individuals may engage in a more extensive information search, other times they may not search very deeply. Moreover, sometimes individuals tend to use information in such a way that the resulting judgments "serve them well." We address these two facets in turn.

Using information and the role of processing intensity

Information accessibility exerts its influence because individuals do not engage in a complete review of all potentially relevant information, but truncate their search processes (see Chapter 2). Given this underlying assumption, it is obvious that the influence of accessible information depends on when the search process is truncated—in other words, how much information individuals retrieve and integrate in their judgment (cf. Bless & Schwarz, 2010). The influence of a given piece of accessible information, for example the influence of the scandal-ridden politician Miller on the evaluations of politicians in general, decreases the more other information is used to represent the judgmental target (Bless, Igou, Schwarz, & Wänke, 2000). Thus, it is no surprise that context effects are usually less pronounced for experts than for novices, because experts can retrieve more judgment-relevant information than non-experts (see e.g., Wänke, Bless, & Schwarz, 1998).

The retrieval of more or less judgment-relevant information is a function not only of expertise in the respective domain, but is also influenced by situational determinants. In particular, processing capacity and processing motivation affect how much information is considered for a judgment. In the domain of person perception, abundant research has demonstrated that when individuals evaluate other persons, stereotype information will come to mind and this stereotype information is less influential when individuals have ample processing resources available and processing motivation is high (cf. Bodenhausen et al., 1999; S. T. Fiske, 1998). For example, in an intriguing set of studies, Bodenhausen (1990) assessed individuals' circadian rhythm, that is, whether participants were either "morning people" (most cognitive resources in the morning) or "evening people" (most cognitive resources in the evening). The experiment was then manipulated to take place in the morning or in the afternoon, such that participants' optimal resources matched or mismatched the timing of the experiment. The results demonstrate that making stereotype information accessible was particularly influential when processing resources were low (e.g., when "evening people" needed to participate in the morning sessions), because in this case little information was considered in addition to the easily accessible stereotype information. Relatedly, abundant research has demonstrated that accessible stereotype information has less effect when processing motivation is high (Bodenhausen et al., 1999; S. T. Fiske, 1998). For example, Neuberg and Fiske (1987) asked participants to evaluate a target person and observed that these evaluations were affected by stereotype information that was made accessible. This influence diminished, however, when participants anticipated interacting with the target person in a subsequent situation, presumably because the anticipated interaction increased processing intensity and led individuals to consider more information about the target person (for conceptually related findings in the persuasion domain, see Petty & Wegener, 1999; Vogel & Wänke, 2016).

Not surprisingly, in addition to situational influences on processing intensity, individuals may dispositionally differ with respect to how much they engage in elaborative cognitive processes. Some individuals have a need to think extensively before making a judgment (high in need for cognition), while other individuals may attempt to avoid extensive, effortful processing (low in need for cognition, see Cacioppo & Petty, 1982). Related constructs such as need for closure (Webster & Kruglanski, 1994) or need for validity (Kruglanski & Webster, 1996) have similarly been shown to influence individuals' engagement in judgmental processes.

So far this section has focused on how processing intensity influences the *amount* of information individuals consider for their evaluative judgments. Let us now recall that accessible information can have quite different effects (i.e., assimilation or contrast), as a function of whether or not individuals perceive the accessible information as relevant and representative. It is obvious that evaluating accessible information for its relevance and representativeness requires a sufficient amount of processing capacity and motivation. Thus, it seems a straightforward assumption that when processing capacity or processing motivation are low, individuals should be more likely to base their judgments on what comes to mind (assimilation), whereas contrast effects become more likely when individuals engage in additional processing, which increases the chances that individuals will detect and try to correct for the potential contamination of their judgment. Evidence in this respect was reported by Martin and colleagues (1990), who found assimilation toward activated context information when participants were low in need for cognition, but contrast effects when participants were high in need for cognition. In a similar vein, accessible atypical exemplars elicit a change of the evaluation of the group in general when processing resources are low (assimilation). However, in the case of high processing resources, individuals do not base their judgments on atypical exemplars, presumably because they exclude this information from their mental representation about the group in general (Bless et al., 2001; Yzerbyt et al., 1999). Note the ironic implication of this finding: conditions that decrease stereotype-based judgments of the specific exemplars (e.g., processing capacity in the circadian rhythm studies by Bodenhausen, 1990) seem to inhibit atypical exemplars from changing stereotype judgments about the group in general.

As has become evident, social situations differ substantially with respect to how individuals form judgments, and, more specifically, how much information individuals consider and how they use accessible information. In many cases, individuals may not communicate their judgment for a variety of reasons. For example, social desirability (see e.g., Paulhus, 1984) may prevent you from telling your aunt that you do not like the birthday present she gave you. But there are also situations in which individuals are not only required to communicate their judgment (e.g., when taking part in a survey), but must also justify their judgment. Interestingly, anticipating having to justify your judgment may change how you form it. For example, imagine you are an employee and have purchased a car for your company. Of course, your boss wants to know why you bought this particular car rather than a different one. Most likely, you would not justify your decision by invoking a particular feeling that you had when you purchased the car. Instead, you would come up with arguments that supported your choice. More generally, whenever we have to justify an action to a third person, we typ-ically offer reasons and not subjective experiences. People who expect that they will have to justify their decisions before they generate a judgment will therefore be more likely to use content instead of feelings as their basis. Labeled accountability (Tetlock, 1992), the perceived need to justify one's judgments to others has been investigated with respect to many judgmental domains, and the available evidence suggests that accountability reduces a wide array of cognitive biases (Lerner & Tetlock, 1999).

Ironically, thinking about reasons for one's judgments does not necessarily increase accuracy. Sometimes, thinking more about potential reasons may in fact decrease accuracy (Tetlock, Skitka, & Boettger, 1989). An example of coming up with reasons for a judgment (rather than basing the judgment on a feeling) is provided by Wilson and colleagues (1993). Their participants were asked to select one poster for free from a set of six different ones. Half of the participants were asked to think of reasons for their selection, whereas the other half were not asked to do so. When participants were asked six weeks later about how satisfied they were with their choice, it turned out that participants who had based the selection on their feeling were more satis-fied (e.g., still had the poster on their wall) than participants who had thought about reasons for their selection. This suggests that thinking extensively may not necessarily increase accuracy (for an overview, see Wilson, Dunn, Kraft, & Lisle, 1989).

Using information that serves us well

Much of the research addressed in the present chapter is implicitly or explicitly based on the assumption that individuals are motivated to hold and report accurate judgments—even in situations with high complexity and even when their processing resources are limited. However, we saw in Chapter 1 that the social thinker may have additional motives. Judgmental processes are driven not only by individuals' need for accuracy; individuals also have the need to feel positive about themselves (e.g., Crocker & Wolfe, 2001; W. James, 1890). How does this assumption relate to the present discussion about individuals using information that is on their mind? Perhaps most importantly, when searching for information in the environment, individuals have the tendency to search for information that is consistent with their prior beliefs, in general, and with the beliefs about themselves, in particular (Chapter 10 provides a more detailed discussion of this topic). These mechanisms, in turn, have a very pro-nounced influence on which information can later be retrieved most easily, that is, on which information is most accessible. For example, Sedikides and Green (2000) demonstrated that individuals are more likely to remember information when it has positive implications for themselves, whereas they are less likely to remember infor-mation that has negative implications. Given such a tendency, it is no surprise that individuals hold a wide array of biased judgments about themselves and the world (cf. Taylor & Brown, 1988, 1994). For example, individuals perceive themselves as better-than-average on almost any dimension that can be evaluated (e.g., Weinstein, 1980; Alicke & Govorun, 2005). Most individuals think they are better drivers than the average person (e.g., Svenson, 1981), that they are more selfless and likable (Epley & Dunning, 2000), or that they have better chances of being happily married (Weinstein, 1980). With respect to life at university, Alicke and Govorun (2005) report that 25% of students taking the SAT assumed that their performance would be in the top 1% range. Staying a longer time at university does not help to overcome these illusions. According to data reported by Cross (1977), 94% of university professors believed they had above-average teaching abilities. Interestingly, it seems that the worse a person's actual performance, the more pronounced is the tendency toward overestimation (Kruger & Dunning, 1999).

The better-than-average effect reflects only one variant of illusory positive judgments individuals hold about themselves and the world. Self-enhancement in social judgment has been documented widely and different explanations have been offered (cf. Alicke & Sedikides, 2011). Many of these accounts attribute the observed judgmental effects to one of the two core issues of the present chapter. On the one hand, it is assumed that illusory judgments are driven by a differential retrieval of information. The argument here is that information with positive implications about the Self is more likely to come to mind due to better encoding, due to the way in which memory is organized, or due to individuals' selective search for this information in memory (Davidai & Gilovich, 2016). Thus, these explanations focus on "what comes to mind." On the other hand, it is argued that individuals select their comparison standards in a way that the evaluation of themselves is likely to turn out positive, for example by comparing themselves to others who are doing rather poorly (cf. Alicke & Sedikides, 2011).

Moreover, research on motivated processing of information (Kunda, 1990; Dunning, 1999) implies that individuals may also be motivated to use accessible information differently in order to maintain their world view (including their positive view about themselves). For example, Kunda and Oleson (1995) demonstrated that when presented with information that was clearly not atypical for the judgmental target, participants were highly flexible in "detecting" atypicality in this information when it contradicted their prior beliefs about the world or themselves. This detection provided a basis for excluding the accessible information and thus allowed them to avoid changing their existing representation and judgments about the judgmental target. In combination, the described processes lead to mental conservatism, that is, they contribute to individuals maintaining their existing view about the social world, in general, and their positive views about themselves, in particular.

Automatic judgments

So far, this chapter has addressed how individuals form judgments on the basis of information that is on their mind through processes where the available information (or a subset of it) is examined, evaluated, and used to form a judgment in a deliberative way. Moreover, we have seen how these judgments are influenced by individuals' processing motivation, as well as sometimes by their tendency to feel positive about themselves. Research suggests that this deliberate route is not the only way in which individuals form judgments. As we have seen, deliberative judgments require processing resources, and given that (a) these resources are limited, and (b) very many complex judgments are required in social situations, it is obvious that judgments must also be formed in ways that require very little elaboration. In fact, sometimes judgments may be formed outside individuals' awareness and attention, seeming to emerge *automatically*. The complementary and interactive character of these more automatic judgments, on the one hand, and more deliberative judgment formation, on the other hand, is captured in various models that integrate the two variants. The proposed models differ in their specifics and the labeling of the different processes (e.g., System 1 vs. System 2, Kahneman, 2003; reflective vs. impulsive,

Strack & Deutsch, 2004), and quite a number of different accounts have been offered, with some of them being more general, and others being more domain specific (for reviews see Bodenhausen & Todd, 2010; Moors & De Houwer, 2006; Sherman et al., 2014). With respect to seemingly automatic judgments, one needs to differentiate between two intertwined aspects. First, information may be brought to mind more or less automatically, as discussed in Chapter 4. Second, based on accessible information, *judgments* may emerge through a non-deliberative, automatic way. In the remainder of this chapter we focus primarily, though not exclusively, on this second aspect.

What are the core features of automatic judgmental processes? It has been proposed that automatic processes can be characterized by four core dimensions: *awareness, intention, efficiency,* and *control* (Bargh, 1994). Related to our current focus on judgmental processes, automatic judgment formation would thus imply that judgments are formed unintentionally outside the individual's awareness, and that individuals have no control over these processes that require very few cognitive resources. Importantly, the four aspects do not need to co-vary, and the conceptual discussions often remain silent about whether each of these four aspects constitutes a necessary condition, and/or whether any of these aspects creates a sufficient condition in order to label processes as "automatic" (Moors, 2016). Instead of engaging in such a definitional endeavor, we will illustrate the four core attributes of automaticity with findings from research on judgments.

Awareness

One typical characteristic of automatic mental processes is that they are assumed to occur outside of individuals' conscious awareness. In the context of judgments, different aspects can lie outside awareness. First, individuals may be unaware that they have formed an initial evaluation or judgment of a particular stimulus (which implies that they are also unaware of the processes that led to the judgment). Second, individuals may be aware of the judgment, yet unaware of *which* information influenced their judgment and how the judgment was formed. Third, individuals may be unaware of *why* a particular piece of information came to mind and was subsequently used for their judgment. We discuss these aspects in turn.

At first glance, it may seem rather counterintuitive that individuals are unaware of the fact that they have evaluated or judged a stimulus. Nevertheless, research on the Iowa Gambling Task has demonstrated that this is in fact possible (Bechara, Damasio, Tranel, & Damasio, 1997). In the Iowa Gambling Task, participants start with an endowment of points and aim at maximizing their points by sampling cards that can entail either wins or losses from four decks of cards. What participants do not know is that the card decks are set up in such a way that two of the decks include large wins but are disadvantageous in the long run because they also include large losses. The two other decks, in contrast, include only small wins but are advantageous in the long run because losses are also small. By recording the skin conductance reactions of participants in addition to their decisions and their spoken reports of what is going on in this game, it is possible to demonstrate that (healthy) participants go through a phase in which deciding to sample from the disadvantageous decks elicits stronger anticipatory skin conductance reactions than deciding to sample from the advantageous decks, though participants did not report having preferences for certain decks. Apparently, an evaluation took place without participants being aware of it. Later, participants reached a phase in which they reported having a preference for the advantageous decks without being able to explain why, before they eventually consciously grasped the properties of the different card decks. In combination, these findings suggest that individuals may be unaware that they had formed a judgment, while their skin conductance reactions indicate clearly that they in fact had.

The second aspect of unaware judgment formation pertains to the observation that individuals may be unaware of *which* information influenced their judgment. For example, in a study documented by Nisbett and Wilson (1977), decisions were influenced by whether objects were presented on the right or the left side of a choice array, even though participants never consciously considered this aspect. Other research has demonstrated that repeated presentations of a stimulus can elicit more positive evaluations without individuals being aware that they saw the stimulus before (Zajonc, 1980). Moreover, judgments can be influenced by subliminal cues, as was seen in a study by Winkielman, Berridge, and Wilbarger (2005), where thirsty participants' evaluations of beverages were influenced by displays of happy (vs. angry) faces that were presented at a subliminal level and had no effect on conscious affective states. Consistent with the notion of unawareness, individuals have no insight into these processes, and when asked, they are sometimes strongly convinced that their judgments are the result of deliberative thinking (see Haidt, 2001). For example, in Nisbett and Wilson's (1977) research, participants who preferred the right-most objects were unable to report this influence, and even when they were explicitly asked for a potential effect of the object position, all participants denied this possibility. The seminal work by Nisbett and Wilson (1977) points to the possibility that when asked to justify our judgments we may come up with answers about which information we used, but this (post-judgmental) reasoning reflects a justification of an intuitive judgment rather than the actual determinants of the judgment.

Even when individuals are aware of which information they used for their judgment, they can still be unaware of *why* that piece of information was brought to mind and entered their judgment. For example, a study by Berger, Meredith, and Wheeler (2008) demonstrated that voters assigned to cast their vote in schools were more likely to support a school funding initiative than voters assigned to vote in other polling locations. Most probably, these voters were not aware that their thoughts about the school funding initiative were influenced by the polling location (see Chapter 4 for a detailed discussion of automaticity in the context of information acquisition).

Intentionality

Another, frequently highlighted characteristic of automatic mental processes is that they take place regardless of whether the person wants them to occur or not. Imagine, for example, individuals performing a Stroop task, where they are instructed to name the ink color (e.g., yellow) in which color names (e.g., "RED") are printed. These individuals will experience that they are not able to stop the highly automatized reading process from taking place and interfering with their performance in the actual color naming task (that is, reading "RED" interferes with naming "yellow"). Similar unintentional processes can be observed with respect to judgmental processes. For example, in the domain of person perception it has been argued that individuals form judgments about other persons spontaneously and independently of a particular intention (e.g., Gawronski & Quinn, 2013; Lench & Bench, 2012). In this respect, researchers

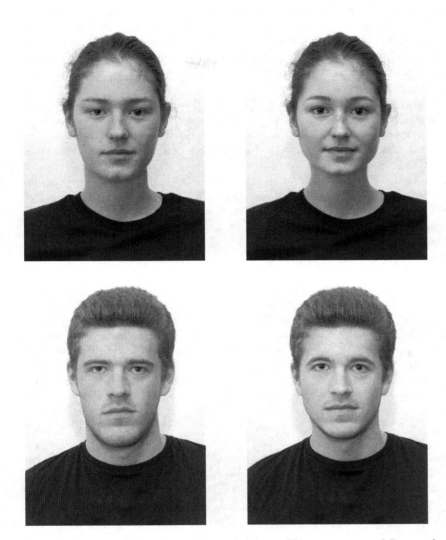

Illustration 5.5 Which person (left or right) would you trust more? Research suggests that people spontaneously and very quickly draw inferences about other people's trustworthiness based on their facial appearance. In the two left pictures, facial features known to be perceived as signals of trustworthiness have been reduced; in the two right pictures, the same features have been enhanced (for details about this мethod, see Walker & Vetter, 2016)

Source: The original photographs belong to the Basel Face Database (Walker, Schönborn, Greifeneder, & Vetter, 2017). © Mirella Walker

have posited that such spontaneous judgments pertain especially to dimensions that are important and central in person perception. When interacting with another person, that person's emotion (e.g., "Is the person angry?), assumed warmth (e.g., "Can I trust the person?"), and competence are critical aspects for future interaction (see e.g., S. T. Fiske, Cuddy, Glick, & Xu, 2002; Oosterhof & Todorov, 2008). Judgments on these dimensions provide answers to whether or not the other person has the potential and the willingness to do harm. Given the importance and centrality of these judgments, it is no surprise that research has documented that such judgments are often formed rather spontaneously, without conscious intention (e.g., Klapper, Dotsch, van Rooij, & Wigboldus, 2016; Todorov & Uleman, 2003; Uleman, Blader, & Todorov, 2005).

Spontaneous judgments are, however, not restricted to these pivotal dimensions. Presumably, judgments on almost any dimension can be performed unintentionally once this judgment is central for the perceiver's current situation and has become automatized through repetition (e.g., Aarts, Verplanken, & Knippenberg, 1998; Duff & Newman, 1997). Thus, we may unintentionally form judgments about, for instance, someone else's goals (Van Overwalle, Van Duynslaeger, Coomans, & Timmermans, 2012), his or her personality (Walker & Vetter, 2016), whether the person looks like a criminal (Funk, Walker, & Todorov, 2016), or whether he or she might be a good roommate.

Controllability

Since automatic mental processes occur outside of awareness and without a person's intention, they are very difficult to control. In fact, the control we have over automatic judgments seems to be at most indirect rather than direct. That is, we may avoid or seek situations where we are likely to encounter stimuli that would trigger certain automatic reactions, or we may engage in a process of unlearning automatic reactions to certain stimuli (e.g., when someone with arachnophobia does behavioral therapy). However, once we are exposed to a target that has the potential of eliciting an automatic judgment, we have no direct control over the process of judgment formation. What we can control, though, is whether we want to turn an implicit automatic judgment into an explicit judgment. Imagine, for example, that you have a negative first impression of another person without even knowing why. Although this judgment has already been formed, you may still decide to "overrule" this judgment and not base your subsequent behavior toward this person on your automatic judgment. Bodenhausen and Todd (2010) addressed various situational and personal factors that influence the degree to which individuals tend to counteract (or at least to scrutinize) their first automatic judgments. For example, individuals high in need for cognition have been found to be more likely to counteract automatic negative associations toward a stereotyped group as compared to individuals low in need for cognition (Florack et al., 2001). Complementary to this motivational factor, individuals are less likely to override their automatic judgments when under a cognitive load (Ferreira, Garcia-Marques, Sherman, & Sherman, 2006), or when self-regulation resources are depleted (Hofmann, Rauch, & Gawronski, 2007; for a more extended discussion, see Bodenhausen & Todd, 2010).

It is important to note that attempts to correct for initial judgments can be successful, but are not invariably so (e.g., Gawronski, Geschke, & Banse, 2003). One reason for the difficulty in overriding the initial automatic judgment may stem from the fact that individuals are often unaware of what caused their judgment. Moreover, first impressions may guide much of subsequent, more deliberative thinking in a hypothesis-confirming fashion. Finally, even though individuals may realize that their first impression needs correction, it is difficult to know just how much the judgment should be corrected.

Efficiency

For cognitive processes to be categorized as efficient, the operation of the cognitive processes should require very little mental resources. For example, with respect to automatic judgments, research on face perception has demonstrated that attributions of personality characteristics from faces are made so rapidly that the process resembles perception more than thinking (Todorov, Olivola, Dotsch, & Mende-Siedlecki, 2015). In an intriguing series of studies, Willis and Todorov (2006) showed their participants unfamiliar faces for 100, 500, or 1,000 milliseconds and asked them to report their impressions on dimensions such as aggressiveness or trustworthiness. Interestingly, a 100 millisecond exposure was enough for participants to make specific judgments. Importantly, with respect to efficiency, these extremely fast judgments were similar to those made when participants were provided with more time to view the faces. These findings illustrate the more general notion that individuals can form judgments and make decisions on the basis of very little information (see also Ambady, Bernieri, & Richeson, 2000).

Because automatic judgments require very few mental resources, their operation is, in contrast to deliberative processes, not affected by individuals' ability and willingness to allocate mental resources to the judgmental task. As a consequence of this differential impact of mental resources on more deliberative versus more automatic processes, constraints on mental resources can increase the impact of automatic judgments on behavior in situations where deliberative and automatic judgments contradict each other. For example, a study by Hofmann and colleagues (2007) demonstrated that the consumption of candies by participants was predicted by their automatic evaluations of candies following a manipulation that depleted their self-regulatory resources, but it was predicted by explicit dietary standards instead of automatic evaluations when they were in full possession of their self-regulatory resources. Note that these findings complement the research related to the controllability aspect discussed above.

Very importantly, in order to be labeled as "efficient," automatic judgments must not only require few mental resources, but must also provide valid results—not in every situation, but in the majority of cases. We address this accuracy aspect in the next section.

Automatic judgments and accuracy

Can automatic judgments be both extremely fast and accurate? Recall the research on person perception in which participants provided judgments even though they saw the other person only for 100 milliseconds (Willis & Todorov, 2006). Interestingly, research suggests that these judgments formed on the basis of brief glimpses of a person's behavior may reflect a surprisingly high accuracy (Ambady, 2010; Ambady et al., 2000). However, there is also conflicting evidence that this optimistic view of the accuracy of thin slice judgments is not always warranted (e.g., Ames, Kammrath, Suppes, & Bolger, 2009; Gray, 2008). Contrary to the assumption that thin slices result in valid judgments, Letzring, Wells, and Funder (2006) reported that accuracy in person perception increased with more information. This mixed pattern of findings suggests that under some conditions thin slices provide a good basis, and under some conditions a poor basis for judgments (see Fiedler & Kareev, 2011, for a conceptual discussion of how relying on small vs. large samples of information influences accuracy).

The discussion on the accuracy of automatic judgments is not restricted to individuals relying on thin slices of information. Even when the situation is more complex and a lot of information is provided, automatic judgment formation may have its benefit. In this respect, Dijksterhuis and colleagues (Dijksterhuis, 2004; Dijksterhuis, Bos, Nordgren, & van Baaren, 2006) proposed the unconscious thought theory. It holds that in complex situations, individuals may form more accurate judgments when they form the judgment without attention as compared to when they think about the judgment consciously. For example, participants were provided with descriptions about different apartments varying on many attributes (price, location, view, etc.). One of these apartments was pre-tested to be clearly superior. After the presentation of the information, participants either deliberatively thought about their decision, or were distracted from deliberative thinking about the apartments. Unconscious thinking (by distracted participants) led to better judgments than deliberate judgment formation (for corresponding evidence in the area of lie detection, see Reinhard, Greifeneder, & Scharmach, 2013).

The research on the advantages of unconscious judgment and decision making has attracted much attention and additional work. The available cumulative evidence is currently rather mixed, with some findings supporting unconscious thought theory (e.g., Ham & van den Bos, 2011; Strick et al., 2011), and some research questioning its reliability (e.g., Acker, 2008; Nieuwenstein et al., 2015). While this debate is still ongoing, the conflicting findings point to some yet unknown moderating conditions. Under some conditions unconscious thought may improve judgments, whereas under some other conditions it seems more advisable to give decisions deliberative thought, and these conditions still need to be explored. Interestingly, research that addresses the accuracy of deliberative versus automatic judgment quite frequently compares automatic judgments to judgments that are reported by participants who were asked to think about the judgment for a given amount of time. In this respect, it has been argued that, particularly outside the laboratory setting, individuals determine themselves how much deliberative thinking they invested in a decision (J. W. Payne, Samper, Bettman, & Luce, 2008). The self-determined versus experimentally determined amount of processing may, in turn, affect accuracy of judgment.

Outlook

Despite all the controversial issues with respect to automatic judgment and decision making, there is a broad consensus that much of our social thinking is determined by more or less non-deliberative processes. The degree to which the four aspects of awareness, intention, efficiency, and control apply to the various processes varies substantially, and it is therefore sometimes difficult to determine whether or not a judgment formation should be labeled "automatic." This is also reflected in the fact that many processes are initially very controlled and become more and more automatized over time with repeated operation (similar to when people are learning to drive a car and driving is far from automatic in the first lessons in driving school).

Research to date still lacks a clear and consensual description of how judgments and decisions are formed automatically and then somehow pop up into consciousness. One potential avenue for addressing this question points to the crucial role of feelings. Some researchers have proposed that individuals' feelings may capture much of unconsciously processed information, and that while the unconsciously processed information remains inaccessible, individuals can become aware of their feeling(s) and use these feelings for judgment and decision making. This important link between automatic and deliberative processes will be addressed in Chapters 7 and 8.

Concluding remarks

Information accessibility plays a key role in social cognition research, because it is assumed that individuals base their judgment on information that comes to mind most easily. Based on the accessible information, individuals may apply different processing strategies and use the accessible information in different ways—either more deliberately or more automatically. It has become obvious that both components are involved in the majority of social judgments, yet the degree of the components differs as a function of the social situation. Sometimes our judgments are more deliberative, and sometimes, when processing resources are low and task complexity and time demands are high, the automatic component carries greater weight. Subscribing to these basic underlying assumptions, this chapter holds two additional messages. First, it is indeed the case that much of social judgment can be explained by determining which information comes to mind most easily at the time the judgment is made. In many cases, this reliance on what is on our mind is a reasonable and valid strategy, as accessibility is usually linked to what is important in a given situation or to what is important for the individual in general. The second, often overlooked message holds that individuals do not rely blindly on what is on their mind. Individuals are well aware that information can come to mind for the wrong reason or can be atypical for the present judgment, and consequently they try to avoid contamination of their judgments. In order to protect themselves against unwanted influences from activated declarative knowledge, individuals solve this task by drawing inferences on the basis of their naive theories about the functioning of their mind (see Bless & Schwarz, 2010; Wegener & Petty, 1997; Wilson & Brekke, 1994). In other words, individuals do hold naive theories about how accessible information might influence their judgment, and they have flexibility in how to use what is on their mind.

It has become evident that detecting potential contamination and applying corrective processes requires cognitive resources. Thus, on the one hand, contamination is more likely under sub-optimal processing conditions, for example due to high complexity or time constraints. On the other hand, we have seen that more processing does not always and under all conditions improve judgmental accuracy. With respect to processing intensity, it is important to point out that processing resources may turn out to be too low to allow for the retrieval and integration of even a small subset of potentially relevant information. In this case, individuals can resort to other, less taxing judgmental processing strategies, such as relying on very simple heuristics or basing their judgments on their feelings. We address these possibilities in the subsequent chapters.

Chapter summary

1   When forming judgments and decisions, individuals do not consider all potentially relevant information but rely on a subset of information that is most accessible in the situation.
2   In many situations, relying on what is on one's mind constitutes a solid strategy, because accessibility is not random but reflects situational as well as dispositional importance.
3   To understand people's judgments in a social context, it is not sufficient to explain what is on their mind. Rather, it is necessary to determine whether information is used and how it is used, given that it is activated.
4   When accessible information is used to represent the judgmental target, assimilation effects emerge, that is, there is a positive relationship between the implications of accessible information and the resulting judgment.

5   Individuals do not rely blindly on accessible information but scrutinize whether accessible information may come to mind for the wrong reason (relevance filter), and whether accessible information is representative for the judgmental target (representativeness filter).

6   When accessible information does not pass the filters, contrast effects are a likely outcome, that is, there is a negative relationship between the implications of accessible information and the resulting judgment. Contrast effects are more likely the more individuals are willing and able to allocate processing resources that are necessary to scrutinize relevance and representativeness.

7   The more information individuals consider for a judgment, the less influence is exerted by any given piece of accessible information.

8   Judgments can be formed rather automatically, meaning that the formation of judgments is sometimes unconscious, unintentional, and the process itself is not controllable.

9   Unconscious judgments are often highly efficient, as they require very few cognitive resources while providing valid judgments in many situations.

Discussion questions/topics

1   Think of examples showing that individuals base their judgment on "what is on their mind" rather than considering all potentially relevant information.

2   What is an assimilation effect? What is a contrast effect? Think of examples of how the same information may elicit both types of effects.

3   Imagine yourself as a salesperson trying to sell a particular product. How could you make use of a contrast effect to increase the perceived attraction of your product?

4   Discuss the possibility of changing stereotypic judgments by making a specific exemplar of that group, for example, a famous celebrity, accessible.

5   Imagine you are asked to conduct a survey on how satisfied employees are with their employer. Would you first ask how satisfied employees are overall, and subsequently for specific issues, such as satisfaction with salary, working conditions, pension regulations, career opportunities, and so on? Or would you prefer the reversed order (overall question at the very end)? Discuss the different orders with respect to what information respondents will use for their judgment.

6   Think of situations in which individuals may form judgments and decisions in either a deliberative or an automatic way. Discuss the potential advantages and disadvantages of the different processing variants.

Recommendations for further reading

Bless, H., & Schwarz, N. (2010). Mental construal and the emergence of assimilation and contrast effects: The inclusion/exclusion model. *Advances in Experimental Social Psychology*, *42*, 319–373. (The paper provides a more in-depth coverage of the underlying mechanisms that determine how individuals use information that is on their mind.)

Schwarz, N. (1996). *Cognition and communication: Judgmental biases, research methods, and the logic of conversation*. Hillsdale, NJ: Lawrence Erlbaum Associates. (This book offers a conceptual integration of the often separately discussed cognitive vs. communicative determinants of information use.)

Wilson, T. D., Wheatley, T. P., Meyers, J. M., Gilbert, D. T., & Axsom, D. (2000). Focalism: A source of durability bias in affective forecasting. *Journal of Personality and Social Psychology*, *78*, 821–836. (This paper reports research on how individuals predict what makes them happy and how relying on the most accessible information may lead them astray.)

6   Using information

Judgmental shortcuts[1]

Rainer Greifeneder & Herbert Bless

It would seem that the best decisions are made when all pertinent information is considered and appropriately weighted. However, individuals often do not have access to all the information and its appropriate weighing—and even if they did, they often lack the time or motivation to process the information thoroughly enough. To illustrate, consider a random set of decisions that you may make tomorrow, such as deciding whether you can trust the person sitting next to you in your Social Psychology class, or whether it is your turn to empty the dishwasher. It is unlikely that you have access to all the information it takes to decide whether another person is trustworthy (do you know everything about the person's past?), and you may not invest all the time and motivation it takes to determine precisely who emptied the dishwasher more often before. If you lack information, capacity, or motivation, but still need to judge and decide, you may resort to judgmental shortcuts. Such shortcuts require less time and effort than the deliberate or extensive judgment formation discussed in the previous chapter; but they also do not qualify as automatic, since their use is quite often deliberate. In the literature, such shortcuts are referred to as heuristics.

What are judgmental heuristics?

To understand the nature of heuristics, imagine that you want to invite a good friend to a gourmet dinner. Since you have just moved to a new city, you do not know many restaurants. How can you decide which restaurant is most suitable for the dinner you have in mind? One possibility is to start sampling all restaurants in the city several months prior to the invitation, rate the food according to criteria important to you, draw up a ranking of the restaurants, and choose the one that comes out on top. While this method may lead to a fairly good decision, it takes up a lot of time, energy, and financial resources.

A much simpler method for solving this task is to rely on a restaurant guide. This would be a reasonable approach, since restaurant guides often offer accurate assessments of a restaurant's quality. However, in some cases the ratings are influenced by factors other than the actual standard of the cuisine. Was the critic perhaps in a bad mood when she visited a particular restaurant? Did the publisher of the guide test only a selected number of restaurants? Was there perhaps a recent change in restaurant ownership, with a marked influence on food quality? Although the restaurant guide is a reasonable rule of thumb, it may result in misjudgments.

---

1 This chapter is based on a previous version authored by Fritz Strack.

This example might help you to understand some essential elements and characteristics of heuristic judgment. First, there is the *judgmental dimension* of interest. For instance, in the above example, the judgmental dimension of interest is food quality, and an individual may wish to locate a specific object of judgment (e.g., a restaurant) on this dimension. Because the first strategy—testing all the restaurants—is beyond the individual's financial possibilities, he or she may use the summary ratings in the restaurant guide as substitute information. This substitute information is linked to the judgment dimension of interest, and is referred to as a *heuristic stimulus or cue*. Strategies that combine cues and judgmental dimensions are called *heuristics*. Heuristics are thus simple "rules of thumb" that are applied to readily available information and allow a person—even when information, capacity, or motivation are lacking—to arrive at a judgment. Depending on the relationship between the cue and the judgmental dimension, the final judgment may be more or less accurate.

What kinds of judgmental heuristics exist? There are a number of heuristics that are highly *general* in nature and can be applied to cues that are available in a great variety of situations. These heuristics are used, for instance, to assess frequency and probability, categorize persons, make value judgments, or estimate numerical quantities. Tversky and Kahneman (1974) were among the first to investigate these rules of thumb. The chapter's next section will focus on three heuristics introduced by these authors.

In addition to such general heuristics, individuals may have evolved content-specific simplifying judgment rules, such as the one about food quality in restaurants described above. These content-specific rules of thumb may result from contingency learning in the environment or be acquired from others, and may apply to all kinds of judgment targets, including objects (such as consumer products) and persons. The chapter's third section provides a brief introduction.

Three general rules of thumb: availability, representativeness, and anchoring

Tversky and Kahneman (1974) placed the idea of judgmental heuristics at the center of their theoretical reflections in the 1970s, providing the impetus behind the heuristics and bias research program that has profoundly influenced the psychology of judgment down to the present day. Our discussion will begin by introducing three cognitive heuristics that were the starting point for the research program. First, we will describe the availability heuristic, originally introduced as a rule of thumb to gauge frequency or probability. Second, we will address the representativeness heuristic, which is used to assign single elements (e.g., persons) to larger categories (e.g., groups), but is also employed to estimate frequency and probability. Third, we will examine the heuristic that has been labeled "anchoring and adjustment."

Availability heuristic

In assessing the frequency or probability of a stimulus or event, individuals may resort to a strategy that is based on the ease or difficulty with which bits of information can be retrieved or generated from memory. To illustrate, read the following list of names: Michelle Obama, Angelina Jolie, Samuel Alito, Andreas Seppi, Sarah Palin, David Paymer, Stefan Franz, Jennifer Lopez, Oprah Winfrey, François Fillon,

Albert Rupprecht, Fredrik Reinfeldt, Joanne K. Rowling, Rober Joy, Naomi Campbell, Markus Hediger, Britney Spears, Carla Bruni, Gary Allen.

Now answer the following question, without reading the names again: Did the above list contain more female or male names?

If your answer is "more female names," your judgment may have been influenced by what Tversky and Kahneman (1973) called the availability heuristic. The availability heuristic holds that judgments of frequency or probability may be influenced by the ease or difficulty with which relevant instances come to mind. In the above list, female names were factually less numerous than male names (9 vs. 10), but the female names may have come to your mind more easily because they are much more famous. In the original experiment, Tversky and Kahneman (1973) used a total of 19 famous and 20 non-famous names and found that about 80% of participants overestimated the proportion of the gender associated with the famous names. Presumably, these participants did not rely on actual name frequency when judging numerosity, but on the ease or difficulty with which the names came to mind.

Let's consider a second example: Are there more English words that start with the letter R than words with the letter R in the third position?

About two-thirds of the participants in one of Tversky and Kahneman's (1973) experiments judged words from the first category (starting with the letter R) to be more frequent than words from the second category (having R in the third position). Presumably, this is because recalling words starting with the letter R feels easier than recalling words having R in the third position. Using this experienced ease as a heuristic cue, participants judge the former word category to be more frequent, despite the second being more numerous.

The underlying logic

What is the logic behind the availability heuristic? Formulated as a rule, the availability heuristic holds: "If I can recall an event with ease, it probably occurs frequently," or "If I can imagine an event with ease, it is likely that the event will occur frequently."

Does this rule make sense? Very often, the answer is "yes," because the rule is based on observed contingencies in our learning environment, in which things that occur frequently are recalled with greater ease. For instance, if you frequently go to a certain restaurant, thinking of this restaurant feels easy. If you have met a person many times, the person's name comes to mind more easily than the name of a person you met only once.

The availability heuristic inverts this observed contingency of frequency and ease by drawing conclusions from experienced ease (e.g., I can recall the name easily) to frequency (e.g., I must have met the person frequently). In formal terms, the availability heuristic inverts the observed "when p then q," to "when q then p."

If the link between frequency and ease were bidirectionally true, this inversion would be unproblematic. However, the fact that things that are frequent can be recalled with greater ease (p then q) does not imply that everything that can be recalled with greater ease is necessarily more frequent (q then p). This is because our powers of memory are influenced not only by the frequency of the information to be remembered, but also by factors that are not or only indirectly linked to frequency. For instance, vividness of accounts, salience, or recency of previous encounters all influence the accessibility of information and experienced ease independently of frequency. Moreover, certain characteristics of our memory can cause certain information to be remembered better, even though there is no difference in the frequency with which the information is experienced. For example, we know that information is remembered better if the context of remembering resembles the context of learning.

With this in mind, let's return to the two introductory experiments. Both experiments illustrate nicely that the inversion of "when p then q" may prove problematic. Famous people are featured in the media and are often powerful, and their names are therefore likely to be encoded and recalled with greater ease than non-famous names. Similarly, words starting with a certain consonant can be recalled more easily than words having the same consonant in the third position. Just like a book in a library or a word in a dictionary, the concepts stored in human memory are also catalogued according to the first letter. And just as names that start with a certain letter are easier to find in a phone book than names where the same letter appears as the third letter, concepts can be more easily retrieved from memory with the help of the beginning letters of the words that describe them. Hence, in both experiments, experienced ease was influenced by factors other than frequency.

The two introductory examples show that drawing on experienced ease to evaluate frequency (q then p) may prove fallible. Does this mean that the availability heuristic is generally problematic? Fortunately, there is good reason to assume that the availability heuristic leads to correct conclusions more often than not (e.g., Greifeneder, Bless, & Scholl, 2013; Herzog & Hertwig, 2013). As discussed further later on, the experiments by Tversky and Kahneman (1973) were finely tuned to show biased judgment formation. Because of this fine-tuning, they are not representative of all the situations in which experienced ease may be used to judge frequency. For instance, in the English language, only some consonants (such as the five used by Tversky and Kahneman: K, L, N, R, and V) have more words with the consonant in the third compared to first position (e.g., Sedlmeier, Hertwig, & Gigerenzer, 1998). For the majority of consonants, there are more words that have the consonant in the first compared to third position. Hence, in the majority of cases, the availability heuristic will lead to a correct solution (irrespective of whether experienced ease is influenced by frequency or the architectural properties of our mind).

Experienced ease or content?

Tversky and Kahneman (1973) assigned a key role to experienced ease. However, alternative explanations for the observed evidence are also viable. Let's return to the letter R experiment for an illustration. On the one hand, individuals can use the feeling of experienced *ease* as a heuristic cue, as suggested by Tversky and Kahneman (1973). On the other hand, it could be that participants recalled *more* words with the letter R in the first compared to third position, and that subsequent judgments were made on the basis of this biased sample of *content*. To assess the two explanations, Schwarz, Bless, Strack, and colleagues (1991) conducted the following experiment: participants were given the task of writing down 6 or 12 examples of their own assertive behavior. Retrieving and listing 6 behaviors was pre-tested to be easy, whereas retrieving and listing 12 behaviors was pre-tested to be difficult. Afterwards, participants were asked to rate their own assertiveness. In this situation, the experienced ease explanation and the content explanation make different predictions with respect to participants' judgments. Because retrieving 6 assertive behaviors is easier than retrieving 12 behaviors, individuals may conclude that they are more assertive when retrieving 6 compared to 12 assertive behaviors. After all, if retrieving examples is so easy, there must be many—and conversely, if it feels difficult, there are likely only a few (see Illustration 6.1, left). Different implications are derived from the content explanation: participants should report being more confident after writing down 12 rather than 6 assertive behaviors. After all, 12 is more than 6 (see Illustration 6.1, right).

The results observed by Schwarz, Bless, Strack, and colleagues (1991) are in line with the experienced ease explanation: individuals who recalled many examples of their own assertive behavior (difficult) judged themselves as less assertive than individuals who were asked to report only a few examples (easy). Even though the first group remembered more assertive behaviors, the difficulty they experienced in remembering these examples led them to the conclusion that they could not be all that assertive (for reviews, Greifeneder, Bless, & Pham, 2011; Schwarz, 2008; Wänke, 2013).

Schwarz, Bless, Strack, and colleagues (1991) argue that the feeling of ease or difficulty is used as a piece of information in judgment. To further corroborate this argument, they manipulated whether individuals perceived the experienced ease as informative with respect to the amount of information stored in their memory. Once again, participants listed either 6 or 12 assertive or non-assertive behaviors. In addition, while writing down the behaviors, participants listened to meditation music. Half of the participants were told that the music rendered the retrieval task easier, while the other half were told the music rendered the task more difficult. As a consequence, in some conditions participants could attribute the experienced ease to the music (when the task felt easy and the music ostensibly made the task easy), thus undermining the informational value of the experienced ease. In other conditions, participants could attribute the ease of retrieval to the retrieval itself (when the task felt easy and the music ostensibly made the task difficult). When the informational value was not questioned by the information about the music, individuals judged themselves as more assertive after retrieving 6 rather than 12 self-confident behaviors, presumably

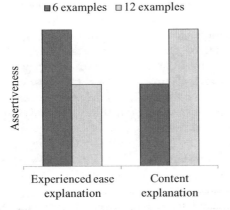

Illustration 6.1 Illustration of the predictions following the experienced ease explanation (left) versus the content explanation (right) in an experiment conducted by Schwarz and colleagues (1991). Results of the original study support the experienced ease explanation. The values reported here are arbitrary to demonstrate the different predictions

because they relied on the experienced ease or difficulty. However, when participants could attribute the experienced ease to the music, thus reducing the informational value of the experienced ease, they based their judgments on the content of the retrieved information and judged themselves as less assertive after retrieving 6 rather than 12 self-confident behaviors (see also Ruder & Bless, 2003).

A third test of the availability heuristic consists in manipulating the feeling of ease directly while keeping the effort associated with the cognitive activity constant. To do so, Stepper and Strack (1993) instructed participants to remember six examples of assertive behavior. Half of the participants were told to furrow their brows, a movement that goes along with feelings of tension and effort. By contrast, the other half of the participants were asked to smile. The result: participants who furrowed their brows and thus experienced a feeling of effort judged themselves to be less assertive than did participants who smiled. This study, along with a number of other experiments, provided impressive confirmation that individuals indeed use perceived ease of retrieval as the basis for judgments (for meta-analytic evidence, see Weingarten & Hutchinson, 2016).

Taken together, when individuals use the availability heuristic in judgment, they presumably use the experienced ease of cognitive processing as a cue for judgment formation: when it feels easy, objects or events are judged to be frequent or probable; when it feels difficult, frequency and probability are judged to be low.

Using the availability heuristic to explain other judgmental phenomena

The availability heuristic has been connected with a range of well-known judgmental phenomena. Here we briefly review three.

ASSESSING RISK

Lichtenstein, Slovic, Fischhoff, Layman, and Combs (1978) reported systematic misperceptions of certain causes of death. While at that time stroke caused 85% more deaths than accidents, only 20% of those surveyed thought that stroke was the greater risk. More generally, the authors observed that the risk of dramatic and sensational events (murder, flood, automobile accident) was overestimated, while the rather inconspicuous causes of death (stroke, heart disease, cancer, diabetes) were underestimated. Presumably, this is because conspicuous events receive a lot of media attention, while silent causes of death do not. Whenever a child dies of measles in Europe (very few cases), there is nation-wide media coverage; in contrast, heart attacks are reported perhaps only as a summary statistic at the end of the year. Importantly, media coverage influences availability irrespective of actual frequency, so that instances of measles may come to mind particularly easily. To the extent that individuals draw on experienced ease when judging the risk of certain events, the availability heuristic helps to understand the evidence reported by Lichtenstein and colleagues (1978).

Tragically, biased risk assessments may result in maladaptive risk behavior. For instance, in the wake of 9/11, it was easy to imagine a plane being hijacked even within the US. As a result, the risk of flying may have been overestimated, and people may have resorted to other ways of transportation, such as their cars. Yet, because road traffic is associated with higher casualties, this would have reflected maladaptive risk behavior (Gigerenzer, 2004).

Illustration 6.2 In April 2010, an explosion occurred on the oil platform Deepwater Horizon, which caused an unprecedented environmental disaster. Before this event, many individuals may have underestimated the probability of such an event. How can the underestimation of probabilities be explained in terms of the availability heuristic?

Source: US Coast Guard 100421-G-XXXXL Deepwater Horizon fire (public domain), https://commons.wiki media.org/w/index.php?curid=10089914

If the risk of events that can be imagined easily is overestimated, the risk of unknown events may be underestimated. As a result, it is conceivable that the risk of catastrophic events such as the explosion of the Deepwater Horizon drilling platform in the Gulf of Mexico in 2010, or the nuclear disaster at Fukushima in March 2011, was underestimated before the event, and overestimated afterwards.

Again, one may ask whether it is indeed the experience of ease or difficulty (accessibility explanation), or the content that comes to mind (availability explanation) that influences risk assessments. The evidence supports the accessibility explanation. For instance, participants asked to list three instead of eight factors that increased their own risk of contracting heart disease estimated their risk to be higher (Rothman & Schwarz, 1998). Relatedly, participants in a study by Grayson and Schwarz (1999) considered the risk of becoming a victim of a sexual crime to be higher when they were asked to list four instead of eight behaviors that increased their risk.

IF ONLY . . . ASSESSING ALTERNATIVE COURSE OF EVENTS

The availability heuristic may also help to understand mechanisms underlying counterfactual thinking. To illustrate, consider the following example: "If I had gotten up two minutes earlier this morning, I would not have missed the train." In this case, the event can be easily undone (only two minutes!), and the person may regard alternative courses as likely. Now imagine that the person is not late by two but by 30 minutes. In this case, mentally undoing the event (missing the train) may be more difficult, and alternative courses perceived as less likely. Hence, the ease with which we can undo an event in our mind may strongly influence judgments. For a detailed account on counterfactual thinking, see Roese (1997).

EGOCENTRIC BIAS

Have you experienced situations in which you felt that your contribution to a group or team was bigger than that of others? Ross and Sicoly (1979) asked spouses separately to list whether the responsibility for 20 activities in daily life (e.g., cleaning the dishes) was primarily theirs or their partners. Interestingly, when the responses were combined, it turned out that for many couples they added up to more than 100% of the activities. This biased perception occurred because each partner overestimated her or his contribution. Because this happened for pleasant and unpleasant activities, it is unlikely that participants just wanted to appear in a positive light. Rather, it is likely that participants' own contributions came to mind more easily than those of their partners. If these experiences of ease or difficulty are then used in judgment, one's own contributions are overestimated simply as a function of the availability heuristic (for further evidence, see e.g., Kruger & Savitsky, 2009). Because one's perceived share of work strongly impacts fairness considerations, the egocentric bias may have negative influences on work satisfaction or cohesion within teams in the workplace (for a review, see Cohen-Charash & Spector, 2001).

Representativeness heuristic

The representative heuristic may be used to answer a specific probability question, namely whether a certain element is part of a larger category. This is a common question in daily life, since we often wish to know how others can be categorized (e.g., Is she an only child? Is he a good tennis player? Are they dangerous?). While finding an answer to questions such as these may prove difficult (how do you know whether someone is dangerous without putting yourself at risk?), the representativeness heuristic provides a frugal solution. Here is how:

Imagine you are having lunch with a fellow student and want to make a bet about the field in which a student at a neighboring table at the cafeteria is majoring. He is wearing a suit and is reading the business section of the paper. How could you determine the most likely major? Short of reliable information, your knowledge of certain characteristics of various groups of people may constitute a basis for judgment. In particular, you may have an idea about the typical student in education, physics, or art history, and could thus assign the student at the next table to the group to which he is most *similar*, that is, *representative* of—in this case perhaps business majors. If you reached your judgment in this way you would have made use of the representativeness heuristic (Kahneman & Tversky, 1972). The term representativeness reflects how similar or typical an element (e.g., the student in question) is for a specific category (e.g., business student), a sample (e.g., a thousand people), a basic entity (e.g., citizens), an effect (e.g., sore throat), or a cause (e.g., viral infection). In more general terms, judging by representativeness means asking how well a concrete case represents an abstract model. The representativeness heuristic uses similarity and typicality as the basis for categorization and probability judgments: the more typical the concrete case is for the model, the greater the assessed probability that the case belongs to this model, and the greater the likelihood that the case will be assigned to this category.

The underlying logic

What is the logic behind the representativeness heuristic? Formulated as a rule, it can be described as follows: "If a person is similar to a certain group, the person is likely a member of this social category," or "If an event is similar to a category, it likely pertains to the category."

Does this rule make sense? Very often, the answer is "yes," because members of a category are often similar to the category prototype. For instance, students of various majors may in fact show different attire, and the stereotype of the business major may contain knowledge about specific clothing characteristics. If our knowledge of the models is sufficiently accurate, judgments on the basis of the representativeness of exemplars may lead to correct judgments. However, the use of representativeness can lead to erroneous judgments if other factors that determine the probability of occurrences are neglected or fundamental principles of probability are ignored. This is because the representative heuristic inverts the observed contingency by drawing conclusions from perceived similarity (e.g., has the look of a business major) to category membership (e.g., is a business major). To the extent that factors other than similarity contribute to category membership, the representativeness heuristic may lead us astray. The following examples will illustrate this.

Ignoring base rates

Judging by representativeness, you may have categorized the student at the neighboring table as a business major. But how meaningful would such a classification be if your university had only a tiny business department, with the proportion of business students in the entire student body below 1%? In this case the probability that the student is, in fact, a business major would be very low, even if he looks like the prototype. Findings suggest that individuals often neglect base rates and tend to judge others by representativeness (e.g., Griffin & Buehler, 1999; Kahneman & Tversky, 1973; Koehler, 1996). To illustrate the pervasiveness of this effect, consider the following example.

Peter is a good friend of the authors of the present book. He is 45 years old, likes poems, reads about old buildings, and spends most of his vacations in Italy. Is Peter more likely to be an art historian or a psychologist? If you opted for art historian, you may have fallen prey to the representativeness heuristic by neglecting the high base-line probability that friends often share the same professional background (and the three authors of this book are all social psychologists).

The Peter example is modeled after a classic experiment carried out by Kahneman and Tversky (1973, p. 241). Participants were presented with brief personality descriptions such as the following one:

> Jack is a 45-year-old man. He is married and has four children. He is generally conservative, careful, and ambitious. He shows no interest in political and social issues and spends most of his free time on his many hobbies, which include home carpentry, sailing, and mathematical puzzles.

In addition, Jack was said to be either an engineer or a lawyer. Importantly, the authors varied the base rates of members of both groups by telling participants that the descriptions were the result of psychological interviews conducted with 70 lawyers and 30 engineers (or 30 lawyers and 70 engineers). Participants were asked the following question: "The probability that Jack is one of the 30 (70) engineers in the sample of 100 is ___%?"

Interestingly, the different base rates (30% or 70% engineers) had minimal effect on probability judgments. Rather, participants relied on the specific description of Jack, thus reflecting judgments by representativeness. This was the case when the description *sounded* like that of an engineer ("many hobbies, which include home carpentry, sailing, and mathematical puzzles"), but also for totally uninformative sketches. Participants' judgments reflected the base rate information quite accurately only if no individuating information was provided, suggesting that representativeness is a fairly powerful source of information in assigning category membership.

The conjunction fallacy: disregarding the principle of extensionality

If a judgment is made on the basis of representativeness, the conjunction of events may appear more likely than each event alone, which violates one fundamental assumption of the theory of probability, that of extensionality. The principle of extensionality maintains that if a result A includes the result B, the probability for B cannot be higher than for A. For instance, the probability that someone is studying biology (B) cannot be greater than the probability that the person is studying the natural sciences (A). Similarly, the probability that a person is a bank teller and an active feminist (B) cannot be greater than the probability that a person is a bank teller (A). In each instance, A is a more general description that contains the specific case B. Although this may seem self-evident, many studies show violations of the principle of extensionality. For example, Tversky and Kahneman (1983, p. 297) gave participants the following description:

> Linda is 31 years old, single, outspoken and very bright. She majored in philosophy. As a student, she was deeply concerned with issues of discrimination and social justice, and also participated in anti-nuclear demonstrations.

Having read the description, participants were asked to arrange eight statements about Linda according to their probability, whereby the following two statements were critical:

A   Linda is a bank teller.

B   Linda is a bank teller and active in the feminist movement.

Given the principle of extensionality, the more specific conjunction B cannot be more likely than A, since A includes the case "bank teller and active in the feminist movement" as well as the case "bank teller and *not* active in the feminist movement." But it is easy to see that the conjunction B shows a greater representativeness for Linda than A. That Linda is active in the feminist movement fits her description, whereas it is hard to imagine her working in a bank. Participants who categorize Linda by way of representativeness should therefore be more likely to select B than A. The results obtained by Tversky and Kahneman (1983) indicate the use of the representativeness heuristic: between 85% and 90% of participants considered conjunction B more likely than statement A. This phenomenon, described as conjunction fallacy or conjunction effect, has been shown in a number of studies (e.g., Bar-Hillel & Neter, 1993; Betsch & Fiedler, 1999; Epstein, Donovan, & Denes-Raj, 1999; Fiedler, 1988; Gavanski & Roskos-Ewoldsen, 1991; Mellers, Hertwig, & Kahneman, 2001). Interestingly, even participants who received training in probability reasoning appear to disregard base rates and show judgments in accordance with the representativeness heuristic. Specifically, irrespective of whether participants were undergraduate students without training in statistics, first-year graduate students with training in statistics, or doctoral students in the area of decision science with advanced training in statistics and probability theory, conjunction B was perceived as more likely than the single event A (see Illustration 6.3; Tversky & Kahneman, 1983).

A part is representative of the whole: misperception of coincidence

Here is a third example where representativeness may result in erroneous category judgments. Let us assume that there is a family with six children. You are asked to judge the probability of the following sequence of births of boys (B) and girls (G):

BGBGBG   GGGBBB   BGGBBG

Which of these sequences do you consider most likely? If you chose the third sequence, your intuition is in line with that of many people. However, all three sequences have

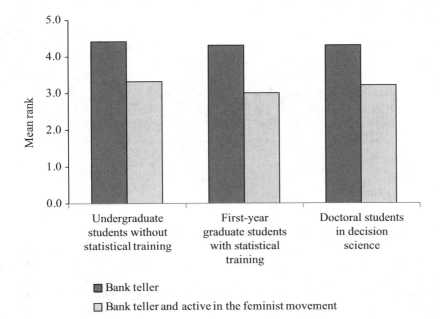

Illustration 6.3 Mean rank assigned to the events A (bank teller) or B (bank teller and active in feminist movement); the lower the rank, the higher the perceived probability (Tversky & Kahneman, 1983)

the same probability (at least if one assumes that as many boys as girls are born and that the gender of one child does not allow any predictions about the gender of the next child). To illustrate, consider the birth of the first child: both B and G have the probability of 50%. Now consider the birth of the second child: again, both B and G have the probability of 50%. Stochastically speaking, the sequences BB, GG, BG, or GB are thus equally likely. Still, mixed sequences such as BG or GB are more in line with what individuals perceive as *representative* of chance than uniform sequences like BB or GG.

To further illustrate this issue, let as assume a lottery where you can pick only one of two series of winning numbers. One week the following series are put out, with the same jackpot for both:

15, 3, 8, 47, 23, 14   1, 2, 3, 4, 5, 6

Which series would you bet on? Once again, both series have the same probability. Still, people tend to think that the probability for the first series is greater. Kahneman and Tversky (1972) maintain that this erroneous judgment indicates the use of the representativeness heuristic. While both sequences are equally likely, they are differently representative for what individuals perceive as random. This is because the intuitive perception of a random sample excludes regularities; indeed, regularities (be it the birth of six boys or the drawing of six sequential numbers) are perceived as highly untypical for random processes. Ironically, individuals even expect more alternations and scattering in sequences than would be normatively expected for a random process (e.g., Falk & Konold, 1997; Scholl & Greifeneder, 2011). As a result, sequences that *appear* representative for random samples are considered to be more probable. For reasons of illustration, try the following:

> Assume that an unbiased coin is tossed three times, and each time heads is up. If you had to bet 100 Euro on the next toss, what side would you choose?

Independent of the previous outcomes, the probability of both sides is equal (.50). Hence, 50% of individuals should prefer heads, and 50% tails. Yet, the majority of individuals prefer to bet on tails because a sequence of four heads appears to be less representative of a random process than a sequence of three heads and one tail.

Anchoring and adjustment

Let us now turn to the third heuristic. To make a judgment in a given situation, it often happens that one selects an initial, rough starting point for the judgment. A student in the first semester who wants to estimate how long it will take to finish her studies can use the normal duration as a starting point, ask herself whether she will require more or fewer semesters, and then adjust her final response. A tourist who wants to gauge the height of a building can draw on the height of other buildings and then increase or reduce his estimate as seems appropriate. A person who wishes to sell her car may first ask her partner whether the asking price is reasonable. If it is too low, she can raise the price in her mind until it seems acceptable. What all these examples have in common is that individuals gauge numerical size by starting from an initial value (an anchor), which they then adjust during the subsequent course of processing to arrive at their final judgment. Importantly, to the extent that adjustment of the judgment is insufficient, it may lead to judgments that are distorted in the direction of the starting value. Tversky and Kahneman (1974) called this phenomenon of assimilating a judgment to a starting value *anchoring and adjustment.*

In one study, Tversky and Kahneman (1974) asked participants to estimate the proportion of African states that are members of the United Nations. In order to establish different anchors for the judgment, this judgment task was preceded by a procedure in which a wheel of fortune with numbers from 1 to 100 was turned. Participants were first asked to indicate whether the outcome of this wheel of fortune (e.g., 10) was larger or smaller than the actual proportion of African member states. Only after this anchor was established did participants provide their estimates of the actual percentage of African member states. The result: if the number 10 was randomly given, the percentage of African states was estimated to be 25%. But if, for example, the number 65 was randomly given, the estimated percentage of member states rose to 45%. Apparently, the randomly selected number served as an anchor from which participants adjusted their response. But because this adjustment was insufficient, the final judgment was assimilated to the wheel's initial outcome.

In many cases, research investigating the anchoring effect is carried out using the above described procedure: first, the anchor information is offered in the form of a comparative question ("Is the true value of the object of judgment larger or smaller than X?"); second, participants are asked to provide an absolute judgment ("What is the true value?"). But anchoring effects are not limited to this sequence. Instead, the anchor can originate from other sources, for example from the partial completion of a task (e.g., when a person deduces the final result from an interim result in a math problem) or from the description of a task ("Enter your answer here, for example, 150 meters"). Moreover, anchoring effects are not limited to laypersons (e.g., Northcraft & Neale, 1987; Whyte & Sebenius, 1997). For instance, in one study, Traud (2000) observed that the provision of anchors may influence economic judgments such as the future exchange rate of the Euro. Participants in this study were advanced students in economics and responded to one of two questions: "Six months from now, will the Euro be higher than 1.30 US Dollars?" (high anchor); or "Six months from now, will the Euro be lower than 0.70 US Dollars?" (low anchor). Subsequently, participants estimated the Euro/US Dollar exchange rate (absolute judgment). Supporting the idea that even experts are influenced by the anchoring heuristic, participants with the high anchor estimated a higher exchange rate (1.16) than participants with the low anchor (0.94).

Intriguingly, research suggests that even incentives to render especially accurate judgments or explicit instructions not to let oneself be influenced by the anchor do not reliably reduce the anchoring effect (e.g., Wilson, Houston, Etling, & Brekke, 1996). All these findings converge in the conclusion that the anchoring effect is remarkably robust.

The underlying logic

Since the original publication by Tversky and Kahneman (1974), researchers have developed a number of theories to explain the anchoring effect (e.g., Chapman & Johnson, 2002; Epley & Gilovich, 2006; Jacowitz & Kahneman, 1995; Wilson et al., 1996). Here we focus on one approach, the selective accessibility model

(SAM; Mussweiler & Strack, 1999a, 1999b; Strack & Mussweiler, 1997). To explain anchoring effects, the SAM invokes two fundamental cognitive processes: selective hypothesis testing and semantic priming.

Selective hypothesis testing occurs during the processing of the anchor information: individuals test the possibility that the anchoring value in fact corresponds to the actual location of the judgmental object on the judgmental scale. That is, individuals test whether a selective hypothesis is correct; researchers therefore also speak of positive testing strategies. For example, confronted with the question of whether the average price of a car in Germany is more or less than 20,000 Euro, individuals will test whether the price is in fact 20,000. In so doing they will try to find information corroborating this possibility. Importantly, independent of whether their answer is affirmative ("Yes, the average price is 20,000 Euro") or not ("No, the average price is lower"), knowledge that supports the correctness of the anchor—so called anchor-consistent knowledge—is retrieved from memory and remains cognitively accessible. Mussweiler and Strack (2000) tested this notion with the following experiment. Participants first decided whether the average price of a German car is more or less than 20,000 Euro (high anchor) or 10,000 Euro (low anchor). Subsequently, they were presented with a series of words and asked to decide as quickly as possible whether each was meaningful or not. In these kinds of lexical decision tasks, individuals are faster at recognizing words that fall into a category previously made accessible (see Chapter 4). The meaningful words included some that were associated with affordable cars ("Rabbit," "Volkswagen") or with expensive cars ("Mercedes," "BMW"). Participants were faster at recognizing expensive cars if they had worked on the high anchor. By contrast, affordable cars were recognized more quickly as meaningful words if participants had been given a low anchor. For an illustration of this experiment, see: www.youtube. com/watch?v=HefjkqKCVpo.

How does selectively heightened accessibility lead to anchoring? According to the SAM, the mediating process is one of *semantic priming*. In order to answer the question proper ("What is the average price?"), individuals draw on the knowledge that is accessible at the time of judgment—and this is anchor-consistent knowledge, as illustrated above. Note that the SAM does not invoke processes of insufficient adjustment. Rather, it is knowledge made accessible through selective hypothesis testing that ultimately produces anchoring effects.

If semantic priming is at the root of anchoring effects, the general principles of priming discussed in Chapter 3 should apply to anchoring effects, such as *applicability*. The applicability principle holds that accessible knowledge needs to be applicable to the judgment target in order to have an impact (for an overview, see Higgins, 1996). Strack and Mussweiler (1997) tested this idea by asking participants first about the *height* of the Brandenburg Gate in Berlin (comparative judgment: "Higher or lower than 150 meters?"), but then focused on the *width* of the Brandenburg Gate in the absolute question. Although testing the first question likely increased the accessibility of hypothesis-consistent knowledge (i.e., indicating a certain height, such as "Double-decker buses can drive through it."), this knowledge is not applicable to judgments of width, and therefore did not result in anchor-consistent assimilation effects. More generally, if the comparative question focuses on one topic, and the absolute question on a different topic, the knowledge made accessible through selective hypothesis testing should have limited applicability for the absolute judgment, thus limiting anchoring effects.

The SAM also suggests that anchoring effects should be diminished when hypothesis-*inconsistent* knowledge is made available in the first step. To test this notion, Mussweiler, Strack, and Pfeiffer (2000) provided participants with different price estimates for a used car (2,800 or 5,000 Euro). Importantly, half of the participants were asked to indicate what argued against this price. For these participants, no significant anchor effects were observed, presumably because considering the opposite did not result in anchor-consistent knowledge.

Anchoring effects in negotiations and at court

The previous examples illustrate that anchoring effects are not limited to questions of knowledge (e.g., Strack & Mussweiler, 1997; Wilson et al., 1996) or probability judgments (e.g., Block & Harper, 1991), but can also occur in situations involving sales. In the context of negotiations, researchers demonstrated that the size of the initial offer had a strong influence on the final outcome (e.g., Neale & Northcraft, 1991; Ritov, 1996). Whyte and Sebenius (1997) observed that even among business students and experienced managers, the initial price offer, the minimum price, and the desired price were strongly influenced by the anchor value. One implication of these results is that it may be beneficial to be the first mover in a negotiation (e.g., Galinsky & Mussweiler, 2001).

In view of the possible consequences, anchoring effects are especially relevant in the formation of legal judgments. Studies on simulated verdicts by jurors (Chapman & Bornstein, 1996) and judges (Englich & Mussweiler, 2001) revealed that the assessment

Illustration 6.4 Twenty-eight or 35 months in jail? The anchoring heuristic may influence legal judgments and decisions

Source: Photo 12/Alamy

of guilt and the severity of punishment could be influenced by anchors. Englich, Mussweiler, and Strack (2006) supplied experienced judges with the usual information for judging a case of rape and asked them to determine the punishment they would impose (absolute judgment). Previously, however, the judges had been asked whether the penalty of either 12 or 36 months in jail allegedly proposed by a journalist was too high or too low (comparative judgment). Notably, judges who had been asked to evaluate the high anchor imposed a sentence of 33.4 months on average, while judges with the lower anchor imposed 25.4 months on average.

Just as being the first mover in negotiations may prove advantageous due to the mechanisms of anchoring, so is having the first word in court. Because in many legal systems the prosecution presents its closing statement first, one could argue that there is a systematic hidden disadvantage for the defense (Englich, Mussweiler, & Strack, 2005).

Using the anchoring paradigm to explain other judgmental phenomena

The anchoring effect has also been invoked to explain other judgmental phenomena, for example the fundamental attribution error (e.g., Leyens, Yzerbyt, & Corneille, 1996; Quattrone, 1982)—that is, the overestimation of the influence of personal factors on the behavior of others and the simultaneous underestimation of the influence of situational factors (Jones & Harris, 1967). Individuals, the thinking goes, usually begin by explaining the behavior of others with reference to their attitudes or personality, and then adjust this evaluation (insufficiently) by taking additional causes into consideration (Gilbert & Malone, 1995).

Another judgmental phenomenon that has been explained through the anchoring effect is the hindsight bias (Fischhoff, 1975; Hawkins & Hastie, 1990). Specifically, having access to the correct solution to a problem, individuals in retrospect overestimate the likelihood that they correctly solved the problem or would have been able to do so. These findings suggest that the correct solution works as an anchor and influences the memory of the answer previously given (e.g., Pohl, 1992).

Alternative explanations and further developments

This discussion of the research program on judgmental heuristics would be incomplete if we failed to point out that researchers have proposed and experimentally tested alternative explanations for some of the judgmental phenomena described above. Two of these are task understanding and presentation format.

Task understanding

Judgments and decisions depend not only on the information provided, but also on how this information is understood or encoded by participants (see Chapter 3; e.g., Bless, Strack, & Schwarz, 1993; D. J. Hilton, 1995; Schwarz, 1996; Strack, 1994). To illustrate, let us revisit the neglect of base rates when deciding whether Jack is a lawyer or engineer (see the section on representativeness). Participants were provided with descriptions of five different persons (such as the one for Jack), while the base rates always remained the same. This could have led participants to believe that the person information was more important and more relevant than the base rates for the judgment they had been asked to make. Schwarz, Strack, Hilton, and Naderer (1991) examined this possibility by varying the base rates and keeping the person descriptions constant in one condition, and keeping the base rates constant and varying the person descriptions in another condition. Result: the influence of the person information was strongly reduced if it was kept constant (for a summary of related evidence, see Koehler, 1996).

Likewise, one alternative explanation of the conjunction effect rests on task understanding. Tversky and Kahneman (1983) considered the possibility that participants may not have understood the global statement "Linda is a bank teller" (A) in a comprehensive sense—that is, one that includes all other cases. Rather, compared to option B ("Linda is a bank teller and active in the feminist movement."), they may have understood option A ("Linda is a bank teller") to mean "Linda is a bank teller and *not* active in the feminist movement." Dulany and Hilton (1991) observed that only 55% of participants interpreted the sentence "Linda is a bank teller" in the comprehensive sense. Among these individuals, the rate of conjunction error was strongly reduced. These results suggest that differences in task understanding may have contributed to the conjunction fallacy (for an informed discussion of conversational influences on reasoning, see D. J. Hilton, 1995).

Presentation format

A second critique of the heuristics and biases approach is aimed at the fact that many problems are expressed in the form of probabilities (see e.g., Cosmides & Tooby, 1996; Gigerenzer, 1991; Gigerenzer & Hoffrage, 1995). Presumably, our cognitive system is adjusted to the processing of frequencies but much less to the processing of probabilities. Whereas humans have dealt with frequency information throughout their history, the concept of probability is rather abstract and its linguistic representation is relatively recent. If this is the case, the fallacies documented in the heuristics and biases program may reflect primarily inadequacies in dealing with probability information. In support of this argument, a number of studies have shown that judgment errors such as the neglect of base rates (e.g., Cosmides & Tooby, 1996) or the conjunction fallacy (e.g., Fiedler, 1988) disappear when information is presented in the form of relative frequencies, or if judgments are solicited in the frequency format. For example, Fiedler (1988) asked one group of participants to rank individual statements about Linda ("Linda is a bank teller" etc.) according to their *probability*. A second group was asked to indicate to *how many* of 100 women each statement of the Linda problem applied. When asked for probability judgments, 73% of participants violated the conjunction rule; in contrast, when asked for frequency judgments, the number dropped to 23%.

In closing this section, it should be noted that the use of the frequency format appears to be less reliable in causing a reduction of judgmental errors than was initially assumed (see Griffin & Buehler, 1999). Moreover, the finding that judgmental errors occur less frequently in the frequency format does not explain their occurrence in the probability format.

Content-specific rules of thumb

The previous section focused on heuristics that are very general in nature and can be applied independent of a particular content. At the heart of each of these heuristics is a certain cognitive type of processing or inference (e.g., relying on experienced ease; semantic priming).

Apart from these general heuristics, individuals also have content-specific rules of thumb at their disposal. Remember the food quality example provided at the beginning of this chapter? Instead of repeatedly sampling all restaurants, individuals might rely on quality ratings in a restaurant guide to determine which place to go to. Here, individuals take a judgmental shortcut by drawing inferences from a heuristic cue. Content-specific rules of thumb imply the use of prior general knowledge, which may result from contingency learning in the environment, or may be acquired from others.

Content-specific rules of thumb have received particular attention in the domains of person perception and attitude change. For example, when evaluating another person, individuals can base their judgments on available individuating information about a specific target person (e.g., Peter has three children and cares a lot about his grandmother). Or they may simplify their processing by basing their judgment on a simple cue, the person's category membership (e.g., Peter is a skinhead).

Similar considerations can be applied when individuals are confronted with a persuasive message and are forming an attitude judgment. On the one hand, they may carefully consider the content of the message, paying close attention to the implications of the presented arguments. Or, they may simplify this task and rely on heuristic cues, such as the communicator's expertise, likableness, attractiveness, or the sheer length of a message.

In both domains, various models have been proposed to conceptualize the different processes of arriving at a judgment. Addressing attitude change, for instance, the elaboration likelihood model (e.g., Petty & Cacioppo, 1981, 1986) and the heuristic systematic model (e.g., Chaiken, 1987; Chen & Chaiken, 1999) distinguish between two conditions of processing. When motivation or capacity are low, the change of attitude depends primarily on content-specific rules of thumb, such as the perceived expertise of a communicator (e.g., Petty, Goldman, & Cacioppo, 1981). In contrast, when motivation and capacity are high, the strength and number of presented arguments affect attitude change. Content-specific rules of thumb include, for instance, "Experts can be trusted" or "More is better than less." They are applicable especially to the context of the communication, since they refer chiefly to characteristics of a communicator or a message (for an extended discussion, see Vogel & Wänke, 2016).

Similar models have been developed in the domain of person perception. Again, these models distinguish between two different processing pathways, one relying on easy-to-process social category cues, and the other on intensive processing of individuating information (e.g., Brewer, 1988; S. T. Fiske & Neuberg, 1990). The key assumption is that judgments based on category membership information are more likely if processing capacity and/or motivation is low, whereas judgments based on individuating information are more likely if both motivation and capacity are sufficiently high (see also Bodenhausen et al., 1999; Hamilton & Sherman, 1996; Kruglanski, 1989).

The duality inherent to the above models may imply an either/or type of processing, such that individuals process *either* the stereotypical cue *or* the individuating information. Many models, however, use this duality to describe extreme ends, while postulating that processing moves along a continuum of either heuristic or systematic processing (e.g., Chen & Chaiken, 1999; S. T. Fiske & Neuberg, 1990). It is the specific situation, along with personality factors, that determines the location on this continuum.

Interestingly, extensive or controlled processing as described in Chapter 5 is akin to what the above models refer to as systematic processing. From this perspective, the above models connect the present and the previous chapter by suggesting two roads to attitude change or person perception. The judging individual may be characterized as a manager or motivated tactician (S. T. Fiske & Taylor, 2017), who pursues various goals with temporally and cognitively limited resources and who must and is able to coordinate these resources. In this picture, both extensive processing and the recruitment of rules of thumb are tools the manager has at his or her disposal to accomplish judgment formation. Which tasks does this resource management entail? First, it is necessary to make sure that more resources are allocated to important judgments than to unimportant judgments. Second, under conditions of strongly constrained resources, more parsimonious judgmental strategies must be employed than under conditions of less constrained resources. Third, a judgmental strategy must be changed when it apparently does not lead to the desired goal, for example when the information to which the judgmental strategy can be applied is not representative or because the strategy proves unsuccessful during its application.

Heuristics: blessing or curse?

In the introductory example on restaurant choice, we briefly discussed that relying on heuristic cues may lead us astray. Most examples provided throughout this chapter appear to support this perspective. As such, heuristics may be a curse. Yet, this perspective itself is biased, since the situations modeled in psychological experiments might not constitute a representative sample of all possible situations. To illustrate, recall Tversky and Kahneman's (1973) letter R experiment, in which reliance on the availability heuristic seemingly resulted in erroneous judgments. Importantly, however, Tversky and Kahneman carefully selected the letter R (and other consonants), for which the availability heuristic will produce an erroneous frequency judgment. For the majority of consonants, the availability heuristic leads to the same conclusion as extensive processing of all words in the lexicon would. The letter R experiment is thus not informative with respect to the totality of situations in which the availability heuristic may be applied.

Before you feel deceived by Tversky and Kahneman, note that there is good reason, from a scientific perspective, to rely on situations that produce error. Let us illustrate. For the majority of consonants in the English alphabet, the availability heuristic leads to the same outcome as extensive processing of all words. Evidence collected with this majority of consonants is thus not very instructive with regard to the underlying process. This is different for the few consonants (e.g., R) where the availability heuristic and extensive processing result in different outcomes. For these consonants, different outcomes result from different underlying processes, so that researchers may draw inferences from the outcome to the underlying process. Ironically, it is by looking at errors that new knowledge can be gained. Errors are thus a source of insight into psychological processes, and the injunction "to learn from mistakes" applies to scientists and researchers, too. For Wilhelm von Helmholtz (1903, p. 96), the pioneer in the psychology of perception, it was "precisely those instances in which external impressions create in us perceptions that do not correspond to reality that are especially revealing when it comes to discovering the processes and means by which normal perception occurs." Importantly, the primary purpose of the study of judgmental errors is therefore not to demonstrate the faulty nature of human thinking, but to gain insight into the mechanisms of normal thought.

Heuristics *may* thus be a curse. But heuristics might also a blessing, because they help to save resources and spare individuals processing effort (such as sampling all possible restaurants). Gigerenzer and colleagues (Gigerenzer, Koehler, & Harvey, 2004; Gigerenzer, Todd, & ABC-Research-Group, 1999) have emphasized the adaptive nature of heuristics, highlighting that heuristics are an important part of our cognitive toolbox, and that simple heuristics may make us smart. And while heuristics may lead astray, this is similarly true for extensive processing (as became apparent in Chapter 5), so neither pathway is inherently better or more accurate. For this and other reasons, the scientific inquiry into heuristics and further conceptual development is ongoing (e.g., Gigerenzer & Gaissmaier, 2011).

Chapter summary

1   The process of generating a judgment can be simplified by using rules of thumb, which are referred to as heuristics. Heuristics allow for fast and frugal decision making.

2   Three heuristics introduced by Tversky and Kahneman were reviewed in more detail. The *availability* heuristic posits that the ease with which information can be brought to mind may be used to form judgments of frequency and probability. The *representativeness* heuristic uses perceived similarity to judge category membership. Finally, the *anchoring and adjustment* heuristic describes how judgments are oriented toward initial pieces of information.

3   Some of the procedures relied on in the study of heuristics have been criticized, and variables that moderate the typical results (such as presentation format) have been identified. Nevertheless, research suggests that the three heuristics are very robust.

4   The three heuristics help us to understand everyday judgment and decision making, and the systematic errors that may arise during this process. Furthermore, other well-known phenomena in social psychological research may be explained in terms of these heuristics.

5   The heuristics introduced by Tversky and Kahneman are very general in nature and build on specific types of cognitive processing or inference (e.g., relying on experienced ease; semantic priming). Apart from these general heuristics, individuals also have content-specific rules of thumb at their disposal.

6   Content-specific rules of thumb are learned through contingencies or are acquired from other individuals.

7   Content-specific rules of thumb have received particular attention in the realm of attitudes and person perception. Models in these areas generally postulate two pathways: one effortful and one effortless. It is on the effortless pathway that heuristic cues have a particular impact when it comes to judgment and decision making.

8   In many scientific experiments, reliance on heuristics results in seemingly faulty judgments. The abundance of biases and mistakes in the literature, however, does not necessarily allow for conclusions about the ecological validity of reliance on heuristics in everyday life. Researchers often choose scientific situations and

material very carefully precisely to show bias, because it is from error that new knowledge can be gained. But this choice of situations is not representative of all the situations in which heuristics can be applied.

9 Rather than being a constant source of error, researchers have argued that heuristics are a blessing, since they require few cognitive resources and still make us smart.

Discussion questions/topics

1 Try to identify situations or judgments in your daily life in which the availability heuristic, the representativeness heuristic, or anchoring and adjustment may be at work.

2 Explain the letter R experiment in your own words.

3 Why did we mention the misperception of random sequences as one instantiation of the representativeness heuristic?

4 Some individuals may believe that Vladimir Putin is not a member of the World Wildlife Fund. How can their belief be explained with one of the heuristics mentioned in this chapter?

5 How does the SAM explain the occurrence of anchoring effects?

6 Some people believe that a powder made from a rhino's horn will be effective as an aphrodisiac. How does this belief reflect the representativeness heuristic?

7 You have found a particularly nice piece of furniture at a garage sale. Would you ask for the price, or make a first offer yourself? Why?

8 Following the elaboration likelihood model or the heuristic systematic model, in which situations will individuals rely on content-specific rules of thumb?

9 Discuss the benefits and costs of relying on heuristics in judgment.

10 After reading the literature on heuristics, some individuals may believe that heuristics are a curse. How could you put this belief in perspective?

Recommendations for further reading

Gigerenzer, G., & Gaissmaier, W. (2011). Heuristic decision making. In S. T. Fiske, D. L. Schacter, & S. E. Taylor (Eds.), *Annual review of psychology* (Vol. 62, pp. 451–482). Palo Alto: Annual Reviews.

Mata, R., Schooler, L., & Rieskamp, J. (2007). The aging decision maker: Cognitive aging and the adaptive selection of decision strategies. *Psychology and Aging, 22*, 796–810.

Tversky, A., & Kahneman, D. (1974). Judgment under uncertainty: Heuristics and biases. *Science, 185*, 1124–1131.

7 The interplay of cognition and feelings
Mood states

Rainer Greifeneder & Herbert Bless

Introduction: feelings in social cognition

In the previous chapters, we discussed a wide spectrum of aspects that are involved in individuals' constructions of social reality. We learned about encoding, retrieval, and judgmental processes, and how they relate to each other. At this point, one might wonder: With all the emphasis on cognitive aspects, is there a place for feelings? After all, the strong focus on information processing within social cognition research and the computer processing metaphor seem to portray the human being as a cold and emotionless information-processing machine. Yet, most individuals know from experience that social reality can look quite different when feelings come into play. For example, when in a negative compared to positive mood state, we may pay more attention to, and be more critical about, what other guests at a party are talking about.

That our social judgments and behaviors are influenced by how we feel in a particular situation is not a new idea. Scientific interest has manifested itself in a long tradition of philosophical (Descartes, 1961/1649) and psychological theorizing (e.g., Freud, 1940–1968; W. James, 1890). Many of these traditional positions hold that feelings impair the ability of individuals to think rationally about the social world (for overviews, see Forgas, 2000b; Solomon, 2008). Challenging such positions, research that started in the 1980s has uncovered that feelings do not necessarily create irrationalities, but often constitute a useful source for the regulation of cognitive and behavioral processes and for the interpretation of a social situation. Since then, research has accumulated a large body of empirical and theoretical contributions, providing enormous evidence that feelings are an integral part of social cognition (for reviews see e.g., Blanchette & Richards, 2010; Bless, 2001; Forgas, 2000a; Greifeneder, Bless, et al., 2011; Martin & Clore, 2001; Unkelbach & Greifeneder, 2013a; Schwarz, 2012; Ziegler, 2014).

This and the next chapter will each focus on one particular type of feeling and its role in social cognition. The present chapter focuses on *affective* feelings, that is, experienced positivity or negativity. Chapter 8 will focus on *cognitive* feelings, that is, experiences that accompany cognitive processing. Though the notion of cognitive feelings may appear surprising at first glance, most individuals are quite familiar with their phenomenology.

Over the two chapters, it will become evident that affective and cognitive feelings share many commonalities (e.g., Bless & Forgas, 2000; Clore, 1992; Greifeneder et al., 2011; Koriat & Levy-Sadot, 1999; Schwarz, 2012; Strack, 1992). It may therefore not come as a surprise that many of the processes discussed in the present chapter will be revisited in Chapter 8.

Mood states and their impact on social cognitive processing

Affective feelings comprise all sorts of valenced experiences, the most prominent of which are emotions and mood states. Whereas emotions have a clear referent (i.e., emotions are always *about* something, such as being angry about a behavior or another person), mood states are usually free of a referent (i.e., we may be in a positive or negative mood, without knowing why). Emotions are often intense, salient, and of limited duration; mood states are more subtle, less salient, and last longer (e.g., Ortony, Clore, & Collins, 1988; W. N. Morris, 1989; Isen, 1987; Schwarz & Clore, 2007).

In what follows, we will place emphasis on *mood states* and their role in social cognition for two reasons. First, though emotions and moods differ in critical aspects as outlined above, they also share many commonalities—reviewing both would result in many redundancies. Second, because mood states are often subtle, they act more in the background of other activities (W. N. Morris, 1989). For example, we may be in a sad mood but still continue all our daily activities. This "background character" constitutes a particularly intriguing facet and may explain why mood states play a critical role in a wide spectrum of social cognitive processes. Of these, we will cover the impact of mood states on individuals' memory, their social judgments, and momentary styles of information processing. Note that we limit this chapter to one direction of the affect–cognition relationship. In particular, we focus on how affective states influence cognitive processes, for example how being in a specific mood influences the extent of stereotyping (Bodenhausen, Kramer, & Süsser, 1994). For reasons of scope, we will not discuss the reversed direction, that is, how different cognitive processes elicit different affective states (see Clore et al., 1994; Manstead, 2010; Niedenthal, Krauth-Gruber, & Ric, 2006).

Illustration 7.1 Think about your kindergarten time. What are the first three memories that come to your mind? Are these mainly positive or mainly negative?

Source: Folio Images/Alamy

Mood and memory

In Chapter 3 we discussed how the accessibility of concepts influences encoding processes, and in Chapter 5 it became clear that the accessibility of information has a pronounced impact on social judgments. One key role that mood states play in social cognitive processing is influencing the accessibility of information that is stored in memory. Put differently, mood states influence what comes to mind (for overviews, see Bower & Forgas, 2001; Forgas, 1995b). For example, Bower (1981) asked individuals about events from their kindergarten time, and observed that more positive events were recalled when individuals were in a happy mood at the time of retrieval. In contrast, when in a sad mood at retrieval, individuals retrieved more negative events (see Illustration 7.2). Results such as these demonstrate that the accessibility of information is *mood-dependent*.

The notion of mood-dependency was first conceptualized in Gordon Bower's (1981) associative network model of human memory. This model builds on prior associative network models (e.g., J. R. Anderson & Bower, 1973), which describe memory as a network of nodes, each representing a particular concept. The nodes are linked to other nodes, and links may be of different strengths. Once a particular concept is activated, activation spreads to associated nodes along the links (see Chapter 4). Compared to earlier associative network models, Bower (1981) assigned a key role to affective states and suggested that they constitute hubs interlinking concepts of correspondent valence. Moreover, these hubs are linked to autonomic activity as well as to muscular and expressive patterns that usually accompany the respective affective state (for an overview of different network models, see Niedenthal, 2008).

Associative network models generally hold that when new material is learned, it is associated and linked with the nodes that are active at the time of learning (encoding).

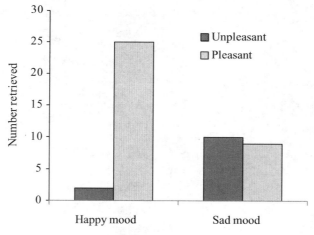

Illustration 7.2 Mood influences information retrieval: number of retrieved incidents as a function of mood at retrieval (happy vs. sad) and valence of incident (unpleasant vs. pleasant)

Source: Bower (1981)

Bower (1981) emphasizes that affective states are among the nodes active at the time of learning, which means that the newly learned material is linked to affective nodes. For example, imagine you meet a person at a party and also happen to be in a good mood at the time. On the level of associative networks (see Illustration 7.3), the (to be formed) node for the new acquaintance and the positive affect node are simultaneously active and therefore become interlinked. If the positive mood node becomes activated again later, activation will spread from the positive mood node to other concepts interlinked with it, including the node for the new acquaintance. As a consequence, being in a happy mood will increase the chance that the new acquaintance is remembered.

Two central hypotheses were derived from Bower's model. First, the *state-dependency hypothesis* holds that recall is improved when individuals are in the same affective state at encoding and retrieval. To illustrate, participants recalled more positive and less negative experiences from their time in kindergarten when they were in a happy rather than in a sad mood (see Illustration 7.2). Note that the state-dependency hypothesis is not restricted to valenced information, that is, positive or negative information. When studying affectively neutral words (e.g., "paper," "window"), these neutral words were also more likely to be recalled when the affective state at encoding matched the affective state at retrieval.

Second, the *mood-congruent recall hypothesis* holds that material is more likely to be recalled if its affective tone matches the individuals' affective state at the time of retrieval. For example, individuals in a positive mood are more likely to recall words with a positive connotation, such as friendly, nice, or beautiful. In contrast, individuals in a negative mood are more likely to recall words with a negative connotation, such as unkind, aggressive, or ugly (Bower, 1981). Note that the mood-congruent recall hypothesis focuses on the match of the affective state at retrieval and the valence of the retrieved information, whereas the state-dependency hypothesis focuses on a match of affective states at encoding and retrieval.

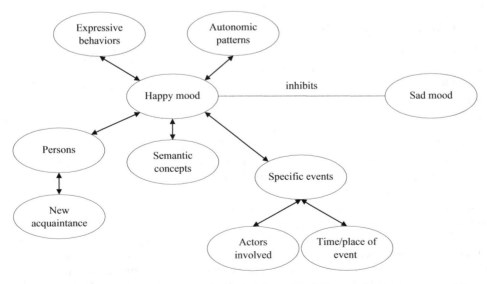

Illustration 7.3 Associative network model (after Bower, 1981). Mood states are part of the network and become interlinked with others nodes, such as a new acquaintance

Initially, both the state-dependency hypothesis and the mood-congruent recall hypothesis received considerable support (see Bower, 1981). However, subsequent research revealed that effects of state dependency and mood-congruent recall are less reliable than initially assumed (see Clore et al., 1994; Eich & Macaulay, 2000). First, state dependency is less likely if the stimulus material is highly structured. In particular, existing strong associations within the material can be so powerful that the impact of mood on accessibility is no longer detectable. To illustrate, imagine two lists of words. One list comprises the word "cat" and is learned in a happy mood state, whereas the other list is learned in a sad mood state and comprises the word "dog." According to the state-dependency hypothesis, "cat" should be more likely recalled in a happy, and "dog" in a sad mood. However, because there is a pre-existing strong association between "cat" and "dog," the two words are likely to be recalled together, although they were learned in different affective states.

Second, mood-congruent recall is asymmetric. In support of the mood-congruent recall hypothesis, findings show that happy moods facilitate the recall of happy memories and inhibit the recall of sad memories. Arguing against the mood-congruent recall hypothesis, however, findings show that sad moods may inhibit the recall of happy memories but often do not increase the recall of sad memories. This asymmetry is already reflected in the results of the "kindergarten" study (see Illustration 7.2). It is evident that happy individuals recalled more positive than negative events, but sad individuals recalled about an equal number of positive and negative events. What is the reason for this asymmetry? One account holds that individuals in negative affective states may be motivated to repair their mood by attempting "to stop the process of thinking about negative material that might be cued by sadness" (Isen, 1987, p. 217). Supporting this assumption, research by Isen (1987) suggests that sad individuals' controlled processes (i.e., their attempts to think of positive rather than negative information) may override the automatic impact of sad moods on the accessibility of sad material.

Mood and evaluative judgments

Try the following exercise: Imagine you are asked to form an evaluative judgment, such as whether you like your university's new merchandising. Would you evaluate that merchandising more or less positively when you are incidentally in a positive or a negative mood state? Just as common sense suggests, individuals form more positive judgments when they are in a positive mood and more negative judgments when they are in a negative mood. This tendency is referred to as *mood-congruent judgments* and has been reported independent of whether the judgmental target pertains to other persons, consumer products, the quality of life, or performance appraisals, to name but a few (see e.g., Cohen, Pham, & Andrade, 2008; Clore et al., 1994; Forgas, 1992, 1995a; Schwarz & Clore, 1996).

How can we explain mood-congruent judgments? One explanation builds on Bower's (1981) associative network model discussed above. It is argued that individuals form judgments on the basis of the information they recall. Due to mood-congruent recall, happy individuals selectively recall positive information and, in turn, their judgments will be more favorable than judgments formed by sad individuals (see Bower, 1991; Forgas, 1992, 1995a). This logic seems straightforward, and mood-congruent judgments have therefore often been treated as evidence for mood-congruent recall.

For instance, Forgas and Bower (1987) presented participants with short descriptions of stimulus characters and induced participants to feel either happy or sad. In accordance with a memory-based explanation for mood congruency, happy participants evaluated the stimulus characters positively more often than did sad participants.

A second explanation for mood-congruent judgments was offered by Schwarz and Clore (1983, 1988). Schwarz and Clore questioned the assumption that mood-congruent judgments are mediated by a mood-congruent *recall*. Rather, they suggested that affective states may themselves serve as relevant information in making a judgment. More specifically, individuals are thought to ask themselves "How do I feel about it?" when evaluating an object, and then use this feeling as information. Think back to your university's new merchandising, mentioned above: not having seen this product before, you could ask yourself: "How do I feel about it?" A positive feeling may tell you that you like the product, whereas a negative feeling may tell you that you dislike it. Notably, though positive mood leads to more positive judgments, in this case, mood congruency does not result from mood-congruent *recall* (i.e., positive mood activates positive material in memory, see above), but from using feelings as pieces of information ("Hey, if I feel positive about it, I probably like it"). Schwarz and Clore's (2003) account is often referred to as mood-as-information, or—more generally—as feelings-as-information (Schwarz & Clore, 2007).

By asking "How do I feel about it?" individuals treat their current affective state as a *reaction* to the judgmental target. In the above example, current positive or negative feelings are treated as a reaction to or result of the merchandising product. In many cases this is an adequate strategy. After all, a positive stimulus is more likely to elicit a positive mood than a negative stimulus. Hence, if we feel positive in the presence of a merchandising product, it is often quite reasonable to conclude that we like the product. However, although currently experienced feelings may arise in reaction to the judgmental target, they may have other reasons, as well. For instance, when evaluating the merchandising product, you may be in a happy or sad mood for a totally unrelated reason, such as finding or losing money five minutes ago. This creates the interesting situation that mood states unrelated to the current judgmental task may nevertheless be used as information.

On the level of psychological processes, what happens here is an *attribution* of current feelings to what is currently in the focus of attention—"Why else would I be feeling that way at this moment?" This attribution mechanism is variously known as the immediacy principle (Clore et al., 2001) or the aboutness principle (Higgins, 1996), and constitutes a particularly parsimonious default. When mood states are *integral* to the judgmental target (e.g., Bodenhausen, 1993)—that is, caused by the target itself (you feel positive because you like the merchandising product)—this default is correct. However, when mood states are *incidental* to the target—that is, caused by a source other than the judgmental target (you found money five minutes ago)—this mechanism may lead individuals astray. Fortunately, attribution is also governed by processes other than temporal contiguity, so that mistaken attribution is likely the exception rather than the rule. This conclusion may appear surprising, given that misattribution of incidental mood states is often documented in mood research. However, settings chosen for research are not randomly sampled from all possible situations, but constitute a very special set. This set is specifically designed to allow researchers to investigate the influence of mood. Researchers may employ, for example, rapid switches between the mood induction (e.g., Task 1 in a study) and the presentation of the judgmental target (e.g., Task 2 in a study). Such rapid shifts may elicit misattributions of mood to the judgmental target, due to the operation of the immediacy or aboutness principle. Of course, such rapid shifts between a mood-eliciting situation and a subsequent social judgment occur in real-life settings, too, but likely with a much lower frequency than in research. Hence, despite the fact that attribution processes may lead us astray, feelings very often provide a useful and valuable source of information (see Schwarz, 2002, on the wisdom of feelings).

Both the mood-as-information approach and the mood-congruent recall hypothesis can account for the observation of mood-congruent judgments. Perhaps most central in the debate over the two approaches, the mood-as-information hypothesis holds that individuals will stop using their affective state as a basis of judgment if the feeling's informational value has been called into question. For instance, should you realize that your current mood is due to finding or losing money five minutes ago, it is unlikely that you will rely on this feeling when evaluating the merchandising product. After all, if what you feel is due to finding money, this feeling has no informational implication for the merchandising product, and hence should not be used in its evaluation.

To illustrate this conceptual difference between the affect-as-information account and mood-congruent recall, let us turn to a classic finding. In a study reported by Schwarz and Clore (1983, Experiment 2), participants were interviewed by telephone either on a sunny or a rainy day. During the interview, participants were asked for their current mood and to assess their life satisfaction. Not surprisingly, participants were happier on a sunny than on a rainy day. Moreover, they reported being more satisfied with their life in general on a sunny rather than on a rainy day (see left part of Illustration 7.5). This mood-congruent judgment is consistent with the affect-as-information account, because participants might have asked themselves "How do I feel

Illustration 7.4 Imagine being called on a rainy day and asked by an interviewer about your current life satisfaction. What would you say?

Source: Gemphoto/Shutterstock.com

about it?" and then concluded from their positive (negative) mood that they are generally satisfied (or not). Note that this finding is also consistent with mood-congruent recall, because individuals in a good mood might have remembered more positive memory content, and individuals in a bad mood more negative content (Bower, 1981). In order to differentiate between the two accounts, Schwarz and Clore (1983) pointed out to some participants that the current weather might be influencing their mood. As can be seen in the right part of Illustration 7.5, these participants no longer showed mood-congruent judgments. Findings such as these are difficult to reconcile with the implications of mood-congruent recall, because telling participants about the source of their current feelings should not decrease the activation of mood-congruent material in an associative network structure (if anything, the surplus attention should increase the feelings' activation potential). In contrast, this finding integrates very well with the notion of affect-as-information, because drawing attention to the weather unmasks weather-induced current positive or negative mood states as incidental to the judgment of life satisfaction, and hence as irrelevant or uninformative.

In addition to differentiating between the affect-as-information and the mood-congruent recall account, the above experiment by Schwarz and Clore (1983) illustrates the operation of the immediacy or aboutness principle: because a weather-induced mood is experienced when life satisfaction is evaluated, it is perceived as informative, despite being incidental and not integral to the judgmental target. However, this default is not destiny, as the effect vanishes when mood is unmasked as incidental. One way to look at this is that the immediacy/aboutness principle works as an automatic default, but is backed up by a safety net (for a related argument in the realm of cognitive feelings, see Greifeneder et al., 2013).

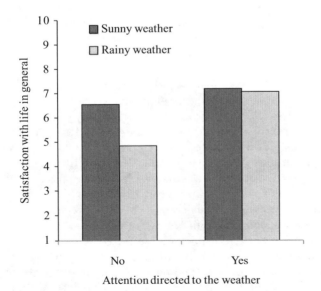

Illustration 7.5 Mood and satisfaction with life. Reported satisfaction with life in general as a function of the weather and participants' attention

Source: Schwarz and Clore (1983, Experiment 2)

That participants in the weather experiment ceased to rely on feelings when the feeling's cause was made salient illustrates one of five variables known to *moderate* reliance on feelings as information: perceived *representativeness*. Representativeness here means that a feeling is perceived to emanate from the target.

Reliance on affect as information is further moderated by the feeling's *salience*, in that reliance on affect as information is more likely when feelings are salient. After all, to be used as information, a feeling has to be identified. On first glance, the two moderators representativeness and salience appear in conflict, because salience plays a role in both. However, the salience of the feeling needs to be differentiated from the salience of the feeling's *cause*—and only the latter triggers representativeness (e.g., Siemer & Reisenzein, 1998). To illustrate, consider again Schwarz and Clore's (1983) weather experiment. Schwarz and Clore increased the *feeling's* salience by first asking participants how they feel and then how satisfied they are. Different from the feeling's salience, the salience of the feeling's *cause* was manipulated by directing participants' attention to the weather.

The third moderator is called *relevance* and holds that feelings need to be perceived as relevant in order to be informative. Whereas representativeness is about the link between the feeling and the target, relevance is about the link between the feeling and the judgment (Greifeneder, Bless, et al., 2011). Pham (1998) induced participants into a positive or negative mood. To manipulate relevance, participants were given either an instrumental motive to see a movie (e.g., to qualify for another study) or a consummatory motive (e.g., to have a good time). Participants' movie-going intentions were influenced by current mood when they had consummatory but not when they had instrumental motives. Presumably, this is because feelings were perceived as relevant only when participants had consummatory motives in mind (see also Yeung & Wyer, 2004).

The fourth moderator pertains to the *evaluative malleability* of judgments and holds that the impact of feelings is stronger when judgments are open to extraneous influences. For example, Gorn, Pham, and Sin (2001) observed that mood states influence the evaluation of an affectively ambiguous ad, but not the evaluation of an ad with a clearly pleasant affective tone.

Finally, reliance on affect-as-information is moderated by *processing motivation and processing capacity*: generally speaking, mood-congruent judgments are more likely when individuals are not strongly motivated (Isbell & Wyer, 1999) or currently lack cognitive resources to process information intensively (e.g., Siemer & Reisenzein, 1998). The five moderators are summarized in Illustration 7.6 (Greifeneder, Bless, et al., 2011).

So far, we have focused on findings that illustrate mood-congruent judgments. But the affect-as-information account can also accommodate mood-*incongruent* judgments, such as negative judgments despite being in a positive mood. This is because the affect-as-information account emphasizes that it is not the affective state per se, but individuals' interpretation of this state that influences further processes. To illustrate, imagine being informed that a particular movie is supposed to make you feel sad. If you then feel happy, the movie is probably bad; but if you feel really sad, the movie did a great job. In this situation, a positive feeling means something negative (bad movie), and a negative feeling something positive (great movie; Martin, Abend, Sedikides, & Green, 1997). More generally, findings such as these suggest that individuals are very flexible in the use of their affective state as a source of information,

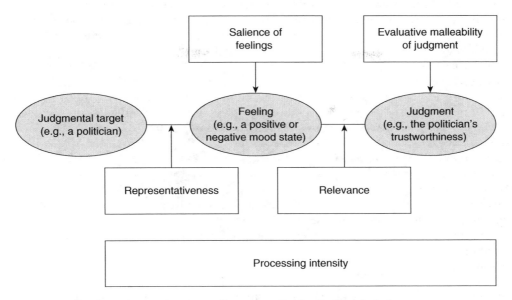

Illustration 7.6 Variables moderating reliance on affective feelings in judgment

Source: Greifeneder, Bless, and Pham (2011)

and that feelings need interpretation in the respective context (for an overview, see Martin, 2001). The implications of experiencing a happy (or sad) mood thus depend on the context.

To summarize, at least two accounts offer explanations for mood-congruent judgments. Mood-congruent recall emphasizes that affective feelings influence what information comes to mind (Forgas, 1995a). In contrast, the affect-as-information account emphasizes that feelings may be used as information when forming judgments. Forgas (1995a) has integrated both perspectives in his affect-infusion model, suggesting that affect-as-information processes are more likely in conditions of low processing intensity, and mood-congruent recall effects in conditions of high processing intensity. In support of this suggestion, he observed that the more individuals think about a judgment (i.e., the more information they retrieve from memory), the more individuals' judgments will reflect their affective state (for further discussion, see Bless, 2001; Forgas, 2001).

Mood and processing style

Above we discussed how affective states may influence individuals' memory and evaluative judgments. In both cases, the primary focus has been on the congruency between the individuals' affective state, on the one hand, and the material retrieved from memory or the evaluative judgment, on the other hand. There is, however, a perhaps more intriguing aspect which suggests that the impact of affective states may extend far beyond this congruency aspect. Affective states may not only influence *what* information is processed, but also *how* information is processed. Indeed, a broad spectrum of research findings has consistently demonstrated that even rather subtle changes in affective states may influence performance on a wide variety of cognitive tasks.

In the previous chapters, we discussed various aspects related to different styles of information processing. One central aspect pertains to the degree to which individuals' processing is guided by their prior knowledge structures (see Theme 2, Chapter 2). In the case of top-down processing, individuals' processing is very strongly based on prior knowledge structures, for example, in the form of stereotypes, scripts, and heuristics. In the case of bottom-up processing, prior knowledge has less impact and individuals' processes are more affected by the data at hand. Interestingly, a series of studies suggests that affective states moderate individuals' reliance on prior knowledge structures. Specifically, happy individuals seem more likely to rely on stereotypes and heuristic processing strategies than sad individuals (for overviews, see Bless, 2001; Isen, 2008; Martin & Clore, 2001; Schwarz, 2012). In the remainder of this section, we discuss major findings on how mood influences cognitive processes in person perception, attitude change, the use of other heuristics, and the level of abstraction. Subsequently, we discuss potential explanations for these findings.

Mood and person perception

As we have seen in previous chapters, individuals may form judgments about other persons via different processing strategies (cf. S. T. Fiske & Neuberg, 1990; Macrae & Quadflieg, 2010). On the one hand, individuals may rely extensively on their prior knowledge, for example, in the form of the stereotype about the social group to which the target person is assigned. To illustrate, if a person is assigned to the social group of librarians, individuals' prior knowledge may imply that the person is more likely to be introverted than extraverted. On the other hand, individuals may form a judgment by attending more to the individuating information of the specific target—in that case, existing stereotypes are less likely to influence judgments. A number of studies have explored whether and how individuals' affective state may impact the different strategies (Bless, Schwarz, & Wieland, 1996; Bodenhausen, Kramer, et al., 1994; Bodenhausen, Sheppard, & Kramer, 1994; Forgas, 2011; Krauth-Gruber & Ric, 2000; Trent & King, 2013). For example, Bodenhausen, Kramer, and Süsser (1994) presented happy or neutral mood participants with a description of an alleged assault on campus. Apparently, a student had beaten up a roommate. The evidence was mixed, however, and participants were asked to judge guilt. The identity of the student was manipulated so that he was either a member of a stereotypically aggressive group or not. In particular, the student had either a Hispanic name ("Juan Garcia") or an ethnically non-descript name ("John Garner"). Because the descriptions were identical except for the names, differences in the perceived guilt can be attributed to participants' reliance on their group stereotypes. As can be seen in Illustration 7.7, the offender's name influenced participants in a happy mood, who judged Juan Garcia as guiltier than John Garner, presumably because the former is a member of a group that is stereotypically associated with aggressiveness. In contrast, no impact of the name was observed for sad or neutral mood participants, presumably because they relied less on stereotypic information.

Conceptually related evidence has also been found in research addressing the perception of ingroups (perceiver and judgmental target belong to the same group) versus outgroups (perceiver and judgmental target belong to different groups).

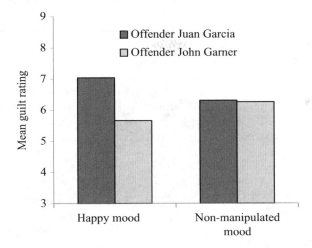

Illustration 7.7 Mood and person perception. Happy participants attributed more guilt
to the offender when his name apparently signaled membership in a
group stereotypically associated with aggression (Juan Garcia), compared
to a group for which no stereotype was applicable (John Garner). This
effect was not observed for individuals in non-manipulated moods

Source: Bodenhausen et al. (1993, Experiment 1)

For instance, Forgas and Fiedler (1996) reported that happy individuals were more
likely to discriminate against the outgroup, unless the situation implied a high relevance of the group membership information. Relatedly, Abele, Gendolla, and Petzold
(1998; see also Abele, 2000) observed that when participants evaluate a target, the
target's group membership (ingroup vs. outgroup) receives more weight when participants are in a happy rather than a neutral mood (see also Ziegler & Burger, 2011,
on the interplay of individuals' mood and the valence of the individuating information). Finally, inducing a positive mood during intergroup contact resulted in less
favorable evaluations of the outgroup when the groups were in immediate competition or had a history of prior conflict (Dovidio, Gaertner, & Loux, 2000).

The above-reviewed evidence suggests that stereotyping is more pronounced
in happy compared to sad mood states. This may appear counter-intuitive at first
glance, given that many theories, such as "scapegoating," hold that negative affective
states trigger stereotyping and outgroup discrimination (for an overview, see Bless,
Schwarz, & Kemmelmeier, 1996). One solution to this puzzle rests on whether individuals perceive their negative affect as a result of the target person (integral) or as
a result of the current situation in general (incidental). If negative affect is integral,
that is, caused by the evaluation target, scapegoating appears likely. However, if negative affect is incidental, it is likely that the processing of information about the target
is based less on stereotypic content. Depending on whether the stereotype is negative
or positive, less reliance on stereotypes may result in more positive or more negative
judgments.

The finding that positive mood is associated with reliance on general knowledge
structures, and negative mood with systematic processing, has important bearings also

for lie detection. Research in this realm often documents that individuals are not much better than chance at discerning lies from the truth (e.g., C. F. Bond, Jr. & DePaulo, 2006; Reinhard et al., 2013). One reason for this poor performance lies in our lay theories about non-verbal cues, which seem to be wrong more often than not. For instance, lay persons often associate gaze aversion with lying, yet empirical evidence suggests that liars do not avoid eye contact more than truth tellers (DePaulo et al., 2003). Interestingly, lie detection performance can be increased if individuals systematically integrate content information. If sad moods foster systematic content integration, negative mood states should therefore help to catch more liars, as documented by Reinhard and Schwarz (2012).

Mood and persuasion

Similar to judgments about other persons, attitude judgments following a persuasive communication may reflect two different processing strategies (Eagly & Chaiken, 1993; Petty & Cacioppo, 1986; for an overview see Vogel & Wänke, 2016).

On the one hand, individuals may elaborate on the presented arguments of a persuasive message. In this case, strong arguments should lead to a greater acceptance of the communication's intention than weak arguments. Alternatively, individuals may base their judgments on peripheral cues, for example, the communicator's attractiveness. In this case, argument quality should play a minor role. To illustrate, consider evidence reported by Bless, Mackie, and Schwarz (1992). These authors asked participants to provide a detailed description of either a positive or a negative life-event, which elicited a positive or a negative mood, respectively. Subsequently, participants listened to a tape-recorded message in which an increase in student fees was announced. Based on pre-testing, arguments in favor of this fee were selected to be either strong or weak. As can be seen in Illustration 7.8, participants in a sad mood were more persuaded by strong than by weak arguments. In contrast, participants in a happy mood state were not influenced by argument quality, suggesting that sad but not happy individuals took the provided arguments into account (for related evidence see e.g., Bless, Bohner, Schwarz, & Strack, 1990; Mackie & Worth, 1989). This evidence was complemented by the observation that attitudes of participants in happy moods—but not those in neutral moods—reflected the presence of peripheral cues (Mackie & Worth, 1989; see also Bohner, Crow, Erb, & Schwarz, 1992, for an extension of this notion from attitudinal judgments to behavior; for a conceptual overview, see Schwarz, Bless, & Bohner, 1991). Moreover, research suggests that the described general interplay of mood and argument quality may be moderated by the affective valence of the presented arguments (see Ziegler, 2014).

Findings such as these allow for two conclusions. First, when communicators have weak arguments, it may pay off to make recipients feel good. Is this perhaps one reason why advertisers often try to make us laugh? Second, and perhaps more surprisingly, when communicators have strong arguments, inducing a positive mood state may hurt the communicator's case, because strong arguments have less impact in conditions of positive mood.

If we equate the reliance on stereotypes with the reliance on peripheral cues, and the reliance on the presented arguments with the reliance on individuating information, the above-reviewed evidence converges with that obtained in the person perception domain. In both cases, individuals in a sad mood are more likely to attend

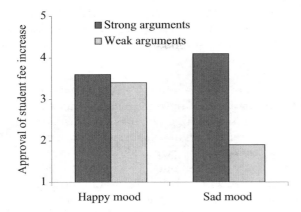

Illustration 7.8 Mood and persuasion. Sad recipients were more strongly influenced by a message comprising strong rather than weak arguments. In contrast, happy recipients were equally persuaded by strong and weak arguments

Source: Bless, Mackie, and Schwarz (1992, Experiment 1)

to the specific information provided in a situation. Given this similarity, one may also ask whether individuals in a happy mood are more likely to rely on heuristic cues in persuasion, just as they are more likely to rely on stereotypes in person judgments. Evidence supports this notion. For instance, Greifeneder, Bless, and Kuschmann (2007) investigated brand extensions, that is, the marketing of new products under an existing brand name. Brand extensions are a particularly popular marketing strategy, because marketers hope that positive associations with the brand will transfer to the new product (think of Calvin Klein selling perfumes). According to the findings on person perception, however, this hope is likely to be fulfilled in conditions of positive but not negative mood, because positive but not negative mood fosters reliance on stereotypes or heuristic cues, such as brand information. Supporting these conjectures, Greifeneder and colleagues (2007) observed that attitudes toward a new van marketed as an extension to a positive brand were more positive for happy compared to sad participants (see also Adaval, 2003).

Mood and other heuristics

The conclusion that happy individuals are more likely to rely on heuristic processing strategies is not restricted to the domains of person perception and persuasion. For example, Isen and colleagues report that happy moods increase the likelihood that individuals rely on the availability heuristic (Tversky & Kahneman, 1973) when making frequency judgments (Isen, Means, Patrick, & Nowicki, 1982; Ruder & Bless, 2003). In a related vein, happy moods increase reliance on general knowledge structures. For example, when encoding a sequence of events that characterize typical activities, happy individuals are more likely than sad individuals to rely on pre-existing scripts. When subsequently confronted with a recognition test, happy individuals more readily recognize information that is consistent with the script, resulting in more hits (i.e., correct identification of items that were presented), but also more intrusion errors (i.e., erroneous identification of items that are consistent with the script, but were not presented; Bless, Clore, et al., 1996). This recall pattern suggests that happy individuals are more likely than sad individuals to rely on their prior knowledge in the form of a pre-existing script when encoding new information.

Mood and level of abstraction

Interestingly, much of the evidence reported above converges with the idea that happy individuals are likely to categorize and represent information more abstractly than individuals in sad moods. Happy participants rely more on categorical information in the form of scripts, stereotypes, or brands, as well as on general heuristic cues. Moreover, research has documented that more inclusive, that is, more abstract categories are used when individuals are in a happy mood (e.g., Isen, Niedenthal, & Cantor, 1992; Hirt, Levine, McDonald, Melton, & Martin, 1997; Murray, Sujan, Hirt, & Sujan, 1990; see also Bolte, Goschke, & Kuhl, 2003; Rowe, Hirsh, & Anderson, 2007). In line with this relationship between mood and mental abstraction, a happy mood elicits a focus on global configurations rather than on specific details (Curby, Johnson, & Tyson, 2012; Fredrickson, 2001; Fredrickson & Branigan, 2005; Gasper, 2004; Gasper & Clore, 2002). Moreover, more abstract interpretations of social situations are provided by happy rather than sad individuals (Beukeboom & Semin, 2005, 2006; Labroo & Patrick, 2009; Pyone & Isen, 2011). In combination, one may conclude that different levels of construal (Trope & Liberman, 2010; see Chapter 3) constitute one core feature of the differential processing styles elicited by happy versus sad mood (for a direct test, see Burger & Bless, 2016), especially if one assumes that global processing constitutes the default (see Huntsinger, Clore, & Bar-Anan, 2010).

Explaining mood effects on processing style

The reported research on the impact of mood on processing style suggests that rather minor changes of individuals' affective states can have a pronounced impact on how social information is processed. How can we account for these findings? The explanations offered emphasize different aspects, such as processing capacity, processing motivation, mood management, or a general reliance on heuristics under happy moods. Each will be briefly reviewed in what follows.

First, it has been suggested that individuals in a happy compared to neutral mood may have fewer cognitive resources (Mackie & Worth, 1989). This line of reasoning holds that individuals usually have stored more positive than negative material in memory. As a consequence, more material is potentially activated in memory if individuals are in a happy rather than a sad mood (see considerations on mood-dependent memory outlined above). Due to this activation, happy individuals have fewer resources available for other tasks, and are more likely to rely on less taxing strategies, that is, on top-down or heuristic processing. In line with this reasoning, providing extra processing time, presumably reducing the processing load, eliminates the differences between happy and sad mood participants (Mackie & Worth, 1989).

Second, it has been argued that happy moods may reduce individuals' processing motivation. The reduced processing motivation in turn increases the likelihood that happy individuals rely on their prior knowledge structure in the form of stereotypes or heuristics. Different assumptions have been made about why being happy should reduce processing motivation. Focusing on *mood management*, it has been argued that individuals are motivated to maintain positive affective states and to eliminate negative affective states (Isen, 1987; Wegener & Petty, 1994). Assuming that strenuous cognitive processes interfere with the goal of maintaining positive mood states, researchers have argued that individuals in happy moods are less motivated to invest cognitive effort than sad individuals—and in turn rely on heuristic processing strategies (see also Ziegler, 2014, for an extension on how processing effort is influenced by the congruence between individuals' mood and the processed materials).

A third approach emphasizes the *informative function of affective states*. It is proposed that the affective state may inform the individual about the nature of the current situation (Schwarz, 1990, 2012). Individuals usually feel good in situations that are characterized by positive outcomes and/or in situations that do not threaten their current goals. In contrast, individuals usually feel bad in situations that threaten their current goals because of the presence of negative outcomes or the lack of positive outcomes. Reversing this logic, individuals may consult their affect as an often valid and quick indicator as to the nature of the current situation. Feeling good would imply that the situation poses no problem, while feeling bad would imply that the current situation is problematic. It is now assumed that individuals in a bad mood are more motivated to engage in detail-oriented systematic processing strategies, which is typically adaptive to handling problematic situations. In contrast, individuals in a good mood may see little reason to spontaneously engage in strenuous processing strategies, unless this is called for by other goals (Schwarz, 2012). As a consequence, happy individuals will rely more strongly on top-down or heuristic processing, whereas sad individuals will attend more to the specifics of the situation and bottom-up processing. Supporting this line of reasoning, it has been found that increasing participants' processing motivation—for example, by telling participants that they would later need to justify their judgments—eliminated the differences between happy and sad mood participants in person perception (Bodenhausen, Kramer, et al., 1994; Bless et al., 1990).

Fourth, it has been suggested that the observed processing differences between happy and sad individuals are not mediated by differences in either processing motivation or processing capacity. Again, it is argued that happy moods signal an unproblematic situation. In contrast to the previous account, an unproblematic situation is thought to *directly* imply that it is OK to rely on prior knowledge when constructing social reality (see also Burger & Bless, in press, for relating these considerations to level of construal). Thus, as before, happy individuals may rely on their prior knowledge, yet not because they lack cognitive resources or processing motivation, but because relying on prior knowledge structures appears appropriate in happy mood states (Bless, Clore, et al., 1996; for a similar perspective, see Fiedler, 2000b). In a study supporting this assumption (Bless, Clore, et al., 1996), participants listened to a tape-recorded story about a scripted activity. When later asked to recall the provided information, happy participants committed more intrusion errors than sad participants, that is, they recalled script-consistent information that was not actually presented. This suggests that happy participants relied more strongly on top-down processing than sad participants. Notably, participants in this study simultaneously worked on a second task, a concentration test, while they were listening to the scripted information. The results of this test showed that happy participants outperformed sad participants on this secondary task. The combination of the results of the recall test and the concentration test suggests that by relying on top-down processing, happy participants spared resources they could allocate to the secondary task. The finding of improved performance on the secondary task is difficult to reconcile with accounts suggesting that happy moods reduce processing capacity or motivation.

Taken together, at least four accounts offer explanations for why mood states may influence processing style. Researchers have provided evidence for each of the outlined theoretical positions. Future research will tell whether the four accounts work in unison, or whether their operation perhaps depends on other situational factors. Despite differences in the presumed mechanisms, it should be kept in mind that the four accounts make very similar predictions for a wide spectrum of phenomena. This underscores that the impact of mood states on the reliance on heuristic versus systematic processing strategies is a rather robust finding.

Interestingly, a recent theoretical account questions whether specific mood states (e.g., positive mood) and specific processing strategies (e.g., heuristic processing) are directly linked. This affect-as-cognitive-feedback account (e.g., Clore & Huntsinger, 2009; Huntsinger, 2012, 2013; Huntsinger, Isbell, & Clore, 2014) holds that mood states confer value on ongoing information processing strategies, with positive mood signaling that the currently ongoing processing (whatever it is) is fine, whereas negative mood states constitute a stop signal. Whenever currently ongoing processing is heuristic or top-down, the affect-as-cognitive-feedback account predicts results similar to those reviewed above. However, when currently ongoing processing is bottom-up, the affect-as-cognitive-feedback account yields opposite predictions: those in a positive mood go on with what they were doing and therefore process bottom-up, whereas those in a negative mood stop what they were doing and now process top-down. To illustrate, consider evidence reported by Huntsinger (2012), who first primed participants to process information either globally ("the forest") or locally ("the trees") and then induced them into either a happy or a sad mood state. Huntsinger assessed whether participants subsequently processed information either globally or locally. The results offer support for the affect-as-cognitive-feedback account: when participants were first primed to process information globally, positive mood led to a global focus and negative mood to a local focus; however, when participants were first primed to process information locally, positive mood led to a local focus, and negative mood to a global focus.

How can the affect-as-cognitive-feedback account be reconciled with the wealth of evidence suggesting a direct link between positive mood and reliance on general knowledge structures? One way is to take ecological frequencies of global and local processing into account. Specifically, if we assume that top-down is generally more frequent than bottom-up processing (for instance, because cognitive capacity is limited, see Theme 1, Chapter 2), the affect-as-cognitive-feedback account dovetails with the robust finding that positive affect is often associated with top-down processing, and negative affect with bottom-up processing.

Conclusion

Let us return to this chapter's starting question: With all the emphasis on cognitive aspects in social cognition research, is there a place for feelings? Although the reported evidence reflects only a small selection of research from the affect and cognition domain (see recommendations for further reading for broader coverage), it has become obvious that many of our social judgments and behaviors are profoundly influenced by affective feelings. Social cognition research therefore strongly emphasizes the important role of affective states and provides models of how affective states influence social thinking. Most importantly, much of the available current research suggests that affect does not necessarily create irrationalities, but that in most cases individuals' affective states provide a very useful source for the regulation of cognitive processes and for the interpretation of the social situation. Social cognition research is thus far from conceptualizing the human being as a cold and emotionless information-processing machine. Quite the contrary: affective feelings, whether as an antecedent to or as a consequence of cognitive processes, are at the very heart of social cognition.

Chapter summary

1   The impact of affective states on cognitive processes is a widely acknowledged phenomenon, and research has accumulated substantive evidence to that effect. In contrast to the notion that affective states impede individuals' cognitive abilities, this research suggests that affective states play an important adaptive role and support individuals in their construction of social reality. Affective states have been demonstrated to influence many aspects of cognition, among them memory, evaluative judgments, and the style of information processing.

2   Affective states may automatically influence the accessibility of information stored in memory. Information is more likely to be recalled when it is congruent with the current affective state (mood-congruent recall hypothesis), or when it was initially stored in a similar affective state (state-dependency hypothesis). This impact of affective states on memory is less likely with highly structured compared to unstructured material. Individuals may be motivated to repair their negative affective states. They may do so by retrieving positive rather than negative information from memory.

3   The finding that evaluative judgments are often congruent with individuals' current affective state is very robust and has been observed in a wide spectrum of domains. One explanation rests on the increased accessibility of mood-congruent material. Another explanation holds that individuals ask themselves "How do I feel about it?" and thus use their affective feelings as information.

4   Subtle differences in individuals' affective state have been demonstrated to influence the style of information processing. Happy compared to sad individuals have been shown to rely more on heuristics and general knowledge structures. Several explanations have been offered to explain such differences, each highlighting a different mediating mechanism. Recent evidence further suggests that the link between mood states and specific styles of processing may be more variable than previously assumed.

Discussion questions/topics

1   What is the difference between the state-dependency hypothesis and the mood-congruent recall hypothesis? Can you think of examples where it is difficult to distinguish the two theoretical mechanisms?

2   Discuss the two explanations for mood-congruent judgments. Think of everyday examples and consider the implications of mood-congruent judgments.

3   Consider the automatic activation of mood-congruent material in memory. What would happen if we were unable to counteract this automatic activation, in particular when we are in a sad, depressed mood?

4   What kind of impact does mood have on individuals' reliance on stereotypes? Discuss the findings obtained by Bodenhausen, Kramer, and Süsser (1994).

5   What explanations can account for individuals' reliance on heuristics and general knowledge structures as a function of their affective state? What evidence is reported in support of each position?

6   In supermarkets, many attempts are made to put shoppers in a better mood (e.g., music, small gifts). Discuss why this might be an effective strategy. Under which circumstances would this strategy be less effective?

Recommendations for further reading

Schwarz, N. (2012). Feelings-as-information theory. In P. A. Van Lange, A. W. Kruglanski, & E. Higgins (Eds.), *Handbook of theories of social psychology* (pp. 289–308). Thousand Oaks, CA: Sage. (The chapter provides on overview on a wide spectrum of research findings, thereby emphasizing the informative function of affective states.)

8 The interplay of cognition and feelings

Fluency

Rainer Greifeneder & Herbert Bless

Chapter 7 focused on the interplay of cognition and *affective feelings*. The present chapter focuses on the interplay of cognition and *cognitive feelings*. The term cognitive feelings may appear surprising at first glance, because in daily language the terms *feelings* and *affect* are often used synonymously. Yet affective experiences are but one category of the broader concept of feelings, which additionally encompasses bodily (e.g., Meier et al., 2012) and cognitive experiences (e.g., Schwarz & Clore, 2007). This terminology is justified not only from a scientific and conceptual perspective, but also against the background of individuals' language use: when asked, individuals can readily state that recalling some piece of information from memory *felt* easy, or that reading or understanding some content *felt* difficult. It is thus part of our daily language to refer to cognitive processes in terms of feelings.

Perhaps the best way to get in touch with cognitive feelings is by way of an example. Consider the tip-of-the-tongue phenomenon (e.g., Schwartz, 2002), which many individuals are familiar with. Something is said to be on the tip of one's tongue if one can *feel* that it is there, but is unable to retrieve it at that moment. Perhaps you have already had the experience, for instance, that the name of an acquaintance, politician, or town was literally on the tip of your tongue: you could *feel* that you knew the name but were unable to produce it. Here you had experiential access to the working of your mind—you could feel a cognitive state of knowledge. Interestingly, quite often this experiential access may be the only access individuals have to otherwise inaccessible processes or states of knowledge: for what else did you know beyond your *feeling of knowing*?

It is this privileged access to the working of our mind that may explain why cognitive feelings play a key role in social cognition, and it justifies devoting a whole chapter to them. We start with a definition and characterization of cognitive feelings, or more specifically: fluency. Subsequently, we provide a selective review of findings illustrating that judgments of all kinds are informed by fluency. Finally, we discuss findings suggesting that fluency may even tune or change subsequent processing. This chapter structure bears many similarities to the previous chapter's structure, which further underscores that both affective and cognitive experiences are part of the same larger category: feelings.

Fluency: a cognitive feeling

Fluency is the subjective experience of ease or difficulty associated with mental processing (e.g., Greifeneder & Unkelbach, 2013). Compare reading "lpnae" with reading "plane." To the extent that English is your native language (or one that

Illustration 8.1 Just as road traffic can be experienced as fluent or disfluent, so can cognitive processes

Source: Dave Porter/Alamy

you have learned very well), reading "lpnae" likely felt more difficult than reading "plane." Merely using a word or non-word thus produced differences in perceived ease or difficulty, which individuals can readily report when asked. Yet what exactly is this experience of ease or difficulty, and where does it come from? We offer answers by way of four characteristics.

Many sources, one unitary fluency experience

Experiences of fluency can arise from all kinds of different cognitive processes and states of knowledge, including perceiving, encoding, storing, retrieving, or using information (for a review, see Alter & Oppenheimer, 2009). For instance, content presented in high perceptual contrast (e.g., Reber & Schwarz, 1999), content that is repeated (e.g., Jacoby & Dallas, 1981), and content that is coherent (e.g., Topolinski & Strack, 2009) is experienced as fluent. In fact, it has been suggested that fluency arises as a continuous by-product of *every* mental process (Whittlesea & Leboe, 2003). Sometimes, the associated mental processes are apparent in specific labels such as *perceptual* fluency (which refers to the ease or difficulty of perceiving) or *retrieval* fluency (which refers to the ease or difficulty of retrieval). But irrespective of such specific labels and sources, fluency is always felt as an experience of ease or difficulty, which researchers therefore refer to as one unitary experience (Alter & Oppenheimer, 2009). This unitary experience can be located on a continuum from easy to difficult (in everyday language), or fluent to disfluent (in scientific terminology). To assess individuals' fluency experiences, researchers ask questions such as "How easy or difficult was it to . . . ?"

Always there, but not always aware

If fluency arises as a by-product of every mental operation, it follows that our cognitive system not only processes information, but also monitors its own processing (Whittlesea & Williams, 2000). Given this constant monitoring, why are individuals not constantly aware of fluency? The reason is that availability and awareness need not go together. By way of analogy, consider that the state of your stomach is constantly monitored too, but individuals are not constantly aware of being satiated. Likewise, cognitive processing can be constantly monitored, but may be perceived only in specific circumstances. These specific circumstances are, among other contributing factors, a function of prior experiences and expectations, against which ongoing processing may stand out and therefore be noticed (e.g., Hansen & Wänke, 2008; Whittlesea & Williams, 1998).

Fluency experiences are variable

Fluency experiences are a function of your own learning history and the current situational environment. They are therefore not a property of the stimulus itself, but vary with persons and situations. For instance, reading "plane" feels easier than reading "lpnae," but only for those proficient in the English language; if you are not proficient in the French language, reading "élov" (a non-word in French) may be just as difficult as reading "vélo" (bike). As a second example, read the following sentence: *"The latest eruption of Láscar volcano was on 18th April"* (statement taken from Scholl, Greifeneder, & Bless, 2014). Most likely reading it felt difficult because we used the font Mistral. Now read the same sentence again: "The latest eruption of Láscar volcano was on 18th April." Most likely reading it felt easier the second time because deciphering was easier the second time.

Fluency is an efficient piece of information

Fluency experiences summarize the state of ongoing processes in *one* single piece of information, one feeling of ease or difficulty. As a result of this efficiency, fluency may be used effortlessly in judgment formation (e.g., Greifeneder & Bless, 2007; Schwarz, 1998), which has important bearings on the conditions in which fluency is relied on in judgment (see Greifeneder, Bless, et al., 2011; Schwarz, 2004).

With this set of characteristics in mind, we now review two separate sets of findings. We start with fluency's role in judgment, and then report on how fluency tunes subsequent cognitive processing.

Fluency in judgment

Fluency has been shown to inform a seemingly endless number of judgments (see examples in Unkelbach & Greifeneder, 2013b). Because reviewing everything is impossible, we focus on a selective, representative sample of findings. After presenting these examples, we focus on the process level and explain why one unitary experience may inform so many different judgments, and when this influence is likely to occur.

Selective examples of fluency's impact

In this section we review a selective set of findings taken from a variety of literature. At first glance, these examples may appear quite heterogeneous. However, you will recognize the common thread running through all examples, and thereby come to appreciate just how important fluency is in judgment formation.

Feelings of familiarity

There is a strong body of research that addresses the role of fluency in cognitions about *cognitive processing*. Fluency here affords us a peek into our cognitive control room and allows us to assess, for instance, the state of our memory (e.g., Whittlesea & Williams, 2000). Consider feelings of familiarity, which denote the subjective experience of *having prior experience* and play a key role in various kinds of judgments, including recognition (e.g., Jacoby & Dallas, 1981). Our judgments about recognition thus depend, at least in part, on how familiar a stimulus feels. Familiarity, in turn, depends on processing fluency: the more fluently the stimulus is processed, the more it is perceived as familiar, and hence the more individuals indicate recognition. In a demonstration of familiarity effects, participants read aloud a list of non-famous names (such as Sebastian Weisdorf) taken from a telephone book (Jacoby, Kelley, Brown, & Jasechko, 1989). One day later, participants made fame judgments about a set of names that included the previously presented (and therefore old) and new non-famous names. Intriguingly, the old non-famous names were rated as more famous than the new non-famous names, because "reading a nonfamous name [on the first day] has the unconscious influence of increasing the familiarity of that name [on the second day]" (Jacoby, Kelley, Brown, et al., 1989, p. 327). Thus, the previous exposure to a list of non-famous names resulted in a higher likelihood of erroneous fame judgments, presumably because the old non-famous names felt more familiar than the new non-famous names.

Feelings of familiarity are not confined to famous and non-famous names in telephone books, but are constant companions of most individuals. Have you ever met a person in the railway tram who *felt* familiar, but you had no idea where you knew this person from? Only to realize later that it was the clerk from the local supermarket (example adapted from Whittlesea & Williams, 1998)? Or have you ever had the experience that some piece of information felt more familiar than something unknown should? These are but two of a multitude of encounters you may have had with feelings of familiarity.

Feelings of knowing

Let's assume that you have to write an exam about social cognition, and that this exam is coming up soon. You therefore want to gauge how well you know the present book's content. To do so, you could try to recall what you have learned so far, and then draw inferences about the extent of your knowledge. For instance, if recalling information feels difficult, you may infer that your knowledge is scanty; in contrast, if relevant pieces of information come to your mind easily, you may infer that you know quite a bit already. Notably, fluency plays a key role in this chain of events, because it is the felt ease or difficulty of recall (and not the actual recalled content) that inferences about knowledge are based on. Emphasizing the critical role of feelings, these inferences are referred to as *feelings of knowing* (e.g., Hart, 1965; Koriat, 1993, 1997, 2012).

Research suggests that feelings of knowing are quite accurate predictors of future recall (Koriat, 1993). Consider an experiment conducted by Hart (1967, p. 194), who asked participants to answer 75 general knowledge questions such as "What is the capital city of New Mexico?" In the first round, participants were given three seconds to answer each question. For those questions they failed to answer, participants indicated whether they would be able to remember the answer given more time (feeling of knowing). In the second round, participants again answered all questions, but this time without time limit. Interestingly, their feelings of knowing predicted rather well which items they additionally recalled in the second round. The intriguing conclusion following from this evidence is that feelings of knowing provide an indication about what is stored in our memory system even before the memories can be produced. In a third round, participants did not recall answers, but were provided with four alternatives per question and were thus probed for recognition. Feelings of knowing predicted recognition even better than recall. Together these findings illustrate that the feeling of knowing monitors memory quite accurately and may thus be a good guide for students (see Reber & Greifeneder, 2017; for a different conclusion, see Finn & Tauber, 2015).

Judgments of learning

When trying to learn, you may ask yourself for every new piece of information that you have tried to commit to memory: "What are the chances that I will recall this information later?" Such judgments are referred to as *judgments of learning* (JOLs, e.g., Koriat & Ma'ayan, 2005) and once again depend strongly on fluency.

When JOLs are assessed directly after knowledge acquisition, fluency primarily reflects the ease or difficulty at encoding. But when JOLs are assessed directly before recall, fluency may additionally reflect the ease or difficulty at retrieval. To the extent that fluency at encoding and fluency at retrieval differ, JOLs may vary substantially by time of assessment. This may have strong consequences for the predictive validity of JOLs. Research suggests that JOLs are more accurate predictors of future recall, the more fluency is based on retrieval processes. For instance, it has been shown that delayed JOLs allow for quite accurate predictions of future recall (Nelson & Dunlosky, 1991), presumably because experienced fluency here is a function of those processes that are active at recall.

The flipside is that JOLs are likely poor predictors of future recall the more fluency is based on processes that are at odds with the probability of later recall. To illustrate, consider evidence reported by Simon and Bjork (2001), who asked participants to learn to type predefined key sequences on the keyboard number pad in a predefined time. This learning occurred either in homogenous stimuli blocks (i.e., the same key sequences were repeated several times before the next key sequences were learned), or mixed stimuli blocks. Results suggest that homogenous stimuli blocks enhance acquisition and therefore result in higher JOLs—but they cause poorer performance at retrieval, because the stimuli are committed less well to long-term memory (see Illustration 8.2). This example thus illustrates a situation in which fluency at acquisition is at odds with the probability of later retrieval, and hence a situation in which JOLs are poor predictors of future recall.

The findings reported by Simon and Bjork (2001) exemplify a situation in which some difficulties at acquisition are desirable, because they enhance later retrieval. Bjork and Bjork (2011) conclude from findings such as these that it may be desirable to render learning difficult. In direct support, one study found that rendering learning materials difficult to read resulted in better learning outcomes (Diemand-Yauman, Oppenheimer, & Vaughan, 2011). It is critical that the difficulties enhance learning by, for instance, increasing processing depth; just adding extraneous load, such as having the TV running while learning, is likely not helpful (see Reber & Greifeneder, 2017).

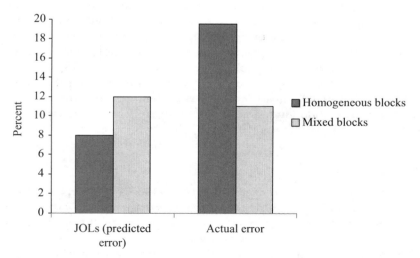

Illustration 8.2 Predicted and actual error following blocked or random schedule acquisition

Source: Simon and Bjork (2001)

The crux with desirable difficulties is that they are beneficial for learning but result in lower levels of fluency at acquisition, and thus in less liking (we will address the hedonic marking of fluency later; see Winkielman, Schwarz, Fazendeiro, & Reber, 2003). Poignantly illustrating this crux, one early study observed that postal workers' learning performance was higher after distributed learning (more difficult) than after blocked learning (easier). Yet the postal workers enjoyed the blocked learning more (Baddeley & Longman, 1978), presumably because acquisition felt more fluent. Hence, though some difficulties in learning are desirable because they may enhance long-term retention, they cause lower levels of fluency at acquisition and thus lower liking.

This crux may constitute not only a motivational hindrance that keeps students from using more efficient learning strategies, but may also create the wrong incentive for those who teach. This is because subjective teaching evaluations are generally assessed after acquisition (e.g., at the end of the semester), and not at retrieval (i.e., after the test, or even after several years). A course that makes learning easy compared to difficult may thus be evaluated more positively. But exactly this ease may come at the price of poor recall performance later. In support, experimental evidence suggests that more positive teaching evaluations go along with poorer student performance in tasks independent of the course under evaluation (Braga, Paccagnella, & Pellizzari, 2014). Another consequence of subjective teaching evaluations assessed at acquisition is equally noteworthy: because fluency at acquisition is often different from fluency at recall (e.g., Koriat & Ma'ayan, 2005), a subjective teaching evaluation today may tell little about how well the course really fostered the long-term retention of new knowledge.

This crux also constitutes a challenge for those who program apps intended to help learning. This is because apps that increase processing depth may be experienced as less fun, and therefore stand a high chance of being uninstalled quickly.

That fluency at encoding increases liking but reduces long-term retention is relevant in realms beyond the educational context. Consider advertising, for instance, where marketers strive to convince customers to buy their products or services. A campaign that is processed easily may enhance liking. This is often highly desirable, because the product or service becomes associated with positivity. But the downside of easy processing may be that the information is not remembered later, which is undesirable (for related evidence, see Labroo & Pocheptsova, 2016). In contrast, a campaign that requires some processing to be understood may not be liked, but may be better remembered. Balancing liking and retention should thus be important managerial decisions in advertising. Decisional complexity arises here if the same ad is repeatedly aired, thereby becoming more fluent over time simply by virtue of repetition.

Judgments of truth and confidence

Consider again the following statement *"The latest eruption of Láscar volcano was on 18th April."* True or false? This is the third time we have presented this statement, and even if you believed this sentence to be wrong in the beginning, you may have changed your mind by now, as a function of repetition and fluency. Why is that?

To navigate in a complex social world, individuals need to know whether information is true or false. How do individuals assess truth? Research has uncovered that one cue individuals rely on is the ease or difficulty with which the information can be processed. For instance, one study observed that a statement presented repeatedly is more likely to be judged true (Hasher, Goldstein, & Toppino, 1977), presumably because it is easier to mentally process repeated statements than new statements (Begg, Anas, & Farinacci, 1992). Corroborating this fluency–truth hypothesis, research suggests that increasing processing fluency independent of repetition produces truth effects, too. In particular, it has been shown that statements printed in high compared to low color contrast are processed more fluently, and that this fluency translates into higher ratings of truth (e.g., Reber & Schwarz, 1999; Unkelbach, 2007; Scholl et al., 2014; for an important qualification, see Dechêne, Stahl, Hansen, & Wänke, 2010). Hence, whether we believe some information to be true depends on the fluency with which the statement is processed.

Conceptually close to truth judgments are judgments of confidence. One important ingredient in these judgments is again fluency, or more specifically, the ease or difficulty of content processing (e.g., Wänke, Bless, & Biller, 1996). In one experiment (C. M. Kelley & Lindsay, 1993, p. 4), participants first read a list of names, things, and places (acquisition list). In a second step, they answered 90 general knowledge questions such as "What was Buffalo Bill's last name?" The acquisition list contained the correct answers to 30 general knowledge questions, incorrect answers to another 30 general knowledge questions, and 30 fillers. As may be expected, participants answered more general knowledge questions correctly if the correct solution was part of the acquisition list, and they performed poorest on items for which related but incorrect answers were provided in the acquisition list. Of more interest here is a second finding: participants were quite confident in their answers both when the correct and the incorrect answers were part of the acquisition list. Thus, although correct answers in the acquisition list led to high performance and incorrect answers to poor performance, participants were equally confident in having provided the correct answer. Presumably this is because prior exposure increased fluency, which in turn increased confidence, independent of actual performance.

Judgments of confidence contribute to an interesting phenomenon called unintentional plagiarism (Jacoby, Kelley, & Dywan, 1989), which holds that writers may unintentionally plagiarize others because someone else's way of phrasing an idea comes to their mind with particular fluency. Presumably, this is because the previous exposure to a sentence may influence the relative fluency with which the sentence presents itself later, thereby rendering the sentence particularly compelling when writers put their "own" thoughts into words. This unintentional plagiarism may occur not only at the semantic level, but also at the abstract level of ideas: an idea processed for the second time may result in higher levels of fluency, and hence be held with higher confidence.

Credibility and trust

Just as statements are perceived to be more likely true if processed fluently, one may expect that individuals associated with fluent processing are perceived to be more credible. Supporting this argument, it has been shown that the perceived ease or difficulty with which individuals can identify clues signaling the truthfulness of a target's account can influence the target's perceived credibility (Ask, Greifeneder, & Reinhard, 2012). Conceptually related evidence further suggests that non-native speakers may be believed less, presumably because a foreign accent reduces processing fluency (Lev-Ari & Keysar, 2010). On both studies, fluency is linked to credibility; what is different is the source of fluency, which is either retrieval or understanding. Going beyond perceived credibility, but building on the same train of thought, fluency has been shown to guide trustful (Greifeneder, Müller, Stahlberg, Van den Bos, & Bless, 2011b) and cooperative behavior toward others (Müller, Greifeneder, Stahlberg, Van den Bos, & Bless, 2010).

Fairness considerations

Being treated fairly is important to individuals, both in their private and work life. Fairness considerations affect, for instance, key organizational outcomes such as organizational identification or job satisfaction (for a review, see Cohen-Charash & Spector, 2001). But how are fairness or justice considerations formed? Several sets of findings converge in suggesting that not only relevant pieces of information (e.g., the characteristics of a selection procedure), but also the fluency associated with processing this information plays an important role. For instance, participants in one study were asked to list either two or four unfair aspects of a nation-wide university selection procedure, and subsequently they evaluated the procedure (Greifeneder, Müller, Stahlberg, Van den Bos, & Bless, 2011a). Reflecting reliance on fluency, participants judged the procedure to be more just after recalling many rather than few *unfair* aspects—after all, if recall of unfair aspects feels difficult (many aspects condition), it is likely that there are few unfair aspects in general, reflecting a fair procedure (see also Janssen, Müller, & Greifeneder, 2011).

Frequency

So far, we have reviewed evidence demonstrating that fluency affects evaluations of memory content (e.g., feelings of knowing), or the extent to which we put faith in our thoughts, other people, or even organizations. Now we turn to a different set of findings that links fluency with frequency and probability. This link is prominently stated in Tversky and Kahneman's (1973) availability heuristic, which we introduced in Chapter 6. To recapitulate, the availability heuristic holds that individuals may evaluate the frequency or probability of events "by the ease with which relevant instances come to mind" (Tversky & Kahneman, 1973, p. 207). For instance, participants in one study were asked to recall three (which was pre-tested to be easy) or eight travel destinations (difficult) for which they had used their bike in the previous month (Aarts & Dijksterhuis, 1999). Subsequently, participants were asked how often they had traveled by bike during the previous month. Participants gave higher frequency judgments in the three- compared to the eight-destinations condition. At first glance, this finding may appear puzzling, given that participants in the eight-destinations condition had factually recalled more destinations. But a fluency perspective resolves this puzzle if we assume that participants inferred from experienced ease that the category "travel destinations by bike" was large, and from experienced difficulty that the category was small (for more on this reasoning, see Chapter 6; Schwarz et al., 1991). Hence, even though participants in the three-destinations condition recalled factually fewer instances, a fluency account can explain why they gave higher frequency judgments (for related evidence, see Greifeneder & Bless, 2008).

Liking

The link between fluency and frequency reviewed in the previous paragraph is quite strong. Perhaps stronger still is the link between fluency and liking. Some authors even argue that fluency and liking are inextricably associated (Winkielman & Cacioppo, 2001; Winkielman et al., 2003). In support of this fluency–liking link, Reber, Winkielman, and Schwarz (1998) asked participants to rate the prettiness of a set of circles. Fluency was manipulated by varying the figure–ground contrast between the circles and the background. A black circle on a white background has a high figure–ground contrast and can be processed fluently; a light grey circle on the same white background has a low figure–ground contrast and can be processed less fluently. Results indicate a close relationship between figure–ground contrast and rated prettiness, thus supporting the idea that fluency may be used as an indicator for prettiness (see also e.g., Reber & Schwarz, 2001; Whittlesea, 1993).

Findings such as those by Reber and colleagues (1998) fit well with the observation that many characteristics associated with prettiness or beauty, such as prototypicality or symmetry, are also associated with increased processing fluency (e.g., Halberstadt & Rhodes, 2000; for a review, see Reber, Schwarz, & Winkielman, 2004). Moreover, findings such as these allow for a different perspective on the robust evidence that repeated presentation increases liking, generally referred to as the mere-exposure effect (Zajonc, 1968). A fluency account of mere exposure stresses that repeated presentation increases the fluency of subsequent processing, which is then used as a basis to evaluate liking (e.g., Bornstein & D'Agostino, 1994). Perhaps this matches with your own experience: sometimes we don't like a product on the first encounter, but gradually come to appreciate and like it with repeated exposure. Think of a new song. That it matches everyone's taste is rather unlikely. Still, after being on the charts for several weeks, more and more people come to like it. Of course, many factors may contribute to this phenomenon—but there is also a fair chance that the song is liked more simply because it has been repeated so often. Relatedly, most individuals have had the experience that they do not like the design of a new car when they see it for the first time. But through repeated exposure they come to appreciate it, nevertheless. Think about what this may mean for design and fashion, and for developing taste (see Reber, 2016).

Why are fluency and liking so closely associated? One explanation stresses that the link between repeated exposure, fluency, and liking reflects individuals' processing environment. Assume that individuals are confronted with negative and positive stimuli (e.g., delicious vs. bad-tasting meals, friendly vs. unfriendly people, etc.). Which stimuli do individuals actively try to avoid and which stimuli do they actively seek out? More often than not, individuals self-select positive over negative stimuli and are therefore more frequently exposed to positive compared to negative stimuli (everything else being equal). Our self-selected environment thus produces an association between positivity and frequency, and frequency, in turn, is linked to fluency. By reversing this link, individuals may draw inferences from fluency to frequency to positivity. That is, as fluency is linked to frequent (and most likely positive) stimuli, high fluency may inform about the positivity of a stimulus. Note that while this backward inference results in valid judgments most of the time, it leads us astray when fluency is caused by sources other than the self-selected prior exposure.

Economic value

You may come to like the design of a new car because repeated exposure increases fluency. But fluency may also increase economic value. Try the following: "There are many reasons to drive a BMW. Can you name one?" (Wänke, Bohner, & Jurkowitsch, 1997, p. 172). Most likely you can, and naming that one reason is likely easy. But consider naming ten reasons, which feels more difficult. Participants asked to name one compared to ten reasons for driving a BMW subsequently indicated higher purchase interest, presumably because they relied on fluency to gauge value. A similar conclusion can be drawn based on an analysis of real stock exchange fluctuations reported by Alter and Oppenheimer (2006). The authors differentiated between stock names that can be pronounced easily and stock names that are more difficult to pronounce, and analyzed the performance of shares one day, one week, six months, or one year after being introduced to the New York Stock Exchange. When first released, investors know relatively little about a stock, and therefore incidental factors such as the fluency with which the stock name can be pronounced may be of impact. After the stock has been in the market for some time, however, this influence of incidental variables should diminish. Consistent with this reasoning, the authors observed that investment in the ten most fluently pronounceable stock names compared to the ten most disfluently pronounceable names would have led to a consistent gain, with this effect being strongest in the beginning and diminishing over time.

Illustration 8.3 Research by Alter and Oppenheimer (2006) suggests that the ease with which new stock names can be pronounced may influence their performance, with this impact being particularly pronounced in the first days of trading

Source: Superclic/Alamy

Performance judgments

We have reviewed evidence that fluency may influence how we perceive or judge our own thoughts and cognition (e.g., JOLs). By the same token, fluency may be used to judge the performance of others. Consider evidence that essays in legible versus less legible handwriting are evaluated more positively by a margin of 8 points on a scale from 70 to 100 (H. W. James, 1929). This is more than a quarter on the grading scale, and thus reflects an enormous impact of legibility. Perhaps the most plausible account of this difference is fluency, based on the following logic: legible compared to less legible handwriting can be read with greater ease, and greater ease signals positivity. Because this positivity signal emerges while the essay is being evaluated, it is (misleadingly) used as information when grading the essay (see Illustration 8.4; Greifeneder et al., 2010; Greifeneder, Zelt, Seele, Bottenberg, & Alt, 2012).

In the legibility bias, differences in fluency result from more or less legible hand-writing. Another source of fluency is the ease or difficulty of understanding. Consider the following sentence, which is a translated excerpt from Descartes' Meditation IV (examples taken from Oppenheimer, 2006, p. 155): "Many other matters respecting the attributes of God and my own nature or mind remain for consideration; but I shall possibly on another occasion resume the investigation of these." Compare this translation to the following one: "There remain to be investigated by me many things concerning the attributes of God, and many things concerning me myself or the nature of my mind." The meaning of the two versions is identical, but participants indicated the latter to be considerably more complex. Presumably because the more complex translation could be processed less fluently, Descartes (as the essay's author) was rated as less intelligent by participants who had read the second translation (Oppenheimer, 2006).

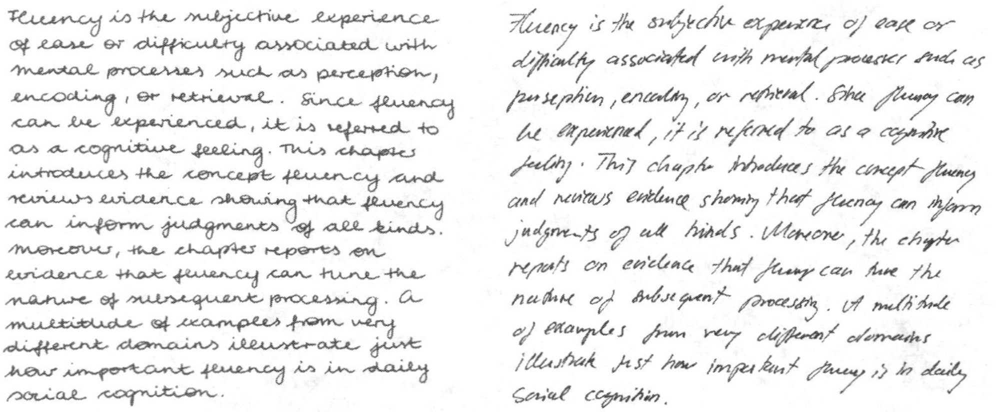

Illustration 8.4 Research suggests that essays are evaluated more positively if written in legible (left) compared to less legible handwriting (right). One explanation holds that legible handwriting can be read more fluently, and fluency signals positivity (e.g., Greifeneder et al., 2010)

Source: © Greifeneder et al. (2010)

Processes underlying fluency's impact on judgment

So far we have reviewed diverse examples illustrating that fluency may inform an enormous multitude of judgments (for reviews, see Greifeneder, Bless, et al., 2011; Schwarz, 1998; Schwarz & Clore, 2007). This multitude may appear surprising, given that we have located fluency on *one* continuum from easy to difficult (see defining characteristics). How is it possible that a unitary construct can be used as a source of information in so many different judgments? To answer this question, we need to get down to the process level that underlies fluency-based judgments. Two process steps are necessary, and they tell a fascinating story about human cognition (e.g., Unkelbach & Greifeneder, 2013a).

Attribution

For fluency to be informative, it needs to be *attributed* to the judgmental target (just as mood needs to be attributed, see Chapter 7). That is, fluency needs to be perceived as emanating from, or being representative of, the processing of the judgmental target (Greifeneder, Bless, et al., 2011). This step is critical, because it links the non-specific fluency experience to a specific judgmental target. The default criterion for attribution is *temporal contiguity*, that is, whether fluency is experienced contiguously to judgment formation (see also Clore et al., 2001; Higgins, 1998). Fluency experienced at the time of judgment thus stands a high chance of being used in judgment. Importantly, this is irrespective of whether fluency is actually caused by the judgmental target. To illustrate, we return to experimental evidence by Schwarz and colleagues (1991), which we introduced in Chapter 6. Participants in this study recalled 6 (12) instances of assertive behavior, a task pre-tested to be easy (difficult), and subsequently assessed their own assertiveness. The authors observed that participants evaluated themselves as more assertive after recalling 6 rather than 12 instances. Presumably this is because they *attributed* the experienced ease (difficulty) of recalling instances of assertive behavior to the judgment in question, and concluded that they were likely assertive (not that assertive) (Schwarz, Bless, Strack, et al., 1991). Here, fluency engendering by retrieval processes was attributed to the judgment at hand, and temporal contiguity served as a criterion.

But temporal contiguity may lead us astray if fluency arises from a process that has no valid bearing on the evaluation target. To illustrate, read again the following sentence and evaluate its intellectual claim: "*Many other matters respecting the attributes of God and my own nature or mind remain for consideration; but I shall possibly on another occasion resume the investigation of these*" (sentence taken from Oppenheimer, 2006, p. 155). Reading this sentence may have felt difficult because the author used a complex grammar structure and wording. But reading this sentence may also have felt difficult because we used the rather disfluent font Mistral. Both sources of fluency happen contiguously to judgment formation and thus stand a high chance of being perceived as representative when evaluating the author's intellect. Yet only the former may be informative, whereas the latter reflects formatting *we chose* and is therefore not informative with respect to any statement concerning the author's intellectual abilities.

Together these examples suggest that while contiguity may be a good criterion, it may also lead us astray. To find out whether the attribution mechanism is adaptive, we need to know how often it is a good criterion, and how often it is not. Though we have no concrete numbers, we can offer two considerations (which are conceptually similar to those offered in Chapters 6 and 7): First, when reading the fluency literature, you may conclude that the attribution principle leads us astray more often than not, because there are many examples when the impact of fluency is specious. Yet this picture is distorted and reflects primarily the fact that researchers strive to mislead the attribution principle (e.g., in so-called misattribution studies) because investigating mistakes often allows for interesting insights. Failed attributions are thus likely overrepresented in the scientific literature, and they tell us little about how well the mechanism performs outside the laboratory (see also Herzog & Hertwig, 2013). Second, even if attribution by contiguity should lead us astray, there are several safety nets in place that protect individuals against relying too much on this swift default (see Greifeneder et al., 2013). For instance, participants in one study were asked to decide which of two surnames is more frequent in the US-American population (Oppenheimer, 2004). One of the surnames was a famous one (e.g., Nixon) and factually more frequent than the other, non-famous one (e.g., Winters). Results revealed that the non-famous name was judged to be more frequent than the famous one. Presumably this is because participants realized that fame may influence fluency and frequency, and therefore guarded against using this information in judgment.

Interpretation

The attribution process discussed above offers an explanation for why fluency can have a bearing on a multitude of different judgments. But it does not explain what fluency *means* in the respective context. Why would you infer that difficulty in recalling 12 examples of assertive behavior means that you are not assertive? To draw this inference, a naive theory linking difficulty with the absence of the respective trait is needed— for instance, the theory that difficulty in recall means that there are few memories of assertive behavior, and that if such memories are scarce you are likely not assertive. Research suggests that individuals hold many naive theories of different kinds.

To illustrate the impact of interpretation, put yourself in the shoes of participants who were asked to list two or ten reasons in favor of implementing senior comprehensive exams at their university (Briñol, Petty, & Tormala, 2006). Naming two is easy for most participants; naming ten feels difficult. Naive theories were manipulated by telling some participants that feeling ease is a bad sign, because ease indicates that thoughts are not very complex. Difficulty, in turn, was said to be a good sign, because it indicates complex thinking. Other participants were told the reverse, so that they had reason to interpret felt ease in a positive way and felt difficulty in a negative way. Results are depicted in Illustration 8.5 and illustrate that the meaning assigned to fluency matters: those participants who interpreted felt ease as something positive, and felt difficulty as something negative, were more in favor of the exam policy after recalling two compared to ten reasons.

But the pattern was reversed for participants who were given the opposite interpretation of ease, that is, felt ease indicated something negative and felt difficulty something positive (for conceptually related evidence, see Winkielman & Schwarz, 2001). In this study, naive theories were provided by the experimenter. But naive theories can also

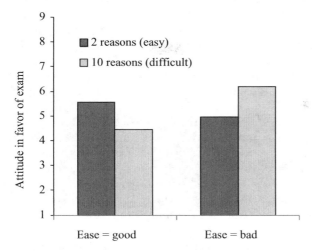

Illustration 8.5 Mean attitude in favor of senior comprehensive exams as a function of fluency and naive theory

Source: Briñol et al. (2006, Experiment 1)

be brought to bear simply by the question asked. For instance, Mandler, Nakamura, and Van Zandt (1987) presented participants with sets of two grey-colored geometric shapes. One of the shapes had been presented before and could therefore be processed more fluently than the other shape, which was new. Some participants were asked which of two shapes they liked better, and results revealed that previously presented shapes were liked better. Presumably, this is because these participants inferred liking from fluency. But other participants were asked which of two shapes was lighter in color. Notably, these participants indicated that the previously presented shapes were lighter, thus inferring lightness from fluency. Depending on the question asked, fluency may thus be interpreted in different ways. Together, findings such as these strongly suggest that fluency needs to be interpreted in order to be meaningful, and that interpretation may be prompted by the situational context, including instructions given or questions asked by the experimenter.

Two final considerations about interpretation need to be briefly mentioned. First, though different interpretations are possible, there seems to be a strong default linking fluency to positivity. Without manipulation of interpretation, fluency is usually taken as an indication of favorableness (and not unfavorableness, e.g., Briñol et al., 2006), frequency (and not scarcity, e.g., Greifeneder & Bless, 2008), as something pleasant or aesthetic (and not hideous, e.g., Reber et al., 2004), or as a signal for truth (and not falsehood, e.g., Reber & Schwarz, 1999). Some authors even suggest that fluency is *hedonically marked* (Winkielman et al., 2003; see also, Garcia Marques, Mackie, Claypool, & Garcia Marques, 2013), that is, fluency and liking are inextricably associated.

Second, if naive theories exist, one may reasonably ask where they come from. One explanation stresses learning, in that individuals associate fluency with various outcomes by way of repeated pairing (Unkelbach, 2006). For instance, individuals may experience that exemplars of large categories can be recalled from memory with ease (e.g., times you abided by the law), whereas exemplars from small categories are difficult to recall (e.g., times you violated the law). Over time, similar experiences result in a naive theory about how category size and retrieval fluency are linked, and this naive theory may be applied the next time you want to estimate frequencies. Similarly, individuals may experience that truthful statements can be processed more fluently, for instance, because they are familiar. If truth and fluency become associated over time, individuals may draw on fluency when judging truth. From such a learning perspective, fluency is not inextricably hedonically marked, but the association between fluency and positivity is learned and can thus be unlearned if truth and disfluency are paired. Evidence in support was provided by Unkelbach (2007), who arranged the learning environment in such a way that participants associated truth and fluency (default naive theory), or truth and disfluency (reverse naive theory). Importantly, participants' truth judgments in a subsequent test phase reflected these contingencies, in that previously presented compared to new stimuli (the former being more fluent than the latter) were judged to be more true for default participants, whereas reverse naive theory participants judged the new compared to previously presented statements to be more true (see also Scholl et al., 2014). Interestingly, a learning perspective of naive theories suggests that naive theories should be socially shared, that is, people hold similar naive theories to the extent that they share the same learning environment. If this learning environment reflects, for instance, regularities of our cognitive system (e.g., exemplars from larger categories can be recalled more easily), the resulting naive theories should even be universal.

Variables that moderate fluency's impact on judgment

By now you know that fluency may influence all kinds of judgments, and you know about the psychological processes that underlie this influence. We now turn to variables that moderate whether fluency is used as information in judgment or not. The overall picture here is identical to the variables that moderate reliance on *affective* feelings, as reviewed in Chapter 7 (see Illustration 7.6). Reliance on fluency in evaluative judgments is more likely when fluency is perceived as *representative* for the target, when fluency is *salient* in the processing context, when fluency is *relevant* for the judgment, when the judgment is *malleable*, and more often than not when processing intensity is low (for a review, see Greifeneder, Bless, et al., 2011). Rather than reiterating these moderating variables in detail, we turn to one variable not addressed before, which is *prior learning experiences*. The idea is as follows: to the extent that individuals strive to provide accurate judgments (e.g., about truth), they should rely on fluency, particularly if fluency proved useful in discerning truth from falsehood before. To test this assumption, Scholl and colleagues (2014) varied during a learning phase whether reliance on fluency resulted in valid truth judgments or not. Participants' behavior in a subsequent test phase reflected this learning experience, in that fluent compared to non-fluent statements were judged to be more likely true particularly by those participants who had experienced fluency as a useful source of information before. These findings draw an intriguing picture of a finely tuned process that adaptively channels whether fluency is relied on in evaluative judgment or not.

Fluency and processing style

In this final section we review evidence that links fluency and processing style. Recall that in Chapter 7 we reported evidence suggesting that *mood* changes the style of cognitive processing, with positive mood fostering heuristic or shallow processing, and negative mood fostering systematic or deep processing (see feelings-as-information theory, e.g., Schwarz, 2012). Presumably, this is because mood provides information about the current situation, with positive mood signaling that everything is fine and benign, and negative mood that something is wrong and problematic. A situation that is perceived as benign may constitute a go-signal and suggest that individuals should continue processing as before (and more often than not, individuals process heuristically). In contrast, a situation that is perceived as problematic may constitute a stop-signal and suggest changing strategies (which then is systematic or detail-oriented processing, e.g., Clore & Huntsinger, 2009). Why do we repeat all this here? Simply because the very same logic applies to fluency, too: all else being equal, experienced ease suggests that everything is going well, that is, the situation is benign, so that heuristic processing is a suitable strategy. In contrast, experienced difficulty suggests that something is wrong and problematic, and therefore requires detail-oriented and systematic processing.

To illustrate, answer the following question for yourself: "How many animals of each kind did Moses take on the Ark?" Most individuals answer "two," failing to realize that *Noah* was piloting the boat. But when this question was presented in one study in a difficult-to-read font, the error rate was considerably lower (see Illustration 8.6; Song & Schwarz, 2008, p. 794). Presumably, this is because low fluency signaled that the situation is problematic and needs attention, resulting in greater scrutiny and the realization that Moses was not on that boat. For such misleading questions, the first association is not the correct one, so a higher level of scrutiny is beneficial. The situation is different for questions where the first reaction is correct, such as "Which country is famous for cuckoo clocks, banks, and pocket knives?" (Switzerland). Here, further scrutiny may yield an incorrect response. Attesting to the notion that fluency tunes processing, low fluency led to a higher error rate on this second type of question (see Illustration 8.6).

If low fluency fosters scrutinizing and analytical thinking, it should prove beneficial for all kinds of problems that require intensive thought. Evidence in support was provided in a study on syllogistic and logical reasoning (Alter, Oppenheimer, Epley, & Eyre, 2007), in which participants were asked to work on three problems such as the following: "A bat and a ball cost $1.10 in total. The bat costs $1.00 more than the ball. How much does the ball cost? _____ cents" (taken from Frederick, 2005). Most individuals answered 10 cents, but the correct solution is 5 cents. Across a series of such tasks, the error rate was higher when the task was printed in a font that was easy rather than difficult to read; again, the reason was presumably that perceived ease fostered heuristic processing, and perceived difficulty systematic processing (note that this evidence could not be replicated by other authors, A. Meyer et al., 2015; but for conceptually related evidence on foreign language processing, see Keysar, Hayakawa, & An, 2012). These findings are strongly related to the evidence on the relationship between fluency and learning outcomes discussed earlier (Diemand-Yauman et al., 2011).

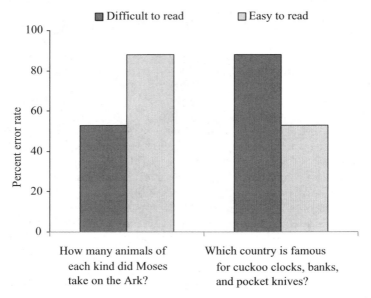

Illustration 8.6 Percentage error rate for misleading and non-misleading questions as a function of fluency

Source: Song and Schwarz (2008, Experiment 1)

The two previous examples pertain to the realm of analytic thinking. Yet fluency's impact on downstream processing is not confined to this specific arena but is general, and should thus also influence, for instance, which information is used in evaluative judgments. Participants in one study read a strong or weak persuasive appeal, either once or several times (Garcia-Marques & Mackie, 2001). When the appeal was presented only once, attitudinal judgments reflected the pre-tested differences in persuasiveness. However, when the appeal was presented several times, attitudinal judgments were not influenced by differences in persuasiveness. Presumably, this is because multiple presentations increased fluency, which in turn resulted in more superficial and less elaborate processing. As a result, differences in argument strength were of lower impact.

If experienced ease fosters reliance on general knowledge structures, one may further expect that fluency might affect the extent of stereotyping. Participants in one study were presented with 12 person descriptions, each accompanied by a photo (E. R. Smith et al., 2006). Half of the photos had been presented previously and could thus be processed more fluently. The person descriptions included both categorical information about professions (i.e., stereotypic knowledge) and individuating information; and the individuating information was worded in such a way that it moderately disconfirmed the categorical information. Participants answered three questions per person description. Analyses revealed more stereotypical judgments for those person descriptions that were accompanied by a previously presented and therefore more fluent photograph. Intriguingly, these results suggest that familiarity may increase stereotyping, and that people we have met before stand a higher chance of being judged based on categorical knowledge. It should be noted, however, that familiarity may boost other processes as well, such as liking or the quantity of individuating knowledge, which may counteract the effect of fluency documented here.

In sum, several lines of research suggest that fluency may regulate downstream processing, with experienced ease fostering more superficial and experienced difficulty more analytical processing. This evidence dovetails with findings on *mood and processing* (see Chapter 7), which lends additional support. At the same time, it needs to be acknowledged that fluency's impact on downstream processing has not always been documented (see A. Meyer et al., 2015), so that further research addressing the nature of this relationship is needed.

Conclusion

This chapter has selectively reviewed evidence about how fluency may serve as information in judgments across all kinds of domains, including judgments about your cognitive system (e.g., feelings of knowing), judgments about others (e.g., credibility), judgments about liking, and judgments of frequency, to name but a few. Furthermore, fluency was shown to serve as an active regulator of subsequent processing. That one unitary feeling—the cognitive experience of ease or difficulty—may be so powerful is noteworthy and allows for critical insights into how individuals construct their social reality.

Chapter summary

1   Fluency is a cognitive feeling and refers to the subjective experience of ease or difficulty associated with mental processing. Fluency may be engendered by all kinds of sources; in fact, it has been suggested that fluency arises as a continuous by-product of every mental process. Nevertheless, researchers refer to one unitary experience that can be located on a continuum from easy to difficult (daily language), or fluent to disfluent (scientific language).
2   Fluency grants experiential access to the working of our mind—with fluency, one can feel a cognitive process or state of knowledge. Interestingly, quite often this experiential access may be the only access individuals have to otherwise inaccessible processes or states of knowledge.
3   Fluency has been shown to inform a seemingly endless number of judgments, including judgments pertaining to our memory, judgments about ourselves and others, and judgments of liking. Fluency is thus an important source of information in social judgment formation.
4   That fluency may inform so many different judgments can be explained by the joint consideration of two mechanisms: attribution and interpretation. Fluency first needs to be attributed to the respective process, and then interpreted. Both mechanisms are finely tuned.
5   Fluency may inform not only judgments, but also the regulation of subsequent processing. In particular, perceived ease may signal that the environment is fine and benign and does not require intensive processing; in contrast, perceived difficulty may signal that intensive processing is in order.

Discussion questions/topics

1   Think about telling your friends about fluency: Which example would you rely on to make it easier to understand? Which of the defining characteristics would they need to know?

2   How could you make use of the feelings of knowing and JOLs in regulating your own learning? When would these two be particularly accurate guides?

3   Let's assume that you would like to create an urban myth, such as having spotted flying saucers with turquoise dots. Why could simply repeating this myth over and over again prove to be a good strategy?

4   We have discussed that marketers may wish to balance the effect of fluency on liking a new product versus the effect of fluency on learning the product's features. What would you do? And why?

5   The mechanisms of attribution and interpretation are critical to understanding fluency's impact on judgment formation. Can you explain the two in your own words?

6   Fluency may regulate downstream processing, with experienced ease leading to more superficial processing, and experienced difficulty to more intensive processing. What should you do if you want someone to read what you have written superficially as opposed to closely? To illustrate, assume that you have a brilliant idea and want your course instructor to realize it.

Recommendations for further reading

Reber, R., & Greifeneder, R. (2017). Processing fluency in education: How metacognitive feelings shape learning, belief formation, and affect. *Educational Psychologist, 52*, 84–103. (This contribution focuses on the various roles of fluency in educational settings and illustrates how students may benefit from knowing about fluency.)

Unkelbach, C., & Greifeneder, R. (Eds.). (2013). *The experience of thinking: How the fluency of mental processes influences cognition and behavior.* Hove: Psychology Press. (This book provides an in-depth perspective on a wide spectrum of research findings, emphasizing the informative function of fluency.)

9   Communicating information

Klaus Fiedler & Rainer Greifeneder

If we take the attribute "social" in social cognition seriously, we should expect language and communication to represent a core area of research and a central topic of the present volume. There is hardly anything more social than communication between people. Whereas attitudes, attributions, stereotypes, person memories, mood states, motives, personality attributes, and other major facets of social cognition can all be studied and measured at the level of a single individual, communication transcends the individual as the unit of analysis. Communication always involves two or more people, who must coordinate their utterances, listen to each other, tailor their words and symbols to the knowledge of others, empathize with their communication partners' needs and prior knowledge, find a way to get along with each other, and attract each other's attention.

There are additional reasons why language and communication ought to occupy a central position in social cognition. Virtually all psychological experiments, questionnaires, interviews, and study techniques involve verbal instructions, linguistic

Illustration 9.1 There is hardly anything more social than communication between people
Source: Jacob Lund/Shutterstock.com

stimulus materials, and verbal responding, and most theories are encoded in language. Empirical evidence is represented semantically in the literature, and psychological education is acquired through communication in lectures, seminars, or face-to-face interactions. In modern societies, all consequential decisions—legislative, executive, and judicial—rely on linguistic terms and critical idioms. And last but not least, a similar point could be made for many everyday behaviors, such as expressing love or hate, trust or distrust, all of which involve linguistic (and sometimes non-linguistic) communication.

And yet, there is a conspicuous neglect of language research in social psychology. As evident from the table of contents in journals and textbooks, theories of social cognition rarely take a communication perspective or include linguistic concepts referring to semantics, syntax, figurative meaning, speech acts, or grammar learning. The few notable exceptions of established findings on language in social cognition have attained no more than a marginal status in the literature. However, as the next sections will show, these findings can be fascinating, enlightening, and of great explanatory value.

Social information processing across individuals: an epitome of truly social cognition

Bartlett (1932) was one of the first scholars who noted that social cognition often rests on collective memories distributed across many different individuals. Rather than keeping all our knowledge in our own private memory, we often build up collective memories together with our partners, friends, and colleagues, who are specialized in certain knowledge domains. Or we consult previous users, customers and experts, dictionaries, Wikipedia, and social networks that jointly form our transactive memory system (Wegner, Erber, & Raymond, 1991). Social stereotypes, in particular, are only to a small extent learned through direct personal experience. To a much greater extent, they reflect distributed and socially shared knowledge from hearsay or mass media. To understand the nature of stereotypes, it is thus necessary to understand that social information varies markedly in communicability and sharability (Kashima & Lan, 2013; Schaller, Conway, & Tanchuk, 2002). Some pieces of information are more likely than others to be communicated among friends, colleagues, and discussion groups (Wittenbaum & Park, 2001), to become part of culture (literature, movies), and to enter the mass media and the history books; and, most importantly, some aspects are more likely to be understood and remembered by our communication partners than others. Social cognition depends heavily on these differences in communicability.

Communicability as a source of stereotyping

Empirical support for this basic assumption was provided by Schaller, Conway, and Tanchuk (2002). They asked participants to rate 76 trait terms that had been used in previous stereotype research (particularly in the seminal studies by Katz & Braly, 1933) for two criteria: their commonness and likelihood of being used in communications about other people. Because both ratings were highly correlated across the 76 traits, they were combined into a communicability index, which was also substantially correlated with a rating of interestingness. However, communicability was shown to bear only little correlation with word frequency, positive versus negative valence, or confirmability of traits from behavioral observations. Schaller and colleagues found that the communicability of traits, which could be assessed at a high rate of reliability, predicted the traits' stereotypicality for four different Canadian population groups, especially for those groups that were highest in conversational prominence (i.e., well represented in linguistic conversation). Thus, the formation and maintenance of stereotypes reflects to a notable extent a linguistic property of trait words. Some words (e.g., intelligent, athletic, quick-tempered, stubborn, quiet, or honest) are more suitable for communication and more likely to be included in collective knowledge than others (e.g., meditative, conventional, alert, rhythmic, methodical, or poor). Because of these differences in communicability, the former become social stereotypes more often than the latter.

Even more compelling than Bartlett's (1932) theoretical notion of collective remembering was his provision of an experimental method: serial reproduction. As in a Chinese whispers game, each member in a chain of participants is asked to remember a received message and convey it to the next person, who passes it on to the next, and so forth. At the end of the chain, a comparison of the final and initial version shows that the message is no longer the same. It has undergone substantial changes, but, importantly, these changes are far from random or unpredictable. For example, the end product of a serial reproduction chain is typically closer to common stereotypes than the original message. In other words, stereotype-consistent utterances are (at least under specific conditions) more likely to be transmitted than stereotype-inconsistent utterances, suggesting, conversely, that stereotypes may reflect what is likely to be transmitted as a rumor, as a humorous story or joke, or as a communication believed to please or help others.

The underlying principles can be quite simple and unsurprising. Being a student of memory, Bartlett (1932) expected familiar and jointly known information to have a reproduction advantage. What is familiar to many people is not only unlikely to be missed at any position in the chain, it can also be reconstructed from shared knowledge when it happens to be forgotten once or twice in a chain. As a consequence, serial communication should often serve to convey and to maintain stereotypically meaningful, familiar knowledge, whereas a variety of socially unshared, stereotype-inconsistent information will be lost.

This basic prediction was tested by Kashima (2000) in a modern version of a serial reproduction experiment. At the beginning of the chain, participants read a story about Sarah and James, who were planning to invite James's employer for a dinner party. The story consisted of 59 propositions that varied in plot relevance (relevant for the gist of the story vs. representing only background information) and stereotype consistency (consistent vs. inconsistent with gender stereotypes vs. neutral). For instance, background propositions consistent with the general gender stereotype at that time were "James takes the opportunity to choose the appropriate wine" and "Sarah even gets her hair done for the occasion." (Inconsistent background propositions included "That morning, James also cleans the house," and "She yells to James that the girls are down at the Royal (a pub)" (Kashima, 2000, p. 598).

Not surprisingly, memory for all types of propositions decreased over serial chain positions. For plot-relevant information, stereotype-inconsistent propositions were more readily reproduced in early positions, whereas stereotype-consistent propositions showed a slight recall advantage in later positions. For background information that was not of central importance to the story plot, a marked recall advantage for stereotype-consistent propositions was obtained across all five chain positions. Thus, gender stereotypes were accentuated through serial reproduction; typically female behaviors by Sarah and typically male behaviors by James were more likely to have been preserved at the end of the serial reproduction game than James's female and Sarah's male behaviors. This sort of stereotype amplification over time was most pronounced when background information was attended to less than plot-relevant information.

In another series of experimental studies by Lyons and Kashima (2003), the impact of serial reproduction on stereotyping was shown to depend on whether communicators believed that their communication partners shared and endorsed their stereotypes, and also on the extent to which they actually shared the stereotypes. The tendency for serial reproduction to render stories more and more stereotypical was shown to be strengthened when stereotypes were based on shared knowledge.

Shared information advantage

Beyond the domain of stereotyping, a general bias to communicate sharable information has been shown to restrict decisions and actions in small groups. A large body of research (Kerr & Tindale, 2004) shows a distinct bias toward including more shared than unshared arguments in group discussions (Stasser, 1999). In other words, discussants tend to communicate arguments that are shared with other communication partners rather than provide unshared information that might actually raise new aspects and previously unrecognized facts. Thus, just like the information conveyed in serial communication chains, the arguments sampled in groups and discussion forums are also biased in favor of shared information and against unexpected and unshared arguments that might work against the prevailing collective knowledge. This so-called shared-information effect (Wittenbaum & Park, 2004) clearly serves an affirmative function, reinforcing collective beliefs and majority positions while neglecting original information held by single persons and minorities. In any case, the pertinent research highlights the selective nature of social communication. Some pieces of information are clearly more likely to be discussed than others.

Snyder (1984) argues that the bias toward communicating what is of interest to other people serves a social function—getting along with others—which is as important as knowledge acquisition. Wittenbaum, Hollingshead, and Botero (2004) emphasize the social-reward value and the confidence-increasing value of information sharing, which serves a mutual enhancement function. In particular, group members who are not yet regarded as high in capability can improve their positive social standing and their positive evaluation by others when they communicate shared information. High-status members who are already respected as high in capability are less dependent on bolstering their image by communicating what others expect to hear (Wittenbaum & Park, 2001).

Apart from such motives of mutual enhancement and social desirability, the shared-information bias can also be justified on rational grounds. After all, when opinions, preferences, or facts are held by two or more individuals, they can be hardly discounted as reflecting erroneous or idiosyncratic beliefs of weird or quixotic persons; they are socially validated (Greitemeyer & Schulz-Hardt, 2003). Moreover, even when the sampling of discussion items is completely unbiased, such that every item residing in any discussant's mind is included in the discussion with the same likelihood, shared items have a higher chance than unshared items of being mentioned by at least one discussant (Larson, Foster-Fishman, & Franz, 1998). Thus, independent of any motive or intention, shared items simply have a higher chance of being communicated. Social desirability or mutual enhancement may be sufficient conditions, but they are not necessary to explain the tendency of social communication to support common and stereotypical expectancies.

Failure to solve hidden-profile tasks

Many experiments have been conducted on one striking consequence of the shared-information bias: the failure to solve so-called hidden-profile tasks (Mojzisch & Schulz-Hardt, 2006; Stasser & Titus, 1985). In this task setting, which is typical of the division of labor in modern democratic societies, each member of a group or committee is provided with a subset of all information that is available on a decision problem. However, the subsets provided to individual group members do not reveal the optimal preference order of the decision alternatives. In order to figure out the best alternative, it is necessary to uncover the "hidden profile" of the advantages and disadvantages of all alternatives through effective group communication.

For illustration, imagine an experiment in which four group members (Persons 1 to 4 in Table 9.1) are presented with subsets of positive and negative arguments about three decision options A, B, and C. The options might be applicants for a job or financial investment funds. As apparent from the bottom row, the overall rates of positive and negative arguments clearly indicate that option A (12+/6−) is the best, followed by option B (14+/14−) and C (6+/12−). However, because A's 12 assets are unshared whereas the 6 deficits are shared, every single group member knows of more deficits than assets for option A (3+/6−). A's superiority can only be discovered in an effective discussion revealing that altogether A has 12 independent assets but only 6 independent deficits. The opposite is the case for option C, for which a lower number of assets is shared (6+), whereas a higher number of deficits are unshared (12−). Compared to the clearly negative shared perspective on A, each individual may hold too positive an impression of C. Option B lies in between; while all 14 assets and 14 deficits are unshared, Persons 1 and 2 know more about the assets, whereas Persons 3 and 4 know more about the deficits. As a result, the individual preference orders are B > C > A for Persons 1 and 2, and C > A > B for Persons 3 and 4. But no one prioritizes A and discards C as most unattractive, despite A > B > C being the correct preference order in this hidden profile. For the group to uncover this order, an effective group discussion is needed.

Table 9.1 Illustration of a hidden-profile task

	Option A	*Option B*	*Option C*
Person 1	3+/6−	6+/1−	6+/3−
Person 2	3+/6−	6+/1−	6+/3−
Person 3	3+/6−	1+/6−	6+/3−
Person 4	3+/6−	1+/6−	6+/3−
Overall	12+/6−	14+/14−	6+/12−

Note: The information provided to each group member (Person 1 to 4) and to the group altogether about the decision options (A, B, C) consists of specific numbers of positive (+)/negative (−) arguments. Bold numbers indicate information that is socially shared across all individuals.

Three decades of insightful research have drawn a pessimistic picture about the ability of people and groups to solve such hidden profiles. Discussion groups rarely manage to discover the hidden profile, especially when individual profiles diverge consistently from the hidden profile. As explained in a comprehensive review by Schulz-Hardt and Mojzisch (2012), this irrational communication failure can be explained by combinations of several factors: (a) basing group decisions on pre-discussion preferences, without discussing the raw arguments; (b) discussion bias toward shared arguments; (c) discussion bias toward preference-consistent arguments; (d) enhanced validity ascribed to shared arguments; and (e) enhanced validity ascribed to preference-consistent arguments. As already mentioned, even in the absence of any bias, (f) the failure to solve such problems may also reflect the sampling advantage of shared arguments, which are more likely than unshared arguments to be recalled and mentioned by at least one group member.

While some of these factors may be unrelated to communication, such as the ascription of higher validity to repeated arguments, other factors, such as the selective communication of shared information, highlight the role of communication barriers. Consistent with this interpretation, hidden profiles have been shown to be solved more often when deviant dissenters force discussion groups to take unshared and unexpected arguments into account (Schulz-Hardt, Brodbeck, Mojzisch, Kerschreiter, & Frey, 2006).

The long-known phenomenon of group polarization (Moscovici & Zavalloni, 1969; Myers & Lamm, 1976; Sunstein, 2007) can be subsumed under the same principle. Group discussions have been shown to reinforce and polarize pre-discussion tendencies among group members. For instance, when judging the guilt of a defendant in court trials, it has been shown that group discussions result in even harsher judgments of the defendant's guilt when there is a prior bias toward aggravating arguments. In contrast, group discussions support more lenient judgments in groups that start from a bias toward ameliorating arguments. This polarizing influence of group discussions

Illustration 9.2 Groups often fail to accurately incorporate information unshared between various group members, resulting in sub-optimal group decision performance

Source: NurPhoto/Getty Images

toward implicit group norms is consistent with the notion that shared arguments in line with the group's initial orientation determine the course and the outcome of group discussion.

Advice taking

A related paradigm is advice taking. Although this paradigm was developed in applied research on decision making rather than in traditional social psychological labs, it offers a strong and telling message to students of social cognition. In the modern information society, when many everyday problems exceed individual people's world knowledge, individuals often base their decisions and actions on the advice of experts or the experiences of others with similar problems. We not only ask medical experts, lawyers, or stock brokers for their expert advice in specific knowledge domains. We also draw on other customers' experiences with hotels, restaurants, or universities as documented on frequently visited Internet sites when making consumer decisions or applying for admission.

In a typical advice-taking experiment (cf. Yaniv & Choshen-Hillel, 2012), participants are presented with knowledge questions for which a correct answer is available, such as "How many calories are there in a baked potato?" After providing their own quantitative estimate, participants are presented judgments provided by other people, who serve the role of advice givers. A typical finding is that participants fail to exploit the wisdom of crowds (Surowiecki, 2004), that is, the fact that the average judgment of many individuals is often more accurate than one's own personal judgment. The deviations from such a wise averaging strategy are not due to random error but reflect systematic biases. One systematic cause of inaccuracy on advice-taking tasks is egocentrism (Yaniv, 2004; Yaniv, Choshen-Hillel, & Milyavsky, 2009). Participants tend to give more weight to their own estimate over those of their advice givers. Because this egocentric bias holds across all participants, from the most accurate to the most inaccurate one, it makes judgments inaccurate. Another systematic reason for ineffective advice taking is again related to the shared-information bias. Advice takers give more weight to those advisors who share their opinions and information sources. In other words, they are more inclined to trust redundant sources that create a sense of consistency and an illusion of validity (Kahneman & Tversky, 1972), than to trust independent sources that might add logically new information and thereby exploit the wisdom of crowds.

Just as the quality of discussion in the hidden-profile paradigm profits from dissenters expressing alternative views, the accuracy of quantitative knowledge estimates has been shown to increase when those receiving advice from others take their perspective. For instance, when participants in an experiment conducted by Yaniv and Choshen-Hillel (2012, Study 1, p. 1023) received five other participants' calorie estimates (randomly drawn from the database of all estimates), their egocentric over-weighting of their own opinions led to rather inaccurate judgments (self-perspective condition). By contrast, in a condition labeled other-perspective, participants were asked to get into another participant's "mindset and give us your guess of his or her best estimate." They were further instructed that "your gain depends on your success in predicting that person's estimate." Such training in interpersonal perspective succeeded in reducing the egocentrism and the inaccuracy declined markedly, as evident from a comparison of the dark grey and light grey bars in Illustration 9.3.

The right-most pair of bars in Illustration 9.3 shows that averaging all six estimates would produce the least inaccurate estimates, superior to individual judges' revised judgments in the middle.

However, the accuracy gain that can be obtained through the exchange of diverse opinions is not strictly bound to advice communicated between people. A similar advantage can result from "silent communication" with oneself. Herzog and Hertwig (2009) called this phenomenon dialectical bootstrapping. After providing an initial estimate of historical dates, participants were asked to provide a second estimate from a deliberately divergent perspective—one that offered an antithesis to their initial thesis. In this way it was possible to emulate the wisdom of crowds within a single individual, and the average of both judgments did in fact come systematically closer to the true value than did the initial judgment. These findings and many others obtained in the advice-taking paradigm highlight the importance of open-minded discussion and information exchange for optimal judgment and decision making.

Cooperative communication and logic of conversation

Common to all the phenomena included so far in this chapter—serial reproduction, group discussion and decision making, and advice taking—is the notion that social cognition often transcends the individual. The knowledge used by individuals for judgments, decisions, and actions is often prepared collectively, based on a division of labor between two or more persons playing distinct roles in communication games. For an informed and comprehensive approach to social cognition, it is essential to understand the coordination and integration of information that resides in the minds of different people. Beyond the assessment of the cumulative knowledge possessed by different members of groups and cultures, it is important to understand the rules that guide the exchange of knowledge and preferences. In what follows, we focus on the rules of the communication games that restrict the exchange of information between individual people.

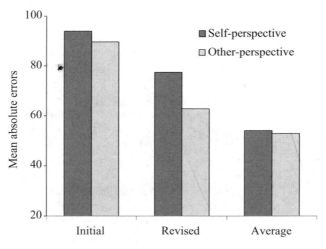

Illustration 9.3 Mean absolute errors of calorie estimates as a function of self- versus other-perspective

Source: Yaniv and Choshen-Hillel (2012, Experiment 1)

Cooperative communication

Paul Grice's (1975) seminal writings on pragma-linguistics and the logic of conversation have led to enlightening answers to this intriguing issue. Even though real social interaction may serve several motives, virtually all communication has to meet a number of requirements.

For communication to remain informative, relevant, and socially rewarding, communication partners must be aware of, and adhere to, four distinct maxims. The *maxim of quantity* obliges communication partners to provide enough information to be understood, but not more information than is really needed by the conversation partner. Thus, the content of verbal messages must be neither too impoverished nor too long-winded and circumstantial. The *maxim of quality* expects communication partners to provide information that is reliable and consistent with the empirical facts of the extra-verbal reality. The *maxim of relation* says that communication partners should use words and phrases that are relevant to antecedent content and references in the ongoing communication goal and to pragmatic context. Finally, the *maxim of manner* prohibits communication partners from bizarre and awkward utterances that create confusion and undermine the effective transmission of information (see Box 9.1).

Box 9.1   Grice's maxims of cooperative communication (Grice, 1975)

Maxim of quantity

1   Make your contribution as informative as required
2   Do not make your contribution more informative than is required

Maxim of quality

1   Do not say what you believe to be false
2   Do not say that for which you lack adequate evidence

Maxim of relation

1   Be relevant

Maxim of manner

1   Avoid obscurity of expression
2   Avoid ambiguity
3   Be brief (avoid unnecessary prolixity)
4   Be orderly

Without these rules of the game, most people would sooner or later lose their interest in communication, or the ongoing social interaction would break down completely. For example, eyewitness reports in a courtroom are expected to be detailed and exhaustive, but they should not include more detail than is really of interest, and the critical information should not be lost in a long-winded report (maxim of quantity). Every utterance made by the eyewitness, even when it is not entirely true, will be interpreted as reflecting some actually existing cause or motive. Why would he or she report something for which there is no underlying reason or motive to do so (maxim of quality)? It is tacitly assumed that every reported observation by an eyewitness in a court trial refers to the same specific crime and to the same perpetrator, even when these references are not explicitly repeated in each and every sentence (maxim of relation). And of course, the eyewitness will not be taken seriously if he or she acts like a mad or drunk person (maxim of manner).

Pragmatic influences in survey research

Let us complement these anecdotal examples with some prominent research results, which testify to the importance of taking Grice's (1975) communication rules into account. In a classical demonstration of the vicissitudes of survey research, Schwarz, Hippler, Deutsch, and Strack (1985) varied the range of response alternatives in survey questions. For instance, respondents were asked to estimate their daily TV consumption on one of two categorical scales that ranged from less than ½ an hour to more than 2½ hours (Scale A: short durations), or from less than 2½ hours to more than 4½ hours (Scale B: longer durations). Analyses revealed clearly higher TV consumption estimates for Scale B than Scale A. For instance, the proportion of respondents who reported watching TV for more than 2½ hours amounted to 37.5% on Scale B, as compared to 16.7% on Scale A.

A Gricean interpretation starts from the premise that individuals do not know exactly how many hours they spend watching TV every day, but have an idea of how much they watch in relation to others. For instance, respondents may know from social comparisons that their TV consumption is halfway between the average and top consumption. In accordance with the maxim of quality, respondents may assume that the response anchors in a survey or questionnaire afford reasonable information about the quantitative distribution of estimates. In particular, they may take it for granted that their virtual communication partner (i.e., the survey researcher) knows about the actual range of TV consumption in the population and has chosen the response options in such a way that a high (or medium or low) option reflects relatively high (or medium or low) TV consumption. Corresponding to their self-evaluation as "between average and top consumption," they may therefore choose a response in the upper half of the response scale. Yet because the upper half of the response scales means very different things for Scale A and Scale B, different consumption estimates are obtained.

An entire research program on survey methodology was motivated by the notion that even standardized communication settings, such as responses to surveys or interviews, are subject to Grice's principles of cooperative communication (Schwarz, 1995; Strack & Schwarz, 1992). Because, as we have seen, the maxim of quality causes a bias toward the response options provided for closed-format questions, open response formats are often superior, soliciting more useful data than closed formats in survey research, witness reports, and clinical interviews (cf. Schwarz & Sudman, 1996).

In a similar vein, the impact of the maxim of quantity was illustrated by Strack, Martin, and Schwarz (1988), who varied the ordering of two survey questions: satisfaction with one's dating experiences, and overall satisfaction with one's life. Responses to both questions were highly correlated ($r = .55$) when the specific question (dating) preceded the more general question (overall satisfaction), but only when the two were presented in separate communication contexts. In contrast, when the two questions were presented in one communication context, the correlation dropped markedly (to $r = .26$). Having already indicated their dating satisfaction, respondents apparently interpreted the subsequent question as referring to all sources of satisfaction other than dating. According to the maxim of quantity, it seems sensible to exclude a specific question that was already addressed from a subsequent general question. Further evidence for this interpretation comes from the demonstration that question order effects disappear when the conversation context is eliminated, that is, when the questions of interest are not presented in close temporal succession, but are separated by other parts of a questionnaire (Strack & Schwarz, 1992).

Pragmatic influences in behavioral research

Of course, communication rules and the logic of conversation can influence not only survey and interview data, but more generally the results of almost all empirical research. Given the major role played by language in providing instructions, communicating experimental tasks, and measuring performance, attitudes, and motives, it seems obvious that the validity of research findings relies heavily on an appropriate understanding of language. On the one hand, task instructions may be misunderstood, and the wording of verbal dependent measures may be ambiguous. On the other hand, language users' logic of conversation diverges in various ways from the rules of propositional logic that provide the normative standards in research on cognitive psychology (for an overview, see Bless et al., 1993).

To illustrate, go back to Chapter 1, Box 1.1, where we introduced Wason's (1966) selection task (which of four cards—4, A, L, 7—need to be turned to check the rule: *If there is a vowel on one side of the card, then there is an even number on the other side of the card*). Hundreds of experiments have shown that even intelligent and highly educated student participants have a hard time solving this reasoning problem. At least part of the difficulty arises because the logic of conversation that determines the understanding of experimental task instructions diverges in important ways from the propositional logic underlying the experimenter's normative model.

On the one hand, in the context of real-life conversations, most implications are governed by different pragmatic constraints. When a father says to the son "If you mow the lawn, you'll get 10 Euro," the if–then statement is not meant as a logical implication. Both the father and the son, as well as all social observers of the episode, know that the principle of social exchange (Homans, 1967) is invoked: if the son did not mow the lawn by the evening, it would not make much sense for him to ask the father for the 10 Euro by pointing out that, logically, the father's implicational statement said nothing about whether not mowing the lawn might not also result in 10 Euro. The pragmatics of social exchange restrict the meaning of the implication: you receive the 10 Euro *if, and only if,* you mow the lawn.

On the other hand, when the logic of conversation does support propositional reasoning, a majority of participants are capable of applying the logic of implications in accordance with the normative structure of the Wason selection task. As reviewed in Box 1.1, when social conversation refers to deontological rules (i.e., rules involving promises or obligations), the uni-directional meaning of an implication is naturally understood (Cheng & Holyoak, 1985; Cosmides, 1989).

Framing effects causing preference reversals

A number of so-called framing effects testify to the power of subtle linguistic cues in rational decision and choice. At first sight, one might be inclined to believe that it is equivalent to hear either that "25% of the people died" or that "75% of the people survived." However, just as in ordinary language saying that "the glass is half full" is not the same as "the glass is half empty," modern research on (ir)rational decision making is replete with linguistic framing effects leading to preference reversals. The preference A > B for one decision option A over another option B may not be maintained, or may even be reversed (A < B), when the available information is simply reframed or paraphrased in different words. Preferences for lotteries may shift when uncertainty is expressed in terms of winning or losing rates, or the perceived danger of diseases or medical interventions may shift when risks are framed in terms of survival or mortality rates, even when these convey the same statistical information.

Tversky and Kahneman's (1981) Asian disease problem outlined in Box 9.2 constitutes one of the most prominent and most frequently studied examples of such a framing effect. When the effectiveness of a new medical program against an epidemic disease is expressed in terms of survival rates, most people tend to be risk-averse. They prefer saving 200 (out of 600) people guaranteed to saving all 600 people with a probability of ⅓. However, when the same existential decision is framed in terms of mortality rates, they no longer prefer the guaranteed event of 400 people dying to the uncertain outcome of 600 dying with a probability of ⅔. That is, reframing the same outcomes in terms of losses (mortality) rather than gains (survival) encourages risk-seeking decision strategies.

Box 9.2   The Asian disease problem (Tversky & Kahneman, 1981)

Imagine that the US is preparing for the outbreak of an unusual Asian disease, which is expected to kill 600 people. Two alternative programs to combat the disease have been proposed. Assume that the exact scientific estimate of the consequences of the programs are as follows:

> If Program A is adopted, 200 people will be saved.
>
> If Program B is adopted, there is ⅓ probability that 600 people will be saved, and ⅔ probability that no people will be saved.
> (Tversky & Kahneman, 1981, p. 453)

When participants were asked which of the two programs they would favor, 72% selected Program A and 28% selected Program B.

> Now consider a slightly different wording of the two programs:
>
> If Program C is adopted 400 people will die.
>
> If Program D is adopted there is ⅓ probability that nobody will die, and ⅔ probability that 600 people will die.
> (Tversky & Kahneman, 1981, p. 453)

Of those participants presented with Programs C and D, 22% selected Program C and 78% selected Program D.

Assuming a total of 600 people, Programs A versus C, and Programs B versus D are equivalent in terms of the outcome and risk. The difference is that Programs A and B are framed as a gain (increasing risk-avoidance tendencies and a preference of A over B), whereas Programs C and D are framed as a loss (increasing risk-seeking tendencies and a preference of D over C).

Why should the mere exchange of complementary wording styles influence judgments of risk related to serious health issues? The common explanation within the context of Kahneman and Tversky's (1979) prospect theory is that subjective value functions are sublinear: the subjective increase in the positive or negative value of surviving or dying people, respectively, is not proportional to the respective objective increase in the number of surviving or dying persons. As the subjective value of 600 survivors is less than three times the subjective value of 200 survivors, reducing the probability from certainty to ⅓ does not appear justified. In contrast, an increase in mortality from 400 to 600 people may appear subjectively justified by the corresponding probability decrease from certainty to ⅔. As a consequence of this discrepancy between the subjective and objective values of decision options, it is only plausible that framing in terms of gains induces risk-avoidance tendencies (e.g., an increase from 200 to 600 survivors does not justify a reduction of survival rates from 100% to 33%).

While this widely shared explanation for the reflection effect on the Asian disease problem explains the impact of linguistic framing in terms of unequal value functions, McKenzie and Nelson (2003) have suggested a pragma-linguistic alternative account. Analogous to the demonstration that a half-full glass implies an increasing change from a reference point of an originally empty glass, whereas a half-empty glass implies a change from an originally full glass to an increasingly empty state, the reference to gains (survival) and losses (mortality) also implies a reference point. Specifically, they showed that receivers of risk communications were more likely to infer a positive reference point (i.e., survival) when new evidence was framed as "50% die" rather than as "50% survive," suggesting that pragmatic language understanding alone might explain why mortality framing encourages more risk acceptance than survival framing. Further evidence on the process underlying framing effects can be found in Igou and Bless (2007).

Communication pragmatics and social influence

One intriguing implication from a pragmatic-communication approach says that one cannot "not-communicate" (Watzlawick, Beavin, & Jackson, 1969). Keeping silent in a discussion about moral values or faithfulness will be understood as a conspicuous sign of guilt or a bad conscience. If a politician evades the topic raised in a journalist's question, he or she will not appear neutral but suspicious. A humorous story among lawyers refers to a court judge who would not allow witnesses to provide qualifying answers and insisted that it was always possible to answer either Yes or No. When asked by one witness if he himself could always respond with a clear-cut Yes or No, the judge said "Yes, of course—go ahead and ask me a question." So the shrewd witness asked the judge, "Mr. xxxx, do you continue to beat your wife?"

This anecdote highlights that one often cannot prevent communication partners from drawing unwanted and often unwarranted inferences. In an innuendo effect, the communication goal is typically to smear the target of the innuendo by bringing about irrevocable changes in the belief systems of those receiving the communication. For instance, by asking the innuendo question "Was politician X seen in the red-light district?" (Wegner, Wenzlaff, Kerker, & Beattie, 1981), a belief system is created that constructs the politician in the context of immoral behavior (Bell, 1997). It is then almost impossible for the politician to remain unharmed unless there is perfectly valid evidence to falsify the very possibility of a kernel of truth. Thus, merely raising the possibility may create a communicative reality that is very hard to refute. Two paradigms that highlight this insight provide the topics for the next two subsections.

The answer is in the question

In asymmetric communication settings, involving interviewers and interviewees, interrogators and witnesses, or advice givers and clients, the providers of information are typically more knowledgeable than their communication partners. Yet, in such asymmetric encounters the answer is often in the question (Semin & De Poot, 1997; Semin, Rubini, & Fiedler, 1995). Answers from those providing information are to a considerable extent constrained or even predetermined by the questions posed by those soliciting the information.

For an illustration, consider the phenomenon of implicit verb causality (R. Brown & Fish, 1983; Rudolph & Försterling, 1997). An otherwise identical question might be asked in slightly different ways, using different verbs. One might either ask "Why do you read the *New York Times*?" or "Why do you like the *New York Times*?" The first question uses an *action verb* that implies intentional, self-determined action. An actor who chooses to "read" is himself or herself perceived as the causal origin of such intentional behaviour. In technical terms, action verbs imply an internal attribution of behaviors to the sentence subjects, who take the role of agents (cf. R. Brown & Fish, 1983). In contrast, the second question uses an affective state verb that implies external causation acting upon the sentence object. Saying that somebody "likes" the *Times* points to a causal origin in the *Times*. The sentence subject serves the role of a patient or experiencer who exhibits an emotional reaction to the stimulus object.

These different causal schemas triggered by action verbs and state verbs reflect a highly regular phenomenon that generalizes to almost all words in the English lexicon (Kanouse & Abelson, 1967; R. Brown & Fish, 1983; Semin & De Poot, 1997), as well as the lexicon of other languages (Fiedler & Semin, 1988; Rudolph & Försterling, 1997). An interviewer (or journalist) can therefore solicit different answers from the interviewee, which then lead to different causal attributions, simply by using different verbs in the questions. This kind of social influence is so subtle that communication partners hardly ever notice how they are being manipulated.

Indeed, the impact of questions on communication partners and observers is so strong that one does not even have to wait for the answers from the person being questioned. Swann, Giuliano, and Wegner (1982) presented their participants with interview protocols that consisted mainly of questions about extraverted behaviors or introverted behaviors. Some participants were provided with (a) only the questions asked by the interviewers, (b) only the interviewees' answers, or (c) full information about the interviewers' questions as well as the interviewees' answers. All participants were then asked to evaluate the interviewees. Interestingly, interviewees were judged to be more extraverted in the extraversion condition but more introverted in the introversion condition, regardless of whether judges had seen both questions and answers, only the answers, or merely the interviewers' questions without the answers (see Illustration 9.4). Thus, consistent with the notion that the "answer is in the question," a focus on extraversion or introversion in the question was sufficient to induce a corresponding impression. Judges apparently did not consider the possibility that interviewees' answers might disconfirm the question content.

From a pragmatic point of view, the uncritical inferences of interviewee attributes from interviewer questions may not be completely irrational or "surrealistic." Participants might interpret the interviewers' deliberate focus on either extraversion or introversion as a reflection of prior knowledge: why would interviewers focus on one particular pole of the extraversion–introversion dimension, unless they had relevant background knowledge? Thus, the very focus of the questions might inform pragmatic inferences about the kind of person the interviewee seems to represent.

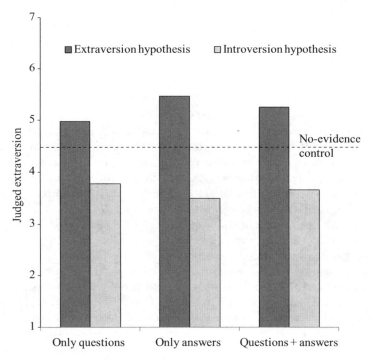

Illustration 9.4 Influence of hypothesis focus extraversion vs. introversion on judged extraversion under three different information conditions: when only interview questions, only answers, or questions and answers were provided

Source: Swann et al. (1982, Experiment 1)

Recent evidence by Wänke and colleagues (Wänke & Fiedler, 2007; Wänke & Reutner, 2010) points to similar pragmatic inferences in the context of persuasive communication. Regardless of whether descriptions of consumer products included the phrase "with Recitin" or "without Recitin," its inclusion led to more positive evaluations by communication recipients, even though they did not know anything about the substance "Recitin." Evidently, the very inclusion of an adverbial phrase (whether "with" or "without" an unknown substance) implies, pragmatically, that it must reflect high quality and a positive evaluation. Otherwise, such a qualifying phrase would hardly be included in an attempt at persuasive communication, the pragmatic goal of which can only be the promotion of advertised products.

All three examples illustrate that the simple communicative act can inform pragmatic inferences that go far beyond the information that is explicitly stated in the actual communication. In a persuasion context, insufficiently understood text phrases likely reflect positively valued attributes—why else would they be mentioned? The same can be expected to hold for phrases used in the context of flirting, dating, and mating, when speech acts aim at ingratiation and the creation of positive and intimate relationships. In this context, fillers and ambivalent phrases can only reflect positive feelings and evaluations. By contrast, in police interrogations or in hostile debates, ambiguous verbal or non-verbal expressions are unlikely to reflect positive intentions; they will typically be interpreted as expressions of suspicion, anger, or accusation. As a general rule, the semantic meaning of ambivalent or poorly understood utterances will often be assimilated to the pragmatic meaning of the communication goal, which is inherent in the question content.

Saying is believing

The impact of pragmatic inferences affects not only the subsequent attitudes and behaviors of communication recipients and observers, but also the communicators themselves. This is the take-home message of research conducted in another paradigm, which has been denoted the "communication-game approach" (Higgins, McCann, & Fondacaro, 1982). Higgins and Rholes' (1978) demonstration of the "saying-is-believing" phenomenon illustrates a typical finding from this paradigm. In this experiment, participants were presented with either ambiguous or unambiguously positive and negative descriptions of a target person. The participants' task was to summarize this information for a communication recipient who was known to either like or dislike the target person. Consistent with Zajonc's (1960) notion of cognitive-tuning effects, the evaluative tone of the messages was tuned toward the message recipients' attitudes. Participants wrote more positive (negative) messages to recipients who purportedly liked (disliked) the target person. Crucially, this tuning effect also influenced the communicators' own memory representations, which were biased toward positive (negative) evaluations after they had written positive (negative) messages. No such effects were observed in a control condition, in which participants had received the same target person information but had not written a tuned message. Moreover, these distortions in communicators' memories, which increased over a period of two weeks, were correlated with subsequent evaluations of the target person described in the message.

Other findings from the communication-game approach showed that communicators' memories were distorted not only toward the affective tone, but also toward other aspects of the messages they had produced. For example, Higgins, McCann, and Fondacaro (1982) asked participants to produce communications to people who differed in prior knowledge of the message content. When communicating to informed experts, communicators used a more abstract style and much less detail than when communicating to uninformed laypersons. As a consequence, the communicators' resulting memory representations were characterized by either more abstract or more concrete and detailed content.

More recent research has aimed at theoretical explanations and practical applications of saying-is-believing effects. Echterhoff, Higgins, and Levine (2009) gathered evidence that seems to support an explanation in terms of a desire to create shared realities in interpersonal communication.

In applied work, research has shown that saying-is-believing can generalize to audiences larger than single communication recipients (Hausmann, Levine, & Higgins, 2008), and that communication treatment can be combined with other interventions to optimize learning and instruction. In one impressive research project, Canning and Harackiewicz (2015) demonstrated in a series of experiments that having students generate communications about the utility of learning content in academic settings is a more effective intervention than providing students with explicit information about the utility of a novel mental math technique. The latter intervention actually undermined students' performance.

Summing up, the research we have been discussing so far highlights the role of interpersonal communication for social cognition. What we know about other people and groups and their motives and goals, about our attitudes, stereotypes, and social sentiments depends not only on cognitive processes of perception, learning, retrieval, reasoning, and motivated inferences within the mind of individual persons. Our knowledge depends also in distinct ways on the rules of the game that constrain the communication between persons. If people wish to understand each other and to get along, the communication game obliges them to focus on information that is communicable and sharable, to be sensitive to the logic of conversation, and to draw pragmatic inferences beyond the manifest message content. Moreover, the selective content and the focus of the resulting conversations determine the knowledge and the judgments of all participants in the communication games: the recipients, the audience, and even the communicators themselves.

The power of lexical stimuli

Complementing the previous pragmatic perspective on language and cognition, the chapter's next section is devoted to the lexical perspective, which emphasizes the social knowledge that is wired into the semantic meaning of words. Our shared world knowledge about what is good or bad, safe or dangerous, obvious or disputable, controllable, confirmable, and stable is to a considerable extent inherent in the semantics of the words used to verbalize and represent the world symbolically.

Diagnosticity and confirmability

Let us explain and illustrate this statement with anecdotal examples and empirical evidence. In a previous subsection, we were already concerned with linguistic framing effects. Decisions and actions under risk depend on whether the task instruction focuses on gains or losses, advantages or disadvantages, on motives of approach or avoidance. The lexicon is full of implicit framing effects that trigger different thoughts and thought processes. For example, consider the following pairs of positive and negative traits: honest versus dishonest; tolerant versus intolerant; polite versus rude; fair versus unfair. All these trait antonyms differ systematically in their implicit quantifiers (Gidron, Koehler, & Tversky, 1993). Using the positive trait word "honest" implies that somebody behaves honestly most of the time. By contrast, merely a single act of dishonesty or just a few dishonest behaviors would justify calling somebody "dishonest." The same holds for a majority of antonymous adjectives and nouns in the lexicon. To be a "murderer," one murder is sufficient; to be a "saint" one has to be nice and decent all the time. Social norms generally let us expect people to exhibit honest, tolerant, polite, and fair behaviors most of the time, whereas dishonest, intolerant, impolite, and unfair behaviors are expected to represent exceptional violations of the norm. It is due to this imbalance that negative traits are more diagnostic than positive terms. A single act of dishonest behavior (e.g., a lie) is more diagnostic than a single act of honest behavior (e.g., true statement), simply because the normative threshold (implicit quantifier) is much higher in the latter case.

Thus, in the domain of morality or communion, verbal descriptions of negative behaviors are more likely to result in trait attributions, compared to the less diagnostic descriptions of positive behaviors. As a result, it is relatively easy to confirm, and rather difficult to disconfirm, negative impressions or stereotypes. By comparison, it is difficult to confirm and easy to disconfirm positive trait inferences. In an early attempt to assess these differences in confirmability and disconfirmability more systematically, based on semantic ratings of 150 trait adjectives, Rothbart and Park (1986) obtained the results summarized in Illustration 9.5. Obviously, the difference between positive and negative traits is quite compelling.

It should be noted, though, that negative behavioral evidence does not always generate stronger inferences than positive behavioral evidence. The traits summarized in Illustration 9.5 belong almost exclusively to the domain of morality or *communion*. In the domain of ability or *agency*, the difference in diagnosticity is reversed (Reeder & Brewer, 1979; Skowronski & Carlston, 1987; Tausch, Kenworthy, & Hewstone, 2007). For instance, a single demonstration of high ability (e.g., a double somersault; a juggling act; the solution to a difficult mathematical problem) is enough to confirm that a person is athletic, a good performer, or very smart, even when the same person does not exhibit the same performance on many other occasions. Apparently, then, the fundamental difference of the "big two" in personality assessment and judgment, communion and agency (Abele & Wojciszke, 2013), or warmth and competence on the level of social groups (e.g., S. T. Fiske, Cuddy, & Glick, 2007), seems to be built into the lexicon of our language.

Linguistic abstractness

The potential for stereotypical inferences and prejudice depends on the thresholds entailed in the semantic meaning of positive and negative trait words. After all, stereotypical inferences can be conceived of as inferences of abstract and generalized trait attributes from more specific and contextualized behaviors observed in members of a group or culture (McCauley & Stitt, 1978). Accordingly, two verbal strategies suggest themselves as effective means for inducing social stereotypes: (a) describing target groups in terms

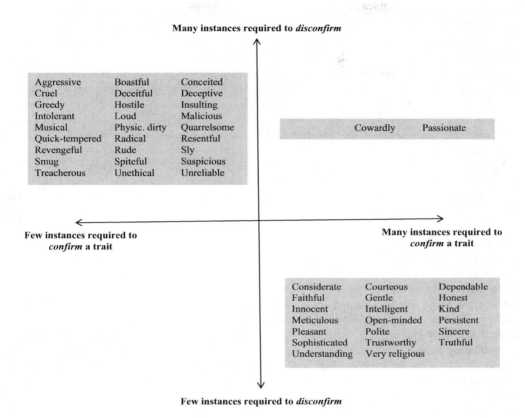

Illustration 9.5 Traits vary in the amount of information required for confirmation and for disconfirmation

Source: Rothbart and Park (1986)

of abstract adjectives and nouns rather than specific verbs and adverbs in the first place, and (b) describing target groups in terms of specific verbs that have a low threshold for stereotypical inferences. Let us first review some prominent findings on selective abstraction before we return to research on trait inferences from observed behavior.

Action-identification theory

In Chapter 3 we outlined that individuals may represent social reality on different levels of abstraction. In the present section we elaborate on and extend our prior considerations with a more in-depth discussion. The basic premise of Vallacher and Wegner's (1987) action identification theory is that the same behavior can almost always be represented in different degrees of abstractness and meaningfulness. For example, an act of moral integrity and resistance to temptation can be described at a very low, descriptive level (*saying "No"*), at a medium level (*standing firm*), or at a very high level of abstraction (*being morally strong* or even *being a moral role model or martyr*). Raising the verbal representation used for behavior identification to an increasingly high level of abstractness amounts to increasing the meaning, importance, and generality of the attribution. Characterizing somebody as "morally strong" or as a "martyr" entails much stronger evaluation and dispositional attribution than simply describing the same person, in the same behavioral situation, as "saying 'No.'"

Vallacher and Wegner (1987) suggested that language users show a general preference for abstract, high-level representations over concrete low-level representations, which are clearly less communicative. However, a shift toward lower identification levels and more concrete language should typically occur when more abstract verbal statements are not easily understood or accepted. Resorting to a lighter and less implicational language style may then increase the chances of reaching and convincing a recipient who lacks sufficient background knowledge, or whose prior attitude is not compatible with strong abstraction. Most of the time, though, a general preference for abstract identification levels should facilitate stereotypical inferences.

Linguistic category model

The lexicon offers four different word classes that can be used as predicates of sentences to describe persons or groups with language at different levels of abstractness. In the taxonomy of the linguistic category model (Semin & Fiedler, 1988), these word classes are called descriptive action verbs (DAV), interpretive action verbs (IAV), state verbs (SV), and adjectives (ADJ). The most important differences between these word classes on two semantic dimensions are presented in Illustration 9.7, along with a few common examples.

For an example, imagine a person whose behavior toward the boss is observed and verbalized by his colleagues. Different words might be used by different colleagues to

Illustration 9.6 The same behavior may be described very differently as holding the door open (DAV), ingratiating oneself with the boss (IAV), liking the boss (SV), or being polite (ADJ)

Source: Westend61 GmbH/Alamy

describe the same behavior as holding the door open (DAV), ingratiating oneself with the boss (IAV), liking the boss (SV), or being polite (ADJ). A defining feature for the lowest level (DAV) is that verbs describe behaviors in objective ways, with reference to concrete physical features, but refrain from evaluation and interpretation beyond the physical content. Holding the door open per se is neither positive nor negative (it could be both in different contexts), and it is not bound to a particular speech act (it could be part of an accusation, a memory test, a joke, or a deception attempt).

Without further information about the context, it is impossible to determine the evaluative, semantic, and pragmatic meaning of verbs from the DAV category. The causal origin of a DAV sentence (e.g., "Bill holds the door open for his boss") seems to lie in the subject (Bill) rather than the object (boss). However, depending on the context (e.g., if the boss is carrying a heavy pile of books, or if the boss explicitly asked for the favor), the causal constraints are pretty low and it is easy to imagine a causal origin in the object person (boss) or in the situation. As a result, the social meaning of DAV sentences is highly dependent on the social and physical context. DAVs are local and temporary, refer to specific behaviors that could be found in most people and therefore allow for few trait inferences, and involve little interpretation beyond the descriptive contents. DAVs are therefore located in Illustration 9.7 at the bottom (i.e., the lowest level of abstractness) and slightly on the left (i.e., by default they are caused by the subject, but causal inferences are context-dependent and not very strong).

In contrast, the semantic meaning of IAVs strongly constrains the causal and pragmatic interpretation and in most cases also the (positive or negative) evaluation of the described behavior. Saying that "Bill is ingratiating himself with his boss" clearly reflects a causal origin in the subject's (Bill's) intentional behavior, and it is essentially negative (though perhaps not as negative as other IAVs like *sliming* or *sucking up*). The interpretation is essential in that it hardly depends on the situational context and it is not bound to any specific physical feature or procedure; there are countless ways of displaying ingratiating behavior that do not have a single physical feature in common. However, although IAVs represent classes of interpretive actions, they can be interpreted at a high level of objectiveness, that is, there will be high agreement among different observers when discriminating between different IAVs such as ingratiate oneself, flirt, praise, embarrass, ridicule, or deceive. Moreover, they imply intentional control and therefore permit imperative statements like "Do not ingratiate yourself!" or "Help me!" In Illustration 9.7, therefore, IAVs are located in a slightly higher vertical position (moderately high abstractness) and on the left pole of the horizontal axis (reflecting a distinct causal origin in the sentence subject's own intention).

At the next higher level of abstractness, SVs no longer express individual acts with a clear-cut beginning and end that can be assessed objectively. For instance, the sentence "Bill likes his boss" refers to a more enduring mental or cognitive state that is no longer bound to one distinct, observable episode. SVs are no longer amenable to objective identification by other people, and they hardly allow for an imperative. Thus, "Like me!" or "Abhor me!" would represent linguistic anomalies because such imperatives do not tell the recipient how to accomplish the affective state in a distinct, observable action. Moreover, because the subject (Bill) does not have voluntary control over his affective states, most SVs strongly suggest a causal attribution to the sentence object. It must be something about the boss if "Bill likes his boss," or something about his neighbor if "Bill abhors his neighbor."

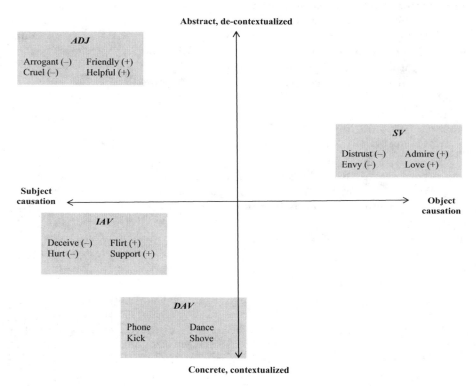

Illustration 9.7 Two semantic dimensions underlying the linguistic category model

Source: Semin and Fiedler (1988)

The reader may recognize that the opposite causal inferences triggered by IAVs and SVs account for the phenomenon of implicit verb causality that was already introduced in the subsection on communication pragmatics. Whereas most IAVs in the lexicon suggest a cause within the subject and an affective reaction in the object of a sentence, the semantic meaning of most SVs locates the affective reaction in the subject and the causal origin in the object. Moreover, SVs are presented in an even higher vertical position (reflecting increased abstractness) and in a horizontal position opposite IAVs.

At the uppermost level of the hierarchy in Illustration 9.7, ADJs are not only abstracted from the physical, temporal, and spatial context, and from controllable action plans; they are also detached from the dyadic relation between subject and object. If "Bill is polite," he will probably exhibit this general disposition not only toward his boss but also toward many other people. Moreover, the disposition can be expected to be stable and largely independent of the context, and it will bear a consistent relationship to other traits such as fairness, reliability, friendliness, and agreeableness. As a consequence, ADJ sentences entail the most abstract and, hence, the strongest and most diagnostic implications about the kind of person denoted by the sentence subject.

Linguistic categories can bias stereotypical inferences

Not surprisingly, empirical research shows that ADJs and IAVs are the most effective linguistic tools for inducing stereotypic inferences about the focal subject of a communication, while SVs afford a rhetorical means for excuses and attribution to external circumstances. For example, Schmid and Fiedler (1998) analyzed the predicates used by defense attorneys and prosecutors in their closing statements at trials. When talking about the same defendants' guilt, defense attorneys' speeches were characterized by a clearly elevated prevalence of positive ADJs, thus referring to nice person dispositions that largely abstract from the specific criminal behavior but may still trigger ameliorating conditions and benevolent guilt attributions. In contrast, prosecutors' final speeches focused on negative action verbs that highlight subject causation and controlled intentional actions by the defendant, thus calling for enhanced guilt and punishment. Although the differential rhetoric of defense attorneys and prosecutors appears to be plausible and functional and was actually successful in triggering different guilt attributions, it seems very unlikely that defense attorneys and prosecutors actually know what they are doing at the linguistic level.

Even when stimulus behavior is observed in a film rather than being merely presented in a verbal format, linguistic categories can exert a strong impact on trait inferences. A series of experiments by Fiedler, Armbruster, Nickel, Walther, and Asbeck (1996) demonstrated both the facilitation of trait inferences from behaviors recoded as IAVs, and the excuse function of recoding behaviors as SVs. Participants in these experiments saw a videotaped TV talk show that revolved around the marketing tricks of the food industry. Immediately after they had viewed the lively and adversarial discussion, the participants were asked whether they had observed a set of 12 distinct behaviors. In different experimental conditions, the behaviors used in the questions were positive IAVs (e.g., Did the protagonist *support* others?), negative IAVs (e.g., Did he *insult* others?), positive SVs (e.g., Did he *respect* others?), or negative SVs (e.g., Did he *abhor* others?). Later on, all participants rated the protagonist on a profile of trait dimensions that were matched to the meaning of the verbs used for the questions.

Merely asking the participants to verify the behaviors described as positive IAVs led to more positive trait ratings than verifying behaviors described as negative IAVs. Even when participants correctly denied behaviors that were not shown in the film, the mere verbal representation of such (correctly denied) behaviors at the IAV level led to systematically different trait ratings. In contrast, questions using SVs exerted a reverse influence. Reconstructing the protagonist's behavior in terms of negative SVs, which suggested external reasons and excuses for negative behaviors, led to relatively more positive ratings, whereas questions using positive SVs led to relatively more negative trait ratings.

Linguistic intergroup bias

By far the most widely known demonstration of lexical stimulus effects on stereotyping and intergroup relations is the linguistic-intergroup bias (LIB, cf. Maass, 1999; Maass et al., 1989). The characteristic pattern of the LIB is as follows: In verbal descriptions of outgroups, people tend to use abstract terms for negative behaviors and concrete terms for positive behaviors, whereas ingroup descriptions tend to represent positive behaviors at higher levels of linguistic abstractness than negative behaviors. Of course, the LIB serves to induce an ingroup-serving bias, because the differential abstraction trend raises positive ingroup behavior and negative outgroup behavior to a higher level of generality and importance than negative ingroup and positive outgroup behavior.

However, later research by Maass, Milesi, Zabbini, and Stahlberg (1995) and by Wigboldus, Semin, and Spears (2000) cast the interpretation of the LIB as a motivated ingroup-serving bias into doubt. Rather than reflecting a tendency to express desired information at a higher level than undesired information, the LIB might actually reflect the tendency to express expected behavior at a more abstract level than unexpected behavior. To be sure, expectedness and valence are confounded in the ingroup–outgroup distinction: most people expect their ingroup's behavior to be positive in most respects and the behavior of their outgroups to be relatively more negative. However, they would also concede that a few ingroup behaviors are negative and a few outgroup behaviors positive. By asking participants to describe ingroups and outgroups on all four types of attribute combinations (positive-expected; negative-expected; positive-unexpected; negative-unexpected), Maass et al. (1995) as well as Wigboldus et al. (2000) found that the expectedness principle dominated the desirability principle. More abstract predicates were used to verbalize expected than unexpected behaviors, regardless of whether expected behaviors served to benefit the ingroup or the outgroup.

For instance, in the Maass et al. (1995) study, Northern Italian participants from the Veneto region and Southern Italian participants from Sicily were presented with eight vignettes in which Northern and Southern protagonists exhibited desirable and undesirable behaviors and traits that were typically expected of Northern Italians (industriousness, emancipation; materialism, intolerance) or Southern Italians (hospitality, warmth/friendliness; sexism, intrusiveness). For each vignette, four verbal descriptions were offered, representing the four levels of abstraction of the linguistic

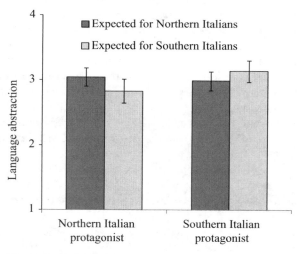

Illustration 9.8 Abstractness of descriptions of behaviors expected and unexpected by Northern Italian and Southern Italian behavior protagonists

Source: Maass et al. (1995, Experiment 1)

category model, and participants were asked to choose the most appropriate description. The dependent measure was the average abstract level of the chosen descriptions, coding 1, 2, 3, and 4 for DAV, IAV, SV, and ADJ descriptions, respectively. Using a counterbalanced design in which all combinations of desirability and expectedness occurred equally often with Southern and Northern protagonists, no ingroup-serving bias was obtained. That is, the descriptions chosen by Northern participants for positive Northern and negative Southern protagonists were no more abstract than the descriptions chosen for negative Northern and positive Southern protagonists. However, more abstract descriptions were chosen for expected than for unexpected behaviors (see Illustration 9.8).

Nomina sunt omina

Going beyond different classes of verbs and adjectives, a recent set of studies by Carnaghi and colleagues (2008) investigated the inductive consequences of nouns on attributions generated by listeners. Providing participants with expectancy-consistent nouns (e.g., artist, athlete, genius) instead of trait adjectives (e.g., artistic, athletic, brilliant) in descriptions of fictitious target persons led to stronger inferences of stereotypical person attributes. In other words, noun phrases like "is a criminal" or "is a homosexual" caused more far-reaching stereotypical inferences than ADJ phrases like "is criminal" or "is homosexual."

Together, these examples illustrate that lexical stimuli themselves are replete with (hidden) social knowledge, which message senders (unknowingly) use and message recipients (unknowingly) decode. Lexical stimuli themselves thus strongly affect how individuals construct social reality, and may be part of the explanation for why stereotypes about social groups have a strong tendency to persist.

Chapter summary

1   Some things are more easily communicated than others. These differences in communicability affect the communication content.
2   Information that is shared by several members of a group has a higher chance of being communicated. As a result, unshared information is often not weighted appropriately in group decision situations, which proves problematic in so-called hidden profile situations.
3   Grice (1975) introduced a set of four rules or maxims that guide social communication: the maxim of quantity, the maxim of quality, the maxim of relation, and the maxim of manner.
4   These maxims are relied on in direct communication between individuals, but also in survey and interview responses and research participation. For instance, estimates of TV consumption may vary depending on the response options provided by researchers.
5   Individuals often draw conclusions from the question to the answer, because they assume that the question reflects prior (tacit) knowledge.
6   Lexical stimuli vary on many linguistic dimensions, including diagnosticity or confirmability. For instance, whereas having murdered one person is enough to be called a murderer, it takes many holy acts to be called a saint.

7   Lexical stimuli also vary in abstractness, as explained by the linguistic category model. Whereas expected behavior is often described in an abstract way, unexpected behavior is described in a concrete way. Because individuals often expect more positive than negative things from their ingroup, but more negative than positive things from an outgroup, an interesting linguistic bias emerges at the intergroup level: positive ingroup behavior is communicated more abstractly than positive outgroup behavior, and negative ingroup behavior is communicated more concretely than negative outgroup behavior.

Discussion questions/topics

1   Think of two social groups and write down the first five associations that come to mind. Are these rather frequent and common words, or infrequent and rare words?
2   Describe in your own words the reasons why groups often fail to solve hidden profiles.
3   Imagine being the leader of a group and wishing to come up with a correct solution to a hidden profile. What could you do to solve this task given your knowledge of social cognition?
4   What are the four conversation maxims that Grice (1975) introduced?
5   How can these maxims be used to create different questions in standardized surveys? Use the general-question (life satisfaction) versus specific-question (dating satisfaction) example to illustrate your reasoning.
6   How can the maxims help to explain why the two opposite advertisements "with ingredient XXX" versus "without ingredient XXX" can both result in a positive impression of the advertised product?
7   Why should saying have an effect on believing? Where would you expect this to occur in your own life? Let's assume that you wish to sell used cars: how could you take advantage of this phenomenon?
8   The linguistic category model distinguishes four categories of words. How can the four be differentiated? Think of members of a selection committee: which kind of words would you expect to dominate the speech of Member A, who strongly supports one candidate, and Member B, who strongly opposes the same candidate?
9   Many cities and universities have perceived "rivals," which are often close by. Think of such a rivalry of your own city or university, and describe your own and the rival social group in a list of elementary sentences. Do you see a similar pattern of language use as the linguistic intergroup bias observed for expected and unexpected behaviors of Italian protagonists?

Recommendations for further reading

Clark, H. H. (1996). *Using language.* Cambridge: Cambridge University Press.
Hauser, D. J., & Schwarz, N. (2016). Semantic prosody and judgment. *Journal of Experimental Psychology: General, 145*(7), 882–896.
Kashima, Y., & Lan, Y. (2013). Communication and language use in social cognition. In D. E. Carlston (Ed.), *The Oxford handbook of social cognition* (pp. 729–748). New York: Oxford University Press.
Maass, A. (1999). Linguistic intergroup bias: Stereotype perpetuation through language. In M. P. Zanna (Ed.), *Advances in experimental social psychology* (Vol. 31, pp. 79–121). San Diego, CA: Academic Press.

10 How the environment constrains social cognitive processing

Klaus Fiedler

In the broad definition introduced in Chapter 1, social cognition was defined as the construction of social reality, spanning the whole cycle from the input originating in the social environment to cognitive, motivational, and affective processes within the individual, and back to the social consequences of the resulting attitudes, judgments, and actions. In Chapter 2, we outlined three ingredients for the construction of social reality: input from the situation, input in the form of prior knowledge, and processes that operate on the input. The preceding chapters focused on general knowledge structures and on processes within the individual, while silently presupposing that cognitive and affective processes within the individual determine the manner in which stimulus information triggers social behavior. Let us now turn to intriguing research findings that demonstrate how the environment constrains the processes within the individual. In other words, let us delineate the intriguing interplay of environmental and cognitive factors that characterizes human interaction in distinct situations and institutions.

Social hypothesis testing: updating knowledge in the light of environmental data

Throughout the preceding chapters, we got to know a variety of experimental tasks that have been constructed to study social-cognitive phenomena. For instance, recall or recognition tasks have been used to study person memory, courtroom sentencing scenarios to study guilt attribution, priming procedures to study social stereotypes, and probability judgment tasks to investigate heuristics and cognitive biases. Outside the scientific laboratory, however, these various tasks are not presented in isolation by an experimenter. Rather, they appear intertwined with and embedded in diverse kinds of social interactions—as people try to get acquainted with each other, to achieve social influence, to buy or sell products, to evaluate performance or moral conduct; as they compare themselves and their own group to others and other groups, in dating, fighting, or deception episodes.

One feature that all of these task environments have in common is the *testing of social hypotheses*. Social hypothesis testing is the unifying paradigm used in the present chapter to illuminate the impact of environmental constraints on social cognition. As people interact with one another, they are permanently involved in asking questions or testing hypotheses related to all kinds of problems: How much interest does the other person show in my personality, in my private thoughts, in my feelings? How much can I attract the other? How much are the goods worth that I want to sell? How far can I go in pursuing my interests without appearing unfair? How do I compare to others in terms of morality and ability? And how does my ingroup compare to various outgroups? Does my conversation partner tell the truth or try to deceive me? Is that person my friend or my enemy?

Social life is replete with such hypothesis tests. In fact, we might be justified in saying that a great proportion of all social interaction can be subsumed under this paradigm. This central role assigned to hypothesis testing is nothing but a logical consequence of the generalized assumption, emphasized throughout this book, that social cognition is an active, knowledge-guided construction process, rather than a merely passive reaction to given stimuli. To the extent that people approach the world with prior knowledge and meaningful expectations in mind, the resulting process takes the form of dynamic hypothesis testing. Many prominent phenomena in social cognition—such as person memory, attribution, stereotypes, probability judgments, cognitive fallacies—are all embedded in this dynamic interplay between what information is available in the environment and what information is relevant to the individual's hypothesis-testing goals.

Confirmation bias

Hypothesis-testing episodes have their own internal structure and rules. One of the most intriguing features is that the hypotheses people use to explore their social ecology seem to have a built-in device for confirmation. All other things being equal, hypothesis tests are more likely to end up with an affirmative than with a negative answer (Hernandez & Preston, 2013; Nickerson, 1998). If we want to find out whether somebody else is mad, it is not unlikely that we find some supportive evidence. If we try to find out whether somebody is ingenious, we will presumably find some pertinent evidence. Tests for dishonesty will likely reveal dishonest people; tests for fairness and altruism will identify fair and helpful people. It is this affirmative, yes-responding echo of the social environment (Snyder, 1984) that makes experimental approaches to social hypothesis testing so interesting (Trope & Liberman, 1996). Testing suitable hypotheses, and avoiding others, can be used to confirm social stereotypes (Slusher & Anderson, 1987), to support attributions (Trope, 1986), to attain social influence (Wegner et al., 1981), and to justify performance evaluation (Rosenthal, 1991) and group decisions (Jonas, Schulz-Hardt, Frey, & Thelen, 2001). An analysis of this persistent tendency toward confirmation in social hypothesis testing reveals distinct ways in which the environment constrains social cognition.

Motivational versus environmental origins of confirmation bias

A substantial part of social interaction is driven by two prominent classes of hypotheses that have intrigued philosophers and psychologists alike (Greve, 2001): *beliefs* and *desires*. People are either concerned with hypotheses about the truth of some belief, or about the means of fulfilling some desire. Some problem situations involve a mixture of both goals; people must find a compromise between an accuracy goal (find the truth about beliefs) and a motivational goal (realize some desire). In other words, cognitive as well as motivational influences suggest themselves as explanations of the pervasive tendency toward confirmation (Kunda, 1990; Pyszczynski & Greenberg, 1987; Snyder, 1984). Obviously, many hypotheses are verified in order to fulfil the individual's prior beliefs or personal motives.

Prominent examples of such "motivated cognition" phenomena include self-enhancement, unrealistic optimism, wishful thinking, and egocentric bias. Patients refuse to learn information about a terminal disease; we are more prone to recognize our own success and the failure of others than our own failure and the success of others; parents wish to preserve the belief that their son or daughter is high in academic achievement and not involved in drug abuse; individuals overestimate their own compared to their spouses' household responsibilities (see Chapter 6, egocentric bias); and researchers selectively expose themselves to evidence that confirms their own theory and disconfirms alternative theories.

Controlled experiments provide systematic empirical evidence for such motivated biases. In one study by Dawson, Gilovich, and Regan (2002), participants learned that they (allegedly) obtained a high or a low score on a test of emotional lability, and were then engaged in a test of a hypothesis that could have threatening implications for themselves; when participants with a high emotional lability score were asked to gather information to test the hypothesis "If someone is high in emotional lability, he or she is likely to die early," they avoided looking at cases that might have confirmed the unpleasant hypothesis. Evidence such as this supports the conclusion that individuals' hypothesis-testing behavior is sometimes driven by self-serving motives such as avoiding ego-threat or enhancing self-esteem.

However, at other times, individuals' hypothesis-testing behavior is not determined by self-serving motives. Under more auspicious [favorable] conditions, they may try to do their best to test a hypothesis as rationally and accurately as possible. But the enigmatic confirmation bias persists even then. The outcomes of social hypothesis testing may still be subject to systematic biases, even when all cognitive processes within the individual are unbiased, simply because the social and physical environment does not make all information equally accessible. In other words, confirmation biases may be rooted in certain properties of the information environment (Fiedler, 2000a).

Analyzing the environmental input to social cognition

The next sections are devoted to three research approaches that all highlight the need to analyze the environmental stimulus input that impinges on the individual's mind, as distinguished from cognitive and motivated influences within the human mind. First, hypothesis testers may be more likely to be exposed to certain kinds of data because of the individual's social role or his or her selective information-search strategies (referred to as "self-generated data" in what follows). For instance, a journalist with an affinity toward one political party may be selectively exposed to information related to this particular party. Second, hypothesis testers may inadvertently *produce*, in the target person, the data needed to support a hypothesis (referred to as "self-produced data" in what follows). The journalist, for instance, may unintentionally apply an interview strategy that leads or misleads a politician to provide confirming evidence for the guiding hypothesis. Third, the external environment may afford more opportunities to learn some stimulus data rather than other kinds (referred to as "externally constrained data" in what follows).

For instance, as undesirable information about political activities is more likely to be concealed than desirable information, a positivity bias in publication will mainly benefit the one party that constitutes the majority of a journalist's work environment. Let us see how these three types of influences together impose constraints on social hypothesis testing, making confirmation more likely than disconfirmation.

Self-generated data: the information-search paradigm

One classical investigation of information search leading to confirmation bias was conducted four decades ago by Snyder and Swann (1978), using a simulated interview task that was later adopted in many subsequent studies. In a kind of get-acquainted interview, some participants were instructed to find out whether their interview target was extraverted, and others whether their interview partner was introverted. For this purpose, participants would select suitable interview questions from an extended list, and target persons replied to these questions. Based on the resulting sequence of interview questions and answers, impression judgments of the interviewees were provided by the interviewers themselves as well as by third-person observers who were not themselves involved in the information-search process.

The focus of interview questions and the resulting person impressions were systematically biased toward the interviewer's starting hypothesis. Across four experiments, interviewers who tested the extraversion hypothesis asked more questions about such extraverted behaviors as partying, making friends, chatting, and joking. In contrast, when interviewers focused on the introversion hypothesis, their questions invited respondents to talk about such introverted topics as spending time alone, silence, or reading a book (see Illustration 10.1). Because the question focus facilitated confirming responses by the interviewees—they could provide some evidence for virtually all questions—there was a general tendency to find confirmation for whatever hypothesis the participants happened to test. This confirming tendency was also apparent in subsequent impression judgments made by the interviewers themselves as well as by the passive observers.

Personal desires and prior beliefs could not account for these findings, because the direction of hypothesis was manipulated and participants were randomly assigned to the two experimental groups. Note also that the communication partners could not directly see or hear each other, so that interviewers could not subtly communicate the hypothesis through non-verbal or para-verbal communication as in Rosenthal's (1966) seminal work on experimenter effects. Moreover, the results did not reflect selective memory for hypothesis-confirming interview responses or distorted judgment processes that were only sensitive to observations congruent with the starting hypothesis. Rather, the resulting impressions were largely determined by an information-search process that provided more evidence for extraverted behavior in the extraversion condition, and for introverted behavior in the introversion condition.

How could this happen? Analyses of the questions selected as suitable for the interview revealed that the hypothesis confirmation effect was already apparent in the initial stage of information search (see Illustration 10.1). In accordance with the task instructions, interviewers of the extraversion group typically asked questions that created rich opportunities for targets to exhibit extraverted responses. Examples of such questions are "What would you do if you wanted to liven things up at a party?" or "What kind of situation do you seek out if you want to meet new people?"

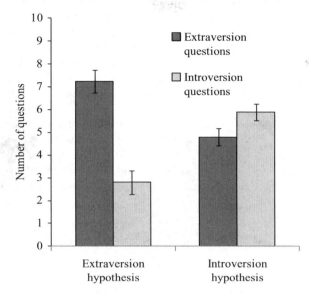

Illustration 10.1 Mean number of extraversion and introversion questions when testing an extraversion hypothesis (interview partner is an extravert) versus an introversion hypothesis (interview partner is an introvert), as reported by Snyder and Swann (1978, Investigation 2)

In contrast, interviewers of the introversion group typically asked questions such as "In what situations do you wish you could be more outgoing?" or "What things do you dislike about loud parties?" Such questions would typically elicit more introverted and less extraverted responses in the interview target.

For several reasons, though, the hypothesis testers' personal motives or biased expectations do not provide a sufficient explanation of the confirmation bias. After all, interviewers had no vested interest or need to confirm their personal expectations. Moreover, they did not prescribe the interviewees' responses. Thus, rather than blaming the interviewers and their internal motives, we must look for additional factors in the hypothesis verification process. Even though the interviewers were apparently not driven by strong beliefs or motives to confirm either extraversion or introversion, they may have been influenced by what they *believed* to be the experimenter's expectancy or the purpose of the experimental game. Thus, in spite of the randomized allocation to hypothesis conditions, they may have internalized the task hypothesis they were assigned to, assuming that "If I am to look for extraversion, extraversion must be a reasonable guess. The experimenter must know why the task is chosen this way." So, does the verification effect reflect the influence of directly or subtly conveyed demands or expectancies?

Prior expectancy or hypothesis focus?

This question was soon tackled by Semin and Strack (1980), who demonstrated that no expectancies need to underlie the hypotheses that tend to be verified. Semin and

Strack (1980) manipulated expectancies and hypothesis focus in an orthogonal design. In two experimental conditions, information about the interview target's profession was used to create the expectancy that the target is probably an extravert (salesman) or an introvert (librarian). Within both expectancy groups, different subgroups of participants received instructions to find out whether their interview partner was an extravert or an introvert. The latter manipulation of the externally defined task purpose clearly governed the process of information search; the expectancy manipulation had little influence. Regardless of whether the target was a salesman or a librarian, interviewers instructed to test the extraversion hypothesis asked more questions about extraverted topics (parties, jokes, friends), whereas interviewers in the introversion condition asked relatively more questions about introverted topics (privacy, meditation, contemplation). Thus, even when interviewers were not biased toward prior expectancies or beliefs but simply cooperated with the experimental task instructions, they asked different questions that solicited different interview responses.

Presuppositions and the logic of conversation

Another aspect of Snyder and Swann's (1978) original paradigm that might have influenced the interviewers' information search is that the pool of questions offered by the experimental materials contained rather blatant *presuppositions*. For instance, rather than asking, in an open format, whether the target is occasionally the one who livens up the party, the question presupposed that the target does and merely asked *how* the target filled this role. Presuppositions, as opposed to open, unbiased questions, afford a common linguistic device used for leading questions and suggestive manipulation, as evident from research on eyewitness testimony (Loftus, 1979; Roper & Shewan, 2002). This aspect of the linguistic task environment should have also contributed to the confirmation bias.

   However, the phenomenon of hypothesis confirmation is by no means confined to presuppositions or similar conversation tricks. When similar experiments were conducted using open questions rather than presuppositions (e.g., Fiedler, Walther, & Nickel, 1999; Zuckerman, Knee, Hodgins, & Miyake, 1995), the outcome remained largely the same. Depending on the hypothesis focus, participants would search for more information about typically extraverted situations when testing the extraversion hypothesis, and for more information about typically introverted behaviors when testing the introversion hypothesis.

Positive testing

Klayman and Ha (1987) suggested the term *positive testing* to denote the prevailing tendency in information search to concentrate on positive examples of the hypothesis being tested (e.g., for examples of extraverted behavior when testing the extraversion hypothesis). Questions about extraverted situations (like parties) promise to provide direct and diagnostic information about extraversion, rather than only indirect information about the absence of introversion. Positive observations about the target's multiple social contacts or his or her ability to tell jokes provide more cogent evidence for extraversion than the failure to observe behaviors in private or lonely situations. Indeed, the absence of introversion does not imply high extraversion, simply because the social world is not strictly dichotomous. Somebody may be neither introverted nor extraverted, or high in both extraversion and introversion. Therefore, because the dimensional constraints on antonyms are very weak (e.g., extraversion and introversion are not mutually exclusive), performing direct positive tests is a rational and effective strategy most of the time (Oaksford & Chater, 1994).

Thus, rather than reflecting personal motives or irrational biases, the interviewers' positive testing may reflect a rational strategy tailored to the demands of the experimental task: to diagnose extraversion (introversion), concentrating on extraverted (introverted) behaviors and situations is simply more informative than gathering indirect information about the opposite pole of the dimension. Note also that such positive testing need not automatically result in an unwarranted confirmation bias. Rather, the outcome of the hypothesis-testing process depends, eventually, on whether the target person (i.e., the interviewee) provides confirming or disconfirming responses.

Self-produced data: self-fulfilling prophecies

The aforementioned findings corroborate the contention that a bias in the questions selected by the participant alone cannot provide a satisfying explanation of the resulting confirmation bias. Questions alone can provide neither confirmation nor disconfirmation. The outcome of information search depends obviously on the target person's answers.

So let us consider the object role in the social environment, played by the targets or interviewees. Complementary to the findings presented in the last section, emphasizing that hypothesis confirmation can reflect the hypothesis tester's "normal" and "rational" search behaviors, other evidence highlights the critical role played by the hypothesis target. Persons or groups, or even animal targets, often do exhibit the kind of behavior with which they are associated in a hypothesis. For instance, in demonstrations of self-fulfilling prophecies (Jussim, 1991; Madon, Jussim, & Eccles, 1997; Rosenthal & Jacobson, 1968), such as when experimenters expect white rats to outperform grey rats or when teachers expect middle-class children to outperform lower-class children, the rats or children actually end up confirming the expectations, justifying and actually supporting hypothesis confirmation. Let us now turn to empirical evidence for these kinds of self-fulfilling prophecies, with an emphasis on the role of the hypothesis target.

Acquiescence tendency

For the hypothesis tester's one-sided test strategies to bring about a confirmation bias, the targets have to provide answers that complete the confirmation cycle. However, by what rule is the target "obliged" to follow the hypothesis tester's question content? The answer suggested in a series of studies by Zuckerman et al. (1995) refers to a long-known phenomenon called acquiescence.

Using the same simulated interview paradigm as in Snyder's early work, Zuckerman et al. (1995) demonstrated that the interviewer's strategy to ask positive questions is complemented by the interviewee's tendency to give positive answers. In one condition, the hypothesis to be tested focused on the *positive* poles of four trait dimensions: trusting/suspicious, calm/worried, extraverted/introverted, optimistic/pessimistic.

In a second condition, the task focus was on the *negative* poles. In a third condition, both hypotheses were presented and participants had to find out which one of the two hypotheses was correct. As in previous work, most participants who tested one-sided hypotheses applied a positive-test strategy, asking more questions about the hypothesis under investigation than about the opposite hypothesis. Thus, when testing positive attributes, they tended to ask more questions about positive attributes and fewer questions about negative attributes than when focusing on the negative poles. However, at the same time, the interviewees exhibited a so-called *acquiescence* tendency: regardless of which type of questions they were asked, they tended to provide confirming answers. Such a yes-responding bias has been long known in survey research and interview methodology (Ray, 1983). It may reflect the basic cooperative attitude that characterizes survey respondents much like communication participants in general (Grice, 1975; see also Chapter 9, this volume). Together, these two tendencies, interviewers' positive-test focus and interviewees' acquiescence bias to provide positive responses, create a pattern of social interaction rules that eventually results in confirmation for the hypothesis under investigation (see Illustration 10.2).

The cooperation principle

Again, it is important to note that this interplay of two strategies, the interviewer's positive testing and the interviewee's acquiescence, is independent of personal motives, beliefs, or desires. On the contrary, the ubiquitous tendency to confirm and maintain hypotheses can be partially understood as a byproduct of an essentially cooperative communication process (Grice, 1975), driven by pro-social motives. According to Snyder (1984), social interaction is essentially cooperative, and by extension confirmative (Misyak, Melkonyan, Zeitoun, & Chater, 2014; Tomasello, Melis, Tennie, Wyman, & Herrmann, 2012). Interviewers cooperate by asking informative questions and interviewees cooperate by filling the interviewers' questions with positive content. The confirmation bias, at least to some degree, can be a side effect of such intrinsically cooperative behavior.

Targets' hedonic value

Last but not least, targets (i.e., interviewees) can constrain the hypothesis-testing process by virtue of their hedonic value. Whereas attractive targets bind the individual's attention and encourage continued interaction, aversive or painful targets tend to repel the individual and to truncate the process of information search.

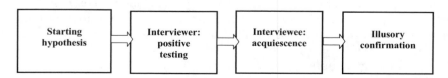

Illustration 10.2 Positive testing and acquiescence response tendency as mediating factors in the illusory confirmation of social hypotheses

Source: After Zuckerman et al. (1995)

This phenomenon has been termed the "hot-stove effect" (Denrell & March, 2001). Just as we avoid future contact with the hot-stove after we have burnt our hands, we avoid future interaction with a person or a setting experienced as unpleasant or even traumatic. Thus, we will probably not return to a restaurant where we have experienced very bad service or even sickness (even when the sickness was caused by a virus rather than the food served in the restaurant). As a consequence of this truncated interaction, there will be no chance to correct for the negative impression of the target. Because there are so many alternative restaurants (at least in urban environments), why should we return to a place that was the source of such displeasure?

Following the analogy to a hot stove, Denrell (2005) developed a hedonic-sampling model that predicts persistent negativity effects when further interaction with unpleasant targets is truncated so that negative initial or intermediate impressions cannot be corrected. In contrast, there are usually many opportunities to correct for premature positive impressions, because positive targets will very likely continue to be attended to and experienced in the future.

An intriguing and inspiring experimental demonstration of this asymmetric negative effect was provided by Fazio, Eiser, and Shook (2004) in an attitude learning paradigm called "BeanFest." Analogous to the foraging task of animals to increase the energy supply of their food, participants were asked to learn to discriminate between good beans (supplying high energy) and bad beans (supplying low energy). The graphically represented beans varied across ten levels in two dimensions, shape (slender vs. rotund) and surface (number of speckles); that is, there were $10 \times 10 = 100$ sorts of beans altogether. On every trial of the learning game, participants clicked with the computer mouse on one bean and received feedback about the value of the selected bean. As they were motivated to maximize the energy supply (transformed into performance-contingent payment at the end of the experiment), they successfully learned to discriminate between good and bad beans. Crucially, however, learning was asymmetrically stronger for negative than for positive beans. Participants not only very effectively learned to avoid clicking again on beans that had been directly linked with negative feedback, they also learned to avoid beans that resembled the carriers of negative feedback in terms of similar shape and surface pattern. Thus, once particular beans were charged with negative valence, the resulting negative attitude would persist and spread to similar beans.

Closer inspection of the underlying learning and sampling process clarifies, however, that attitude learning will not always result in such a persistent negativity bias. This will only occur when the avoidance of hedonically unpleasant stimuli is acquired very fast and when the subsequent avoidance of negative sources is then so radical that negative impressions become irreversible. In contrast, when the learning of initially neutral attitudes grows slowly and gradually, a positivity bias may be obtained, reflecting more polarized positive attitudes due to enhanced attention to and sampling from pleasant targets (Fiedler, Wöllert, Tauber, & Hess, 2013).

Externally constrained data: environmental learning processes

Something is still missing in the emerging theoretical account of social hypothesis confirmation. Upon closer inspection, neither selective sampling, nor positive testing, nor acquiescence can fully explain why most social hypotheses are ultimately *confirmed.* For instance, when testing whether the target person is extraverted, asking many extraversion questions (positive testing) that elicit mostly Yes responses (acquiescence) may increase the *absolute* number of observations that seem to support extraversion. However, logically, this may not warrant hypothesis confirmation, simply because the *relative* rate of confirming observations may be the same for extraversion and introversion. Thus, it is possible that clearly fewer introversion questions produce the same proportion of Yes responses, or even a higher proportion. A sufficient account of hypothesis confirmation must therefore explain why the same (or even a slightly higher) proportion of confirmation is worth less in a small than in a large sample. Let us consider this puzzle more closely.

Number of observations or learning trials

Assuming twice as many extraversion as introversion questions and twice as many Yes as No responses (Illustration 10.3), the stimulus input may, for example, consist of 8 Yes responses to 12 extraversion questions and 4 Yes responses to 6 introversion questions. Thus, the relative proportion of confirmation for extraversion and introversion is the same: $8/12 = 4/6 = 67\%$. Only the absolute amount of information is higher in the former case. In order to explain that interviewers and observers arrive at more extraverted impressions of the target, one has to assume that a ratio of $8/12$ observations is worth more, psychologically, than a ratio of $4/6$. Although this may appear strange at first glance, it is easily understood upon some reflection. Just like any learning process, learning that a hypothesis tends to be confirmed increases with increasing number of trials. Even though the ratio of confirmation is the same, there are 12 trials to learn the 67% confirmation rate for extraversion, but only 6 trials to

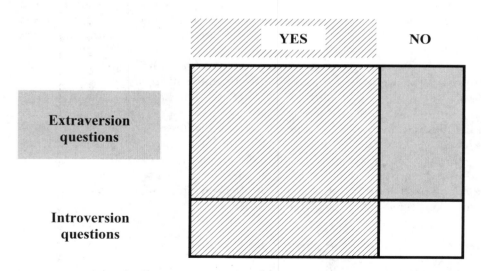

Illustration 10.3 Graphical illustration of the fact that although a high prevalence of extraversion questions (grey area) goes along with a high proportion of Yes responses (dashed area), the relative proportion of Yes responses is the same for extraversion and introversion questions

learn the same rate for introversion, thus allowing for m
focal hypothesis than for the reverse hypothesis.

Such a simple learning principle helps us to underst
cation. The learning principle is more general than the
testing and acquiescence; there are many other possibl
learning trials may not be the same for all targets. An
colleagues (1999) substantiates this point. In a diagno:
were asked to find out whether the problems in a het
Heike, were due to different aggression styles in men :
ticipants had to test the hypothesis that the male par
overt aggression whereas the female partner (Heike) sh
Participants could search information in a database
whether or not particular items of overt or covert aggr
down menu) had been observed in Peter and Heike
select an item of overt or covert aggression and ask whe
observed in Peter or Heike. The feedback rate was held
Yes responses. That is, regardless of whether Peter or F
sion was being considered, the computer confirmed the
75% probability (or acquiescence rate).

After the learning stage was over, participants esti
cies with which overt and covert aggression had been o
They also rated their impressions of Peter and Heike
to overt and covert aggression. As in previous experime
characterized by a marked tendency toward positive 1
asked more questions about overt aggression in Peter :
in Heike than about the reverse combinations. Howev
tion rate for all question topics was held constant at 7£
observations led to illusory verification. Frequency estii
attributed more overt than covert aggression to Peter
aggression to Heike (see Illustration 10.5). This effect w:

Illustration 10.4 There are many kinds of aggression. One way tc
           behaviors is by differentiating overt (e.g., using
           covert aggression (e.g., excluding others, lying).
           aggression is ascribed to men (left), and covert :

Source: After Zuckerman et al. (1995). Ollyy/Shutterstock.com, oliveror

80 —

60 —

40 —

20 —

0 —

Illustra

that a
Heike
Ad
asked
aggre
for th
cover
searc
(ficti
vary
Thus
sion
that 1
ing tl
in thi
In
instr
Pete
cove
ert a
envii
ficati

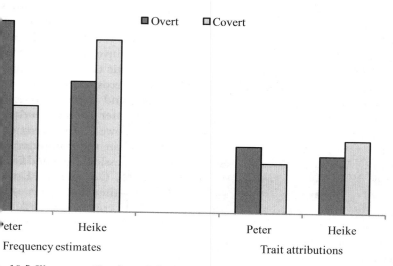

10.5 Illusory verification of the hypothesis that aggression tends to be covert in females (Heike) and overt in males (Peter), as demonstrated by Fiedler and colleagues (1999). Left panel: frequency estimates of overt versus covert aggression behavior; right panel: trait attributions related to overt (violence and peacefulness) versus covert aggression (scheming and frankness)

ger absolute number of observations was available for the Peter–overt and vert combination than for the Peter-covert and Heike-overt combination. onal experiments corroborated this interpretation. When participants were test the opposite hypotheses that Peter's aggression was covert and Heike's n overt (contrary to gender stereotypes), they still found confirmation cal hypotheses. Now participants confirmed that Peter tended to exhibit gression and Heike overt aggression. Moreover, when active information s eliminated and participants could only passively observe how another ·) participant gathered information on Peter and Heike, it was possible to number of observations independently of the direction of the hypothesis. n when the hypothesis asked participants to find out whether Peter's aggres- overt and Heike's covert, it was possible to manipulate *negative testing*, such observations referred to Peter's covert and to Heike's overt aggression (hold- firmation rate constant). What would determine the subsequent judgments dition?

tingly, the crucial determinant was the number of observations. When task ns focused on Peter-overt and Heike-covert, observing larger samples on ·rt and Heike-overt led to an opposite illusion. Peter was judged higher in n overt aggression, and Heike received higher ratings in overt than cov- sion. Apparently, the number of learning trials offered by the information ent can provide a very simple, parsimonious explanation for hypothesis veri- hese findings illustrate what it means to say that social hypothesis testing is constrained by the distribution of stimulus data in the environment, independently of motives and stereotypical beliefs.

Opportunity to learn in the environment

Illusory correlations against minorities

The simple rule that environmental learning increases with the number of trials can explain a very prominent type of illusory correlation. Hamilton and Gifford (1976) created a compelling experimental analogue of minority group derogation that motivated hundreds of follow-up studies using the same basic paradigm. Hamilton and Gifford reasoned that minorities are by definition less numerous than majorities. Moreover, in reality undesirable (i.e., norm-deviant) behaviors are less frequent than desirable (i.e., normative) behaviors. Mapping these realistic assumptions about the social ecology onto a group-judgment experiment, they constructed a stimulus series covering 39 behavior descriptions displayed by members of two social groups, denoted A and B (to avoid associations to real existing groups). The distribution of these 39 stimulus behaviors over the 2 × 2 combinations of groups (A vs. B) and evaluation (desirable vs. undesirable) is given in Illustration 10.6. Group A, the majority, appeared more frequently than Group B, the minority, and desirable behaviors were more frequent than undesirable behaviors, but the proportion of desirable behaviors was exactly the same for both groups (18 out of 26 for Group A → 9 out of 13 for Group B). In other words, the correlation between groups and evaluation was carefully set to zero.

Nevertheless, a systematically more favorable impression was created of the majority than of the minority, in spite of the constant rate of desirable behaviors in both groups. The illusory correlation was evident in several dependent measures. Frequency estimates of the number of positive versus negative behaviors shown by Group A and Group B members were biased in favor of A and against B. Group ratings on trait scales reflected more favorable impressions of A than of B. And in a cued-recall test, erroneous reproductions of the group associations of the stimulus behaviors were

	Majority Group A	Minority Group B
Desirable behaviors	18	9
Undesirable behaviors	8	4

Illustration 10.6 Stimulus distribution leading to illusory correlations, according to Hamilton and Gifford (1976). Although the same high ratio of desirable to undesirable behaviors holds for both groups, the majority Group A is more strongly associated with positive behaviors than the minority Group B

also to the advantage of the majority. These findings—which have been replicated in numerous experiments—are extremely provocative because they suggest a permanent source of bias against minorities. In a world in which norm-deviant behaviors are less frequent than normative behaviors, a systematic illusion will discriminate against minorities—even when there is no factual basis.

Originally, Hamilton and Gifford (1976) explained the illusory correlation phenomenon by assuming that negative behaviors by the minority, the most infrequent combination, is most distinctive and salient in the stimulus list and therefore most likely to be recalled. However, there is little evidence for such a memory advantage of undesirable minority behavior, and the learning perspective offers a simpler explanation. Even when all stimuli are equally distinctive or salient, the high positivity rate should be learned more readily and more completely for the larger group, A, than for the smaller group, B (cf. Illustration 10.6), due to unequal learning opportunities offered by the environment.

Illusory correlations more generally

Positing this interpretation in terms of unequal learning opportunities—that is, more opportunities to observe the prevailing positive behavior in the majority than in the minority—several implications suggest themselves. First, in a predominantly negative environment, when most behaviors are negative, we should expect a reversal: the smaller number of minority observations should then result in less negative minority evaluations. This prediction was indeed supported in several experiments (Fiedler, 1991; Hamilton & Gifford, 1976).

Second, we might expect analogous illusory correlations in many other situations in which the learning environment provides unequal learning opportunities, outside the domain of majority and minority groups. For instance, as a natural consequence of egocentric distance from one's self, our learning experience about our self is much richer and denser than that about other people. Assuming that everyday behavior is by default positive and norm-abiding, and that negative or norm-violating behavior is the exception, such an asymmetric learning environment affords more opportunities to learn about one's own than about others' predominantly positive behavior. The common self-serving bias to evaluate oneself in more positive terms than other people (Sedikides & Strube, 1995) can thus be explained as a predictable consequence of the same illusory correlation that causes the devaluation of minorities in the studies reviewed above.

Self-serving biases

Unrealistic optimism (Shepperd, Klein, Waters, & Weinstein, 2013; Weinstein, 1980), for instance, is the tendency to overestimate one's own abilities and positive outcomes and to underestimate one's risk of contracting a disease or suffering an accident. The risk associated with particular behaviors (e.g., breaking a leg, being robbed, getting divorced) is perceived to be lower for oneself than for other people. Most people agree that driving entails a sizable accident risk, but they assume that this risk is higher for other people than for themselves. Similarly, the probability of contracting AIDS from unsafe sexual contact is generally acknowledged, but much less for oneself than for other people.

In one study (Radcliffe & Klein, 2002), participants were asked to estimate whether they are more likely, less likely, or equally likely to experience a fatal heart attack compared to the average person. These estimates were then compared to an epidemiologically based assessment of their personal heart-attack risk. As it turned out, 56% of all participants were unrealistically optimistic and only 19% of the participants were accurate in estimating their risk. The remaining 25% were unrealistically pessimistic; they overestimated their heart attack risk.

According to the present environmental learning account, this variant of a self-serving bias might simply reflect the larger sample of self-referent than other-referent observations. Heart attacks, just like other diseases or accidents, are rare events with clearly lower base rates than healthy states. Granting a sufficiently large sample of participants in a study, the same base rates hold for the participants themselves as well as the others' in their life. However, because of the enhanced opportunity to gather self-related experience, the consistently high prevalence of positive and healthy outcomes should be more easily detected in themselves than in others. Consistent with this ecological account, the optimistic belief of being healthier and "better than average" (Alicke & Govorun, 2005) has been found to be reversed in situations in which negative outcomes are more likely and therefore more likely to be observed in oneself than in others.

For instance, Moore and Small (2007) found that people typically believe that they are better than others on easy tasks (when success is frequent), but they also tend to believe that they are worse than others on difficult tasks (when failure is frequent). Moore and Small explain this reversal in terms of the simple asymmetry of self- and other-related information: because the environment provides people with better and richer information about themselves than about others, self-referent judgments reflect the actually existing base rates of easy and difficult outcomes more accurately than other-referent judgments. Note also that this ecological explanation might account for the 25% pessimistic participants in Radcliffe and Klein (2002), who may simply find more evidence for certain pessimistic health outcomes in themselves than in others.

The same environmental learning approach allows further insight into otherwise confusing evidence on overconfidence. Moore and Healey (2008) distinguish between three different phenomena for which the same label, overconfidence, is commonly used: *overestimation* of one's own ability, performance, level of control, or likelihood of success relative to the actual values; *overplacement* of oneself relative to other people; and *overprecision* defined as exaggerated estimates of one's own correctness rates in subjective confidence judgments. The ecological impact of the hard–easy effect (according to the aforementioned research by Moore & Small, 2007) is largely confined to the first two phenomena. On difficult tasks, when failure outcomes prevail, people overestimate their own success but underplace themselves relative to others, whereas on easy tasks, when the modal outcome is success, people underestimate their success but overplace themselves relative to others.

A third implication says that illusory correlations should be reduced or fully disappear when the learning task is deprived of its uncertainty. Thus, although a majority described by a sample of 20 different extraverted behaviors and 10 introverted behaviors appears to be more extraverted than a minority described by a sample of 10 extraverted and 5 introverted behaviors, the illusion disappears when the different behavioral descriptions are replaced by constant repetitions of the terms "extraverted" and "introverted" (Kutzner & Fiedler, 2015). With this replacement, the learning process quickly reaches an asymptote even with ten behaviors, and even the least attentive participants notice the higher prevalence of extraversion over introversion. Repeating the same constant trait labels ten more times in the majority condition will hardly produce further learning.

The adaptive value of environmental constraints on social cognition

So far, we have treated environmental constraints—such as unequal base rates or learning opportunities—as causes of illusions and biases. We have pointed out environmental origins for a variety of biases and shortcomings that are independent of the individual's beliefs and desires. However, importantly, the same environmental factors that lead to cognitive illusions can also be quite helpful and useful. Like all perceptual and cognitive illusions, they often serve useful adaptive functions (Armor, Massey, & Sackett, 2008). Unequal base rates, for example, not only lead to biased learning about majorities and minorities or about the Self and others, they also afford a proxy for many everyday purposes. Let us first illustrate the wisdom of base rates with respect to the amazing accuracy of person judgments based on no acquaintance at all (Levesque & Kenny, 1993).

The amazing accuracy of judgments based on minimal information

Over two decades ago, Ambady and Rosenthal (1992) for the first time reviewed the impressive evidence for the accuracy of person judgments informed by "thin slices of expressive behavior": this might be a very brief film clip (Ambady, 2010) or even a still photograph of a face (Samochowiec, Wänke, & Fiedler, 2010). Oftentimes, the diagnostic and prognostic value of these minimal information samples is almost as high as the validity reached through extended diagnostic investigations or assessment centers (but there is also conflicting evidence, see Chapter 5). Lie detection provides a good example for high validity. When the task is to distinguish between lies and true statements in a series of communications where half of the statements are lies, the chance rate of accurate responses is 50%. For participants in a thin-slices experiment, however, accuracy rates significantly different from chance are observed (Albrechtsen, Meissner, & Susa, 2009). Similar findings have been reported for intuitive judgments of personality characteristics (Levesque & Kenny, 1993), and political orientation (Samochowiec et al., 2010; Todorov, Mandisodza, Goren, & Hall, 2005).

Environmental base rates

What strategy might enable non-expert participants to provide accurate diagnostic judgments informed by minimal data, without engaging in laborious diagnostic investigations? One possible answer is that accurate intuitive judgments may rely on very common knowledge about the most prevalent base rates. When classifying unknown

Box 10.1 Accuracy rates of inferences about dichotomous person attributes observed by Olivola and Todorov (2010)

Olivola and Todorov (2010) based their study on "big data" from a popular website called "What's my image?" (www.whatsmyimage.com), which invites users to make inferences about person images from photos. From an initial sample of 1,005,406 guesses about 901 target photos, they selected data referring to the 11 dichotomous characteristics included in the graph below. In addition to the accuracy of these website guesses (medium grey bars), which provide interesting evidence for the "wisdom of crowds" (Surowiecki, 2004), the figure also provides, for comparison, the accuracy of two measures of a base rate driven strategy. The light grey bars indicate the percentage of accurate guesses that would be reached by always predicting the dichotomy level with the objectively higher base rate. Moreover, the dark grey bars indicate the accuracy of a strategy that relies on 98 students' subjective base rate estimates.

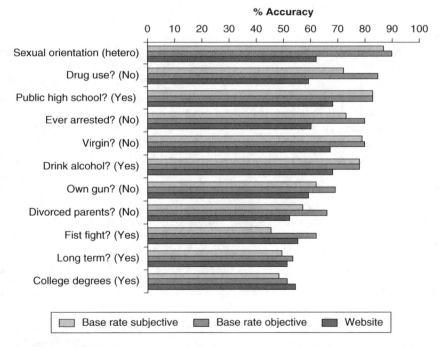

Accuracy rates of inferences about dichotomous person attributes observed by Olivola and Todorov (2010), either from facial appearance in a website or by predicting the attribute level with the higher subjective or objective base rate (as indicated in parentheses).

Apparently, both base rate strategies, whether relying on objective data or on subjective estimates, clearly outperform the collective wisdom in the webpage,

(continued)

(continued)

except for characteristics with base rates close to 50% (items 10 and 11 in the bottom part of the diagram). On the one hand, this means that ecological base rates contain more diagnostic information than the facial features contained in the photos. On the other hand, the ease and accuracy with which base rates can be estimated subjectively underscores the adaptive value of base rate strategies.

target persons on dichotomous attributes such as homosexual versus heterosexual, left-handed versus right-handed, or being a twin versus not, the best strategy may be to go for the option with the higher base rate. As the base rates of heterosexual orientation, right-handed people, and non-twins are much higher than the base rates of homosexual orientation, left-handed people, and twins, consistently predicting the high base rate option affords a maximizing strategy.

Box 10.1 presents a study by Olivola and Todorov (2010) that corroborates the prognostic value of base rate driven strategies when it comes to inferring personality characteristics from faces.

Thus, returning to the earlier topic of lie detection, a good strategy might be to rely on the base rate of behaviors or events reported in communications: classify a statement as a lie if the base rate of the reported event or behavior is low (e.g., "I have been a world champion in judo," "This morning, I came late because the bus driver forgot the direction"); classify a statement as true if it asserts high base rate facts (e.g., "I have downloaded a weather app to my smartphone," "As a student, I greatly enjoyed apartment sharing"). Hardly any other strategy that attempts to exploit the predictive value of specific linguistic or emotional symptoms can enhance accuracy beyond the level that can be reached with a simple and agnostic base rate driven strategy.

At the most general level, the so-called truth bias in lie detection, that is, the bias to classify too many communications as truthful rather than deceptive (Street, Bischof, Vadillo, & Kingstone, 2015), may reflect a justified base rate driven adaptive strategy. Because in reality truth is the norm (Grice, 1975), so that the base rate of true statements is much higher than the base rate of lies, a reasonable strategy under high uncertainty is to assume what is more prevalent. Although the truth bias is indeed a bias, it may nevertheless reflect an adaptive strategy.

Impact of facial appearance

While these findings highlight the low diagnostic value of facial appearance cues relative to ecological base rates, facial cues are by no means irrelevant. Indeed, regardless of their diagnostic accuracy, facial features may function as carriers of social stereotypes and biased hypothesis testing (e.g., Dotsch, Wigboldus, Langner, & van Knippenberg, 2008; Dotsch, Wigboldus, & van Knippenberg, 2011). To illustrate, Mannes (2013) showed that, consistent with a common stereotypical hypothesis, men with shaved heads are perceived to be more dominant, taller, and stronger than men with full heads of hair. Shaving was also shown to afford a successful means of improving the social impression of men with natural hair loss.

Impressive evidence for the impact of facial appearance comes from research on the babyface stereotype. Adult people whose appearance fits the babyface schema (i.e., large, round eyes, high, wide forehead, narrow cheeks, cf. Berry & Zebrowitz-McArthur, 1988) are perceived to be more childlike, naive, and suggestible than people with a more mature-looking face. As a consequence, when a defendant's guilt is tested in court trials, the defendant's facial appearance has a profound effect on the perceived guilt and the severity of the suggested punishment. Crimes committed by delinquents with a babyface are judged less severely than the same crimes committed by mature-looking people, especially when the crime is based on naive complicity (Zebrowitz, Voinescu, & Collins, 1996). The babyface effect may reflect a deeply inherited instinct, but research by Zebrowitz and Franklin (2014) stresses the impact of learning experiences, pointing to distinct associations of babyfaceness in older and younger judges.

Thus, although faces constitute a rich source of information in the social environment—signaling emotions, intentions, and dispositions (e.g., Knutson, 1996; Walker, Schönborn, Greifeneder, & Vetter, 2017; Walker & Vetter, 2016)—facial cues may often be misleading and mediators of systematic bias. In game-theoretical task contexts, such as an ultimatum game (Reed, DeScioli, & Pinker, 2014), facial stimuli may trigger strategic hypothesis testing. In the ultimatum game, proposers must decide what part of an endowment they offer the responder, who may either accept or reject the offer. If the responder rejects the offer, neither the proposer nor the responder will receive anything. When presented with an angry facial expression, proposers in an ultimatum game offered a larger proportion of their endowment to responders than when exposed to neutral facial expressions. The authors interpreted this finding as evidence for the notion that angry expressions function as honest signals that enhance the credibility of threats.

Likewise, in the context of political judgment, research by Samochowiec et al. (2010) and by Todorov et al. (2005) suggests that the readiness to vote for a politician increases when his or her face is easily associated with the party he or she represents.

Conclusion

The research reviewed in this chapter highlights the insight that it is worthwhile taking the environment into account. Environmental constraints imposed on the input to social cognition—such as the frequency distribution of persons and groups and their attributes, psychological distance, and opportunities to learn—often predetermine judgments, decisions, and behaviors before the human mind comes into play. Therefore, the structure of the environment offers alternative accounts for many social-cognitive phenomena.

Chapter summary

1   Environmental information provides the input for social-cognitive processes. To understand cognitive processes, we have to understand the content and the structure of the stimulus input that impinges on the cognitive system.
2   Social individuals interact in distinct ways with their social environment. For various reasons, the outcome of this interaction often serves to confirm the hypothesis driving the interaction.

3   This pervasive confirmation bias, which is evident at virtually all stages of cognitive functioning, need not originate in cognitive or motivational biases.

4   Completely unbiased, regular processes of environmental learning can account for biased judgments and decisions, because social and physical reality is skewed in manifold ways, offering more opportunities to learn about some targets than about others.

5   Statistical base rates constitute a simple but very powerful ecological variable, which underlies distinct judgment biases, but which also affords a useful proxy for making accurate judgments under many conditions.

Discussion questions/topics

1   Are there fundamental differences in the nature of the stimulus information available about ingroups and outgroups? If so, try to characterize these differences.

2   What information environments (media, social networks, literature, communication habits, etc.) facilitate the development of prejudiced versus tolerant attitudes?

3   Under which circumstances does predicting the outcome with the highest base rate afford a useful judgment strategy?

4   Try to develop an alternative account of conformity in terms of the unequal role played by majority (mainstream) and minority (dissenter) positions in politics, social media, or science.

Recommendations for further reading

Fiedler, K. (2000). Beware of samples! A cognitive-ecological sampling approach to judgment biases. *Psychological Review, 107*(4), 659–676.

Galesic, M., Olsson, H., & Rieskamp, J. (2012). Social sampling explains apparent biases in judgments of social environments. *Psychological Science, 23*(12), 1515–1523.

Nickerson, R. S. (1998). Confirmation bias: A ubiquitous phenomenon in many guises. *Review of General Psychology, 2*(2), 175–220.

Snyder, M. (1984). When belief creates reality. In L. Berkowitz (Ed.), *Advances in experimental social psychology* (Vol. 18, pp. 247–305). New York: Academic Press.

Todd, P. M., & Gigerenzer, G. (2012). *Ecological rationality: Intelligence in the world.* New York: Oxford University Press.

Trope, Y., & Liberman, A. (1996). Social hypothesis testing: Cognitive and motivational mechanisms. In E. T. Higgins, A. W. Kruglanski, E. T. Higgins, A. W. Kruglanski (Eds.), *Social psychology: Handbook of basic principles* (pp. 239–270). New York: Guilford Press.

Glossary

Aboutness principle   Tendency to perceive information that comes to mind (including feelings) as being about judgmental targets that are currently in the focus of attention.

Accessibility   The ease and speed with which information stored in memory is found and retrieved.

Accountability   Procedure to have research participants expect to be held accountable for a generated judgment to others. Used to foster systematic (as opposed to heuristic) information processing.

Acquiescence bias   Tendency to provide more Yes than No responses in interviews and survey research.

Action priming   Facilitation of manifest actions in accordance with the pragmatic implications of a preceding prime stimulus.

Activation   Transfer of information from inactive long-term memory to active working memory.

Affect as information   The notion that affective states may serve as information in judgment and decision making.

Affect misattribution procedure   In the affect misattribution procedure, affective reactions to neutral stimuli (e.g., holograms) are used to infer implicit attitudes toward the preceding prime stimuli.

Anchoring and adjustment   An assimilation of a judgment toward a numeric value that has previously been considered.

Applicability   Applicability refers to whether a concept can potentially be used to give meaning to a specific stimulus. Whether or not the concept is actually used depends also on the accessibility of the concept.

Assimilation effect   Judgments of a stimulus are biased toward the implications of a context stimulus (cf. contrast effect).

Associative network   In an associative network, associations between concepts are represented as links between network nodes; the smaller the distance between nodes, the stronger the association between concepts.

Attention   Processes that enable individuals to selectively attend to the (social) environment.

Attribution   Individuals' inferences about the cause of behaviors or events.

Attribution theories   Theories that describe the processes involved when individuals try to explain behaviors or events.

Automatic processes   Cognitive processes that are not consciously initiated, requiring no or very little attentional resources (cf. controlled processes).

Availability heuristic   Rule of thumb for judging the frequency or probability of events on the basis of the ease with which relevant memories come to mind.

Base rate   Frequency of a characteristic in a relevant population or sample.

Bottom-up processing   Information processing that is driven by new stimulus input rather than by abstract knowledge structures in memory (cf. top-down processing).

Categorical priming   Facilitation of categorical judgments or decisions after a category has been primed in a preceding stage of the task.

Category   Elementary knowledge structure; class of functionally similar objects sharing one or more features.

Cognitive consistency   The extent to which different cognitions are compatible with each other, rather than having conflicting implications.

Cognitive feelings   Subjective experiences resulting from cognitive processing. For instance, the feeling of familiarity denotes the subjective experience of having prior experience (cf. fluency).

Cognitive interview   Non-directive interview technique developed to improve the quality of interview data and witness reports in the legal context. In a cognitive interview, the interviewer refrains from imposing fixed questions and response restrictions on the interview, leaving it up to the interviewee to develop his or her own retrieval structure

Cognitive miser   Metaphor for the assumption that individuals try to avoid elaborative and extensive information processing and often rely on simplifying short-cuts and heuristics.

Concept-driven processing   See top-down processing.

Confirmation bias   Systematic tendency in social hypothesis testing to confirm the hypothesis being tested. A variety of causal factors contribute to producing confirmation biases.

Conjunction fallacy   Overestimating the likelihood of a joint (conjunct) occurrence of characteristics on the basis of the similarity between the conjunct characteristics and the judgmental target.

Consistency seekers   Perspective on the social thinker which emphasizes that individuals experience an aversive state when they hold inconsistent beliefs about the social world. Because individuals try to avoid or eliminate this aversive state, they process information in a biased fashion so that perceived inconsistencies are reduced.

Construal level theory   The basic tenet of this theory holds that with increasing psychological distance from the social individual, targets are construed at increasingly abstract levels. Differences in construal may produce systematic differences in judgments and decisions.

Constructive memory   Self-generated, imagined, or inferred information is erroneously remembered as if it had been actually experienced.

Context dependency   The notion that social judgments (and the underlying processes) are highly dependent on the situational context in which they are formed. For example, a person may be judged more positively in one situation than in another situation simply because different standards of comparisons are accessible and applied.

Contrast effect   Judgments of a stimulus are biased in the direction opposite to the implications of a context stimulus (cf. assimilation effect).

Controlled processes   Cognitive processes that are consciously initiated by the individual, usually requiring substantial cognitive resources (cf. automatic processes).

Conversational norms   Implicit principles of communication that facilitate communication and serve as a basis for inferring the meaning of statements beyond what is said explicitly (cf. maxims of communication).

Correspondence bias   Tendency to interpret observed behavior as caused by dispositions of the actor rather than the situation (also called the fundamental attribution error).

Cue   Stimulus that is used as a signal or hint in a cognitive process (e.g., heuristic or retrieval cue).

Data-driven processing   See bottom-up processing.

Ease of retrieval   The ease or difficulty associated with retrieving information from memory. For instance, it may feel easy or difficulty to recall the name of a person you have only met once before (cf. fluency).

Emotions   One type of affective feelings. Emotions usually have a clear referent (i.e., emotions are always *about* something, such as being angry about the behavior of another person); compared to mood states, emotions are more intense, salient, and of limited duration.

Encoding   Various processes that are involved when an external stimulus is transformed into an internal representation. This requires that the external stimulus is given some meaning by relating the new stimulus to prior knowledge.

Episodic memory   Memory of experienced events that are tied to particular times and places.

Evaluative priming   Facilitation of cognitive processing and responding after a preceding prime stimulus of the same valence.

Feeling of knowing   The experience of knowing some particular piece of information although it cannot be recalled at this very moment.

Fluency   The ease or difficulty associated with any kind of cognitive processing.

Framing effects   Preferences of decision alternatives depend on the wording and the format in which the decision options are framed, inviting different comparisons and cognitive representations of logically invariant outcomes and probabilities. Framing effects are essential to understanding prospect theory.

Frequency principle   Chronically increased accessibility of information in long-term memory due to frequent activation in the past.

Fundamental attribution error   See correspondence bias.

Hedonic marking   Notion that fluency is hedonically marked, in that easy processing is affectively positive.

Heuristic   Rule of thumb that allows quick and parsimonious judgment formation and decision making.

Heuristic cue   Information that is generally easily available and easily processed, and is linked (though not necessarily causally) to the judgment dimension of interest. It serves as a substitute. For instance, in the availability heuristic, perceived ease or difficulty serves as substitute information to judge frequency.

Hypothesis testing   The perception and learning of social knowledge about other people and objects in the environment can be characterized as an active hypothesis testing process, analogous to hypothesis testing in empirical science.

Illusory correlations   Observers believe to have seen a correlation in a series of stimulus events despite co-variation between events being nil or clearly lower.

Implicit Association Test (IAT)   Computerized procedure for measuring association tendencies related to attitudes and prejudice, based on the sorting speed for attitude objects and relevant attributes.

Incidental affect   Affective state that is caused by a source other than the judgmental target (cf. integral affect).

Integral affect   Affective state that is caused by the judgmental target (cf. incidental affect).

Judgmental target   Any object, event, or person that a judgment is formed about.

Judgments of learning   Judged likelihood that some piece of information can be later recalled from memory.

Linguistic category model   Taxonomy of four word classes that can be used as predicates to describe behaviors and events: descriptive action verbs, interpretive action verbs, state verbs, and adjectives. Different linguistic categories trigger systematically different attributions and cognitive inferences.

Linguistic intergroup bias   The tendency to describe positive ingroup behavior and negative outgroup behavior in more abstract linguistic terms than negative ingroup and positive outgroup behavior.

Knowledge structure   A super-ordinate term to denote mental knowledge representations such as concepts, schemas, scripts, or associative networks.

Maxims of communication   Four rules or maxims that underlie communication: the maxim of quality, the maxim of quantity, the maxim of relation, and the maxim of manner (cf. conversational norms).

Metacognition   Cognitive processes that involve the knowledge about knowledge or processes, for example knowing that we do not know the answer to a specific question.

Misattribution   Attributing some information such as a feeling to the judgmental target, even though it has a different cause (cf. incidental affect).

Mood   One type of affective feelings. Mood states usually are free of a referent (i.e., we may be in a positive or negative mood, without knowing why); compared to emotions, mood states are more subtle, less salient, and last longer.

Mood as information   See affect as information.

Mood-congruent judgment   The tendency to provide more positive judgments in positive rather than negative affective states.

Mood-congruent recall   The tendency to recall information that is congruent with one's current affective state, for example recalling positive events in happy moods and negative events in sad moods (cf. state dependency).

Mood management   The notion that individuals are motivated to maintain positive affective states and to eliminate negative affective states and consequently engage in cognitive processes that allow them to attain these goals; for example to intentionally think of positive events when being in a sad mood.

Motivated reasoning   Reasoning that is influenced by some motivation that shifts the conclusion in a particular direction (as opposed to non-directional motivational influences toward accuracy).

Motivated tacticians   This perspective on the social thinker reflects that individuals are quite flexible in their strategies when constructing subjective social reality. Sometimes they act as consistency seekers, sometimes as naive scientist, and sometimes as cognitive misers.

Naive scientists   Denotes one perspective on the social thinker, which holds that individuals gather all relevant information unselectively and construct social reality in an unbiased manner. The interpretation of the world is barely influenced by any form of wishful thinking, and conclusions are drawn in an almost logical, scientific manner. This perspective is particularly articulated in attribution theories.

Need for cognition   A person's chronic tendency to engage in effortful cognitive activities and to experience such activities as intrinsically rewarding.

Need for cognitive closure   A person's chronic tendency to perceive ambiguous situations as unpleasant and to desire definite answers and clear-cut interpretations that reduce ambiguity.

Network models   Conceptualizations of human memory that assume a system of nodes and connections.

Part-list cueing   Recall of the remaining stimuli in a list is impaired when part of the list is presented as a retrieval cue.

Positive testing   Selective information search for those events or behaviors that are stated in the hypothesis under focus.

Priming effect   The finding that a schema is more accessible when it has recently been presented or used in the past.

Recency principle   (a) Temporarily increased accessibility of information in long-term memory due to recent activation in the past (i.e., priming). (b) Increased probability of information to be remembered due to presentation at the end of a sequence.

Representativeness heuristic   A heuristic for judging category membership on the basis of various aspects of similarity.

Retrieval   Processes that are involved when individuals retrieve information from long-term memory into working memory.

Retrieval cue   External stimulus or internally generated response that is used to recall other pieces of information from memory.

Salience   The distinctiveness of a stimulus relative to the context reflected in its ability to attract attention (e.g., one male in group of females; a yellow dot among blue ones).

Schema   Knowledge structure linked to adaptive function. Once a schema is activated by specific events, specific reactions are triggered.

Script   Chronologically organized behavioral routine.

Self-fulfilling prophecy   An expectancy-based illusion in social hypothesis testing. Subject persons treat object persons in such a fashion that object persons eventually verify their original (often unjustified) expectations.

Self-serving bias   Motivated tendency to perceive and interpret social information in a self-serving manner, serving to support a positive image of the Self and of one's ingroup.

Semantic priming effect   Facilitation of cognitive processing and responding after a preceding semantically related prime stimulus.

Self-reference effect   Memory advantage for stimuli that have been encoded or judged in relation to the Self.

Shared-information effect   In group decision making, information shared by different group members is more likely to be considered, and is given more weight, than unshared information that is exclusively available to individual members.

State dependency   Describes the general finding that memory performance is enhanced if individuals are in the same psychological state (e.g., the same mood) at both, the time of encoding and the time of retrieval (cf. mood-congruent recall).

Stereotype   Category-like knowledge structure associated with a social group.

Stimulus   Person, object, or event which is external or internal and may elicit a response.

Stroop effect   Decreased performance in a task in which providing the correct answer requires ignoring an automatic reaction that is elicited by the stimulus. Such a task may be to name the ink color (e.g., yellow) in which a color name (e.g., "RED") is printed.

Subliminal   On a subconscious level, out of awareness.

Temporal contiguity   Co-occurrence of events in time.

Thin slices judgments   Judgments about enduring characteristics of individuals that are made on the basis of brief (typically less than a minute long) samples of behavior.

Top-down processing   Information processing that is driven by general, super-ordinate knowledge structures in memory (e.g., schema, stereotype) which influence the perception of new stimuli (cf. bottom-up processing).

Truncated search process   When searching in memory for applicable information (e.g., for encoding, or for computing a judgment) individuals are unlikely to search for all potentially relevant information but instead truncate the search processes. Due to this truncation, information that has a higher accessibility is more influential.

Working memory   The part of our memory system that is currently activated. It has little processing capacity. In order to enter into long-term memory, information has to pass the working memory. Conversely, information from long-term memory needs to enter into working memory in order to affect ongoing processes, judgments, and behaviors.

References

Aarts, H., Chartrand, T. L., Custers, R., Danner, U., Dik, G., Jefferis, V. E., & Cheng, C. M. (2005). Social stereotypes and automatic goal pursuit. *Social Cognition, 23,* 465–490. doi:10.1521/soco.2005.23.6.465.

Aarts, H., & Dijksterhuis, A. (1999). How often did I do it? Experienced ease of retrieval and frequency estimates of past behavior. *Acta Psychologica, 103,* 77–89. doi:10.1016/S0001-6918(99)00035-9.

Aarts, H., Verplanken, B., & Knippenberg, A. (1998). Predicting behavior from actions in the past: Repeated decision making or a matter of habit? *Journal of Applied Social Psychology, 28,* 1355–1374. doi:10.1111/j.1559-1816.1998.tb01681.x.

Abele, A. E. (2000). The experience of a positive mood and its impact on intergroup differentiation and stereotyping. In H. Bless & J. P. Forgas (Eds.), *The message within: The role of subjective experience in social cognition and behavior* (pp. 322–339). Philadelphia, PA: Psychology Press.

Abele, A. E., Gendolla, G. H. E., & Petzold, P. (1998). Positive mood and in-group–out-group differentiation in a minimal group setting. *Personality & Social Psychology Bulletin, 24,* 1343–1357. doi:10.1177/01461672982412008.

Abele, A. E., & Wojciszke, B. (2013). The Big Two in social judgment and behavior. *Social Psychology, 44,* 61–62. doi:10.1027/1864-9335/a000137.

Abelson, R. P., Aronson, E., McGuire, W. J., Newcomb, T. M., Rosenberg, M. J., & Tannenbaum, P. H. (Eds.). (1968). *Theories of cognitive consistency: A sourcebook.* Chicago: Rand-McNally.

Acker, F. (2008). New findings on unconscious versus conscious thought in decision making: Additional empirical data and meta-analysis. *Judgment and Decision Making, 3,* 292–303. doi:10.1037/0096-3445.136.4.569.

Adaval, R. (2003). How good gets better and bad gets worse: Understanding the impact of affect on evaluations of known brands. *Journal of Consumer Research, 30,* 352–367. doi:10.1086/378614.

Ajzen, I., & Fishbein, M. (1980). *Understanding attitudes and predicting social behaviour.* Englewood Cliffs, NJ: Prentice Hall.

Albrechtsen, J. S., Meissner, C. A., & Susa, K. J. (2009). Can intuition improve deception detection performance? *Journal of Experimental Social Psychology, 45,* 1052–1055. doi:10.1016/j.jesp.2009.05.017.

Alexopoulos, T., Fiedler, K., & Freytag, P. (2012). The impact of open and closed mindsets on evaluative priming. *Cognition & Emotion, 26,* 978–994. doi:10.1080/02699931.2011.630991.

Alicke, M. D., & Govorun, O. (2005). The better-than-average effect. In M. D. Alicke, D. Dunning & J. Kueger (Eds.), *The self in social judgment* (Vol. 1, pp. 85–106). New York: Psychology Press.

Alicke, M. D., & Sedikides, C. (Eds.). (2011). *Self-enhancement and self-protection motives.* New York: Oxford University Press.

Alter, A. L., & Oppenheimer, D. M. (2006). Predicting short-term stock fluctuations by using processing fluency. *Proceedings of the National Academy of Sciences, 103,* 9369–9372. doi:10.1073/pnas.0601071103.

Alter, A. L., & Oppenheimer, D. M. (2009). Uniting the tribes of fluency to form a metacognitive nation. *Personality and Social Psychology Review, 13,* 219–235. doi:10.1177/1088868309341564.

Alter, A. L., Oppenheimer, D. M., Epley, N., & Eyre, R. N. (2007). Overcoming intuition: Metacognitive difficulty activates analytic reasoning. *Journal of Experimental Psychology: General, 136,* 569–576. doi:10.1037/0096-3445.136.4.569.

Ambady, N. (2010). The perils of pondering: Intuition and thin slice judgments. *Psychological Inquiry, 21,* 271–278. doi:10.1080/1047840X.2010.524882.

Ambady, N., Bernieri, F. J., & Richeson, J. A. (2000). Toward a histology of social behavior: Judgmental accuracy from thin slices of the behavioral stream. In P. Z. Mark (Ed.), *Advances in experimental social psychology* (Vol. 32, pp. 201–271). San Diego, CA: Academic Press.

Ambady, N., & Rosenthal, R. (1992). Thin slices of expressive behavior as predictors of interpersonal consequences: A meta-analysis. *Psychological Bulletin, 111,* 256–274. doi:10.1037/0033-2909.111.2.256.

Ames, D. R., Kammrath, L. K., Suppes, A., & Bolger, N. (2009). Not so fast: The (not-quite-complete) dissociation between accuracy and confidence in thin-slice impressions. *Personality and Social Psychology Bulletin.* doi:10.1177/0146167209354519.

Anderson, C. A., Benjamin, A. J., & Bartholow, B. D. (1998). Does the gun pull the trigger? Automatic priming effects of weapon pictures and weapon names. *Psychological Science, 9,* 308–314. doi:10.1111/1467-9280.00061.

Anderson, J. R. (1990). *Cognitive psychology and its implications* (7th ed.). New York: Worth Publishing.

Anderson, J. R., & Bower, G. H. (1973). *Human associative memory.* Washington DC: Winston.

Anderson, N. H. (1981). *Foundations of information integration theory.* New York: Academic Press.

Armor, D. A., Massey, C., & Sackett, A. M. (2008). Prescribed optimism: Is it right to be wrong about the future? *Psychological Science, 19,* 329–331. doi:10.1111/j.1467-9280.2008.02089.x.

Ask, K., Greifeneder, R., & Reinhard, M.-A. (2012). On the ease of (dis)believing: The role of accessibility experiences in credibility judgments. *Applied Cognitive Psychology, 26,* 779–784. doi:10.1002/acp.2859.

Baddeley, A. D., & Longman, D. J. A. (1978). The influence of length and frequency of training session on the rate of learning to type. *Ergonomics, 21,* 627–635. doi:10.1080/00140137808931764.

Banaji, M. R., & Hardin, C. D. (1996). Automatic stereotyping. *Psychological Science, 7,* 136–141. doi:10.1111/j.1467-9280.1996.tb00346.x.

Banse, R. (1999). Automatic evaluation of self and significant others: Affective priming in close relationships. *Journal of Social and Personal Relationships, 16,* 803–821. doi:10.1177/0265407599166007.

Bargh, J. A. (1994). The four horsemen of automaticity: Intention, awareness, efficiency, and control as separate issues. In R. S. Wyer Jr. & T. K. Srull (Eds.), *Handbook of social cognition* (pp. 1–40). Hillsdale, NJ: Lawrence Erlbaum Associates.

Bargh, J. A. (1999). The cognitive monster: The case against the controllability of automatic stereotype effects. In S. Chaiken & Y. Trope (Eds.), *Dual process theories in social psychology* (pp. 361–382). New York: Guilford Press.

Bargh, J. A. (2006). Agenda 2006: What have we been priming all these years? On the development, mechanisms, and ecology of nonconscious social behavior. *European Journal of Social Psychology, 36,* 147–168. doi:10.1002/ejsp.336.

Bargh, J. A. (2014). Our unconscious mind. *Scientific American, 310,* 30–37. doi:10.1038/scientificamerican0114-30.

Bargh, J. A., Chen, M., & Burrows, L. (1996). Automaticity of social behavior: Direct effects of trait construct and stereotype activation on action. *Journal of Personality and Social Psychology, 71,* 230–244. doi:10.1037//0022-3514.71.2.230.

Bargh, J. A., Gollwitzer, P. M., Lee-Chai, A., Barndollar, K., & Trötschel, R. (2001). The automated will: Nonconscious activation and pursuit of behavioral goals. *Journal of Personality and Social Psychology, 81*, 1014–1027. doi:10.1037/0022-3514.81.6.1014.

Bargh, J. A., & Pietromonaco, P. (1982). Automatic information processing and social perception: The influence of trait information presented outside of conscious awareness on impression formation. *Journal of Personality and Social Psychology, 43*, 437–449. doi:10.1037//0022-3514.43.3.437.

Bar-Hillel, M., & Neter, E. (1993). How alike is it versus how likely is it: A disjunction fallacy in probability judgments. *Journal of Personality and Social Psychology, 65*, 1119–1131. doi:10.1037/0022-3514.65.6.1119.

Barsalou, L. W. (1985). Ideals, central tendency, and frequency of instantiation as determinants of graded structure in categories. *Journal of Experimental Psychology: Learning, Memory, and Cognition, 11*, 629. doi:10.1037/0278-7393.11.1-4.629.

Bartlett, F. C. (1932). *Remembering: An experimental and social study.* Cambridge: Cambridge University Press.

Bechara, A., Damasio, H., Tranel, D., & Damasio, A. R. (1997). Deciding advantageously before knowing the advantageous strategy. *Science, 275*, 1293–1295. doi:10.1126/science. 275.5304.1293.

Begg, I. M., Anas, A., & Farinacci, S. (1992). Dissociation of processes in belief: Source recollection, statement familiarity, and the illusion of truth. *Journal of Experimental Psychology: General, 121*, 446–458. doi:10.1037/0096-3445.121.4.446.

Bell, D. M. (1997). Innuendo. *Journal of Pragmatics, 27*, 35–59. doi:10.1016/S0378-2166(97) 88001-0.

Berger, J., Meredith, M., & Wheeler, S. C. (2008). Contextual priming: Where people vote affects how they vote. *Proceedings of the National Academy of Sciences, 105*, 8846–8849. doi:10.1073/ pnas.0711988105.

Berry, D. S., & Zebrowitz-McArthur, L. (1988). What's in a face? Facial maturity and the attribution of legal responsibility. *Personality and Social Psychology Bulletin, 14*, 23–33. doi:10.1177/0146167288141003.

Berscheid, E., Graziano, W., Monson, T., & Dermer, M. (1976). Outcome dependency: Attention, attribution, and attraction. *Journal of Personality and Social Psychology, 34*, 978. doi:10.1037/0022-3514.34.5.978.

Betsch, T., & Fiedler, K. (1999). Understanding conjunction effects in probability judgments: The role of implicit mental models. *European Journal of Social Psychology, 29*, 75–93. doi:10.1002/(SICI)1099-0992(199902)29:1%3C75::AID-EJSP916%3E3.0.CO;2-F.

Bettencourt, B. A., Manning, M., Molix, L., Schlegel, R., Eidelman, S., & Biernat, M. (2016). Explaining extremity in evaluation of group members meta-analytic tests of three theories. *Personality and Social Psychology Review, 20*, 49–74. doi:10.1177/1088868315574461.

Beukeboom, C. J., & Semin, G. (2005). Mood and representations of behaviour: The how and why. *Cognition and Emotion, 19*, 1242–1251. doi:10.1080/02699930500203369.

Beukeboom, C. J., & Semin, G. (2006). How mood turns on language. *Journal of Experimental Social Psychology, 42*, 553–566. doi:10.1016/j.jesp.2005.09.005.

Biernat, M. (2005). *Standards and expectancies: Contrast and assimilation in judgments of self and others.* New York: Psychology Press.

Biernat, M. (2012). Stereotypes and shifting standards: Forming, communicating, and translating person impressions. In M. P. Zanna (Ed.), *Advances in experimental social psychology* (Vol. 45, pp. 1–59). San Diego, CA: Elsevier Academic Press.

Biernat, M., & Manis, M. (1994). Shifting standards and stereotype-based judgments. *Journal of Personality and Social Psychology, 66*, 5–20. doi:10.1037/0022-3514.66.1.5.

Bjork, E. L., & Bjork, R. A. (2011). Making things hard on yourself, but in a good way: Creating desirable difficulties to enhance learning. In M. A. Gernsbacher, R. W. Pew, L. M. Hough & J. R. Pomerantz (Eds.), *Psychology and the real world: Essays illustrating fundamental contributions to society* (pp. 56–64). New York: Worth Publishers.

Blair, I. V., & Banaji, M. R. (1996). Automatic and controlled processes in stereotype priming. *Journal of Personality and Social Psychology, 70,* 1142–1163. doi:10.1037/0022-3514.70.6.1142.

Blanchette, I., & Richards, A. (2010). The influence of affect on higher level cognition: A review of research on interpretation, judgement, decision making and reasoning. *Cognition & Emotion, 24,* 561–595. doi:10.1080/02699930903132496.

Bless, H. (2001). The consequences of mood on the processing of social information. In A. Tesser & N. Schwarz (Eds.), *Blackwell handbook in social psychology* (pp. 391–412). Oxford: Blackwell.

Bless, H., Bohner, G., Schwarz, N., & Strack, F. (1990). Mood and persuasion: A cognitive response analysis. *Personality and Social Psychology Bulletin, 16,* 331–345. doi:10.1177/0146167290162013.

Bless, H., & Burger, A. M. (2016). Assimilation and contrast in social priming. *Current Opinion in Psychology, 12,* 26–31. doi:10.1016/j.copsyc.2016.04.018.

Bless, H., Clore, G. L., Schwarz, N., Golisano, V., Rabe, C., & Wölk, M. (1996). Mood and the use of scripts: Does a happy mood really lead to mindlessness? *Journal of Personality and Social Psychology, 71,* 665–679. doi:10.1037//0022-3514.71.4.665.

Bless, H., & Forgas, J. P. (2000). *The message within: The role of subjective experience in social cognition and behavior.* Philadelphia, PA: Psychology Press.

Bless, H., Igou, E. R., Schwarz, N., & Wänke, M. (2000). Reducing context effects by adding context information: The direction and size of context effects in political judgment. *Personality and Social Psychology Bulletin, 26,* 1036–1045. doi:10.1177/01461672002611002.

Bless, H., Mackie, D. M., & Schwarz, N. (1992). Mood effects on attitude judgments: Independent effects of mood before and after message elaboration. *Journal of Personality and Social Psychology, 63,* 585–595. doi:10.1037/0022-3514.63.4.585.

Bless, H., & Schwarz, N. (2010). Mental construal and the emergence of assimilation and contrast effects: The inclusion/exclusion model. In M. P. Zanna (Ed.), *Advances in experimental social psychology* (Vol. 42, pp. 319–373). San Diego, CA: Elsevier Academic Press.

Bless, H., Schwarz, N., Bodenhausen, G. V., & Thiel, L. (2001). Personalized versus generalized benefits of stereotype disconfirmation: Trade-offs in the evaluation of atypical exemplars and their social groups. *Journal of Experimental Social Psychology, 37,* 386–397. doi:10.1006/jesp.2000.1459.

Bless, H., Schwarz, N., & Kemmelmeier, M. (1996). Mood and stereotyping: Affective states and the use of general knowledge structures. *European Review of Social Psychology, 7,* 63–93. doi:10.1080/14792779443000102.

Bless, H., Schwarz, N., & Wieland, R. (1996). Mood and the impact of category membership and individuating information. *European Journal of Social Psychology, 26,* 935–959. doi:10.1002/(SICI)1099-0992(199611)26:6<935::AID-EJSP798>3.0.CO;2-N.

Bless, H., Strack, F., & Schwarz, N. (1993). The informative functions of research procedures: Bias and the logic of conversation. *European Journal of Social Psychology, 23,* 149–165. doi:10.1002/ejsp.2420230204.

Bless, H., & Wänke, M. (2000). Can the same information be typical and atypical? How perceived typicality moderates assimilation and contrast in evaluative judgments. *Personality and Social Psychology Bulletin, 26,* 306–314. doi:10.1177/0146167200265004.

Block, R. A., & Harper, D. R. (1991). Overconfidence in estimation: Testing the anchoring-and-adjustment hypothesis. *Organizational Behavior and Human Decision Processes, 49,* 188–207. doi:10.1016/0749-5978(91)90048-X.

Bodenhausen, G. V. (1990). Stereotypes as judgmental heuristics: Evidence of circadian variations in discrimination. *Psychological Science, 1,* 319–322. doi:10.1111/j.1467-9280.1990.tb00226.x.

Bodenhausen, G. V. (1993). Emotions, arousal, and stereotypic judgments: A heuristic model of affect and stereotyping. In D. M. Mackie & D. L. Hamilton (Eds.), *Affect, cognition, and stereotyping: Interactive processes in group perception* (pp. 13–37). San Diego, CA: Academic Press, Inc.

Bodenhausen, G. V., Kramer, G. P., & Süsser, K. (1994). Happiness and stereotypic thinking in social judgment. *Journal of Personality and Social Psychology, 66*, 621–632. doi:10.1037//0022-3514.66.4.621.

Bodenhausen, G. V., Macrae, C. N., & Sherman, J. S. (1999). On the dialectics of discrimination: Dual processes in social stereotyping. In S. Chaiken & Y. Trope (Eds.), *Dual-process theories in social psychology* (pp. 271–290). New York: Guilford Press.

Bodenhausen, G. V., Schwarz, N., Bless, H., & Wänke, M. (1995). Effects of atypical exemplars on racial beliefs: Enlightened racism or generalized appraisals. *Journal of Experimental Social Psychology, 31*, 48–63. doi:10.1006/jesp.1995.1003.

Bodenhausen, G. V., Sheppard, L. A., & Kramer, G. P. (1994). Negative affect and social judgement: The differential impact of anger and sadness. *European Journal of Social Psychology, 24*, 45–62. doi:10.1002/ejsp.2420240104.

Bodenhausen, G. V., & Todd, A. R. (2010). Automatic aspects of judgment and decision making. In B. Gawronski & B. K. Payne (Eds.), *Handbook of implicit social cognition* (pp. 278–294). New York: Guilford Press.

Bohner, G., Crow, K., Erb, H.-P., & Schwarz, N. (1992). Affect and persuasion: Mood effects on the processing of message content and context cues and on subsequent behaviour. *European Journal of Social Psychology, 22*. doi:10.1002/ejsp.2420220602.

Bolte, A., Goschke, T., & Kuhl, J. (2003). Emotion and intuition effects of positive and negative mood on implicit judgments of semantic coherence. *Psychological Science, 14*, 416–421. doi:10.1111/1467-9280.01456.

Bond, C. F., Jr., & DePaulo, B. M. (2006). Accuracy of deception judgments. *Personality and Social Psychology Review, 10*, 214–234. doi:10.1207/s15327957pspr1003_2A.

Bond, M. H., & Komai, H. (1976). Targets of gazing and eye contact during interviews: Effect on Japanese nonverbal behavior. *Journal of Personality and Social Psychology, 34*, 1276–1284. doi:10.1037/0022-3514.34.6.1276.

Boring, E. G. (1930). A new ambiguous figure. *American Journal of Psychology, 42*, 444–445. doi:10.2307/1415447.

Bornstein, R. F., & D'Agostino, P. R. (1994). The attribution and discounting of perceptual fluency: Preliminary tests of a perceptual fluency/attributional model of the mere exposure effect. *Social Cognition, 12*, 103–128. doi:10.1521/soco.1994.12.2.103.

Bower, G. H. (1981). Mood and memory. *American Psychologist, 36*, 129–148. doi:10.1037//0003-066X.36.2.129.

Bower, G. H. (1991). Mood congruity of social judgments. In J. P. Forgas (Ed.), *Emotion and social judgments* (pp. 31–53). Oxford: Pergamon Press.

Bower, G. H., & Forgas, J. P. (2001). Mood and social memory. In J. P. Forgas (Ed.), *Handbook of affect and social cognition* (pp. 95–120). Mahwah, NJ: Lawrence Erlbaum Associates.

Bower, G. H., & Karlin, M. B. (1974). Depth of processing pictures of faces and recognition memory. *Journal of Experimental Psychology, 103*, 751–757. doi:10.1037/h0037190.

Braga, M., Paccagnella, M., & Pellizzari, M. (2014). Evaluating students' evaluations of professors. *Economics of Education Review, 41*, 71–88. doi:10.1016/j.econedurev.2014.04.002.

Brewer, M. B. (1988). A dual model of impression formation. In T. K. Srull & R. S. Wyer Jr. (Eds.), *A dual model of impression formation: Advances in social cognition* (Vol. 1, pp. 1–35). Hillsdale, NJ: Lawrence Erlbaum Associates.

Briñol, P., Petty, R. E., & Tormala, Z. L. (2006). The malleable meaning of subjective ease. *Psychological Science, 17*, 200–206. doi:10.1111/j.1467-9280.2006.01686.x.

Broadbent, D. E. (1958). *Perception and communication.* New York: Pergamon.

Brown, A. S., & Hall, L. A. (1979). Part-list cueing inhibition in semantic memory structures. *American Journal of Psychology*, 351–362. doi:10.2307/1421929.

Brown, J. D., Novick, N. J., Lord, K. A., & Richards, J. M. (1992). When Gulliver travels: Social context, psychological closeness, and self-appraisals. *Journal of Personality and Social Psychology, 62*, 717–727. doi:10.1037//0022-3514.62.5.717.

Brown, R., & Fish, D. (1983). The psychological causality implicit in language. *Cognition, 14,* 237–273. doi:10.1016/0010-0277(83)90006-9.

Bruner, J. S. (1957a). Going beyond the information given. In J. S. Bruner, E. Brunswick, L. Festinger, F. Heider, K. F. Muenzinger, C. Osgood, & D. Rapaport (Eds.), *Contemporary approaches to cognition.* Cambridge, MA: Harvard University Press.

Bruner, J. S. (1957b). On perceptual readiness. *Psychological Review, 64,* 123–152. doi:10.1037/h0043805.

Burger, A. M., & Bless, H. (2016). Affect and the weight of idealistic versus pragmatic concerns in decision situations. *European Journal of Social Psychology, 46,* 323–340. doi:10.1002/ejsp.2164.

Burger, A. M., & Bless, H. (in press). Mood and the regulation of mental abstraction. *Current Directions in Psychological Science.*

Bushman, B. J. (1998). Priming effects of media violence on the accessibility of aggressive constructs in memory. *Personality and Social Psychology Bulletin, 24,* 537–545. doi:10.1177/0146167298245009.

Bushman, B. J., & Anderson, C. A. (2001). Media violence and the American public: Scientific facts versus media misinformation. *American Psychologist, 56,* 477–489. doi:10.1037/0003-066X.56.6-7.477.

Cacioppo, J. T., & Petty, R. E. (1982). The need for cognition. *Journal of Personality and Social Psychology, 42,* 116–131. doi:10.1037/0022-3514.42.1.116.

Canning, E. A., & Harackiewicz, J. M. (2015). Teach it, don't preach it: The differential effects of directly-communicated and self-generated utility-value information. *Motivation Science, 1,* 47. doi:10.1037/mot0000015.

Cantor, N., & Mischel, W. (1977). Traits as prototypes: Effects on recognition memory. *Journal of Personality and Social Psychology, 35,* 38. doi:10.1037/0022-3514.35.1.38.

Carlston, D. E. (Ed.). (2013). *The Oxford handbook of social cognition.* New York: Oxford University Press.

Carnaghi, A., Maass, A., Gresta, S., Bianchi, M., Cadinu, M., & Arcuri, L. (2008). Nomina sunt omina: On the inductive potential of nouns and adjectives in person perception. *Journal of Personality and Social Psychology, 94,* 839–859. doi:10.1037/0022-3514.94.5.839.

Cesario, J., Plaks, J. E., & Higgins, E. T. (2006). Automatic social behavior as motivated preparation to interact. *Journal of Personality and Social Psychology, 90,* 893–910. doi:10.1037/0022-3514.90.6.893.

Chaiken, S. (1987). The heuristic model of persuasion. In M. P. Zanna, J. M. Olson & C. P. Herman (Eds.), *Social influence: The Ontario symposium* (Vol. 5, pp. 3–39). Hillsdale, NJ: Erlbaum.

Chaiken, S., & Trope, Y. (1999). *Dual-process theories in social psychology.* New York: Guilford Press.

Chan, E., Ybarra, O., & Schwarz, N. (2006). Reversing the affective congruency effect: The role of target word frequency of occurrence. *Journal of Experimental Social Psychology, 42,* 365–372. doi:10.1016/j.jesp.2005.04.008.

Chapman, G. B., & Bornstein, B. H. (1996). The more you ask for, the more you get: Anchoring in personal injury verdicts. *Applied Cognitive Psychology, 10,* 519–540. doi:10.1002/(SICI)1099-0720(199612)10:6%3C519::AID-ACP417%3E3.0.CO;2-5.

Chapman, G. B., & Johnson, E. J. (2002). Incorporating the irrelevant: Anchors in judgments of belief and value. In T. Gilovich, D. W. Griffin & D. Kahneman (Eds.), *Heuristics and biases: The psychology of intuitive judgment* (pp. 120–138). New York: Cambridge University Press.

Chen, S., & Chaiken, S. (1999). The heuristic-systematic model in its broader context. In S. Chaiken & Y. Trope (Eds.), *Dual process theories in social psychology* (pp. 73–96). New York: Guilford Press.

Cheng, P. W., & Holyoak, K. J. (1985). Pragmatic reasoning schemas. *Cognitive Psychology, 17,* 391–416. doi:10.1017/CBO9780511814273.042.

Cherry, E. C. (1953). Some experiments on the recognition of speach, with one and with two ears. *Journal of the Acoustical Society of America, 25*, 975–979. doi:10.1121/1.1907229.

Chiu, C.-Y., & Hong, Y.-Y. (2007). Cultural processes: Basic principles. In E. T. Higgins & A. W. Kruglanski (Eds.), *Social psychology: Handbook of basic principles* (pp. 785–804). New York: Guilford Press.

Choi, I., Nisbett, R. E., & Norenzayan, A. (1999). Causal attribution across cultures: Variation and universality. *Psychological Bulletin, 125*, 47. doi:10.1037/0033-2909.125.1.47.

Chua, H. F., Boland, J. E., & Nisbett, R. E. (2005). Cultural variation in eye movements during scene perception. *Proceedings of the National Academy of Sciences of the United States of America, 102*, 12629–12633. doi:10.1073/pnas.0506162102.

Cialdini, R. B., & Goldstein, N. J. (2004). Social influence: Compliance and conformity. *Annual Review of Psychology, 55*, 591–621. doi:10.1146/annurev.psych.55.090902.142015.

Cialdini, R. B., Reno, R. R., & Kallgren, C. A. (1990). A focus theory of normative conduct: Recycling the concept of norms to reduce littering in public places. *Journal of Personality and Social Psychology, 58*, 1015–1026. doi:10.1037/0022-3514.58.6.1015.

Clark, H. H. (1996). *Using language*. Cambridge: Cambridge University Press. doi:10.1017/CBO9780511620539.

Clore, G. L. (1992). Cognitive phenomenology: Feelings and the construction of judgment. In L. L. Martin & A. Tesser (Eds.), *The construction of social judgments* (pp. 133–163). Hillsdale, NJ: Erlbaum.

Clore, G. L., Ellsworth, P. C., Frijda, N. H., Izard, C. E., Lazarus, R., LeDoux, J. E., ... Ekman, P. (1994). What are the minimal cognitive prerequisites for emotion? In P. Ekman & R. J. Davidson (Eds.), *The nature of emotion: Fundamental questions* (pp. 181–191). New York: Oxford University Press.

Clore, G. L., & Huntsinger, J. R. (2009). How the object of affect guides its impact. *Emotion Review, 1*, 39–54. doi:10.1177/1754073908097185.

Clore, G. L., Wyer, R. S., Dienes, B. P. A., Gasper, K., Gohm, C., & Isbell, L. (2001). Affective feelings as feedback: Some cognitive consequences. In L. L. Martin & G. L. Clore (Eds.), *Theories of mood and cognition: A user's guidebook* (pp. 27–62). Mahwah, NJ: Lawrence Erlbaum Associates.

Cohen-Charash, Y., & Spector, P. E. (2001). The role of justice in organizations: A meta-analysis. *Organizational Behavior and Human Decision Processes, 86*, 278–321. doi:10.1006/obhd.2001.2958.

Cohen, J. B., Pham, M. T., & Andrade, E. B. (2008). The nature and role of affect in consumer behavior. In C. P. Haugtvedt, P. M. Herr & F. R. Kardes (Eds.), *Handbook of consumer psychology* (pp. 297–348). New York: Lawrence Erlbaum Associates.

Correll, J., Park, B., Judd, C. M., & Wittenbrink, B. (2002). The police officer's dilemma: Using ethnicity to disambiguate potentially threatening individuals. *Journal of Personality and Social Psychology, 83*, 1314–1329. doi:10.1037/0022-3514.83.6.1314.

Cosmides, L. (1989). The logic of social exchange: Has natural selection shaped how humans reason? Studies with the Wason selection task. *Cognition, 31*, 187–276. doi:10.1016/0010-0277(89)90023-1.

Cosmides, L., & Tooby, J. (1996). Are humans good intuitive statisticians after all? Rethinking some conclusions from the literature on judgment under uncertainty. *Cognition, 58*, 1–73. doi:10.1016/0010-0277(95)00664-8.

Crocker, J., & Wolfe, C. T. (2001). Contingencies of self-worth. *Psychological Review, 108*, 593–623. doi:10.1037/0033-295X.108.3.593.

Cross, K. P. (1977). Not can, but will college teaching be improved? *New Directions for Higher Education, 1977*, 1–15. doi:10.1002/he.36919771703.

Curby, K. M., Johnson, K. J., & Tyson, A. (2012). Face to face with emotion: Holistic face processing is modulated by emotional state. *Cognition & Emotion, 26*, 93–102. doi:10.1080/02699931.2011.555752.

Custers, R., & Aarts, H. (2007). In search of the nonconscious sources of goal pursuit: Accessibility and positive affective valence of the goal state. *Journal of Experimental Social Psychology, 43*, 312–318. doi:10.1016/j.jesp.2006.02.005.

Davidai, S., & Gilovich, T. (2016). The headwinds/tailwinds asymmetry: An availability bias in assessments of barriers and blessings. *Journal of Personality and Social Psychology, 111*, 835. doi:10.1037/pspa0000066.

Dawson, E., Gilovich, T., & Regan, D. T. (2002). Motivated reasoning and performance on the Wason selection task. *Personality and Social Psychology Bulletin, 28*, 1379–1387. doi:10.1177/014616702236869.

Dechêne, A., Stahl, C., Hansen, J., & Wänke, M. (2010). The truth about the truth: A meta-analytic review of the truth-effect. *Personality and Social Psychology Review, 14*, 238–257. doi:10.1177/1088868309352251.

Degner, J. (2009). On the (un-)controllability of affective priming: Strategic manipulation is feasible but can possibly be prevented. *Cognition and Emotion, 23*, 327–354. doi:10.1080/02699930801993924.

Degner, J., & Wentura, D. (2011). Types of automatically activated prejudice: Assessing possessor-versus other-relevant valence in the evaluative priming task. *Social Cognition, 29*, 182–209. doi:10.1521/soco.2011.29.2.182.

Denrell, J. (2005). Why most people disapprove of me: Experience sampling in impression formation. *Psychological Review, 112*, 951–978.

Denrell, J., & March, J. G. (2001). Adaptation as information restriction: The hot stove effect. *Organization Science, 12*, 523–538. doi:10.1287/orsc.12.5.523.10092.

DePaulo, B. M., Lindsay, J. J., Malone, B. E., Muhlenbruck, L., Charlton, K., & Cooper, H. (2003). Cues to deception. *Psychological Bulletin, 129*, 74. doi:10.1037/0033-2909.129.1.74.

Descartes, R. (1961/1649). *Passions of the soul: Essential works of Descartes* (L. Blair, trans.). New York: Bantam Books.

De Soto, C. B. (1960). Learning a social structure. *Journal of Abnormal and Social Psychology, 60*, 417–421. doi:10.1037/h0047511.

Devine, P. G. (1989). Stereotypes and prejudice: Their automatic and controlled components. *Journal of Personality and Social Psychology, 56*, 5–18. doi:10.1037/0022-3514.56.1.5.

Diemand-Yauman, C., Oppenheimer, D. M., & Vaughan, E. B. (2011). Fortune favors the bold (and the italicized): Effects of disfluency on educational outcomes. *Cognition, 118*, 114–118.

Dijksterhuis, A. (2004). Think different: The merits of unconscious thought in preference development and decision making. *Journal of Personality and Social Psychology, 87*, 586–598. doi:10.1037/0022-3514.87.5.586.

Dijksterhuis, A. (2010). *Das kluge Unbewusste: Denken mit Gefühl und Intuition.* Stuttgart: Klett-Cotta.

Dijksterhuis, A., & Aarts, H. (2010). Goals, attention, and (un)consciousness. *Annual Review of Psychology, 61*, 467–490. doi:10.1146/annurev.psych.093008.100445.

Dijksterhuis, A., Aarts, H., & Smith, P. K. (2005). The power of the subliminal: On subliminal persuasion and other potential applications. In R. R. Hassin, J. S. Uleman & J. A. Bargh (Eds.), *The new unconscious* (Vol. 1, pp. 77–106). New York: Oxford University Press.

Dijksterhuis, A., Bos, M. W., Nordgren, L. F., & van Baaren, R. B. (2006). On making the right choice: The deliberation-without-attention effect. *Science, 311*, 1005–1007. doi:10.1126/science.1121629.

Dijksterhuis, A., & van Knippenberg, A. (1995). Timing of schema activation and memory: Inhibited access to inconsistent information. *European Journal of Social Psychology, 25*, 383–390. doi:10.1002/ejsp.2420250403.

Dijksterhuis, A., & van Knippenberg, A. (1998). The relation between perception and behavior, or how to win a game of Trivial Pursuit. *Journal of Personality and Social Psychology, 74*, 865–877. doi:10.1037/0022-3514.74.4.865.

Dotsch, R., Wigboldus, D. H. J., Langner, O., & van Knippenberg, A. (2008). Ethnic out-group faces are biased in the prejudiced mind. *Psychological Science, 19*, 978–980. doi:10.1111/j.1467-9280.2008.02186.x.

Dotsch, R., Wigboldus, D. H. J., & van Knippenberg, A. (2011). Biased allocation of faces to social categories. *Journal of Personality and Social Psychology, 100*, 999–1014. doi:10.1037/a0023026.

Dovidio, J. F., Gaertner, S. L., & Loux, S. (2000). Subjective experiences and intergroup relations: The role of positive affect. In H. Bless & J. P. Forgas (Eds.), *The message within: The role of subjective experience in social cognition and behavior* (pp. 340–371). Philadelphia, PA: Psychology Press.

Doyen, S., Klein, O., Pichon, C.-L., & Cleeremans, A. (2012). Behavioral priming: It's all in the mind, but whose mind? *PloS One, 7*, e29081. doi:10.1371/journal.pone.0029081.

Duff, K. J., & Newman, L. S. (1997). Individual differences in the spontaneous construal of behavior: Idiocentrism and the automatization of the trait inference process. *Social Cognition, 15*, 217. doi:10.1521/soco.1997.15.3.217.

Dulany, D. E., & Hilton, D. J. (1991). Conversational implicature, conscious representation, and the conjunction fallacy. *Social Cognition, 9*, 85–110. doi:10.1521/soco.1991.9.1.85.

Dunning, D. (1999). A newer look: Motivated social cognition and the schematic representation of social concepts. *Psychological Inquiry, 10*, 1–11. doi:10.1207/s15327965pli1001_1.

Dunning, D. (2015). Motivated cognition in self and social thought. In M. Mikulincer, P. R. Shaver, E. Borgida & J. A. Bargh (Eds.), *APA handbook of personality and social psychology* (Vol. 1, pp. 777–803). Washington DC: American Psychological Association.

Eagly, A. H., & Chaiken, S. (1993). *The psychology of attitudes*. Fort Worth: Harcourt Brace Jovanovich.

Echterhoff, G., Higgins, E. T., & Levine, J. M. (2009). Shared reality experiencing commonality with others' inner states about the world. *Perspectives on Psychological Science, 4*, 496–521. doi:10.1111/j.1745-6924.2009.01161.x.

Eich, E., & Macaulay, D. (2000). Cognitive and clinical perspectives on mood-dependent memory. In J. P. Forgas (Ed.), *Feeling and thinking: The role of affect in social cognition* (pp. 105–122). New York: Cambridge University Press.

Einstein, G. O., & McDaniel, M. A. (2005). Prospective memory multiple retrieval processes. *Current Directions in Psychological Science, 14*, 286–290. doi:10.1111/j.0963-7214.2005.00382.x.

Engelhardt, C. R., & Bartholow, B. D. (2013). Effects of situational cues on aggressive behavior. *Social and Personality Psychology Compass, 7*, 762–774. doi:10.1111/spc3.12067.

Englich, B., & Mussweiler, T. (2001). Sentencing under uncertainty: Anchoring effects in the courtroom. *Journal of Applied Social Psychology, 31*, 1535–1551. doi:10.1111/j.1559-1816.2001.tb02687.x.

Englich, B., Mussweiler, T., & Strack, F. (2005). The last word in court: A hidden disadvantage for the defense. *Law and Human Behavior, 29*, 705–722. doi:10.1007/s10979-005-8380-7.

Englich, B., Mussweiler, T., & Strack, F. (2006). Playing dice with criminal sentences: The influence of irrelevant anchors on experts' judicial decision making. *Personality and Social Psychology Bulletin, 32*, 188–200. doi:10.1177/0146167205282152.

Epley, N., & Dunning, D. (2000). Feeling "holier than thou": Are self-serving assessments produced by errors in self- or social prediction? *Journal of Personality and Social Psychology, 79*, 861–875. doi:10.1037/0022-3514.79.6.861.

Epley, N., & Gilovich, T. (2006). The anchoring-and-adjustment heuristic: Why the adjustments are insufficient. *Psychological Science, 17*, 311–318. doi:10.1111/j.1467-9280.2006.01704.x.

Epstein, S., Donovan, S., & Denes-Raj, V. (1999). The missing link in the paradox of the Linda conjunction problem: Beyond knowing and thinking of the conjunction rule, the intrinsic appeal of heuristic processing. *Personality and Social Psychology Bulletin, 25*, 204–214. doi:10.1177/0146167299025002006.

Erber, R., & Fiske, S. T. (1984). Outcome dependency and attention to inconsistent information. *Journal of Personality and Social Psychology, 47*, 709. doi:10.1037/0022-3514.47.4.709.

Falk, R., & Konold, C. (1997). Making sense of randomness: Implicit encoding as a basis for judgment. *Psychological Review, 104*, 301. doi:10.1037/0033-295X.104.2.301.

Fazio, R. H., Eiser, J. R., & Shook, N. J. (2004). Attitude formation through exploration: Valence asymmetries. *Journal of Personality and Social Psychology, 87*, 293. doi:10.1037/0022-3514.87.3.293.

Fazio, R. H., & Towles-Schwen, T. (1999). The MODE model of attitude-behavior processes. In S. Chaiken & Y. Trope (Eds.), *Dual process theories in social psychology* (pp. 97–116). New York: Guilford Press.

Ferreira, M. B., Garcia-Marques, L., Sherman, S. J., & Sherman, J. W. (2006). Automatic and controlled components of judgment and decision making. *Journal of Personality and Social Psychology, 91*, 797. doi:10.1037/0022-3514.91.5.797.

Festinger, L. (1954). A theory of social comparison processes. *Human Relations, 7*, 117–140. doi:10.1177/001872675400700202.

Festinger, L. (1957). *A theory of cognitive dissonance.* Stanford, CA: Stanford University Press.

Fiedler, K. (1988). The dependence of the conjunction fallacy on subtle linguistic factors. *Psychological Research, 50*, 123–129. doi:10.1007/BF00309212.

Fiedler, K. (1991). On the task, the measures and the mood in research on affect and social cognition. In J. P. Forgas (Ed.), *Emotion and social judgments* (pp. 83–104). Oxford: Pergamon Press.

Fiedler, K. (2000a). Beware of samples! A cognitive-ecological sampling approach to judgment biases. *Psychological Review, 107*, 659. doi:10.1037/0033-295X.107.4.659.

Fiedler, K. (2000b). Explaining major findings and their boundary conditions in terms of mood dependent assimilation and accommodation. In L. L. Martin & G. L. Clore (Eds.), *Mood and social cognition: Contrasting theories.* Mahwah, NJ: Lawrence Erlbaum Associates.

Fiedler, K. (2010). The asymmetry of causal and diagnostic inferences: A challenge for the study of implicit attitudes. In J. P. Forgas, J. Cooper & W. D. Crano (Eds.), *The psychology of attitudes and attitude change* (pp. 75–92). New York: Psychology Press.

Fiedler, K., Armbruster, T., Nickel, S., Walther, E., & Asbeck, J. (1996). Constructive biases in social judgment: Experiments on the self-verification of question contents. *Journal of Personality and Social Psychology, 71*, 861–73. doi:10.1037/0022-3514.71.5.861.

Fiedler, K., & Bluemke, M. (2005). Faking the IAT: Aided and unaided response control on the Implicit Association Tests. *Basic and Applied Social Psychology, 27*, 307–316. doi:10.1207/s15324834basp2704_3.

Fiedler, K., Bluemke, M., & Unkelbach, C. (2011). On the adaptive flexibility of evaluative priming. *Memory & Cognition, 39*, 557–572. doi:10.3758/s13421-010-0056-x.

Fiedler, K., & Kareev, Y. (2011). Clarifying the advantage of small samples: As it relates to statistical wisdom and Cahan's (2010) normative intuitions. *Journal of Experimental Psychology: Learning, Memory, and Cognition, 37*, 1039–1043. doi:10.1037/a0023259.

Fiedler, K., Messner, C., & Bluemke, M. (2006). Unresolved problems with the "I," the "A," and the "T": A logical and psychometric critique of the Implicit Association Test (IAT). *European Review of Social Psychology, 17*, 74–147. doi:10.1080/10463280600681248.

Fiedler, K., & Semin, G. R. (1988). On the causal information conveyed by different interpersonal verbs: The role of implicit sentence context. *Social Cognition, 6*, 21. doi:10.1521/soco.1988.6.1.21.

Fiedler, K., Walther, E., & Nickel, S. (1999). The auto-verification of social hypotheses: Stereotyping and the power of sample size. *Journal of Personality and Social Psychology, 77*, 5. doi:10.1037/0022-3514.77.1.5.

Fiedler, K., Wöllert, F., Tauber, B., & Hess, P. (2013). Applying sampling theories to attitude learning in a virtual school class environment. *Organizational Behavior and Human Decision Processes, 122*, 222–231. doi:10.1016/j.obhdp.2013.08.001.

Finn, B., & Tauber, S. K. (2015). When confidence is not a signal of knowing: How students' experiences and beliefs about processing fluency can lead to miscalibrated confidence. *Educational Psychology Review, 27*, 567–586. doi:10.1007/s10648-015-9313-7.

Fischer, P., Kastenmüller, A., & Greitemeyer, T. (2010). Media violence and the self: The impact of personalized gaming characters in aggressive video games on aggressive behavior. *Journal of Experimental Social Psychology, 46*, 192–195. doi:10.1016/j.jesp.2009.06.010.

Fischhoff, B. (1975). Hindsight is not equal to foresight: The effect of outcome knowledge on judgment under uncertainty. *Journal of Experimental Psychology: Human Perception and Performance, 1*, 288. doi:10.1037/0096-1523.1.3.288.

Fishbein, M., & Ajzen, I. (1974). Attitudes towards objects as predictors of single and multiple behavioral criteria. *Psychological Review, 81*, 59. doi:10.1037/h0035872.

Fisher, R. P., Geiselman, R. E., & Amador, M. (1989). Field test of the cognitive interview: Enhancing the recollection of the actual victims and witnesses of crime. *Journal of Applied Psychology, 74*, 722–727. doi:10.1037/0021-9010.74.5.722.

Fiske, A. P., Kitayama, S., Markus, H. R., & Nisbett, R. E. (1998). The cultural matrix of social psychology. In D. T. Gilbert, S. T. Fiske & G. Lindzey (Eds.), *The handbook of social psychology* (pp. 915–981). New York: McGraw-Hill.

Fiske, S. T. (1992). Thinking is for doing: Portraits of social cognition from daguerreotype to laserphoto. *Journal of Personality and Social Psychology, 63*, 877. doi:10.1037/0022-3514.63.6.877.

Fiske, S. T. (1998). Stereotyping, prejudice, and discrimination. In D. T. Gilbert, S. T. Fiske & G. Lindzey (Eds.), *The handbook of social psychology* (Vol. 2, pp. 357–411): Boston, MA: McGraw-Hill.

Fiske, S. T., Cuddy, A. J. C., & Glick, P. (2007). Universal dimensions of social cognition: Warmth and competence. *Trends in Cognitive Sciences, 11*, 77–83. doi:10.1016/j.tics.2006.11.005.

Fiske, S. T., Cuddy, A. J. C., Glick, P., & Xu, J. (2002). A model of (often mixed) stereotype content: Competence and warmth respectively follow from perceived status and competition. *Journal of Personality and Social Psychology, 82*, 878–902. doi:10.1037/0022-3514.82.6.878.

Fiske, S. T., & Neuberg, S. L. (1990). A continuum of impression formation from category-based to individuating processing: Influences of information and motivation on attention and interpretation. In M. P. Zanna (Ed.), *Advances in experimental social psychology* (Vol. 23, pp. 1–74). Orlando, FL: Academic Press.

Fiske, S. T., & Taylor, S. E. (2017). *Social cognition: From brains to culture* (3rd ed.). New York: McGraw-Hill.

Florack, A., Scarabis, M., & Bless, H. (2001). When do associations matter? The use of automatic associations toward ethnic groups in person judgments. *Journal of Experimental Social Psychology, 37*, 518–524. doi:10.1006/jesp.2001.1477.

Ford, T. E., & Kruglanski, A. W. (1995). Effects of epistemic motivations on the use of accessible constructs in social judgment. *Personality and Social Psychology Bulletin, 21*, 950–962. doi:10.1177/0146167295219009.

Forgas, J. P. (1992). Affect in social judgments and decisions: A multiprocess model. In M. P. Zanna (Ed.), *Advances in experimental social psychology* (Volume 25, pp. 227–275). San Diego, CA: Elsevier Academic Press.

Forgas, J. P. (1995a). Mood and judgment: The affect infusion model (AIM). *Psychological Bulletin, 117*, 39–66. doi:10.1037/0033-2909.117.1.39.

Forgas, J. P. (1995b). Strange couples: Mood effects on judgments and memory about prototypical and atypical relationships. *Personality and Social Psychology Bulletin, 21*, 747–765. doi:10.1177/0146167295217009.

Forgas, J. P. (2000a). Affect and information processing strategies: An interactive relationship. In J. P. Forgas & K. D. Williams (Eds.), *Feeling and thinking: The role of affect in social cognition*. New York: Cambridge University Press.

Forgas, J. P. (2000b). *Feeling and thinking: The role of affect in social cognition*. New York: Cambridge University Press.

Forgas, J. P. (2001). Affect and the "social mind": Affective influences on strategic interpersonal behaviors. In J. P. Forgas & K. D. Williams (Eds.), *The social mind: Cognitive and motivational aspects of interpersonal behavior* (pp. 46–71). New York: Cambridge University Press.

Forgas, J. P. (2011). Can negative affect eliminate the power of first impressions? Affective influences on primacy and recency effects in impression formation. *Journal of Experimental Social Psychology, 47*, 425–429. doi:10.1016/j.jesp.2010.11.005.

Forgas, J. P., & Bower, G. H. (1987). Mood effects on person-perception judgments. *Journal of Personality and Social Psychology, 53*, 53–60. doi:10.1037/0022-3514.53.1.53.

Forgas, J. P., & Fiedler, K. (1996). Us and them: Mood effects on intergroup discrimination. *Journal of Personality and Social Psychology, 70*, 28. doi:10.1037/0022-3514.70.1.28.

Förster, J., & Liberman, N. (2007). Knowledge activation. In A. W. Kruglanski & E. T. Higgins (Eds.), *Social psychology: Handbook of basic principles* (2nd ed., pp. 201–231). New York: Guilford Press.

Frank, M. G., & Gilovich, T. (1988). The dark side of self- and social perception: Black uniforms and aggression in professional sports. *Journal of Personality and Social Psychology, 54*, 74–85. doi:10.1037/0022-3514.54.1.74.

Frederick, S. (2005). Cognitive reflection and decision making. *Journal of Economic Perspectives, 19*, 25–42. doi:10.1257/089533005775196732.

Fredrickson, B. L. (2001). The role of positive emotions in positive psychology: The broaden-and-build theory of positive emotions. *American Psychologist, 56*, 218. doi:10.1037/0003-066X.56.3.218.

Fredrickson, B. L., & Branigan, C. (2005). Positive emotions broaden the scope of attention and thought-action repertoires. *Cognition & Emotion, 19*, 313–332. doi:10.1080/02699930441000238.

Freud, S. (1940–1968). *Gesammelte Werke.* Frankfurt, Germany: Fischer.

Friese, M., Wänke, M., & Plessner, H. (2006). Implicit consumer preferences and their influence on product choice. *Psychology & Marketing, 23*, 727–740. doi:10.1002/mar.20126.

Fujita, K., Trope, Y., & Liberman, N. (2010). Seeing the big picture: A construal level analysis of self-control. In R. R. Hassin, K. N. Ochsner & Y. Trope (Eds.), *Self control in society, mind, and brain* (pp. 408–427). New York: Oxford University Press.

Funder, D. C. (1987). Errors and mistakes: Evaluating the accuracy of social judgment. *Psychological Bulletin, 101*, 75. doi:10.1037/0033-2909.101.1.75.

Funk, F., Walker, M., & Todorov, A. (2016). Modelling perceptions of criminality and remorse from faces using a data-driven computational approach. *Cognition and Emotion*, 1–13. doi:10.1080/02699931.2016.1227305.

Galesic, M., Olsson, H., & Rieskamp, J. (2012). Social sampling explains apparent biases in judgments of social environments. *Psychological Science, 23*, 1515–1523. doi:10.1177/0956797612445313.

Galinsky, A. D., & Mussweiler, T. (2001). First offers as anchors: The role of perspective-taking and negotiator focus. *Journal of Personality and Social Psychology, 81*, 657–669. doi:10.1037//0022-3514.81.4.657.

Garcia-Marques, T., & Mackie, D. M. (2001). The feeling of familiarity as a regulator of persuasive processing. *Social Cognition, 19*, 9–34. doi:10.1521/soco.19.1.9.18959.

Garcia Marques, T., Mackie, D. M., Claypool, H. M., & Garcia Marques, L. (2013). Once more with feeling! Familiarity and positivity as integral consequences of previous exposure. In C. Unkelbach & R. Greifeneder (Eds.), *The experience of thinking: How the fluency of mental processes influences cognition and behavior* (pp. 50–69). Hove: Psychology Press.

Gasper, K. (2004). Do you see what I see? Affect and visual information processing. *Cognition and Emotion, 18*, 405–421. doi:10.1080/02699930341000068.

Gasper, K., & Clore, G. L. (2002). Attending to the big picture: Mood and global versus local processing of visual information. *Psychological Science, 13*, 34–40. doi:10.1111/1467-9280.00406.

Gavanski, I., & Roskos-Ewoldsen, D. R. (1991). Representativeness and conjoint probability. *Journal of Personality and Social Psychology, 61*, 181. doi:10.1037/0022-3514.61.2.181.

Gawronski, B., & Bodenhausen, G. V. (2006). Associative and propositional processes in evaluation: An integrative review of implicit and explicit attitude change. *Psychological Bulletin, 132*, 692–731. doi:10.1037/0033-2909.132.5.692.

Gawronski, B., Geschke, D., & Banse, R. (2003). Implicit bias in impression formation: Associations influence the construal of individuating information. *European Journal of Social Psychology, 33*, 573–589. doi:10.1002/ejsp.166.

Gawronski, B., & Quinn, K. A. (2013). Guilty by mere similarity: Assimilative effects of facial resemblance on automatic evaluation. *Journal of Experimental Social Psychology, 49*, 120–125. doi:10.1016/j.jesp.2012.07.016.

Gidron, D., Koehler, D. J., & Tversky, A. (1993). Implicit quantification of personality traits. *Personality and Social Psychology Bulletin, 19*, 594–594. doi:10.1177/0146167293195011.

Gigerenzer, G. (1991). How to make cognitive illusions disappear: Beyond "heuristics and biases." In W. Stroebe & M. Hewstone (Eds.), *European review of social psychology* (Vol. 2, pp. 83–115). Chichester: John Wiley & Sons.

Gigerenzer, G. (2004). Dread risk, September 11, and fatal traffic accidents. *Psychological Science, 15*, 286–287. doi:10.1111/j.0956-7976.2004.00668.x.

Gigerenzer, G., & Gaissmaier, W. (2011). Heuristic decision making. In S. T. Fiske, D. L. Schacter, & S. E. Taylor (Eds.), *Annual review of psychology* (Vol. 62, pp. 451–482). Palo Alto: Annual Reviews.

Gigerenzer, G., & Hoffrage, U. (1995). How to improve Bayesian reasoning without instruction: Frequency formats. *Psychological Review, 102*, 684. doi:10.1037/0033-295X.102.4.684.

Gigerenzer, G., & Hug, K. (1992). Domain-specific reasoning: Social contracts, cheating, and perspective change. *Cognition, 43*, 127–171. doi:10.1016/0010-0277(92)90060-U.

Gigerenzer, G., Koehler, D. J., & Harvey, N. (2004). Fast and frugal heuristics: The tools of bounded rationality. In D. J. Koehler and N. Harvey (Eds.), *Blackwell handbook of judgment and decision making* (pp. 62–88). Malden: Blackwell.

Gigerenzer, G., Todd, P. M., & ABC-Research-Group. (1999). *Simple heuristics that make us smart.* Oxford: Oxford University Press.

Gilbert, D. T., & Malone, P. S. (1995). The correspondence bias. *Psychological Bulletin, 117*, 21–38. doi:10.1037/0033-2909.117.1.21.

Gilbert, D. T., Pelham, B. W., & Krull, D. S. (1988). On cognitive busyness: When person perceivers meet persons perceived. *Journal of Personality and Social Psychology, 54*, 733. doi:10.1037/0022-3514.54.5.733.

Gilovich, T. (1981). Seeing the past in the present: The effect of associations to familiar events on judgments and decisions. *Journal of Personality and Social Psychology, 40*, 797–808. doi:10.1037/0022-3514.40.5.797.

Gollwitzer, P. M. (1999). Implementation intentions: Strong effects of simple plans. *American Psychologist, 54*, 493–503. doi:10.1037/0003-066X.54.7.493.

Gollwitzer, P. M., & Moskowitz, G. B. (1996). Goal effects on action and cognition. In E. T. Higgins & A. W. Kruglanski (Eds.), *Social psychology: A handbook of basic principles* (pp. 361–399). New York: Guilford Press.

Gollwitzer, P. M., Sheeran, P., Trötschel, R., & Webb, T. L. (2011). Self-regulation of priming effects on behavior. *Psychological Science, 22*(7), 901–907. doi:10.1177/0956797611411586.

Gorn, G., Pham, M. T., & Sin, L. Y. (2001). When arousal influences ad evaluation and valence does not (and vice versa). *Journal of Consumer Psychology, 11*, 43–55. doi:10.1207/S15327663JCP1101_4.

Graesser, A. C., Gordon, S. E., & Sawyer, J. D. (1979). Recognition memory for typical and atypical actions in scripted activities: Tests of a script pointer+ tag hypothesis. *Journal of Verbal Learning and Verbal Behavior, 18*, 319–332. doi:10.1016/S0022-5371(79)90182-8.

Gray, H. M. (2008). To what extent, and under what conditions, are first impressions valid. In N. Ambady & J. J. Skowronski (Eds.), *First impressions* (pp. 106–128). New York: Guilford Press.

Grayson, C. E., & Schwarz, N. (1999). Beliefs influence information processing strategies: Declarative and experiential information in risk assessment. *Social Cognition, 17*, 1–18. doi:10.1521/soco.1999.17.1.1.

Greenwald, A. G., & Banaji, M. R. (1989). The self as a memory system: Powerful, but ordinary. *Journal of Personality and Social Psychology, 57*, 41–54. doi:10.1037/0022-3514.57.1.41.

Greenwald, A. G., Banaji, M. R., Rudman, L. A., Farnham, S. D., Nosek, B. A., & Mellott, D. S. (2002). A unified theory of implicit attitudes, stereotypes, self-esteem, and self-concept. *Psychological Review, 109*, 3–25. doi:10.1037/0033-295X.109.1.3.

Greenwald, A. G., McGhee, D. E., & Schwartz, J. L. K. (1998). Measuring individual differences in implicit cognition: The Implicit Association Test. *Journal of Personality and Social Psychology, 74*, 1464–1480. doi:10.1037/0022-3514.74.6.1464.

Greenwald, A. G., Poehlman, T. A., Uhlmann, E. L., & Banaji, M. R. (2009). Understanding and using the Implicit Association Test: III: Meta-analysis of predictive validity. *Journal of Personality and Social Psychology, 97*, 17–41. doi:10.1037/a0015575.

Greifeneder, R., Alt, A., Bottenberg, K., Seele, T., Zelt, S., & Wagener, D. (2010). On writing legibly: Processing fluency systematically biases evaluations of handwritten material. *Social Psychological and Personality Science, 1*, 230–237. doi:10.1177/1948550610368434.

Greifeneder, R., & Bless, H. (2007). Relying on accessible content versus accessibility experiences: The case of processing capacity. *Social Cognition, 25*, 853–881. doi:10.1521/soco.2007.25.6.853.

Greifeneder, R., & Bless, H. (2008). Depression and reliance on ease-of-retrieval experiences. *European Journal of Social Psychology, 38*, 213–230. doi:10.1002/ejsp.451.

Greifeneder, R., & Bless, H. (2010). The fate of activated information in impression formation: Fluency of concept activation moderates the emergence of assimilation versus contrast. *British Journal of Social Psychology, 49*, 405–414. doi:10.1348/014466609X479699.

Greifeneder, R., Bless, H., & Kuschmann, T. (2007). Extending the brand image on new products: The facilitative effect of happy mood states. *Journal of Consumer Behavior, 6*, 19–31. doi:10.1002/cb.205.

Greifeneder, R., Bless, H., & Pham, M. T. (2011). When do people rely on affective and cognitive feelings in judgment? A review. *Personality and Social Psychology Review, 15*, 107–141. doi:10.1177/1088868310367640.

Greifeneder, R., Bless, H., & Scholl, S. (2013). About swift defaults and sophisticated safety nets: A process perspective on fluency's validity in judgment. In C. Unkelbach & R. Greifeneder (Eds.), *The experience of thinking: How the fluency of mental processes influences cognition and behavior* (pp. 220–233). Hove: Psychology Press.

Greifeneder, R., Müller, P., Stahlberg, D., Van den Bos, K., & Bless, H. (2011a). Beyond procedure's content: Cognitive subjective experiences in procedural justice judgments. *Experimental Psychology, 58*, 341–352. doi:10.1027/1618-3169/a000101.

Greifeneder, R., Müller, P., Stahlberg, D., Van den Bos, K., & Bless, H. (2011b). Guiding trustful behavior: The role of accessible content and accessibility experiences. *Journal of Behavioral Decision Making, 24*, 498–514. doi:10.1002/bdm.705.

Greifeneder, R., & Unkelbach, C. (2013). Experiencing thinking. In C. Unkelbach & R. Greifeneder (Eds.), *The experience of thinking: How the fluency of mental processes influences cognition and behavior* (pp. 1–7). Hove: Psychology Press.

Greifeneder, R., Zelt, S., Seele, T., Bottenberg, K., & Alt, A. (2012). Towards a better understanding of the legibility bias in performance assessments: The case of gender-based inferences. *British Journal of Educational Psychology, 82*, 361–374. doi:10.1111/j.2044-8279.2011.02029.x.

Greitemeyer, T. (2011). Effects of prosocial media on social behavior when and why does media exposure affect helping and aggression? *Current Directions in Psychological Science, 20*, 251–255. doi:10.1177/0963721411415229.

Greitemeyer, T., & Schulz-Hardt, S. (2003). Preference-consistent evaluation of information in the hidden profile paradigm: Beyond group-level explanations for the dominance of shared information in group decisions. *Journal of Personality and Social Psychology, 84*, 322–339. doi:10.1037/0022-3514.84.2.322.

Greve, W. (2001). Traps and gaps in action explanation: Theoretical problems of a psychology of human action. *Psychological Review, 108*, 435–451. doi:10.1037/0033-295X.108.2.435.

Grice, H. P. (1975). Logic and conversation. In P. Cole & J. L. Morgan (Eds.), *Syntax and semantics, vol. 3: Speech acts* (pp. 41–58). New York: Academic Press.

Griffin, D., & Buehler, R. (1999). Frequency, probability, and prediction: Easy solutions to cognitive illusions? *Cognitive Psychology, 38*, 48–78. doi:10.1006/cogp.1998.0707.

Haidt, J. (2001). The emotional dog and its rational tail: A social intuitionist approach to moral judgment. *Psychological Review, 108*, 814–834. doi:10.1037/0033-295X.108.4.814.

Halberstadt, J., & Rhodes, G. (2000). The attractiveness of nonface averages: Implications for an evolutionary explanation of the attractiveness of average faces. *Psychological Science, 11*, 285–289. doi:10.1111/1467-9280.00257.

Ham, J., & Van den Bos, K. (2011). On unconscious and conscious thought and the accuracy of implicit and explicit judgments. *Social Cognition, 29*, 648–667. doi:10.1521/soco.2011.29.6.648.

Hamilton, D. L., & Gifford, R. K. (1976). Illusory correlation in interpersonal perception: A cognitive basis of stereotypic judgments. *Journal of Experimental Social Psychology, 12*, 392–407. doi:10.1016/S0022-1031(76)80006-6.

Hamilton, D. L., & Sherman, S. J. (1996). Perceiving persons and groups. *Psychological Review, 103*, 336–355. doi:10.1037/0033-295X.103.2.336.

Han, H. A., Olson, M. A., & Fazio, R. H. (2006). The influence of experimentally created extrapersonal associations on the Implicit Association Test. *Journal of Experimental Social Psychology, 42*, 259–272. doi:10.1016/j.jesp.2005.04.006.

Hansen, J., & Wänke, M. (2008). It's the difference that counts: Expectancy/experience discrepancy moderates the use of ease of retrieval in attitude judgments. *Social Cognition, 26*, 447–468. doi:10.1521/soco.2008.26.4.447.

Hart, J. T. (1965). Memory and the feeling-of-knowing experience. *Journal of Educational Psychology, 56*, 208–216. doi:10.1037/h0022263.

Hart, J. T. (1967). Second-try recall, recognition, and the memory-monitoring process. *Journal of Educational Psychology, 58*, 193–197. doi:10.1037/h0024908.

Hasher, L., Goldstein, D., & Toppino, T. (1977). Frequency and the conference of referential validity. *Journal of Verbal Learning and Verbal Behavior, 16*, 107–112. doi:10.1016/S0022-5371(77)80012-1.

Hastie, R., & Kumar, P. A. (1979). Person memory: Personality traits as organizing principles in memory for behaviors. *Journal of Personality and Social Psychology, 37*, 25–38. doi:10.1037//0022-3514.37.1.25.

Hauser, D. J., & Schwarz, N. (2016). Semantic prosody and judgment. *Journal of Experimental Psychology: General, 145*, 882–896.

Hausmann, L. R. M., Levine, J. M., & Higgins, E. T. (2008). Communication and group perception: Extending the "saying is believing" effect. *Group Processes & Intergroup Relations, 11*, 539–554. doi:10.1177/1368430208095405.

Hawkins, S. A., & Hastie, R. (1990). Hindsight: Biased judgments of past events after the outcomes are known. *Psychological Bulletin, 107*, 311. doi:10.1037/0033-2909.107.3.311.

Heider, F. (1946). Attitudes and cognitive organization. *Journal of Psychology, 21*, 107–112. doi:10.1080/00223980.1946.9917275.

Henderson, M. D., & Wakslak, C. (2010). Psychological distance and priming: When do semantic primes impact social evaluations? *Personality and Social Psychology Bulletin, 36*, 975–985. doi:10.1177/0146167210367490.

Hermans, D., Baeyens, F., Lamote, S., Spruyt, A., & Eelen, P. (2005). Affective priming as an indirect measure of food preferences acquired through odor conditioning. *Experimental Psychology, 52*, 180–186. doi:10.1027/1618-3169.52.3.180.

Hernandez, I., & Preston, J. L. (2013). Disfluency disrupts the confirmation bias. *Journal of Experimental Social Psychology, 49*, 178–182. doi:10.1016/j.jesp.2012.08.010.

Herr, P. M. (1986). Consequences of priming: Judgment and behavior. *Journal of Personality and Social Psychology, 51*, 1106–1115. doi:10.1037/0022-3514.51.6.1106.

Herr, P. M., Sherman, S. J., & Fazio, R. H. (1983). On the consequences of priming: Assimilation and contrast effects. *Journal of Experimental Social Psychology, 19*, 323–340. doi:10.1016/0022-1031(83)90026-4.

Hertel, G., & Fiedler, K. (1998). Fair and dependent versus egoistic and free: Effects of semantic and evaluative priming on the "ring measure of social values." *European Journal of Social Psychology, 28*, 49–70. doi:10.1002/(SICI)1099-0992(199801/02)28:1<49::AID-EJSP845>3.3.CO;2-8.

Herzog, S. M., & Hertwig, R. (2009). The wisdom of many in one mind improving individual judgments with dialectical bootstrapping. *Psychological Science, 20*, 231–237. doi:10.1111/j.1467-9280.2009.02271.x.

Herzog, S. M., & Hertwig, R. (2013). The ecological validity of fluency. In C. Unkelbach & R. Greifeneder (Eds.), *The experience of thinking: How the fluency of mental processes influences cognition and behavior* (pp. 190–219). Hove: Psychology Press.

Hewstone, M. (1994). Revising and change of stereotypic beliefs: In search of the elusive subtyping model. In W. Stroebe & M. Hewstone (Eds.), *European review of social psychology* (Vol. 5, pp. 69–109). Chichester, UK: Wiley.

Higgins, E. T. (1996). Knowledge activation: Accessibility, applicability, and salience. In E. T. Higgins & A. W. Kruglanski (Eds.), *Social psychology: Handbook of basic principles* (pp. 133–168). New York: Guilford Press.

Higgins, E. T. (1998). The aboutness principle: A pervasive influence on human inference. *Social Cognition, 16*, 173–198. doi:10.1521/soco.1998.16.1.173.

Higgins, E. T., & Eitam, B. (2014). Priming…Shmiming: It's about knowing when and why stimulated memory representations become active. *Social Cognition, 32*, 225–242. doi:10.1521/soco.2014.32.supp.225.

Higgins, E. T., King, G. A., & Mavin, G. H. (1982). Individual construct accessibility and subjective impressions and recall. *Journal of Personality and Social Psychology, 43*, 35–47. doi:10.1037/0022-3514.43.1.35.

Higgins, E. T., McCann, C. D., & Fondacaro, R. (1982). The "communication game": Goal-directed encoding and cognitive consequences. *Social Cognition, 1*, 21. doi:10.1521/soco.1982.1.1.21.

Higgins, E. T., & Rholes, W. S. (1978). "Saying is believing": Effects of message modification on memory and liking for the person described. *Journal of Experimental Social Psychology, 14*, 363–378. doi:10.1016/0022-1031(78)90032-X.

Higgins, E. T., Rholes, W. S., & Jones, C. R. (1977). Category accessibility and impression formation. *Journal of Experimental Social Psychology, 13*, 141–154. doi:10.1016/S0022-1031(77)80007-3.

Hilton, D. J. (1995). The social context of reasoning: Conversational inference and rational judgment. *Psychological Bulletin, 118*, 248. doi:10.1037/0033-2909.118.2.248.

Hilton, J. L., & Von Hippel, W. (1996). Stereotypes. *Annual Review of Psychology, 47*, 237–271. doi:10.1146/annurev.psych.47.1.237.

Hirt, E. R., Levine, G. M., McDonald, H. E., Melton, R. J., & Martin, L. L. (1997). The role of mood in quantitative and qualitative aspects of performance: Single or multiple mechanisms? *Journal of Experimental Social Psychology, 33*, 602–629. doi:10.1006/jesp.1997.1335.

Hofmann, W., De Houwer, J., Perugini, M., Baeyens, F., & Crombez, G. (2010). Evaluative conditioning in humans: A meta-analysis. *Psychological Bulletin, 136*, 390. doi:10.1037/a0018916.

Hofmann, W., Rauch, W., & Gawronski, B. (2007). And deplete us not into temptation: Automatic attitudes, dietary restraint, and self-regulatory resources as determinants of eating behavior. *Journal of Experimental Social Psychology, 43*, 497–504.

Homans, G. C. (1967). *The nature of social science.* New York: Harcourt, Brace & World.

Hunt, R. R., & McDaniel, M. A. (1993). The enigma of organization and distinctiveness. *Journal of Memory and Language, 32*, 421–445. doi:10.1006/jmla.1993.1023.

Huntsinger, J. R. (2012). Does positive affect broaden and negative affect narrow attentional scope? A new answer to an old question. *Journal of Experimental Psychology: General, 141*, 595–600. doi:10.1037/a0027709.

Huntsinger, J. R. (2013). Does emotion directly tune the scope of attention? *Current Directions in Psychological Science, 22*, 265–270. doi:10.1177/0963721413480364.

Huntsinger, J. R., Clore, G. L., & Bar-Anan, Y. (2010). Mood and global–local focus: Priming a local focus reverses the link between mood and global–local processing. *Emotion, 10*, 722–726. doi:10.1037/a0019356.

Huntsinger, J. R., Isbell, L., & Clore, G. L. (2014). The affective control of thought: Malleable, not fixed. *Psychological Review, 121*, 600–618. doi:10.1037/a0037669.

Igou, E. R., & Bless, H. (2007). On undesirable consequences of thinking: Framing effects as a function of substantive processing. *Journal of Behavioral Decision Making, 20*, 125–142. doi:10.1002/bdm.543.

Isbell, L., & Wyer, R. S. (1999). Correcting for mood-induced bias in the evaluation of political candidates: The roles of intrinsic and extrinsic motivation. *Personality and Social Psychology Bulletin, 25*, 237–249. doi:10.1177/0146167299025002009.

Isen, A. M. (1987). Positive affect, cognitive processes, and social behavior. In L. Berkowitz (Ed.), *Advances in experimental social psychology* (Vol. 20, pp. 203–253). San Diego, CA: Academic Press.

Isen, A. M. (2008). Some ways in which positive affect influences decision making and problem solving. In M. Lewis, J. M. Haviland-Jones & L. Barrett (Eds.), *Handbook of emotions* (Vol. 3, pp. 548–573). New York Guilford Press.

Isen, A. M., Means, B., Patrick, R., & Nowicki, G. (1982). *Some factors influencing decision making strategy and risk-taking.* Paper presented at Affect and Cognition: The 17th annual Carnegie Mellon symposium on cognition.

Isen, A. M., Niedenthal, P. M., & Cantor, N. (1992). An influence of positive affect on social categorization. *Motivation and Emotion, 16*, 65–78. doi:10.1007/BF00996487.

Jacoby, L. L., & Dallas, M. (1981). On the relationship between autobiographical memory and perceptual learning. *Journal of Experimental Psychology: General, 110*, 306–340. doi:10.1037/0096-3445.110.3.306.

Jacoby, L. L., Kelley, C. M., Brown, J., & Jasechko, J. (1989). Becoming famous overnight: Limits of the ability to avoid unconscious influences of the past. *Journal of Personality and Social Psychology, 56*, 326–338. doi:10.1037/0022-3514.56.3.326.

Jacoby, L. L., Kelley, C. M., & Dywan, J. (1989). Memory attributions. In H. L. Roediger III & F. I. M. Craik (Eds.), *Varieties of memory and consciousness: Essays in honour of Endel Tulving* (pp. 391–422). Hillsdale, NJ: Lawrence Erlbaum Associates.

Jacowitz, K. E., & Kahneman, D. (1995). Measures of anchoring in estimation tasks. *Personality and Social Psychology Bulletin, 21*, 1161–1166. doi:10.1177/01461672952111004.

James, H. W. (1929). The effect of handwriting upon grading. *The English Journal, 16*, 180–185. doi:10.2307/803599.

James, W. (1890). The principles of psychology. In R. M. Hutchins (Ed.), *The great book of the Western world* (pp. 348). Chicago: Encyclopaedia Brittanica.

Janiszewski, C., & Wyer, R. S. (2014). Content and process priming: A review. *Journal of Consumer Psychology, 24*, 96–118. doi:10.1016/j.jcps.2013.05.006.

Janssen, J., Müller, P., & Greifeneder, R. (2011). Cognitive processes in procedural justice judgments: The role of ease-of-retrieval, uncertainty, and experience. *Journal of Organizational Behavior, 32*, 726–750. doi:10.1002/job.700.

Johnson, R. D., & Downing, L. L. (1979). Deindividuation and valence of cues: Effects on prosocial and antisocial behavior. *Journal of Personality and Social Psychology, 37*, 1532–1538. doi:10.1037/0022-3514.37.9.1532.

Johnston, L., & Hewstone, M. (1992). Cognitive models of stereotype change: 3. Subtyping and the perceived typicality of disconfirming group members. *Journal of Experimental Social Psychology, 28,* 360–386. doi:10.1016/0022-1031(92)90051-K.

Jonas, E., Schulz-Hardt, S., Frey, D., & Thelen, N. (2001). Confirmation bias in sequential information search after preliminary decisions: An expansion of dissonance theoretical research on selective exposure to information. *Journal of Personality and Social Psychology, 80,* 557–571. doi:10.1037/0022-3514.80.4.557.

Jones, E. E., & Davis, K. E. (1965). From acts to dispositions the attribution process in person perception. In L. Berkowitz (Ed.), *Advances in experimental social psychology* (Vol. 2, pp. 219–266). San Diego, CA: Elsevier Academic Press.

Jones, E. E., & Harris, V. A. (1967). The attribution of attitudes. *Journal of Experimental Social Psychology, 3,* 1–24. doi:10.1016/0022-1031(67)90034-0.

Judd, C. M., & Park, B. (1988). Out-group homogeneity: Judgments of variability at the individual and group levels. *Journal of Personality and Social Psychology, 54,* 778–788. doi:10.1037/0022-3514.54.5.778.

Jussim, L. (1991). Social perception and social reality: A reflection-construction model. *Psychological Review, 98,* 54–73. doi:10.1037/0033-295X.98.1.54.

Kahneman, D. (2003). A perspective on judgment and choice: Mapping bounded rationality. *American Psychologist, 58,* 697–720. doi:10.1037/0003-066X.58.9.697.

Kahneman, D., & Miller, D. T. (1986). Norm theory: Comparing reality to its alternatives. *Psychological Review, 93,* 136–153. doi:10.1037/0033-295X.93.2.136.

Kahneman, D., & Tversky, A. (1972). Subjective probability: A judgment of representativeness. *Cognitive Psychology, 3,* 430–454. doi:10.1016/0010-0285(72)90016-3.

Kahneman, D., & Tversky, A. (1973). On the psychology of prediction. *Psychological Review, 80,* 237–251. doi:10.1037/h0034747.

Kahneman, D., & Tversky, A. (1979). Prospect theory: An analysis of decisions under risk. *Econometrica, 47,* 263–291. doi:10.2307/1914185.

Kanouse, D. E., & Abelson, R. P. (1967). Language variables affecting the persuasiveness of simple communications. *Journal of Personality and Social Psychology, 7,* 158–163. doi:10.1037/h0025003.

Kashima, Y. (2000). Maintaining cultural stereotypes in the serial reproduction of narratives. *Personality and Social Psychology Bulletin, 26,* 594–604. doi:10.1177/0146167200267007.

Kashima, Y., & Lan, Y. (2013). Communication and language use in social cognition. In D. E. Carlston (Ed.), *The Oxford handbook of social cognition* (pp. 729–748). New York: Oxford University Press.

Katz, D., & Braly, K. (1933). Racial stereotypes of one hundred college students. *Journal of Abnormal and Social Psychology, 28,* 280–290. doi:10.1037/h0074049.

Kay, A. C., Wheeler, S. C., Bargh, J. A., & Ross, L. (2004). Material priming: The influence of mundane physical objects on situational construal and competitive behavioral choice. *Organizational Behavior and Human Decision Processes, 95,* 83–96. doi:10.1016/j.obhdp.2004.06.003.

Kelley, C. M., & Lindsay, D. S. (1993). Remembering mistaken for knowing: Ease of retrieval as a basis for confidence in answers to general knowledge questions. *Journal of Memory and Language, 32,* 1–24. doi:10.1006/jmla.1993.1001.

Kelley, H. H. (1987). Attribution in social interaction. In E. E. Jones, D. E. Kanouse, H. H. Kelley, R. E. Nisbett, S. Valins & B. Weiner (Eds.), *Attribution: Perceiving the causes of behavior* (pp. 151–174). Morristown, NJ: General Learning Press.

Kelley, H. H., & Michela, J. L. (1980). Attribution theory and research. *Annual Review of Psychology, 31,* 457–501. doi:10.1146/annurev.ps.31.020180.002325.

Kelley, M. R., Pentz, C., & Reysen, M. B. (2014). The joint influence of collaboration and part-set cueing. *Quarterly Journal of Experimental Psychology, 67,* 1977–1985. doi:10.1080/17470218.2014.881405.

Kenrick, D. T., & Gutierres, S. E. (1980). Contrast effects and judgments of physical attractiveness: When beauty becomes a social problem. *Journal of Personality and Social Psychology, 38*, 131–140. doi:10.1037/0022-3514.38.1.131.

Kerr, N. L., & Tindale, R. S. (2004). Group performance and decision making. *Annual Review of Psychology, 55*, 623–655. doi:10.1146/annurev.psych.55.090902.142009.

Keysar, B., Hayakawa, S., & An, S. (2012). The foreign-language effect: Thinking in a foreign tongue reduces decision biases. *Psychological Science, 23*, 661–668. doi:10.1177/0956797611432178.

Klapper, A., Dotsch, R., van Rooij, I., & Wigboldus, D. H. (2016). Do we spontaneously form stable trustworthiness impressions from facial appearance? *Journal of Personality and Social Psychology, 111*, 655–664. doi:10.1037/pspa0000062.

Klauer, K. C., & Musch, J. (2003). Affective priming: Findings and theories. In J. Musch & K. C. Klauer (Eds.), *The psychology of evaluation: Affective processes in cognition and emotion* (pp. 7–49). Mahwah, NJ: Erlbaum.

Klauer, K. C., & Wegener, I. (1998). Unraveling social categorization in the "Who said what?" paradigm. *Journal of Personality and Social Psychology, 75*, 1155–1178. doi:10.1037/0022-3514.75.5.1155.

Klayman, J., & Ha, Y. (1987). Confirmation, disconfirmation, and information in hypothesis testing. *Psychological Review, 94*, 211–228. doi:10.1037/0033-295X.94.2.211.

Klein, S. B. (2012). A role for self-referential processing in tasks requiring participants to imagine survival on the savannah. *Journal of Experimental Psychology: Learning, Memory, and Cognition, 38*, 1234–1242. doi:10.1037/a0027636.

Klein, S. B., & Loftus, J. (1988). The nature of self-referent encoding: The contributions of elaborative and organizational processes. *Journal of Personality and Social Psychology, 55*, 5–11. doi:10.1037/0022-3514.55.1.5.

Knutson, B. (1996). Facial expressions of emotion influence interpersonal trait inferences. *Journal of Nonverbal Behavior, 20*, 165–182. doi:10.1007/BF02281954.

Koehler, J. J. (1996). The base rate fallacy reconsidered: Descriptive, normative, and methodological challenges. *Behavioral and Brain Sciences, 19*, 1–17. doi:10.1017/S0140525X00041157.

Koffka, K. (1935). *Principles of Gestalt psychology*. New York: Harcourt, Brace, & World.

Konrath, S., Meier, B., & Schwarz, N. (2004). Seeing President Bush: Presidential pictures prime aggressive thoughts, perceptions, & behaviors. Poster presented at American Psychological Society in Chicago, IL.

Koriat, A. (1993). How do we know that we know? The accessibility model of the feeling of knowing. *Psychological Review, 100*, 609–639. doi:10.1037/0033-295X.100.4.609.

Koriat, A. (1997). Monitoring one's own knowledge during study: A cue-utilization approach to judgments of learning. *Journal of Experimental Psychology: General, 126*, 349–370. doi:10.1037/0096-3445.126.4.349.

Koriat, A. (2012). The self-consistency model of subjective confidence. *Psychological Review, 119*, 80–113.

Koriat, A., & Levy-Sadot, R. (1999). Processes underlying metacognitive judgments: Information-based and experience-based monitoring of one's own knowledge. In S. Chaiken & Y. Trope (Eds.), *Dual-process theories in social psychology* (pp. 483–502). New York: Guilford Press.

Koriat, A., & Ma'ayan, H. (2005). The effects of encoding fluency and retrieval fluency on judgments of learning. *Journal of Memory and Language, 52*, 478–492. doi:10.1016/j.jml.2005.01.001.

Krahé, B., Berkowitz, L., Moller, I., Warburton, W., Brockmyer, J. H., Bushman, B. J., ... Warburton, W. (2012). Report of the media violence commission. *Aggressive Behavior, 38*, 335–341. doi:10.1002/ab.21443.

Krauth-Gruber, S., & Ric, F. (2000). Affect and stereotypic thinking: A test of the mood-and-general-knowledge-model. *Personality and Social Psychology Bulletin, 26*, 1587–1597. doi:10.1177/01461672002612012.

Kruger, J., & Dunning, D. (1999). Unskilled and unaware of it: How difficulties in recognizing one's own imcompetence lead to inflated self-assessments. *Journal of Personality and Social Psychology, 77*, 1121–1134. doi:10.1037/0022-3514.77.6.1121.

Kruger, J., & Savitsky, K. (2009). On the genesis of inflated (and deflated) judgments of responsibility. *Organizational Behavior and Human Decision Processes, 108*, 143–152. doi:10.1016/j.obhdp.2008.06.002.

Kruglanski, A. W. (1989). *Lay epistemics and human knowledge: Cognitive and motivational bases.* New York: Plenum Press.

Kruglanski, A. W. (2004). *The psychology of closed mindedness.* New York: Psychology Press.

Kruglanski, A. W., & Webster, D. M. (1996). Motivated closing of the mind: "Seizing" and "freezing." *Psychological Review, 103*, 263–283. doi:10.1037/0033-295X.103.2.263.

Kühnen, U., Hannover, B., & Schubert, B. (2001). The semantic-procedural interface model of the self: The role of self-knowledge for context-dependent versus context-independent modes of thinking. *Journal of Personality and Social Psychology, 80*, 397–409. doi:10.1037/0022-3514.80.3.397.

Kuiper, N. A., & Rogers, T. B. (1979). Encoding of personal information: Self-other differences. *Journal of Personality and Social Psychology, 37*, 499–514. doi:10.1037/0022-3514.37.4.499.

Kunda, Z. (1990). The case for motivated reasoning. *Psychological Bulletin, 108*, 480–498. doi:10.1037/0033-2909.108.3.480.

Kunda, Z., & Oleson, K. C. (1995). Maintaining stereotypes in the face of disconfirmation: Constructing grounds for subtyping deviants. *Journal of Personality and Social Psychology, 68*, 565–579. doi:10.1037/0022-3514.68.4.565.

Kunda, Z., & Oleson, K. C. (1997). When exceptions prove the rule: How extremity of deviance determines the impact of deviant examples on stereotypes. *Journal of Personality and Social Psychology, 72*, 965–979. doi:10.1037/0022-3514.72.5.965.

Kutzner, F. L., & Fiedler, K. (2015). No correlation, no evidence for attention shift in category learning: Different mechanisms behind illusory correlations and the inverse base-rate effect. *Journal of Experimental Psychology: General, 144*, 58–75. doi:10.1037/a0038462.

Labroo, A. A., & Patrick, V. M. (2009). Psychological distancing: Why happiness helps you see the big picture. *Journal of Consumer Research, 35*, 800–809. doi:10.1086/593683.

Labroo, A. A., & Pocheptsova, A. (2016). Metacognition and consumer judgment: Fluency is pleasant but disfluency ignites interest. *Current Opinion in Psychology, 10*, 154–159. doi:10.1016/j.copsyc.2016.01.008.

Lambert, A. J., & Wyer, R. S. (1990). Stereotypes and social judgment: The effects of typicality and group heterogeneity. *Journal of Personality and Social Psychology, 59*, 676–691. doi:10.1037/0022-3514.59.4.676.

Langer, E. J., Fiske, S. T., Taylor, S. E., & Chanowitz, B. (1976). Stigma, staring, and discomfort: A novel-stimulus hypothesis. *Journal of Experimental Social Psychology, 12*, 451–463. doi:10.1016/0022-1031(76)90077-9.

Larson, J. R., Foster-Fishman, P. G., & Franz, T. M. (1998). Leadership style and the discussion of shared and unshared information in decision-making groups. *Personality and Social Psychology Bulletin, 24*, 482–495. doi:10.1177/0146167298245004.

Lench, H. C., & Bench, S. W. (2012). Automatic optimism: Why people assume their futures will be bright. *Social and Personality Psychology Compass, 6*, 347–360. doi:10.1111/j.1751-9004.2012.00430.x.

Lepore, L., & Brown, R. (1997). Category and stereotype activation: Is prejudice inevitable? *Journal of Personality and Social Psychology, 72*, 275–287. doi:10.1037/0022-3514.72.2.275.

Lerner, J. S., & Tetlock, P. E. (1999). Accounting for the effects of accountability. *Psychological Bulletin, 125*, 255–275. doi:10.1037/0033-2909.125.2.255.

Letzring, T. D., Wells, S. M., & Funder, D. C. (2006). Information quantity and quality affect the realistic accuracy of personality judgment. *Journal of Personality and Social Psychology, 91*, 111–123. doi:10.1037/0022-3514.91.1.111.

Lev-Ari, S., & Keysar, B. (2010). Why don't we believe non-native speakers? The influence of accent on credibility. *Journal of Experimental Social Psychology, 46,* 1093–1096. doi:10.1016/j.jesp.2010.05.025.

Levesque, M. J., & Kenny, D. A. (1993). Accuracy of behavioral predictions at zero acquaintance: A social relations analysis. *Journal of Personality and Social Psychology, 65,* 1178–1187. doi:10.1037/0022-3514.65.6.1178.

Leyens, J.-P., Yzerbyt, V. Y., & Corneille, O. (1996). The role of applicability in the emergence of the overattribution bias. *Journal of Personality and Social Psychology, 70,* 219–229. doi:10.1037/0022-3514.70.2.219.

Liberman, N., Sagristano, M. D., & Trope, Y. (2002). The effect of temporal distance on level of mental construal. *Journal of Experimental Social Psychology, 38,* 523–534. doi:10.1016/S0022-1031(02)00013-6.

Liberman, N., & Trope, Y. (1998). The role of feasibility and desirability considerations in near and distant future decisions: A test of temporal construal theory. *Journal of Personality and Social Psychology, 75,* 5–18. doi:10.1037//0022-3514.75.1.5.

Liberman, N., & Trope, Y. (2014). Traversing psychological distance. *Trends in Cognitive Sciences, 18,* 364–369. doi:10.1016/j.tics.2014.03.001.

Liberman, N., Trope, Y., & Stephan, E. (2007). Psychological distance. In A. W. Kruglanski, A. W. Higgins & E. T. Higgins (Eds.), *Social psychology: Handbook of basic principles* (Vol. 2, pp. 353–381). New York: Guilford Press.

Liberman, V., Samuels, S. M., & Ross, L. (2004). The name of the game: Predictive power of reputations versus situational labels in determining prisoner's dilemma game moves. *Personality and Social Psychology Bulletin, 30,* 1175–1185. doi:10.1177/0146167204264004.

Lichtenstein, S., Slovic, P., Fischhoff, B., Layman, M., & Combs, B. (1978). Judged frequency of lethal events. *Journal of Experimental Psychology: Human Learning and Memory, 4,* 551–578. doi:10.1037/0278-7393.4.6.551.

Loftus, E. F. (1979). *Eyewitness testimony.* Cambridge, MA: Harvard University Press.

Lombardi, W. J., Higgins, E. T., & Bargh, J. A. (1987). The role of consciousness in priming effects on categorization: Assimilation versus contrast as a function of awareness of the priming task. *Personality and Social Psychology Bulletin, 13,* 411–429. doi:10.1177/0146167287133009.

Lyons, A., & Kashima, Y. (2003). How are stereotypes maintained through communication? The influence of stereotype sharedness. *Journal of Personality and Social Psychology, 85,* 989–1005. doi:10.1037/0022-3514.85.6.989.

Maass, A. (1999). Linguistic intergroup bias: Stereotype perpetuation through language. In M. P. Zanna (Ed.), *Advances in experimental social psychology* (Vol. 31, pp. 79–121). San Diego, CA: Elsevier Academic Press.

Maass, A., Milesi, A., Zabbini, S., & Stahlberg, D. (1995). Linguistic intergroup bias: Differential expectancies or in-group protection? *Journal of Personality and Social Psychology, 68,* 116–126. doi:10.1037/0022-3514.68.1.116.

Maass, A., Salvi, D., Arcuri, L., & Semin, G. (1989). Language use in intergroup contexts: The linguistic intergroup bias. *Journal of Personality and Social Psychology, 57,* 981–993. doi:10.1037/0022-3514.57.6.981.

Mackie, D. M., & Worth, L. T. (1989). Processing deficits and the mediation of positive affect in persuasion. *Journal of Personality and Social Psychology, 57,* 27–40. doi:10.1037/0022-3514.57.1.27.

Macrae, C. N., Hewstone, M., & Griffiths, R. J. (1993). Processing load and memory for stereotype-based information. *European Journal of Social Psychology, 23,* 77–87. doi:10.1002/ejsp.2420230107.

Macrae, C. N., & Martin, D. (2007). A boy primed Sue: Feature-based processing and person construal. *European Journal of Social Psychology, 37,* 793–805. doi:10.1002/ejsp.406.

Macrae, C. N., & Quadflieg, S. (2010). Perceiving people. In S. T. Fiske, D. T. Gilbert & G. Lindzey (Eds.), *Handbook of social psychology* (pp. 428–463). Hoboken, NJ: Wiley.

Madon, S., Jussim, L., & Eccles, J. (1997). In search of the powerful self-fulfilling prophecy. *Journal of Personality and Social Psychology, 72,* 791–809. doi:10.1037/0022-3514.72.4.791.

Magee, J. C., & Smith, P. K. (2013). The social distance theory of power. *Personality and Social Psychology Review, 17,* 158–186. doi:10.1177/1088868312472732.

Mandler, G. (2011). From association to organization. *Current Directions in Psychological Science, 20,* 232–235. doi:10.1177/0963721411414656.

Mandler, G., Nakamura, Y., & Van Zandt, B. J. (1987). Nonspecific effects of exposure on stimuli that cannot be recognized. *Journal of Experimental Psychology: Learning, Memory, and Cognition, 13,* 646–648. doi:10.1037/0278-7393.13.4.646.

Manktelow, K. (1999). *Reasoning and thinking.* Hove: Psychology Press.

Mannes, A. E. (2013). Shorn scalps and perceptions of male dominance. *Social Psychological and Personality Science, 4,* 198–205. doi:10.1177/1948550612449490.

Manstead, A. S. R. (2010). Social psychology of emotion. In R. Baumeister & E. J. Finkel (Eds.), *Advanced social psychology: The state of the science* (pp. 101–137). New York: Oxford University Press.

Markus, H. R., & Kitayama, S. (1991). Culture and the self: Implications for cognition, emotion, and motivation. *Psychological Review, 98,* 224–253. doi:10.1037/0033-295X.98.2.224.

Martin, L. L. (1986). Set/reset: Use and disuse of concepts in impression formation. *Journal of Personality and Social Psychology, 51,* 493–504. doi:10.1037/0022-3514.51.3.493.

Martin, L. L. (2001). Moods don't cause effects, people do: A mood as input look at mood effects. In L. L. Martin & G. L. Clore (Eds.), *Mood and social cognition: Contrasting theories.* Mahwah, NJ: Lawrence Erlbaum Associates.

Martin, L. L., Abend, T., Sedikides, C., & Green, J. D. (1997). How would it feel if...? Mood as input to a role fulfillment evaluation process. *Journal of Personality and Social Psychology, 73,* 242–253. doi:10.1037/0022-3514.73.2.242.

Martin, L. L., & Clore, G. L. (2001). *Theories of mood and cognition: A user's guidebook.* Mahwah, NJ: Lawrence Erlbaum Associates.

Martin, L. L., Seta, J. J., & Crelia, R. A. (1990). Assimilation and contrast as a function of people's willingness and ability to expend effort in forming an impression. *Journal of Personality and Social Psychology, 59,* 27–37. doi:10.1037/0022-3514.59.1.27.

Martin, L. L., & Tesser, A. (1996). Some ruminative thoughts. In R. S. Wyer (Ed.), *Advances in social cognition* (Vol. 9, pp. 1–47). Mahwah, NJ: Erlbaum.

Masuda, T., & Nisbett, R. E. (2001). Attending holistically versus analytically: Comparing the context sensitivity of Japanese and Americans. *Journal of Personality and Social Psychology, 81,* 922–934. doi:10.1037/0022-3514.81.5.922.

Mata, R., Schooler, L., & Rieskamp, J. (2007). The aging decision maker: Cognitive aging and the adaptive selection of decision strategies. *Psychology and Aging, 22,* 796–810. doi:10.1037/0882-7974.22.4.796.

Matlin, M. W. (2013). *Cognition* (8th ed.). Hoboken, NJ: Wiley & Sons.

Matsumoto, D. (1990). Cultural similarities and differences in display rules. *Motivation and Emotion, 14,* 195–214. doi:10.1007/BF00995569.

Maurer, K. L., Park, B., & Rothbart, M. (1995). Subtyping versus subgrouping processes in stereotype representation. *Journal of Personality and Social Psychology, 69,* 812–824. doi:10.1037/0022-3514.69.5.812.

McArthur, L. Z., & Baron, R. M. (1983). Toward an ecological theory of social perception. *Psychological Review, 90,* 215–238. doi:10.1037/0033-295X.90.3.215.

McArthur, L. Z., & Ginsberg, E. (1981). Causal attribution to salient stimuli an investigation of visual fixation mediators. *Personality and Social Psychology Bulletin, 7,* 547–553. doi:10.1177/014616728174004.

McArthur, L. Z., & Post, D. L. (1977). Figural emphasis and person perception. *Journal of Experimental Social Psychology, 13,* 520–535. doi:10.1016/0022-1031(77)90051-8.

McCauley, C., & Stitt, C. L. (1978). An individual and quantitative measure of stereotypes. *Journal of Personality and Social Psychology, 36*, 929–940. doi:10.1037/0022-3514.36.9.929.

McCrea, S. M., Wieber, F., & Myers, A. L. (2012). Construal level mind-sets moderate self- and social stereotyping. *Journal of Personality and Social Psychology, 102*, 51–68. doi:10.1037/a0026108.

McGuire, W. J. (1985). Attitudes and attitude change. In G. Lindsay & E. Aronson (Eds.), *The handbook of social psychology* (Vol. 2, 3rd ed., pp. 233–346). New York: Random House.

McIntyre, K., Paolini, S., & Hewstone, M. (2016). Changing people's views of outgroups through individual-to-group generalisation: Meta-analytic reviews and theoretical considerations. *European Review of Social Psychology, 27*, 63–115. doi:10.1080/10463283.2016.1201893.

McKenzie, C. R. M., & Nelson, J. D. (2003). What a speaker's choice of frame reveals: Reference points, frame selection, and framing effects. *Psychonomic Bulletin & Review, 10*, 596–602. doi:10.3758/BF03196520.

Meier, B. P., Schnall, S., Schwarz, N., & Bargh, J. A. (2012). Embodiment in social psychology. *Topics in Cognitive Science, 4*, 705–716. doi:10.1111/j.1756-8765.2012.01212.x.

Mellers, B. A., Hertwig, R., & Kahneman, D. (2001). Do frequency representations eliminate conjunction effects? An exercise in adversarial collaboration. *Psychological Science, 12*, 269–275. doi:10.1111/1467-9280.00350.

Meyer, A., Frederick, S., Burnham, T., Guevara Pinto, J., Boyer, T., Ball, L., … Schuldt, J. P. (2015). Disfluent fonts don't help people solve math problems. *Journal of Experimental Psychology: General, 144*, e16–e30. doi:10.1037/xge0000049.

Meyer, D. E., & Schvaneveldt, R. W. (1971). Facilitation in recognizing pairs of words: Evidence of a dependence between retrieval operations. *Journal of Experimental Psychology, 90*, 227–234. doi:10.1037/h0031564.

Misyak, J. B., Melkonyan, T., Zeitoun, H., & Chater, N. (2014). Unwritten rules: Virtual bargaining underpins social interaction, culture, and society. *Trends in Cognitive Sciences, 18*, 512–519. doi:10.1016/j.tics.2014.05.010.

Mojzisch, A., & Schulz-Hardt, S. (2006). Information sampling in group decision making: Sampling biases and their consequences. In K. Fiedler & P. Juslin (Eds.), *Information sampling and adaptive cognition* (pp. 299–325). Cambridge: Cambridge University Press.

Molden, D. C. (Ed.). (2014). *Understanding priming effects in social psychology*. New York: Guilford Press.

Moore, D. A., & Healy, P. J. (2008). The trouble with overconfidence. *Psychological Review, 115*, 502–517. doi:10.1037/0033-295X.115.2.502.

Moore, D. A., & Small, D. A. (2007). Error and bias in comparative judgment: On being both better and worse than we think we are. *Journal of Personality and Social Psychology, 92*, 972–989. doi:10.1037/0022-3514.92.6.972.

Moors, A. (2016). Automaticity: Componential, causal, and mechanistic explanations. *Annual Review of Psychology, 67*, 263–287. doi:10.1146/annurev-psych-122414-033550.

Moors, A., & De Houwer, J. (2006). Automaticity: A theoretical and conceptual analysis. *Psychological Bulletin, 132*, 297–326. doi:10.1037/0033-2909.132.2.297.

Morris, M. W., & Peng, K. (1994). Culture and cause: American and Chinese attributions for social and physical events. *Journal of Personality and Social Psychology, 67*, 949–971. doi:10.1037/0022-3514.67.6.949.

Morris, W. N. (1989). *Mood: The frame of mind*. New York: Springer.

Moscovici, S., & Zavalloni, M. (1969). The group as a polarizer of attitudes. *Journal of Personality and Social Psychology, 12*, 125–135. doi:10.1037/h0027568.

Moskowitz, G. B., & Skurnik, I. W. (1999). Contrast effects as determined by the type of prime: Trait versus exemplar primes initiate processing strategies that differ in how accessible constructs are used. *Journal of Personality and Social Psychology, 76*, 911–927. doi:10.1037/0022-3514.76.6.911.

Müller, P., Greifeneder, R., Stahlberg, D., Van den Bos, K., & Bless, H. (2010). Shaping coop-eration behavior: The role of accessibility experiences. *European Journal of Social Psychology*, *40*, 178–187. doi:10.1002/ejsp.632.

Murray, N., Sujan, H., Hirt, E. R., & Sujan, M. (1990). The influence of mood on categorization: A cognitive flexibility interpretation. *Journal of Personality and Social Psychology*, *59*, 411–425. doi:10.1037/0022-3514.59.3.411.

Mussweiler, T. (2003). Comparison processes in social judgment: Mechanisms and consequences. *Psychological Review*, *110*, 472–489. doi:10.1037/0033-295X.110.3.472.

Mussweiler, T., & Neumann, R. (2000). Sources of mental contamination: Comparing the effects of self-generated versus externally provided primes. *Journal of Experimental Social Psychology*, *36*, 194–206. doi:10.1006/jesp.1999.1415.

Mussweiler, T., & Strack, F. (1999a). Comparing is believing: A selective accessibil-ity model of judgmental anchoring. *European Review of Social Psychology*, *10*, 135–167. doi:10.1080/14792779943000044.

Mussweiler, T., & Strack, F. (1999b). Hypothesis-consistent testing and semantic priming in the anchoring paradigm: A selective accessibility model. *Journal of Experimental Social Psychology*, *35*, 136–164. doi:10.1006/jesp.1998.1364.

Mussweiler, T., & Strack, F. (2000). The use of category and exemplar knowledge in the solution of anchoring tasks. *Journal of Personality and Social Psychology*, *78*, 1038–1052. doi:10.1037/0022-3514.78.6.1038.

Mussweiler, T., Strack, F., & Pfeiffer, T. (2000). Overcoming the inevitable anchoring effect: Considering the opposite compensates for selective accessibility. *Personality and Social Psychology Bulletin*, *26*, 1142–1150. doi:10.1177/01461672002611010.

Myers, D. G., & Lamm, H. (1976). The group polarization phenomenon. *Psychological Bulletin*, *83*, 602–627. doi:10.1037/0033-2909.83.4.602.

Nairne, J. S., & Pandeirada, J. N. S. (2008). Adaptive memory: Is survival processing special? *Journal of Memory and Language*, *59*, 377–385. doi:10.1016/j.jml.2008.06.001.

Nairne, J. S., & Pandeirada, J. N. S. (2016). Adaptive memory: The evolutionary significance of survival processing. *Perspectives on Psychological Science*, *11*, 496–511. doi:10.1177/1745691616635613.

Navon, D. (1977). The forest before trees: The precedence of global features in visual percep-tion. *Cognitive Psychology*, *9*, 353–383.

Neale, M. A., & Northcraft, G. B. (1991). Behavioral negotiation theory. A framework for conceptualizing dyadic bargainig. In L. L. Cummings & B. M. Staw (Eds.), *Research in organi-zational behavior* (pp. 147–190). Greenwich, CT: JAI.

Nelson, T. O., & Dunlosky, J. (1991). When people's judgments of learning (JOLs) are extremely accurate at predicting subsequent recall: The "delayed-JOL effect." *Psychological Science*, *2*, 267–270. doi:10.1111/j.1467-9280.1991.tb00147.x.

Neuberg, S. L., & Fiske, S. T. (1987). Motivational influences on impression formation: Outcome dependency, accuracy-driven attention, and individuating processes. *Journal of Personality and Social Psychology*, *53*, 431–444. doi:10.1037/0022-3514.53.3.431.

Nickerson, R. S. (1998). Confirmation bias: A ubiquitous phenomenon in many guises. *Review of General Psychology*, *2*, 175–220. doi:10.1037/1089-2680.2.2.175.

Niedenthal, P. M. (2008). Emotion concepts. In M. Lewis, J. M. Haviland-Jones & L. Barrett (Eds.), *Handbook of emotions* (Vol. 3, pp. 587–600). New York: Guilford Press.

Niedenthal, P. M., Krauth-Gruber, S., & Ric, F. (2006). *Psychology of emotion: Interpersonal, experi-ential, and cognitive approaches*. New York: Psychology Press.

Nieuwenstein, M. R., Wierenga, T., Morey, R. D., Wicherts, J. M., Blom, T. N., Wagenmakers, E.-J., … van Rijn, H. (2015). On making the right choice: A meta-analysis and large-scale replication attempt of the unconscious thought advantage. *Judgment and Decision Making*, *10*, 1–17.

Nisbett, R. E., & Wilson, T. D. (1977). Telling more than we can know: Verbal reports on mental processes. *Psychological Review, 84*, 231–259. doi:10.1037/0033-295X.84.3.231.

Northcraft, G. B., & Neale, M. A. (1987). Experts, amateurs, and real estate: An anchoring-and-adjustment perspective on property pricing decisions. *Organizational Behavior and Human Decision Processes, 39*, 84–97. doi:10.1016/0749-5978(87)90046-X.

Nussbaum, S., Trope, Y., & Liberman, N. (2003). Creeping dispositionism: The temporal dynamics of behavior prediction. *Journal of Personality and Social Psychology, 84*, 485–497. doi:10.1037/0022-3514.84.3.485.

Oaksford, M., & Chater, N. (1994). A rational analysis of the selection task as optimal data selection. *Psychological Review, 101*, 608–631. doi:10.1037/0033-295X.101.4.608.

Olivola, C. Y., & Todorov, A. (2010). Fooled by first impressions? Reexamining the diagnostic value of appearance-based inferences. *Journal of Experimental Social Psychology, 46*, 315–324. doi:10.1016/j.jesp.2009.12.002.

Oosterhof, N. N., & Todorov, A. (2008). The functional basis of face evaluation. *Proceedings of the National Academy of Sciences, 105*, 11087–11092. doi:10.1073/pnas.0805664105.

Oppenheimer, D. M. (2004). Spontaneous discounting of availability in frequency judgment tasks. *Psychological Science, 15*, 100–105. doi:10.1111/j.0963-7214.2004.01502005.x.

Oppenheimer, D. M. (2006). Consequences of erudite vernacular utilized irrespective of necessity: Problems with using long words needlessly. *Applied Cognitive Psychology, 20*, 139–156. doi:10.1002/acp.1178.

Ortony, A., Clore, G. L., & Collins, A. (1988). *The cognitive structure of emotions.* Cambridge: Cambridge University Press.

Oswald, F. L., Mitchell, G., Blanton, H., Jaccard, J., & Tetlock, P. E. (2013). Predicting ethnic and racial discrimination: A meta-analysis of IAT criterion studies. *Journal of Personality and Social Psychology, 105*, 171–192. doi:10.1037/a0032734.

Oyserman, D., Coon, H. M., & Kemmelmeier, M. (2002). Rethinking individualism and collectivism: Evaluation of theoretical assumptions and meta-analyses. *Psychological Bulletin, 128*, 3–72. doi:10.1037/0033-2909.128.1.3.

Oyserman, D., & Lee, S. W. S. (2008). Does culture influence what and how we think? Effects of priming individualism and collectivism. *Psychological Bulletin, 134*, 311–342. doi:10.1037/0033-2909.134.2.311.

Park, B., Judd, C. M., & Ryan, C. S. (1991). Social categorization and the representation of variability information. *European Review of Social Psychology, 2*, 211–245. doi:10.1080/14792779143000079.

Paulhus, D. L. (1984). Two-component models of socially desirable responding. *Journal of Personality and Social Psychology, 46*, 598–609. doi:10.1037/0022-3514.46.3.598.

Payne, B. K., Cheng, C. M., Govorun, O., & Stewart, B. D. (2005). An inkblot for attitudes: Affect misattribution as implicit measurement. *Journal of Personality and Social Psychology, 89*, 277–293. doi:10.1037/0022-3514.89.3.277.

Payne, J. W., Samper, A., Bettman, J. R., & Luce, M. F. (2008). Boundary conditions on unconscious thought in complex decision making. *Psychological Science, 19*, 1118–1123. doi:10.1111/j.1467-9280.2008.02212.x.

Petty, R. E., & Cacioppo, J. T. (1981). *Attitudes and persuasion: Classic and contemporary approaches.* Dubuque, IA: William C. Brown.

Petty, R. E., & Cacioppo, J. T. (1986). *Communication and persuasion: Central and peripheral routes to attitude change.* New York: Springer.

Petty, R. E., & Cacioppo, J. T. (1996). *Attitudes and persuasion: Classic and contemporary approaches.* Boulder, CO: Westview Press.

Petty, R. E., Goldman, R., & Cacioppo, J. T. (1981). Personal involvement as a determinant of argument-based persuasion. *Journal of Personality and Social Psychology, 41*, 847–855. doi:10.1037/0022-3514.41.5.847.

Petty, R. E., & Wegener, D. T. (1999). The elaboration likelihood model: Current status and controversies. In S. Chaiken & Y. Trope (Eds.), *Dual-process theories in social psychology* (pp. 37–72). New York: Guilford Press.

Pham, M. T. (1998). Representativeness, relevance, and the use of feelings in decision making. *Journal of Consumer Research, 25*, 144–159. doi:10.1086/209532.

Philippot, P., Schwarz, N., Carrera, P., De Vries, N., & Van Yperen, N. W. (1991). Differential effects of priming at the encoding and judgment stage. *European Journal of Social Psychology, 21*, 293–302. doi:10.1002/ejsp.2420210403.

Plessner, H., & Haar, T. (2006). Sports performance judgments from a social cognitive perspective. *Psychology of Sport and Exercise, 7*, 555–575. doi:10.1016/j.psychsport.2006.03.007.

Pohl, R. (1992). Der Rückschau-Fehler: Systematische Verfälschung der Erinnerung bei Experten und Novizen. *Kognitionswissenschaft, 3*, 38–44.

Pyone, J. S., & Isen, A. M. (2011). Positive affect, intertemporal choice, and levels of thinking: Increasing consumers' willingness to wait. *Journal of Marketing Research, 48*, 532–543. doi:10.1509/jmkr.48.3.532.

Pyszczynski, T., & Greenberg, J. (1987). Toward an integration of cognitive and motivational perspectives on social inference: A biased hypothesis-testing model. In L. Berkowitz (Ed.), *Advances in experimental social psychology* (Vol. 20, pp. 297–340). San Diego, CA: Elsevier Academic Press.

Quattrone, G. A. (1982). Overattribution and unit formation: When behavior engulfs the person. *Journal of Personality and Social Psychology, 42*, 593–607. doi:10.1037/0022-3514.42.4.593.

Radcliffe, N. M., & Klein, W. M. P. (2002). Dispositional, unrealistic, and comparative optimism: Differential relations with the knowledge and processing of risk information and beliefs about personal risk. *Personality and Social Psychology Bulletin, 28*, 836–846. doi:10.1177/0146167202289012.

Ray, J. J. (1983). Reviving the problem of acquiescent response bias. *Journal of Social Psychology, 121*, 81–96.

Reber, R. (2016). *Critical feeling: How to use feelings strategically.* Oxford: Oxford University Press.

Reber, R., & Greifeneder, R. (2017). Processing fluency in education: How metacognitive feelings shape learning, belief formation, and affect. *Educational Psychologist, 52*, 84–103. doi:10.1080/00461520.2016.1258173.

Reber, R., & Schwarz, N. (1999). Effects of perceptual fluency on judgments of truth. *Consciousness and Cognition: An International Journal, 8*, 338–342. doi:10.1006/ccog.1999.0386.

Reber, R., & Schwarz, N. (2001). The hot fringes of consciousness: Perceptual fluency and affect. *Consciousness and Emotion, 2*, 223–231. doi:10.1075/ce.2.2.03reb.

Reber, R., Schwarz, N., & Winkielman, P. (2004). Processing fluency and aesthetic pleasure: Is beauty in the perceiver's processing experience? *Personality and Social Psychology Review, 8*, 364–382. doi:10.1207/s15327957pspr0804_3.

Reber, R., Winkielman, P., & Schwarz, N. (1998). Effects of perceptual fluency on affective judgments. *Psychological Science, 9*, 45–48. doi:10.1111/1467-9280.00008.

Reed, L. I., DeScioli, P., & Pinker, S. A. (2014). The commitment function of angry facial expressions. *Psychological Science, 25*, 1511–1517. doi:10.1177/0956797614531027.

Reeder, G. D., & Brewer, M. B. (1979). A schematic model of dispositional attribution in interpersonal perception. *Psychological Review, 86*, 61–79. doi:10.1037/0033-295X.86.1.61.

Reinhard, M.-A., Greifeneder, R., & Scharmach, M. (2013). Unconscious processes improve lie detection. *Journal of Personality and Social Psychology, 105*, 721–739. doi:10.1037/a0034352.

Reinhard, M.-A., & Schwarz, N. (2012). The influence of affective states on the process of lie detection. *Journal of Experimental Psychology: Applied, 18*, 377–389. doi:10.1037/a0030466.

Rim, S., Hansen, J., & Trope, Y. (2013). What happens why? Psychological distance and focusing on causes versus consequences of events. *Journal of Personality and Social Psychology, 104*, 457–472. doi:10.1037/a0031024.

Ritov, I. (1996). Anchoring in simulated competitive market negotiation. *Organizational Behavior and Human Decision Processes, 67,* 16–25. doi:10.1006/obhd.1996.0062.

Roediger, H. L., & McDermott, K. B. (1995). Creating false memories: Remembering words not presented in lists. *Journal of Experimental Psychology: Learning, Memory, and Cognition, 21,* 803–814. doi:10.1037/0278-7393.21.4.803.

Roese, N. J. (1997). Counterfactual thinking. *Psychological Bulletin, 121,* 133–148. doi:10.1037//0033-2909.121.1.133.

Roper, R., & Shewan, D. (2002). Compliance and eyewitness testimony: Do eyewitnesses comply with misleading "expert pressure" during investigative interviewing? *Legal and Criminological Psychology, 7,* 155–163. doi:10.1348/135532502760274765.

Rosch, E., Mervis, C. B., Gray, W. D., Johnson, D. M., & Boyes-Braem, P. (1976). Basic objects in natural categories. *Cognitive Psychology, 8,* 382–439. doi:10.1016/0010-0285(76)90013-X.

Rosenthal, R. (1966). *Experimenter effects in behavioral research.* New York: Appleton-Century Crofts.

Rosenthal, R. (1991). Teacher expectancy effects: A brief update 25 years after the Pygmalion Experiment. *Journal of Research in Education, 1,* 3–12.

Rosenthal, R., & Jacobson, L. (1968). *Pygmalion in the classroom: Teacher expectation and pupils' intellectual development.* New York: Holt, Rinehart & Winston.

Ross, L. (1977). The intuitive psychologist and his shortcomings: Distortions in the attribution process. In L. Berkowitz (Ed.), *Advances in experimental social psychology* (Vol. 10, pp. 173–220). San Diego, CA: Elsevier Academic Press.

Ross, M., & Sicoly, F. (1979). Egocentric biases in availability and attribution. *Journal of Personality and Social Psychology, 37,* 322–336. doi:10.1037/0022-3514.37.3.322.

Rothbart, M., & Park, B. (1986). On the confirmability and disconfirmability of trait concepts. *Journal of Personality and Social Psychology, 50,* 131–142. doi:10.1037/0022-3514.50.1.131.

Rothermund, K., & Wentura, D. (2004). Underlying processes in the Implicit Association Test: Dissociating salience from associations. *Journal of Experimental Psychology: General, 133,* 139–165. doi:10.1037/0096-3445.133.2.139.

Rothman, A. J., & Schwarz, N. (1998). Constructing perceptions of vulnerability: Personal relevance and the use of experiential information in health judgments. *Personality and Social Psychology Bulletin, 24,* 1053–1064. doi:10.1177/01461672982410003.

Rowe, G., Hirsh, J. B., & Anderson, A. K. (2007). Positive affect increases the breadth of attentional selection. *Proceedings of the National Academy of Sciences, 104,* 383–388. doi:10.1073/pnas.0605198104.

Ruder, M., & Bless, H. (2003). Mood and the reliance on the ease of retrieval heuristic. *Journal of Personality and Social Psychology, 85,* 20–32. doi:10.1037/0022-3514.85.1.20.

Rudolph, U., & Försterling, F. (1997). The psychological causality implicit in verbs: A review. *Psychological Bulletin, 121,* 192–218. doi:10.1037/0033-2909.121.2.192.

Ruscher, J. B., & Fiske, S. T. (1990). Interpersonal competition can cause individuating processes. *Journal of Personality and Social Psychology, 58,* 832–843. doi:10.1037/0022-3514.58.5.832.

Sagristano, M. D., Trope, Y., & Liberman, N. (2002). Time-dependent gambling: Odds now, money later. *Journal of Experimental Psychology: General, 131,* 364–376. doi:10.1037/0096-3445.131.3.364.

Samochowiec, J., Wänke, M., & Fiedler, K. (2010). Political ideology at face value. *Social Psychological and Personality Science, 1,* 206–213. doi:10.1177/1948550610372145.

Schaller, M., Conway, L. G., & Tanchuk, T. L. (2002). Selective pressures on the once and future contents of ethnic stereotypes: Effects of the communicability of traits. *Journal of Personality and Social Psychology, 82,* 861–877. doi:10.1037/0022-3514.82.6.861.

Schmid, J., & Fiedler, K. (1998). The backbone of closing speeches: The impact of prosecution versus defense language on judicial attributions. *Journal of Applied Social Psychology, 28,* 1140–1172. doi:10.1111/j.1559-1816.1998.tb01672.x.

Schnall, S., Benton, J., & Harvey, S. (2008). With a clean conscience. *Psychological Science, 19,* 1219–1222. doi:10.1111/j.1467-9280.2008.02227.x.

Scholl, S., & Greifeneder, R. (2011). Disentangling the effects of alternation rate and maximum run length on judgments of randomness. *Judgment and Decision Making, 6,* 531–541.

Scholl, S., Greifeneder, R., & Bless, H. (2014). When fluency signals truth: Prior successful reliance on fluency moderates the impact of fluency on truth judgments. *Journal of Behavioral Decision Making, 27,* 268–280. doi:10.1002/bdm.1805.

Schulz-Hardt, S., Brodbeck, F. C., Mojzisch, A., Kerschreiter, R., & Frey, D. (2006). Group decision making in hidden profile situations: Dissent as a facilitator for decision quality. *Journal of Personality and Social Psychology, 91,* 1080–1093. doi:10.1037/0022-3514.91.6.1080.

Schulz-Hardt, S., & Mojzisch, A. (2012). How to achieve synergy in group decision making: Lessons to be learned from the hidden profile paradigm. *European Review of Social Psychology, 23,* 305–343. doi:10.1080/10463283.2012.744440.

Schwartz, B. L. (2002). *Tip-of-the-tongue states: Phenomenology, mechanism, and lexical retrieval.* Mahwah, NJ: Lawrence Erlbaum Associates.

Schwarz, N. (1990). Feelings as information: Informational and motivational functions of affective states. In E. T. Higgins & R. M. Sorrentino (Eds.), *Handbook of motivation and cognition: Foundations of social behavior* (Vol. 2, pp. 527–561). New York: Guilford Press.

Schwarz, N. (1995). What respondents learn from questionnaires: The survey interview and the logic of conversation. *International Statistical Review/Revue Internationale de Statistique,* 153–168. doi:10.2307/1403610.

Schwarz, N. (1996). *Cognition and communication: Judgmental biases research methods and the logic of conversation.* Hillsdale, NJ: Lawrence Erlbaum Associates.

Schwarz, N. (1998). Accessible content and accessibility experiences: The interplay of declarative and experiential information in judgment. *Personality and Social Psychology Review, 2,* 87–99. doi:10.1207/s15327957pspr0202_2.

Schwarz, N. (2002). Situated cognition and the wisdom in feelings: Cognitive tuning. In L. F. Barrett & P. Salovey (Eds.), *The wisdom in feeling: Psychological processes in emotional intelligence* (pp. 144–166). New York: Guilford Press.

Schwarz, N. (2004). Metacognitive experiences in consumer judgment and decision making. *Journal of Consumer Psychology, 14,* 332–348. doi:10.1207/s15327663jcp1404_2.

Schwarz, N. (2008). Metacognitive experiences: A feelings-as-information perspective. Metacognition and Consumer Behavior Conference. Kellogg School of Management, Northwestern University, Evanston.

Schwarz, N. (2012). Feelings-as-information theory. In P. A. Van Lange, A. W. Kruglanski & E. Higgins (Eds.), *Handbook of theories of social psychology* (pp. 289–308). Thousand Oaks, CA: Sage.

Schwarz, N., & Bless, H. (1992a). Constructing reality and its alternatives: An inclusion/exclusion model of assimilation and contrast effects in social judgment. In L. L. Martin & A. Tesser (Eds.), *The construction of social judgments* (pp. 217–245). Hillsdale, NJ: Lawrence Erlbaum Associates.

Schwarz, N., & Bless, H. (1992b). Scandals and the public's trust in politicians: Assimilation and contrast effects. *Personality and Social Psychology Bulletin, 18,* 574–579. doi:10.1177/0146167292185007.

Schwarz, N., Bless, H., & Bohner, G. (1991). Mood and persuasion: Affective states influence the processing of persuasive communications. In M. P. Zanna (Ed.), *Advances in experimental social psychology* (Vol. 24, pp. 161–199). San Diego, CA: Elsevier Academic Press.

Schwarz, N., Bless, H., Strack, F., Klumpp, G., Rittenauer-Schatka, H., & Simons, A. (1991). Ease of retrieval as information: Another look at the availability heuristic. *Journal of Personality and Social Psychology, 61,* 195–202. doi:10.1037/0022-3514.61.2.195.

Schwarz, N., & Clore, G. L. (1983). Mood, misattribution, and judgment of well-being: Informative and directive functions of affective states. *Journal of Personality and Social Psychology, 45,* 513–523. doi:10.1037/0022-3514.45.3.513.

Schwarz, N., & Clore, G. L. (1988). How do I feel about it? Informative functions of affective states. In K. Fiedler & J. P. Forgas (Eds.), *Affect, cognition, and social behavior* (pp. 44–62). Toronto: Hogrefe International.

Schwarz, N., & Clore, G. L. (1996). Feelings and phenomenal experiences. In E. T. Higgins & A. W. Kruglanski (Eds.), *Social psychology: Handbook of basic principles* (pp. 433–465). New York: Guilford Press.

Schwarz, N., & Clore, G. L. (2003). Mood as information: 20 years later. *Psychological Inquiry, 14*, 296–303.

Schwarz, N., & Clore, G. L. (2007). Feelings and phenomenal experiences. In A. W. Kruglanski & E. T. Higgins (Eds.), *Social psychology: Handbook of basic principles* (2nd ed., pp. 385–407). New York: Guilford Press.

Schwarz, N., Hippler, H.-J., Deutsch, B., & Strack, F. (1985). Response scales: Effects of category range on reported behavior and comparative judgments. *Public Opinion Quarterly, 49*, 388–395. doi:10.1086/268936.

Schwarz, N., & Strack, F. (1999). Reports of subjective well-being: Judgmental processes and their methodological implications. In D. Kahneman, E. Diener & N. Schwarz (Eds.), *Well being: The foundations of hedonic psychology* (pp. 61–84). New York: Russell Sage Foundation.

Schwarz, N., Strack, F., Hilton, D. J., & Naderer, G. (1991). Base rates, representativeness, and the logic of conversation: The contextual relevance of "irrelevant" information. *Social Cognition, 9*, 67–84. doi:10.1521/soco.1991.9.1.67.

Schwarz, N., Strack, F., & Mai, H.-P. (1991). Assimilation and contrast effects in part–whole question sequences: A conversational logic analysis. *Public Opinion Quarterly, 55*, 3–23. doi:10.1086/269239.

Schwarz, N., & Sudman, S. (1996). *Answering questions: Methodology for determining cognitive and communicative processes in survey research.* San Francisco: Jossey-Bass.

Sedikides, C., & Green, J. D. (2000). On the self-protective nature of inconsistency–negativity management: Using the person memory paradigm to examine self-referent memory. *Journal of Personality and Social Psychology, 79*, 906–922. doi:10.1037/0022-3514.79.6.906.

Sedikides, C., & Strube, M. J. (1995). The multiply motivated self. *Personality and Social Psychology Bulletin, 21*, 1330–1335. doi:10.1177/01461672952112010.

Sedlmeier, P., Hertwig, R., & Gigerenzer, G. (1998). Are judgments of the positional frequencies of letters systematically biased due to availability? *Journal of Experimental Psychology: Learning, Memory, and Cognition, 24*, 754–770. doi:10.1037/0278-7393.24.3.754.

Selfridge, O. G. (1955). *Pattern recognition and modern computers.* New York: American Institute of Electrical Engineers.

Semin, G. R., & De Poot, C. J. (1997). The question–answer paradigm: You might regret not noticing how a question is worded. *Journal of Personality and Social Psychology, 73*, 472–480. doi:10.1037/0022-3514.73.3.472.

Semin, G. R., & Fiedler, K. (1988). The cognitive functions of linguistic categories in describing persons: Social cognition and language. *Journal of Personality and Social Psychology, 54*, 558–568. doi:10.1037//0022-3514.54.4.558.

Semin, G. R., & Fiedler, K. (1991). The linguistic category model, its bases, applications and range. *European Review of Social Psychology, 2*, 1–30. doi:10.1080/14792779143000006.

Semin, G. R., Rubini, M., & Fiedler, K. (1995). The answer is in the question: The effect of verb causality on locus of explanation. *Personality and Social Psychology Bulletin, 21*, 834–841. doi:10.1177/0146167295218006.

Semin, G. R., & Strack, F. (1980). The plausibility of the implausible: A critique of Snyder and Swann (1978). *European Journal of Social Psychology, 10*, 379–388. doi:10.1002/ejsp.2420100405.

Shavitt, S., & Wänke, M. (2000). Consumer cognition, marketing, and advertising. In A. Tesser & N. Schwarz (Eds.), *Handbook of social psychology* (pp. 569–590). Oxford: Blackwell.

Shepperd, J. A., Klein, W. M. P., Waters, E. A., & Weinstein, N. D. (2013). Taking stock of unrealistic optimism. *Perspectives on Psychological Science, 8*, 395–411. doi:10.1177/1745691613485247.

Shepperd, J. A., Waters, E. A., Weinstein, N. D., & Klein, W. M. P. (2015). A primer on unrealistic optimism. *Current Directions in Psychological Science, 24,* 232–237. doi:10.1177/0963721414568341.

Sherman, J. W., Gawronski, B., & Trope, Y. (Eds.). (2014). *Dual-process theories of the social mind.* New York: Guilford Publications.

Shiffrin, R. M., & Schneider, W. (1984). Automatic and controlled processing revisited. *Psychological Review, 91,* 269–276. doi:10.1037/0033-295X.91.2.269.

Siemer, M., & Reisenzein, R. (1998). Effects of mood on evaluative judgements: Influence of reduced processing capacity and mood salience. *Cognition & Emotion, 12,* 783–805. doi:10.1080/026999398379439.

Simon, D. A., & Bjork, R. A. (2001). Metacognition in motor learning. *Journal of Experimental Psychology: Learning, Memory, and Cognition, 27,* 907–912. doi:10.1037/0278-7393.27.4.907.

Simons, D. J., & Chabris, C. F. (1999). Gorillas in our midst: Sustained inattentional blindness for dynamic events. *Perception, 28,* 1059–1074. doi:10.1068/p2952.

Skinner, B. F. (1938). *The behavior of organisms: An experimental analysis.* New York: Appleton-Century-Crofts.

Skowronski, J. J., & Carlston, D. E. (1987). Social judgment and social memory: The role of cue diagnosticity in negativity, positivity, and extremity biases. *Journal of Personality and Social Psychology, 52,* 689–699. doi:10.1037/0022-3514.52.4.689.

Slusher, M. P., & Anderson, C. A. (1987). When reality monitoring fails: The role of imagination in stereotype maintenance. *Journal of Personality and Social Psychology, 52,* 653–662. doi:10.1037/0022-3514.52.4.653.

Smeesters, D., Warlop, L., Van Avermaet, E., Corneille, O., & Yzerbyt, V. Y. (2003). Do not prime hawks with doves: The interplay of construct activation and consistency of social value orientation on cooperative behavior. *Journal of personality and social psychology, 84,* 972–987. doi:10.1037/0022-3514.84.5.972.

Smith, C. A. (1989). Dimensions of appraisal and physiological response in emotion. *Journal of Personality and Social Psychology, 56,* 339–353. doi:10.1037/0022-3514.56.3.339.

Smith, E. R. (1994). Procedural knowledge and processing strategies in social cognition. In R. S. Wyer & T. K. Srull (Eds.), *Handbook of social cognition* (Vol. 1, pp. 99–151). Hillsdale: Erlbaum.

Smith, E. R., & DeCoster, J. (2000). Dual-process models in social and cognitive psychology: Conceptual integration and links to underlying memory systems. *Personality and Social Psychology Review, 4,* 108–131. doi:10.1207/S15327957PSPR0402_01.

Smith, E. R., Mackie, D. M., & Claypool, H. M. (2015). *Social psychology* (4th ed.). New York: Psychology Press.

Smith, E. R., Miller, D. A., Maitner, A. T., Crump, S. A., Garcia-Marques, T., & Mackie, D. M. (2006). Familiarity can increase stereotyping. *Journal of Experimental Social Psychology, 42,* 471–478. doi:10.1016/j.jesp.2005.07.002.

Smith, E. R., & Semin, G. R. (2004). Socially situated cognition: Cognition in its social context. In M. P. Zanna (Ed.), *Advances in experimental social psychology* (Vol. 36, pp. 53–117). San Diego, CA: Elsevier Academic Press.

Snyder, M. (1984). When belief creates reality. In L. Berkowitz (Ed.), *Advances in experimental social psychology* (Vol. 18, pp. 247–305). New York: Academic Press.

Snyder, M., & Swann, W. B. (1978). Hypothesis-testing processes in social interaction. *Journal of Personality and Social Psychology, 36,* 1202–1212. doi:10.1037/0022-3514.36.11.1202.

Snyder, M., & Uranowitz, S. W. (1978). Reconstructing the past: Some cognitive consequences of person perception. *Journal of Personality and Social Psychology, 36,* 941–950. doi:10.1037//0022-3514.36.9.941.

Solomon, R. C. (2008). The philosophy of emotions. In M. Lewis, J. M. Haviland-Jones & L. Barrett (Eds.), *Handbook of emotions* (pp. 3–16). New York: Guilford Press.

Song, H., & Schwarz, N. (2008). Fluency and the detection of misleading questions: Low processing fluency attenuates the Moses illusion. *Social Cognition, 26,* 791–799. doi:10.1521/soco.2008.26.6.791.

Spruyt, A., Hermans, D., De Houwer, J., Vandromme, H., & Eelen, P. (2007). On the nature of the affective priming effect: Effects of stimulus onset asynchrony and congruency proportion in naming and evaluative categorization. *Memory & Cognition, 35*, 95–106. doi:10.3758/BF03195946.

Stangor, C., & McMillan, D. (1992). Memory for expectancy-congruent and expectancy-incongruent information: A review of the social and social developmental literatures. *Psychological Bulletin, 111*, 42–61. doi:10.1037//0033-2909.111.1.42.

Stasser, G. (1999). The uncertain role of unshared information in collective choice. In L. L. Thompson, J. M. Levine & D. M. Messick (Eds.), *Shared cognition in organizations: The management of knowledge* (pp. 49–69). Mahwah, NJ: Lawrence Erlbaum Associates.

Stasser, G., & Titus, W. (1985). Pooling of unshared information in group decision making: Biased information sampling during discussion. *Journal of Personality and Social Psychology, 48*, 1467–1478. doi:10.1037/0022-3514.48.6.1467.

Stepper, S., & Strack, F. (1993). Proprioceptive determinants of emotional and nonemotional feelings. *Journal of Personality and Social Psychology, 64*, 211–220. doi:10.1037/0022-3514.64.2.211.

Storbeck, J., & Clore, G. L. (2008). The affective regulation of cognitive priming. *Emotion, 8*, 208–215. doi:10.1037/1528-3542.8.2.208.

Strack, F. (1992). The different routes to social judgments: Experiential versus informational strategies. In L. L. Martin & A. Tesser (Eds.), *The construction of social judgments* (pp. 249–275). Hillsdale, NJ: Lawrence Erlbaum Associates.

Strack, F. (1994). Response processes in social judgment. In R. S. Wyer & T. K. Srull (Eds.), *Handbook of social cognition* (pp. 287–322). Hillsdale, NJ: Lawrence Erlbaum Associates.

Strack, F., & Deutsch, R. (2004). Reflective and impulsive determinants of social behavior. *Personality and Social Psychology Review, 8*, 220–247. doi:10.1207/s15327957pspr0803_1.

Strack, F., Erber, R., & Wicklund, R. A. (1982). Effects of salience and time pressure on ratings of social causality. *Journal of Experimental Social Psychology, 18*, 581–594. doi:10.1016/0022-1031(82)90074-9.

Strack, F., & Hannover, B. (1996). Awareness of influence as a precondition for implementing correctional goals. In P. M. Gollwitzer & J. A. Bargh (Eds.), *The psychology of action: Linking cognition and motivation to behavior* (pp. 579–596). New York: Guilford Press.

Strack, F., Martin, L. L., & Schwarz, N. (1988). Priming and communication: Social determinants of information use in judgments of life satisfaction. *European Journal of Social Psychology, 18*, 429–442. doi:10.1002/ejsp.2420180505.

Strack, F., Martin, L. L., & Stepper, S. (1988). Inhibiting and facilitating conditions of the human smile: A nonobtrusive test of the facial feedback hypothesis. *Journal of Personality and Social Psychology, 54*, 768–777. doi:10.1037/0022-3514.54.5.768.

Strack, F., & Mussweiler, T. (1997). Explaining the enigmatic anchoring effect: Mechanisms of selective accessibility. *Journal of Personality and Social Psychology, 73*, 437–446. doi:10.1037/0022-3514.73.3.437.

Strack, F., & Schwarz, N. (1992). Communicative influences in standardized question situations: The case of implicit collaboration. In G. R. Semin & K. Fiedler (Eds.), *Language, interaction and social cognition* (pp. 173–193). Thousand Oaks, CA: Sage.

Strack, F., & Schwarz, N. (2016). Social priming. *Current Opinion in Psychology, 12*, 1–100. doi:10.1016/j.copsyc.2016.11.001.

Strack, F., Schwarz, N., Bless, H., Kübler, A., & Wänke, M. (1993). Awareness of the influence as a determinant of assimilation versus contrast. *European Journal of Social Psychology, 23*, 53–62. doi:10.1002/ejsp.2420230105.

Strack, F., Schwarz, N., & Gschneidinger, E. (1985). Happiness and reminiscing: The role of time perspective, affect, and mode of thinking. *Journal of Personality and Social Psychology, 49*, 1460–1469. doi:10.1037/0022-3514.49.6.1460.

Street, C. N. H., Bischof, W. F., Vadillo, M. A., & Kingstone, A. (2015). Inferring others' hidden thoughts: Smart guesses in a low diagnostic world. *Journal of Behavioral Decision Making, 29*, 539–549. doi:10.1002/bdm.1904.

Strick, M., Dijksterhuis, A., Bos, M. W., Sjoerdsma, A., van Baaren, R. B., & Nordgren, L. F. (2011). A meta-analysis on unconscious thought effects. *Social Cognition, 29,* 738–762. doi:10.1521/soco.2011.29.6.738.

Suh, E. M., Diener, E., & Fujita, F. (1996). Events and subjective well-being: Only recent events matter. *Journal of Personality and Social Psychology, 70,* 1091–1102. doi:10.1037//0022-3514.70.5.1091.

Suls, J., & Wheeler, L. (2007). Psychological magnetism: A brief history of assimilation and contrast in psychology. In D. Stapel & J. Suls (Eds.), *Assimilation and contrast in social psychology* (pp. 9–44). New York: Psychology Press.

Sunstein, C. R. (2007). Group polarization and 12 angry men. *Negotiation Journal, 23,* 443–447. doi:10.1111/j.1571-9979.2007.00155.x.

Surowiecki, J. (2004). *The wisdom of crowds: Why the many are smarter than the few and how collective wisdom shapes business* (Vol. 296). New York: Doubleday & Co.

Svenson, O. (1981). Are we all less risky and more skillful than our fellow drivers? *Acta Psychologica, 47,* 143–148. doi:10.1016/0001-6918(81)90005-6.

Swann, W. B., Giuliano, T., & Wegner, D. M. (1982). Where leading questions can lead: The power of conjecture in social interaction. *Journal of Personality and Social Psychology, 42,* 1025–1035. doi:10.1037/0022-3514.42.6.1025.

Tajfel, H. (1969). Cognitive aspects of prejudice. *Journal of Social Issues, 25,* 79–97. doi:10.1111/j.1540-4560.1969.tb00620.x.

Tausch, N., Kenworthy, J. B., & Hewstone, M. (2007). The confirmability and disconfirmability of trait concepts revisited: Does content matter? *Journal of Personality and Social Psychology, 92,* 542–556. doi:10.1037/0022-3514.92.3.542.

Taylor, S. E., & Brown, J. D. (1988). Illusion and well-being: A social psychological perspective on mental health. *Psychological Bulletin, 103,* 193–210. doi:10.1037/0033-2909.103.2.193.

Taylor, S. E., & Brown, J. D. (1994). Positive illusions and well-being revisited: Separating fact from fiction. *Psychological Bulletin, 116,* 21–27. doi:10.1037/0033-2909.116.1.21.

Taylor, S. E., & Fiske, S. T. (1975). Point of view and perceptions of causality. *Journal of Personality and Social Psychology, 32,* 439–445. doi:10.1037/h0077095.

Taylor, S. E., & Fiske, S. T. (1978). Salience, attention, and attribution: Top of the head phenomena. In L. Berkowitz (Ed.), *Advances in experimental social psychology* (Vol. 11, pp. 249–288). New York: Academic Press.

Taylor, S. E., Fiske, S. T., Etcoff, N. L., & Ruderman, A. J. (1978). Categorical and contextual bases of person memory and stereotyping. *Journal of Personality and Social Psychology, 36*(7), 778–793.

Teige-Mocigemba, S., & Klauer, K. C. (2013). On the controllability of evaluative-priming effects: Some limits that are none. *Cognition & Emotion, 27,* 632–657. doi:10.1080/02699931.2012.732041.

Tetlock, P. E. (1992). The impact of accountability on judgment and choice: Toward a social contingency model. In M. P. Zanna (Ed.), *Advances in experimental social psychology* (Vol. 25, pp. 331–376). San Diego, CA: Academic Press.

Tetlock, P. E., Skitka, L., & Boettger, R. (1989). Social and cognitive strategies for coping with accountability: Conformity, complexity, and bolstering. *Journal of Personality and Social Psychology, 57,* 632–640. doi:10.1037/0022-3514.57.4.632.

Thompson, E. P., Roman, R. J., Moskowitz, G. B., Chaiken, S., & Bargh, J. A. (1994). Accuracy motivation attenuates covert priming: The systematic reprocessing of social information. *Journal of Personality and Social Psychology, 66,* 474–489. doi:10.1037/0022-3514.66.3.474.

Todd, P. M., & Gigerenzer, G. (2012). *Ecological rationality: Intelligence in the world.* New York: Oxford University Press.

Todorov, A., Mandisodza, A. N., Goren, A., & Hall, C. C. (2005). Inferences of competence from faces predict election outcomes. *Science, 308,* 1623–1626. doi:10.1126/science.1110589.

Todorov, A., Olivola, C. Y., Dotsch, R., & Mende-Siedlecki, P. (2015). Social attributions from faces: Determinants, consequences, accuracy, and functional significance. *Psychology, 66*, 519–545. doi:10.1146/annurev-psych-113011-143831.

Todorov, A., & Uleman, J. S. (2003). The efficiency of binding spontaneous trait inferences to actors' faces. *Journal of Experimental Social Psychology, 39*, 549–562. doi:10.1016/S0022-1031(03)00059-3.

Tomasello, M., Melis, A. P., Tennie, C., Wyman, E., & Herrmann, E. (2012). Two key steps in the evolution of human cooperation. *Current Anthropology, 53*, 673–692. doi:10.1086/668207.

Topolinski, S., & Strack, F. (2009). The architecture of intuition: Fluency and affect determine intuitive judgments of semantic and visual coherence and judgments of grammaticality in artificial grammar learning. *Journal of Experimental Psychology: General, 138*, 39–63. doi:10.1037/a0014678.

Traud, G. R. (2000). Behavioral finance und der Kurs des Euro. In H. Löchel (Ed.), *Finanzmärkte in Euroland* (pp. 139–153). Frankfurt: Bankakademie Verlag.

Trent, J., & King, L. A. (2013). Faith in intuition moderates the effects of positive affect on gender stereotyping. *Personality and Individual Differences, 54*, 865–868. doi:10.1016/j.paid.2012.12.008.

Trope, Y. (1986). Identification and inferential processes in dispositional attribution. *Psychological Review, 93*, 239–257. doi:10.1037/0033-295X.93.3.239.

Trope, Y., & Liberman, A. (1996). Social hypothesis testing: Cognitive and motivational mechanisms. In S. Chaiken & Y. Trope (Eds.), *Dual-process theories in social psychology* (pp. 239–270). New York: Guilford Press.

Trope, Y., & Liberman, N. (2010). Construal-level theory of psychological distance. *Psychological Review, 117*, 440–463. doi:10.1037/a0018963.

Tversky, A., & Kahneman, D. (1973). Availability: A heuristic for judging frequency and probability. *Cognitive Psychology, 5*, 207–232. doi:10.1016/0010-0285(73)90033-9.

Tversky, A., & Kahneman, D. (1974). Judgment under uncertainty: Heuristics and biases. *Science, 185*, 1124–1131. doi:10.1126/science.185.4157.1124.

Tversky, A., & Kahneman, D. (1981). The framing of decisions and the psychology of choice. *Science, 211*, 453–458. doi:10.1126/science.7455683.

Tversky, A., & Kahneman, D. (1983). Extensional versus intuitive reasoning: The conjunction fallacy in probability judgment. *Psychological Review, 90*, 293–315. doi:10.1016/B978-1-4832-1446-7.50038-8.

Uleman, J. S., Blader, S. L., & Todorov, A. (2005). Implicit impressions. In R. Hassin, J. S. Uleman & J. A. Bargh (Eds.), *The new unconscious* (pp. 362–392). New York: Oxford University Press.

Unkelbach, C. (2006). The learned interpretation of cognitive fluency. *Psychological Science, 17*, 339–345. doi:10.1111/j.1467-9280.2006.01708.x.

Unkelbach, C. (2007). Reversing the truth effect: Learning the interpretation of processing fluency in judgments of truth. *Journal of Experimental Psychology: Learning, Memory, and Cognition, 33*, 219–230. doi:10.1037/0278-7393.33.1.219.

Unkelbach, C., & Greifeneder, R. (2013a). A general model of fluency effects in judgment and decision making. In C. Unkelbach & R. Greifeneder (Eds.), *The experience of thinking: How the fluency of mental processes influences cognition and behavior* (pp. 11–32). Hove: Psychology Press.

Unkelbach, C., & Greifeneder, R. (Eds.). (2013b). *The experience of thinking: How the fluency of mental processes influences cognition and behavior.* Hove: Psychology Press.

Vallacher, R. R., & Wegner, D. M. (1987). What do people think they're doing? Action identification and human behavior. *Psychological Review, 94*, 3–15. doi:10.1037/0033-295X.94.1.3.

Van den Bos, K., & Lind, E. A. (2002). Uncertainty management by means of fairness judgments. In M. P. Zanna (Ed.), *Advances in experimental social psychology* (Vol. 34, pp. 1–60). San Diego, CA: Academic Press.

Van Lange, P. A. M., Joireman, J., Parks, C. D., & Van Dijk, E. (2013). The psychology of social dilemmas: A review. *Organizational Behavior and Human Decision Processes, 120,* 125–141. doi:10.1016/j.obhdp.2012.11.003.

Van Overwalle, F., Van Duynslaeger, M., Coomans, D., & Timmermans, B. (2012). Spontaneous goal inferences are often inferred faster than spontaneous trait inferences. *Journal of Experimental Social Psychology, 48,* 13–18. doi:10.1016/j.jesp.2011.06.016.

Vogel, T., & Wänke, M. (2016). *Attitudes and attitude change (Social psychology: A modular course).* London: Psychology Press.

Vohs, K. D., Mead, N. L., & Goode, M. R. (2006). The psychological consequences of money. *Science, 314,* 1154–1156. doi:10.1126/science.1132491.

von Helmholtz, H. (1903). Optisches über Malerei: Umarbeitung von Vorträgen, gehalten zu Berlin, Düsseldorf und Köln a. Rh. 1871 bis 1873. In H. von Helmholtz (Ed.), *Vorträge und Reden* (pp. 93–135). Braunschweig: Vieweg und Sohn.

Walker, M., Schönborn, S., Greifeneder, R., & Vetter, T. (2017). *The Basel face database: A validated set of photographs reflecting systematic differences in Big Two and Big Five personality dimensions.* Unpublished manuscript, University of Basel.

Walker, M., & Vetter, T. (2016). Changing the personality of a face: Perceived Big Two and Big Five personality factors modeled in real photographs. *Journal of Personality and Social Psychology, 110,* 609–624. doi:10.1037/pspp0000064.

Wänke, M. (2013). Almost everything you always wanted to know about ease-of-retrieval effects. In C. Unkelbach & R. Greifeneder (Eds.), *The experience of thinking: How the fluency of mental processes influences cognition and behavior* (pp. 151–169). Hove: Psychology Press.

Wänke, M., Bless, H., & Biller, B. (1996). Subjective experience versus content of information in the construction of attitude judgments. *Personality and Social Psychology Bulletin, 22,* 1105–1113. doi:10.1177/01461672962211002.

Wänke, M., Bless, H., & Igou, E. R. (2001). Next to a star: Paling, shining, or both? Turning interexemplar contrast into interexemplar assimilation. *Personality and Social Psychology Bulletin, 27,* 14–29. doi:10.1177/0146167201271002.

Wänke, M., Bless, H., & Schwarz, N. (1998). Context effects in product line extensions: Context is not destiny. *Journal of Consumer Psychology, 7,* 299–322. doi:10.1207/s15327663jcp0704_01.

Wänke, M., Bohner, G., & Jurkowitsch, A. (1997). There are many reasons to drive a BMW: Does imagined ease of argument generation influence attitudes? *Journal of Consumer Research, 24,* 170–177. doi:10.1086/209502.

Wänke, M., & Fiedler, K. (2007). What is said and what is meant: Conversational implicatures in natural conversations, research settings, media and advertising. In K. Fiedler (Ed.), *Frontiers in social psychology: Social communication* (pp. 223–256). New York: Psychology Press.

Wänke, M., & Reutner, L. (2010). Pragmatic persuasion or the persuasion paradox. In J. P. Forgas, W. Crano & J. Cooper (Eds.), *The psychology of attitudes & attitude change* (pp. 183–198). New York: Psychology Press.

Wason, P. C. (1966). Reasoning. In B. Foss (Ed.), *New horizons in psychology* (pp. 135–151). London: Penguin.

Watson, J. B. (1930). *Behaviorism.* New York: Norton.

Watzlawick, P., Beavin, J. H., & Jackson, D. D. (1969). *Human communication: Forms, disturbances, paradoxes.* Oxford, UK: Hans Huber Publishers.

Weber, R., & Crocker, J. (1983). Cognitive processes in the revision of stereotypic beliefs. *Journal of Personality and Social Psychology, 45,* 961–977. doi:10.1037/0022-3514.45.5.961.

Webster, D. M., & Kruglanski, A. W. (1994). Individual differences in need for cognitive closure. *Journal of Personality and Social Psychology, 67,* 1049–1062. doi:10.1037/0022-3514.67.6.1049.

Wegener, D. T., & Petty, R. E. (1994). Mood management across affective states: The hedonic contingency hypothesis. *Journal of Personality and Social Psychology, 66,* 1034–1048. doi:10.1037/0022-3514.66.6.1034.

Wegener, D. T., & Petty, R. E. (1997). The flexible correction model: The role of naive theories of bias in bias correction. In M. P. Zanna (Ed.), *Advances in experimental social psychology* (Vol. 29, pp. 142–208). San Diego, CA: Elsevier Academic Press.

Wegner, D. M. (1994). Ironic processes of mental control. *Psychological Review, 101,* 34–52. doi:10.1037/0033-295X.101.1.34.

Wegner, D. M., Erber, R., & Raymond, P. (1991). Transactive memory in close relationships. *Journal of Personality and Social Psychology, 61,* 923–929. doi:10.1037/0022-3514.61.6.923.

Wegner, D. M., Wenzlaff, R., Kerker, R. M., & Beattie, A. E. (1981). Incrimination through innuendo: Can media questions become public answers? *Journal of Personality and Social Psychology, 40,* 822–832. doi:10.1037/0022-3514.40.5.822.

Weingarten, E., & Hutchinson, W. (2016). *Does ease mediate the ease-of-retrieval effect? A meta-analysis.* Unpublished manuscript, Marketing Department, Wharton School of the University of Pennsylvania, Philadelphia, PA.

Weinstein, N. D. (1980). Unrealistic optimism about future life events. *Journal of Personality and Social Psychology, 39,* 806–820. doi:10.1037/0022-3514.39.5.806.

Wentura, D., & Degner, J. (2010). A practical guide to sequential priming and related tasks. In B. Gawronski & B. K. Payne (Eds.), *Handbook of implicit social cognition: Measurement, theory, and applications* (pp. 95–116). New York: Guilford Press.

Wertheimer, M. (1945). *Productive thinking.* New York: Harper.

Whittlesea, B. W. A. (1993). Illusions of familiarity. *Journal of Experimental Psychology: Learning, Memory, and Cognition, 19,* 1235–1253. doi:10.1037//0278-7393.19.6.1235.

Whittlesea, B. W. A., & Leboe, J. P. (2003). Two fluency heuristics (and how to tell them apart). *Journal of Memory and Language, 49,* 62–79. doi:10.1016/S0749-596X(03)00009-3.

Whittlesea, B. W. A., & Williams, L. D. (1998). Why do strangers feel familiar, but friends don't? A discrepancy-attribution account of feelings of familiarity. *Acta Psychologica, 98,* 141–165. doi:10.1016/S0001-6918(97)00040-1.

Whittlesea, B. W. A., & Williams, L. D. (2000). The source of feelings of familiarity: The discrepancy-attribution hypothesis. *Journal of Experimental Psychology: Learning, Memory, and Cognition, 26,* 547–565. doi:10.1037//0278-7393.26.3.547.

Whyte, G., & Sebenius, J. K. (1997). The effect of multiple anchors on anchoring individual and group judgment. *Organizational Behavior and Human Decision Processes, 69,* 75–85. doi:10.1006/obhd.1996.2674.

Wigboldus, D. H. J., Semin, G. R., & Spears, R. (2000). How do we communicate stereotypes? Linguistic bases and inferential consequences. *Journal of Personality and Social Psychology, 78,* 5–18. doi:10.1037/0022-3514.78.1.5.

Willis, J., & Todorov, A. (2006). First impressions: Making up your mind after a 100-ms exposure to a face. *Psychological Science, 17,* 592–598. doi:10.1111/j.1467-9280.2006.01750.x.

Wilson, T. D., & Brekke, N. (1994). Mental contamination and mental correction: Unwanted influences on judgments and evaluations. *Psychological Bulletin, 116,* 117–142. doi:10.1037/0033-2909.116.1.117.

Wilson, T. D., Dunn, D. S., Kraft, D., & Lisle, D. J. (1989). Introspection, attitude change, and attitude-behavior consistency: The disruptive effects of explaining why we feel the way we do. In L. Berkowitz (Ed.), *Advances in experimental social psychology* (Vol. 22, pp. 287–343). San Diego, CA: Academic Press.

Wilson, T. D., Gilbert, D. T., & Wheatley, T. P. (1998). Protecting our minds: The role of lay beliefs. In V. Y. Yzerbyt & G. Lories (Eds.), *Metacognition: Cognitive and social dimension* (pp. 171–201). Thousand Oaks, CA: Sage.

Wilson, T. D., Houston, C. E., Etling, K. M., & Brekke, N. (1996). A new look at anchoring effects: Basic anchoring and its antecedents. *Journal of Experimental Psychology: General, 125,* 387–402. doi:10.1037/0096-3445.125.4.387.

Wilson, T. D., Lisle, D. J., Schooler, J. W., Hodges, S. D., Klaaren, K. J., & LaFleur, S. J. (1993). Introspecting about reasons can reduce post-choice satisfaction. *Personality and Social Psychology Bulletin, 19,* 331–339. doi:10.1177/0146167293193010.

Wilson, T. D., Wheatley, T., Meyers, J. M., Gilbert, D. T., & Axsom, D. (2000). Focalism: A source of durability bias in affective forecasting. *Journal of Personality and Social Psychology, 78*, 821–836. doi:10.1037/0022-3514.78.5.821.

Winkielman, P., Berridge, K. C., & Wilbarger, J. L. (2005). Unconscious affective reactions to masked happy versus angry faces influence consumption behavior and judgments of value. *Personality and Social Psychology Bulletin, 31*, 121–135. doi:10.1177/0146167204271309.

Winkielman, P., & Cacioppo, J. T. (2001). Mind at ease puts a smile on the face: Psychophysiological evidence that processing facilitation elicits positive affect. *Journal of Personality and Social Psychology, 81*, 989–1000. doi:10.1037/0022-3514.81.6.989.

Winkielman, P., & Schwarz, N. (2001). How pleasant was your childhood? Beliefs about memory shape inferences from experienced difficulty of recall. *Psychological Science, 12*, 176–179. doi:10.1111/1467-9280.00330.

Winkielman, P., Schwarz, N., Fazendeiro, T. A., & Reber, R. (2003). The hedonic marking of processing fluency: Implications for evaluative judgment. In J. Musch & K. C. Klauer (Eds.), *The psychology of evaluation: Affective processes in cognition and emotion* (pp. 189–217). Mahwah, NJ: Lawrence Erlbaum Associates.

Winograd, E. (1981). Elaboration and distinctiveness in memory for faces. *Journal of Experimental Psychology: Human Learning and Memory, 7*, 181–190. doi:10.1037/0278-7393.7.3.181.

Wittenbaum, G. M., & Park, E. S. (2001). The collective preference for shared information. *Current Directions in Psychological Science, 10*, 70–73. doi:10.1111/1467-8721.00118.

Wittenbaum, G. M., Hollingshead, A. B., & Botero, I. C. (2004). From cooperative to motivated information sharing in groups: Moving beyond the hidden profile paradigm. *Communication Monographs, 71*(3), 286–310.

Wittenbrink, B., Judd, C. M., & Park, B. (1997). Evidence for racial prejudice at the implicit level and its relationship with questionnaire measures. *Journal of Personality and Social Psychology, 72*, 262–274. doi:10.1037/0022-3514.72.2.262.

Wittenbrink, B., & Schwarz, N. (Eds.). (2007). *Implicit measures of attitudes.* New York: Guilford Press.

Wyer, R. S., & Srull, T. K. (1989). *Memory and cognition in its social context.* Hillsdale, NJ, England: Lawrence Erlbaum Associates.

Yaniv, I. (2004). Receiving other people's advice: Influence and benefit. *Organizational Behavior and Human Decision Processes, 93*, 1–13. doi:10.1016/j.obhdp.2003.08.002.

Yaniv, I., & Choshen-Hillel, S. (2012). When guessing what another person would say is better than giving your own opinion: Using perspective-taking to improve advice-taking. *Journal of Experimental Social Psychology, 48*, 1022–1028. doi:10.1016/j.jesp.2012.03.016.

Yaniv, I., Choshen-Hillel, S., & Milyavsky, M. (2009). Spurious consensus and opinion revision: Why might people be more confident in their less accurate judgments? *Journal of Experimental Psychology: Learning, Memory, and Cognition, 35*, 558–563. doi:10.1037/a0014589.

Yeung, C. W. M., & Wyer, R. S. (2004). Affect, appraisal, and consumer judgment. *Journal of Consumer Research, 31*, 412–424. doi:10.1086/422119.

Yzerbyt, V. Y., & Carnaghi, A. (2008). Stereotype change in the social context. In Y. Kashima, K. Fiedler & P. Freitag (Eds.), *Stereotype dynamics: Language-based approaches to the formation, maintenance, and transformation of stereotypes* (pp. 29–57). Mahwah, NJ: Lawrence Erlbaum Associates.

Yzerbyt, V. Y., Coull, A., & Rocher, S. J. (1999). Fencing off the deviant: The role of cognitive resources in the maintenance of stereotypes. *Journal of Personality and Social Psychology, 77*, 449–462. doi:10.1037/0022-3514.77.3.449.

Zajonc, R. B. (1960). The process of cognitive tuning in communication. *Journal of Abnormal and Social Psychology, 61*, 159–167. doi:10.1037/h0047987.

Zajonc, R. B. (1968). Attitudinal effects of mere exposure. *Journal of Personality and Social Psychology, 9*, 1–27. doi:10.1037/h0025848.

Zajonc, R. B. (1980). Feeling and thinking: Preferences need no inferences. *American Psychologist, 35*, 151–175. doi:10.1037/0003-066X.35.2.151.

Zebrowitz, L. A., & Franklin, R. G. (2014). The attractiveness halo effect and the babyface stereotype in older and younger adults: Similarities, own-age accentuation, and older adult positivity effects. *Experimental Aging Research, 40*, 375–393. doi:10.1080/0361073x.2014.897151.

Zebrowitz, L. A., & Montepare, J. M. (1992). Impressions of babyfaced individuals across the life span. *Developmental Psychology, 28*, 1143–1143.

Zebrowitz, L. A., Voinescu, L., & Collins, M. A. (1996). "Wide-eyed" and "crooked-faced": Determinants of perceived and real honesty across the life span. *Personality and Social Psychology Bulletin, 22*, 1258–1269. doi:10.1177/01461672962212006.

Ziegler, R. (2014). Mood and processing effort: The mood-congruent expectancies approach. In M. P. Zanna and J. M. Olson (Ed.), *Advances in experimental social psychology* (Vol. 49, pp. 287–355). San Diego, CA: Elsevier Academic Press.

Ziegler, R., & Burger, A. M. (2011). Mood and the impact of individuating information on the evaluation of ingroup and outgroup members: The role of mood-based expectancies. *Journal of Experimental Social Psychology, 47*, 1000–1006. doi:10.1016/j.jesp.2011.04.002.

Zuckerman, M., Knee, C. R., Hodgins, H. S., & Miyake, K. (1995). Hypothesis confirmation: The joint effect of positive test strategy and acquiescence response set. *Journal of Personality and Social Psychology, 68*, 52–60. doi:10.1037/0022-3514.68.1.52.

Author index

Subject index

PGIL2021USA